The Dhofar Conflict

The Dhofar Conflict

The SAS and Counterinsurgency

Stephen Quick

Pen & Sword
MILITARY

First published in Great Britain in 2025 by
Pen & Sword Military
An imprint of Pen & Sword Books Limited
Yorkshire – Philadelphia

Copyright © Stephen Quick 2025

ISBN 978 1 03610 887 8

The right of Stephen Quick to be identified as
Author of this Work has been asserted by him in accordance
with the Copyright, Designs and Patents Act 1988.

A CIP catalogue record for this book is
available from the British Library.

All rights reserved. No part of this book may be reproduced, transmitted, downloaded, decompiled or reverse engineered in any form or by any means, electronic or mechanical including photocopying, recording or by any information storage and retrieval system, without permission from the Publisher in writing. NO AI TRAINING: Without in any way limiting the Author's and Publisher's exclusive rights under copyright, any use of this publication to "train" generative artificial intelligence (AI) technologies to generate text is expressly prohibited. The Author and Publisher reserve all rights to license uses of this work for generative AI training and development of machine learning language models.

Typeset by Mac Style
Printed in the UK by CPI Group (UK) Ltd, Croydon, CR0 4YY.

The Publisher's authorised representative in the EU for product safety is Authorised Rep Compliance Ltd., Ground Floor, 71 Lower Baggot Street, Dublin D02 P593, Ireland.
www.arccompliance.com

For a complete list of Pen & Sword titles please contact

PEN & SWORD BOOKS LIMITED
47 Church Street, Barnsley, South Yorkshire, S70 2AS, England
E-mail: enquiries@pen-and-sword.co.uk
Website: www.pen-and-sword.co.uk
or
PEN AND SWORD BOOKS
1950 Lawrence Road, Havertown, PA 19083, USA
E-mail: uspen-and-sword@casematepublishers.com
Website: www.penandswordbooks.com

For Dodilee and Luke

Contents

Abstract ix
Tables xi
Figures xi
Acknowledgements xii
Foreword xiii
Glossary & Abbreviations xv

Chapter 1   Introduction   1

Chapter 2   The Dhofar War: Background, and Literature Representation   7

Part I: The Dhofar War: A Classical British COIN Campaign?   25

Chapter 3   Background and Strategic Level Similarities   34

Chapter 4   Campaign-Specific Aspects Similarities   42

Part II: Campaign Differences   65

Chapter 5   Background and Strategic Level Differences   67

Chapter 6   Campaign-Specific Aspects Differences   70

Part III: The Dhofar War: Typical in Terms of Success?   85

Chapter 7   A Military Success?   92

Chapter 8   A Strategic Counterinsurgency Success?   111

Chapter 9   A Cost-Effective Campaign?   115

Chapter 10   Other Evidence of Success – Continuing UK influence in Oman post-campaign   125

Part IV: A Truly British Counter-insurgency Action?		139
Chapter 11	The Changing Nature of the British Role	155
Chapter 12	Evolution of British Political and Economic Influence	164
Chapter 13	British-Linked War Strategy	189
Chapter 14	Operational Control, Training & War Fighting	199
Chapter 15	Conclusion	215
Notes		221
Bibliography		267

Abstract

The Dhofar Conflict, the SAS, and Counterinsurgency

Taking place in Oman's most remote westerly province, the Dhofar War (1965–1975) was one of the most strategically significant Middle Eastern conflicts of the Cold War era. It also was one of the most important Counterinsurgency (COIN) actions which involved Britain's elite Special Air Services (SAS) Regiment, and alongside the long war in Northern Ireland it defined its role and reputation throughout the first half of the 1970s. Overall, the Dhofar War was one of the most strategically successful British COIN actions of the post-Second World War era. This was a period in history which was dominated by rising nationalism and the superpower stand-off of the Cold War. These two factors were often inextricably linked, and were the driving force behind numerous bitterly fought insurgencies the world over.

The theory of COIN that developed due to the campaigns which took place from the closing period of the Second World War to the 1980s (and with Northern Ireland arguably into the 1990s) is often referred to as 'classical counterinsurgency'.[1] From a causative perspective, these 'classical-era' insurgencies occurred due largely to either nationalist or ideological – often Communist – underpinnings, or a combination of both. The Dhofar War displayed many characteristics in common with such previous 'classical-era' or 'post imperial' campaigns undertaken by the British state and indeed further afield via the campaigns of several other nations including France, Belgium, Portugal, and the United States.[2] On the surface this would suggest that it could be considered archetypal or typical in this respect. This book explores this issue in depth by assessing whether it resembles these historic UK COIN campaigns from different perspectives, to what level it can be considered successful considering the historical record, and to what extent it can actually be properly classified as a 'British' campaign.

This book shows that although often similar in numerous respects including the large-scale covert use of British Special Forces, the Dhofar War was not an archetypal British COIN campaign. For several reasons it can in fact be considered unique or rather in a class of its own. Despite this, although also far from model or ideal in execution and notwithstanding an overall decline in UK influence over the duration of the campaign, it was, however, ultimately one of Britain's most significant historical COIN wins. This success was achieved not by sole, sovereign UK prosecution of the campaign as was largely the case in the past. Instead, it was achieved via an increasingly more distanced, hands-off support or 'consultancy-type' role, which has arguably remained the core British *modus operandi* with regards to COIN to date.

Tables

Table 1	Evolution of the Dhofar Insurgent Organisation.	16
Table 2	COIN and Warfare Experience of Key Commanders Relating to the Dhofar War.	56
Table 3	Classical-Era British COIN Win/Loss Record.	88
Table 4	Britain and Dhofar COIN Campaign – 'Sliding Scale of Influence' Phases.	163
Table 5	Key British Indirect Military Support/COIN Assistance to Oman and the Dhofar War.	176
Table 6	Key British COIN Training and Warfighting Contributions to Dhofar Campaign.	211

Figures

Figure 1	Map of Dhofar and the Arabian Peninsula (from 1971)	xvi
Figure 2	Text of 1958 'Exchange of Letters' Agreement Between British Government and Sultan of Muscat and Oman	175
Figure 3	Map of Dhofar Operational Area – Final Operations	213

Acknowledgements

This book is the product of research undertaken for a PhD. at King's College London and an endless fascination for a small, largely overlooked or sidelined war in the Arabian Peninsula which made an outsized impact on the outcome of the wider Cold War. The research for this project was undertaken in several archives worldwide, including the UK, Oman, and the United Arab Emirates. Perhaps just as importantly it is a product of visits to Muscat in Oman and Dhofar Province itself. Here, I had the privilege to see or walk many of the key sites and battlefields associated with the war. I was also able to experience the unique annual Khareef monsoon conditions which keep Dhofar almost refreshingly cool in the searing heat of the Arabian Peninsula summer. The annual Khareef also had a significant bearing on the war, including the development of fighting 'seasons' and the restrictive effects on operations carried out by both sides.

I would like to highlight my thanks to Dr. Lester Crook and his team at Pen & Sword for their support in seeing this project through to publication. Thanks are also due to the many people with a hand in advising on concepts, drafts, proofreading, formatting, and the like. Among these I would like to highlight Professor Nikolas Gardner, Professor Joel Hayward, Dr. Ash Rossiter, Dr. Martha Dillman, Mr. Firasse Beale. and my father, Mr. Roger Quick; the latter whose former-teacher's forensic-like critical eye was invaluable. I would also like to highlight my appreciation to Dhofar War veteran, Mr. Sid Pass, for the generous permission to utilise images from his collection of personal wartime photographs for this book.

Special thanks is also due to fellow Dhofar veteran and celebrated explorer Colonel (ret'd) John Blashford-Snell CBE, for his kind review of the work and foreword. His words and insights (including that his team of Royal Engineers latterly repaired damage to Mirbat Fort – as featured on the cover of this book – as sustained in the momentous 1972 battle waged in that small, coastal settlement) bring home the importance of this small-scale, secretive, yet vitally important war. They also highlight the key role of British military forces and (both serving and ex-) personnel in the Dhofar campaign's successful conclusion, including the central role played by the SAS Regiment.

Finally, it should be stated that the responsibility for any inaccuracies or oversights contained within this book are my own, and that any opinions expressed are those of the author alone, and do not reflect the view of Rabdan Academy (University) or the Abu Dhabi Government.

Dr. Stephen Quick
April 2025

Foreword

During the few months my Royal Engineers Squadron supported the Sultan's Armed Forces (SAF) in 1974 during the Dhofar conflict and on a couple of short visits in later years, I came to respect and admire the people and the Military of this Sultanate. However, I did not have the opportunity to study the full history of the country in great depth nor to comprehend the political and strategic background to the Dhofar conflict. Thus it has been an education to read Dr. Quick's work, for which he has conducted much in-depth research.

The three sections of the book collectively discuss the Dhofar Campaign's place within the wider topic of 'counterinsurgency', the pros and cons and especially the level of 'success' of the campaign, and the extent to which it can actually be considered 'British' as such. Where appropriate, the book also outlines the criticisms and views of Nation States who sought to take over Oman and close the Strait of Hormuz to the free flow of Gulf oil, so vital to the global economy.

There is no doubt that much credit is due to the inspiration provided by HM Sultan Qaboos Bin Said, who had been trained at Sandhurst and served for a while in the British Army. His wisdom in providing aid for the Jebali people and thus winning their 'hearts and minds' was of special value. The courage and skill of the SAF, so ably supported and led by British and Omani officers is also rightly recognised as a major factor in the success of the war. Happily, the close relationship between them continues to this day. Dr. Quick also shows that the assistance of the Iranian and Jordanian forces was of key importance as were the vital efforts, unique skill sets and expertise of the often-courageous British SAS, who worked closely with the Omani tribal Firqa units.

Visiting Salalah with a group of British veterans a few years ago, I was approached by a young Omani gentleman, who was enjoying a swim in one of the new luxury hotel pools with his family. "What are all you English doing here?" he enquired. When I had explained, he shook my hand and said, "I read about that at school. Thank you for helping to save our country."

This book puts forward the persuasive argument that whilst unique in several respects, the Dhofar COIN campaign should be clearly considered both a 'British' counterinsurgency win and a hitherto underrated success in strategic terms. As such, it shows how the SAF, the British-led campaign, and the support of Oman's allies secured the stability of the country for future generations.

Colonel John Blashford-Snell CBE
April 2025

Glossary & Abbreviations

Abbreviation	Meaning
BATT	British Army Training Team (cover name for covert SAS deployment to Dhofar)
BBME	British Bank of the Middle East
CAT	Civil Aid Team
CENTO	The Central Treaty Organization (formerly Baghdad Pact)
DF	Dhofar Force
DLF	Dhofar Liberation Front
DR	Desert Regiment
FO/FCO	Foreign Office/Foreign & Commonwealth Office (UK)
FST	Field Surgical Team
IIBG	Imperial Iranian Battle Group
JR	Jebel Regiment
LFA	Land Freedom Army
LSP	Loan Service Personnel
MAN	Movement of Arab Nationalists
MCP	Malayan Communist Party
MOFF	Muscat and Oman Field Force
MPAJA	Malayan People's Anti-Japanese Army
MR	Muscat Regiment
NDFLOAG	National Democratic Front for the Liberation of the Occupied Arabian Gulf (formed from the Popular Revolutionary Movement)
NKNA	North Kalimantan National Army
OG	Oman Gendarmerie
OR	Oman Regiment
PD(O)	Petroleum Development (Oman)
PDRY	People's Democratic Republic of Yemen
PFLO	Popular Front for the Liberation of Oman
PFLOAG	Popular Front for the Liberation of the Occupied Arabian Gulf and Popular Front for the Liberation of Oman and the Arabian Gulf (formed from merger between PFLOAG and NDFLOAG)

Abbreviation	Meaning
RA	Royal Artillery (UK)
RAF	Royal Air Force (UK)
RAFO	Royal Air Force of Oman
RE	Royal Engineers (UK)
ROP	Royal Oman Police
(C) SAF	(Commander) Sultan's Armed Forces
SAS	Special Air Service Regiment (UK)
SEP	Surrendered Enemy Personnel
SOAF	Sultan of Oman's Air Force
SON	Sultan of Oman's Navy
TOS	Trucial Oman Scouts
UAR	United Arab Republic

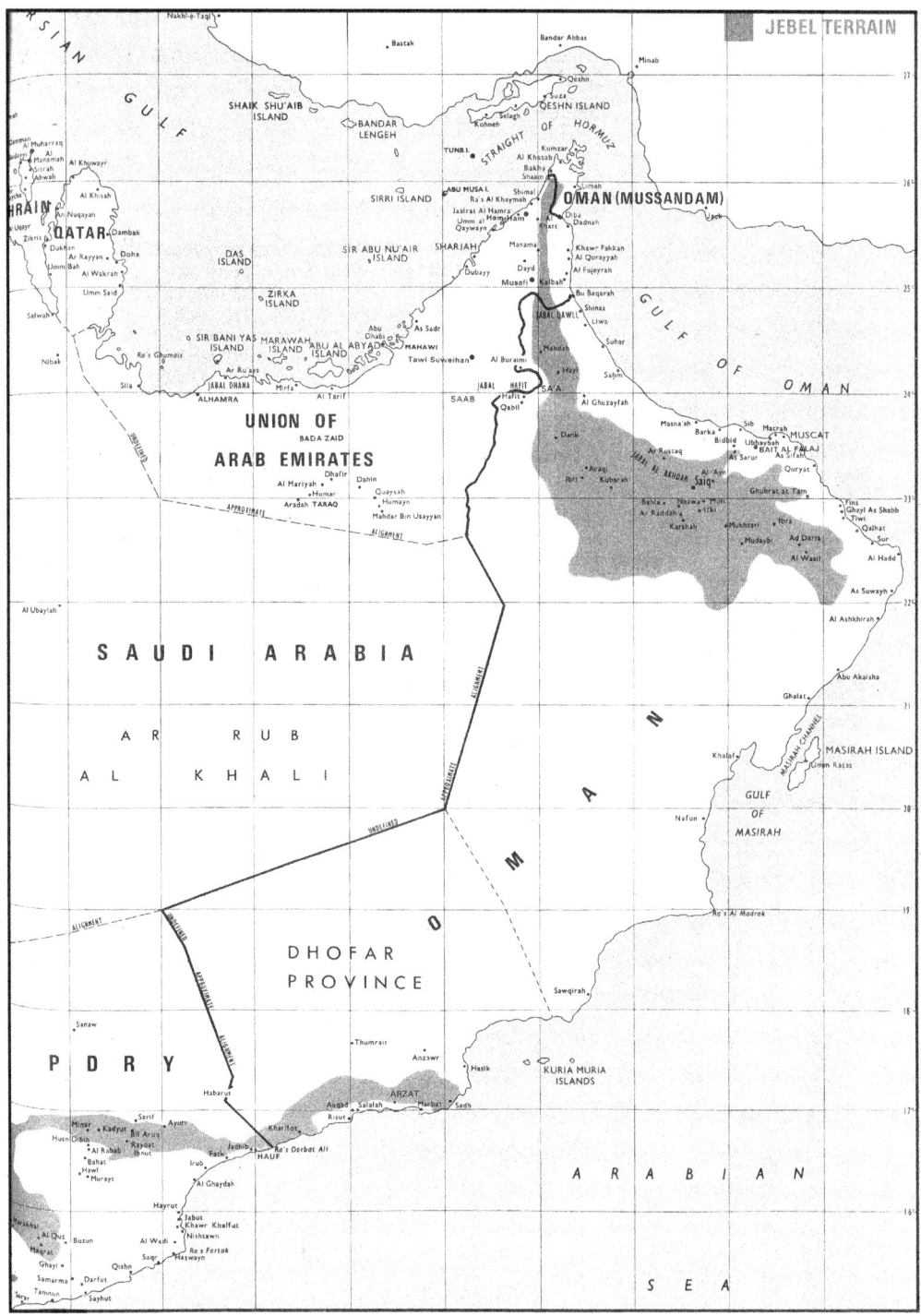

Figure 1: Map of Dhofar and the Arabian Peninsula (from 1971). (*Source: TNA – CAB 186/11 – Cabinet Joint Intelligence Committee Report: 'The Outlook for Oman (Delicate Source), 1 Mar 1972, p.494.*
Reproduced courtesy of The National Archives (Kew, UK))

Chapter 1

Introduction

The Dhofar War of 1965–1975 in many ways closely resembled previous post-Second World War 'classical-era' British anti-insurgency operations undertaken the world over. This included with the covert presence of the UK's elite SAS Special Forces Regiment in theatre. Fundamental differences, however, identify the Dhofar War as being different in key ways which makes it largely unique within the historical British COIN record. This book aims to justify this 'unique' designation, and present a more balanced and considered verdict of the history of the war than has perhaps been the case in print to date. As such this book aims to highlight the unique characteristics of the COIN campaign carried out in Oman's remote, but strategically important Dhofar Province.

Conducted in virtual secrecy for most of its duration and overshadowed in historical importance by higher-profile contemporary conflicts, the Dhofar War was nonetheless one of the most strategically significant confrontations of the 1960s and 1970s.[1] The Dhofar COIN campaign arguably prevented the collapse of Dhofar province and subsequently the whole of Oman to a Communist-backed insurgency. As a result, it also helped to halt the spread of Marxist doctrine and mitigate Communist great power (both Chinese and later Soviet) influence, as well as the worst effects of radical Arab nationalism in the Arabian Gulf region.[2] These developments all took place with the backdrop of the ideological turmoil, and revolutionary forces unleashed throughout the world during the Cold War looming large. The campaign also allowed Britain to support a long-term ally with both formal treaty and informal links between the two countries going back centuries, and therefore fulfil long-held historical responsibilities towards the Sultanate and its rulers. It also enabled a relatively smooth and orderly implementation of the UK's military and political withdrawal 'East of Suez' in 1971. This was considered a relatively successful initiative as compared to the chaotic, politically-implemented withdrawal from Britain's largest overseas military presence and base areas located in Aden in 1967.[3] Success in Dhofar also helped cement the stability and survival of the Western, and wider world's largely carbon-dependent economic systems. It achieved this by maintaining the vital flow of Gulf oil supplies via the Strait of Hormuz through the survival of the governing status quo in Oman and its control over the Musandam Peninsula and effectively one half of this strategically situated geographic bottleneck. As remains the case, in the contemporary Dhofar War timeframe of the 1960s and 1970s, Oman controlled one half of this strategic waterway chokepoint. As then, the Strait remains the initial maritime bottleneck required to be negotiated before exiting the Arabian Gulf, allowing the region to supply "the precious life-blood for the West", and a majority of the industrialised world's crude oil requirements.[4]

Publications on the Dhofar campaign to date have collectively been largely polarised in their portrayal of the war and explanations of how it fits into the wider field of COIN. The literature has also been historically divided on the issue of the relative success or otherwise of the campaign, and who was responsible ultimately for its prosecution and achieving the 'win'. The traditional historical view portrays the Dhofar COIN undertaking as being both a tactical and strategic success, even going as far as to describe it as an ideal or 'model' COIN campaign comparable in success terms to the 1948–1960 Malayan Emergency.[5] In contrast, revolutionary-oriented and revisionist narratives tend to portray the Dhofar campaign as reflecting the wider post-Second World War British COIN record as being somewhat 'hyped' in terms of success, intertwined with colonial-era excesses with the term 'oppression' being the key descriptor. It also raises the issue of competence of campaign execution before, during and after the war with views apparent such as "The British had no reason to feel proud of their attempts at running the Sultan's Armed Forces."[6] The revisionist narrative of recent years also encompasses the view that the UK's role was far from singular or decisive but was actually supportive at most as compared to other actors such as Iran, with its influence merely preventing the war from being lost.[7] It also incorporates the Omani 'official' interpretation of events which purports that it was not Britain, but the Sultan of Oman who guided his armed forces to victory primarily through his own skills and leadership abilities.[8]

This book focuses on cutting through these competing views to present a more balanced and considered verdict of the history of the Dhofar War, the actors involved, and its wider relationship to other post-1945 or 'classical era' UK (and further afield) COIN campaigns. As such it will re-examine many of the traditional literature views as well as reinterpreting some of the more recent revisionist interpretations of Britain's involvement in the war and notions of its success. The British role in the Dhofar War is covered in depth, and highlights the remarkable levels of assistance provided by the UK to Oman both prior to, and over a decade of fighting including the provision of troops and the rare, long-term deployment of Britain's foremost Special Forces unit, the Special Air Services (SAS) Regiment.

This book is comprised of three broad sections, the first concentrating on establishing if the Dhofar War can properly be considered a classical British COIN campaign in terms of characteristics. Much of the body of scholarship on the subject to date points to the Dhofar case being a typical example of a classical British counterinsurgency campaign. What such narratives often neglect are the key differences which highlight the Dhofar War as being distinct in comparison with other British (and non-UK) COIN campaigns in the post-Second World War-era. This section ascertains how the Dhofar campaign fits into overall COIN literature with regards to British campaigns carried out since 1945. Initially, the section will clarify if there are certain similarities linking all post-war British COIN campaigns or whether they are all completely standalone in their main background circumstances and campaign-specific factors involved in their prosecution. It is then clarified whether, and to what extent, the Dhofar War differed from other classical-era British operations in these respects. As such, section 1 then establishes whether the Dhofar War should, therefore, be considered part of the same general 'classical' narrative regarding UK COIN or a standalone or unique example.

Britain is widely lauded as being historically successful at prosecuting COIN campaigns. This is reflected in a "largely celebratory literature", and that, "While certainly not flawless, the British approach to counterinsurgency has been more successful than that of any other nation" with only Palestine and Aden considered clear defeats.[9] Section 2's purpose is to ascertain whether the Dhofar COIN campaign replicates the perceived successes or otherwise of previous British classical-era anti-insurgency undertakings, and to what extent the Dhofar campaign can therefore actually be considered a relative and absolute success in its own right. The section will, furthermore, re-evaluate existing narratives to clarify the level of success achieved by the UK in the Dhofar campaign. This is viewed in the context relative to previous British and COIN campaigns conducted by other states and indeed whether the view that, "In short, were Britain's post-1945 won-lost record that of a football team, the coach would most assuredly be searching for alternative employment" rings true, or whether the record should be viewed in a more positive light.[10] The level of success, from both a UK and other campaign actor perspective, is judged primarily, but not exclusively, in military terms, therefore giving a more balanced and nuanced view of the notion of 'success'.

Section 3 then follows to establish whether the Dhofar War can properly be considered a British COIN action. Initially the British level of influence or control of the campaign is clarified, and secondly the type or manifestation of such influence. This section therefore provides a more nuanced explanation of the scale of British influence which is largely absent in the subject literature to date. The argument for the campaign not being primarily a British undertaking is initially addressed, followed by an alternative perspective on how to best classify the UK role and its level of influence. Positive and negative factors of British influence on the campaign are then explored to clarify whether the campaign was a British operation, an Omani Sovereign-run undertaking, an Iranian-forced result, or whether it was a more nuanced situation where the UK's role evolved during the campaign's duration, and whether it was primarily actually British influence which finally brought the campaign to a successful conclusion.[11]

This book argues that although highly similar in many respects, the Dhofar War was fundamentally different in background and operational aspects, levels of success and in terms of UK identity or influence when compared to previous British COIN campaigns. Britain utilised similar tactical or operational approaches across its various COIN campaigns, and often utilised covert means such as the use of its renowned Special Forces capabilities to pursue objectives incorporating a shield of 'plausible deniability'. Although it should be considered part of the UK historical COIN narrative, in such respects it was different to the extent that the Dhofar campaign should be considered a standalone or largely unique example. From a background classification level most of Britain's post-Second World War COIN campaigns took place in the era of the Cold War and that of global decolonisation which affected the reasons for UK involvement. Likewise, from a campaign-specific background factor perspective the Dhofar campaign was also very similar to previous British COIN undertakings. There were, however, several fundamental differences relating to the Dhofar case. Importantly, it was technically not a campaign undertaken by the British state in a politically controlled territory as other classical-era British COIN campaigns were. In addition, the campaign was not primarily prosecuted directly by British, or UK government-controlled COIN forces but by the military forces of the Sultan of Oman. This book will therefore establish that whilst the Dhofar War should be considered part of the British COIN historical narrative, it retains its own unique status within this overall classification.

Contrary to the 'best ever' narrative as found in some quarters of the subject literature to date, the Dhofar COIN campaign could have been much more successfully prosecuted and was not a model or ideal operation from tactical, operational, or strategic perspectives. The war persisted too long (a decade-plus), cost more in terms of resources and lives than perhaps 'necessary' and resulted in more suffering to both sides than should have been the case. This book therefore counters the traditionalist view that the Dhofar War was effectively an unmitigated success and an ideal or 'model' campaign in almost every way; to be emulated and in future such conflicts by both British and the forces of other nations.[12] Conversely, although it cannot be considered a complete success from a tactical and operational level (absolute) perspective the Dhofar campaign was, however, from a wider strategic (relative) standpoint a great success in many ways for Britain, and for the state, ruler and people of Oman. It can also be considered a considerable success for the major campaign allies in the latter years of the war. It was also a successful COIN undertaking from the perspective of the West in general in the context of the Cold War, and for the Middle East as a whole as a facilitator of stability. From a wider strategic standpoint, its successful conclusion was central to preventing a progressive 'domino theory-like' communist takeover of the Gulf region and for securing continued access to crucial Gulf oil supplies for Western economies including that of Japan. From this perspective, therefore, the Dhofar campaign can actually be considered similar in terms of wider UK COIN. This is because it continued the overall level and narrative of a mixed British success 'scoresheet' in its classical-era COIN campaigns.

Contrary to much of the historical record to date, the Dhofar War was not, however, a wholly British fought war. It was the SAF troops – largely Baluchi ("there was an important but often unacknowledged contribution from another group of expatriates: they came from a place called Makran, in the Pakistan Province of Baluchistan") as well as Omani soldiers and later a variety of foreign troops who undertook the vast majority of the combat-related actions against the insurgents.[13] Britain did, however, at the operational and most importantly at the strategic level operate the levers of influence to the extent that it can still be considered a highly UK-influenced COIN undertaking. This influence was one of the prime contributors towards the SAF's ability to defeat the insurgents and win the war. Only a relatively small number of British officers and non-commissioned military personnel were involved directly in the campaign and casualties sustained were relatively low, totalling 35 only (including 16 suffered by the SAS in theatre).[14] Additionally, in the latter stages of the war Jordan had similar numbers of troops on the ground in Oman as the UK and Iranian troop numbers significantly outnumbered those of British forces.[15] More importantly, the fighting was undertaken by sovereign Omani forces ultimately commanded by the country's absolute monarch. Britain, did, however, have strong historical links to Oman stretching over centuries and held significant influence within the country at governmental, private business, and personnel levels.

The campaign was eventually won by utilising the collective wide experience and skill of the British officers in leadership positions within the SAF and UK civilians employed in the Omani regime. This was backed by the generally very sparing (arguably 'tight-fisted' from the Omani perspective), yet highly targeted and effective support from the British government. This included the vital deployment of support troops including significant numbers of the SAS

Regiment. As such, Britain was essentially the driving force behind the strategy and overall conduct of the campaign which has been described as a unique approach in the contemporary era, and ultimately of the overall victory.[16] It would be somewhat misleading to describe the Dhofar War as a model campaign in a tactical war-fighting sense. If one looks more broadly however and considers how British support facilitated the winning of a campaign by assisting an ally to help itself (instead of the combat actions involving the large-scale use of British troops) in a supportive, mentoring, or 'consultancy'-type role it was a model to emulate.[17] In establishing this, this book essentially refutes the Marxist scholarly 'colonial oppressor'-related narrative that the Dhofar campaign was a neo-Imperial war of oppression imposed by Britain on both Oman and the Dhofari population in collaboration with a 'puppet' local ruler. It also counters the idea that the conduct of the campaign was any more brutal than previous UK classical-era COIN campaigns or that Britain's influence was somehow immoral and generally oppressive.[18] In addition, this book puts into perspective the idea present in the revisionist-slanted literature that the British role was largely irrelevant or was not a major factor in winning the Dhofar War; and as such reverses the modern trend for the UK's key role to be downplayed, sidelined, or sometimes even virtually omitted from the wider historical record.[19]

The Dhofar campaign can therefore ultimately be deemed one of Britain's most significant COIN wins, even though the UK did not undertake the majority of the fighting itself. Although it cannot be considered a typical classical UK COIN campaign, the accumulated experience of the British personnel in leadership roles in the SAF, and the UK government and British military's – and especially that of the SAS's – experience and historical institutional memory was brought to bear. This eventually enabled the insurgency crisis in Dhofar and within wider Oman to be neutered. By achieving this, Britain made a clear and substantial contribution to securing stability in both Oman and in the Gulf Region. Importantly, the COIN win in Dhofar also contributed to maintaining the economic prosperity of the Western and wider world economy as a whole within the contemporary Cold War framework.

Chapter 2

The Dhofar War: Background, and Literature Representation

The purpose of this chapter is firstly to provide a contextual background to the conflict, and secondly to review how the wider subject literature on the war has been presented to date. As such, this chapter is organised into two main sections. Firstly a contextual background to the Dhofar case is set out, covering such topics as the geography of Oman and the Dhofar region, the history of British involvement in the country, the origins of the conflict and the history and general principles of COIN. The second section identifies the key authors, themes and narratives in the literature related to the war and the specific sections of this book. It also acts to identify shortfalls or gaps within the wider literature that this book aims to help remedy.

Dhofar War and Counterinsurgency Subject Background – Geographical Environment (Physical and Population)

Hemmed – in by greater Oman to the east and by modern Yemen to the west, Dhofar has a geography distinct from the rest of the Sultanate. The vast Indian Ocean meets southern Dhofar on a consistently narrow flat coastal belt of approximately a mile wide before the topography changes dramatically via near vertical escarpments to form the looming 'wall' of the Jebel or mountainous region. The virtually unbroken Jebel area is made up largely of the interconnecting Qamar, Qara and Samhan mountain ranges. The only exception to this virtual mountain wall is the approximately 50 miles of coastline of the Salalah plain which surrounds the historic regional capital.[1] Here, there is a wider plateau with the land extending significantly further inland (up to 6 miles) on a fertile plain area before finally transforming – often very abruptly – once again into soaring mountain range.[2] The towering Jebel ranges extend some 20 miles inland where they then flatten out to become the featureless gravelly Negd plains. This barren gravelly plain area eventually morphs into the Rub Al Khali desert or 'Empty Quarter' of intrepid exploration fame (traversed by legendary explorers such as Wilfred Thesiger) which extends over hundreds of miles into the neighbouring state of the Kingdom of Saudi Arabia (KSA).[3]

Dhofar is unique in the Arabian Peninsula, not just from a topographical perspective but also in terms of its climate. When the peninsula is sweltering in the sometimes 50-plus degrees centigrade annual high summer heat between June and September, Dhofar is a much more pleasant place to be. This is due to a large proportion of the province being subject to the meteorological effects of the annual 'Khareef' monsoon season. As such, Dhofar is largely covered in cooling monsoon rains and mists from sea level up to approximately 2,000 feet for around four months or a third of each year. This annual weather phenomenon means Dhofar blossoms into a lush green landscape for several months of the year, with a much more temperate climate than the rest of the Arabian Peninsula. Observed by an SAS soldier who served in Dhofar: "The grass on the Jebel grows at a furious pace once the Khareef fog and rain set in. Sometimes when the mist cleared temporarily the whole place had taken on an emerald green mantle only to be swallowed up minutes later."[4] This has specific relevance because the annual Khareef season not only created distinct 'fighting seasons' which affected the war's chronological development, but influenced decisions at both the tactical as well as overall strategic level in relation to the prosecution of military operations for both sides. Under the cover of the rain, clouds and swirling mists, the insurgents could move more freely and transport supplies than in clear weather conditions. At the same time, the SOAF was often unable to fly in these conditions due to the reduced – or sometimes zero – visibility, therefore the SAF's logistical capability for transporting personnel, ammunition or other war materials was acutely curtailed. The wet, muddy conditions prevented large-scale mechanical or even infantry movements as it was too hazardous to both personnel and equipment. In addition, the large waves on the Dhofari coast brought on by the Khareef usually prevented naval support or supply operations close to any point on the Dhofari coastline. When the mists cleared to reveal the resultant luxuriant vegetation growth pervasive all over the province and especially in wadis (normally dry river beds or valleys) and Jebel approaches, both during the misty Khareef period and the post-monsoon 'green' season, the situation provided the Insurgents with plentiful cover and a strong tactical advantage until the greenery finally died away over the following weeks.[5]

The population of Dhofar was also distinct, and this too affected the development of the insurgency in the province. Partly as a result of large-scale waves of Arab migrations into what is now modern-day Omani territory in the 2nd century AD and the development of the Nizarite and Yemenite tribal affiliations, population-wise the approximately 30,000 residents of Dhofar were both culturally and ethnically separate from the rest of Oman and more akin to contemporary Yemeni tribes[6]. This cultural and ethnic differentiation was a key driver of the insurgency. Both the Sultan, his advisors and the personnel of his armed forces were viewed as outsiders and alien to their normal kinship-based society. In addition to this were the fact that Dhofar only officially became part of in 1879, and its remote location within the territory of the Sultanate, both of which factors had a key impact on the genesis of the original national-oriented insurgency as well as its longevity and the dogged staying power of the insurgent cause.[7]

Omani Historical Perspectives and Britain's Relations with Oman

From early trade-related contact between Oman's rulers and the East India Company in the 1650s, English, and later British, influence grew steadily through an increase in diplomatic interaction to formal treaty. From the British perspective this was undertaken primarily for the purpose of limiting the influence of its bitter contemporary rival, France, in both the Gulf region generally and within strategically-situated Omani territory specifically.[8] Due in part to Emperor Napoleon Bonaparte's Egyptian conquest strategy and suspected designs on India, Britain entered into formal treaty relations with the Sultan in 1798. Britain also provided an annual subsidy to the Omani Sultan. This was paid in gold from 1866 via the UK Indian government which cemented Britain's central economic influence in Oman. In addition, the treaty arrangements also benefitted the Sultan by providing protection to offset the rising influence of the Qawasim Sheikhs and Wahhabis from Ras Al Khaimah in modern day UAE and Saudi Arabia respectively.[9] Discontented Imamate forces attacked Muscat and deposed the Sultan in 1868. This situation lasted until 1871 when forces under Sayyid Turki killed Imam Azzin and captured Muscat with the British government brokering the overall surrender to Turki's forces, ostensibly to avoid further death or destruction.[10] This intervention by British political agent personnel as the broker between competing Sultanic power claims thus helped set the stage for later UK assistance to the Sultans of Oman. Britain later provided military assistance to a beleaguered Sultan of Muscat and Oman in 1913 when Imamate forces rebelled, which included naval bombardment by the Royal Navy, and then garrisoned Bait Al Falaj fort with British Indian troops to deter further challenges to the Sultan's authority. Britain played an even bigger role in 1915 whilst still embroiled in the turmoil of the First World War, when over 3000 rebels attacked Muscat (Bait Al Falaj Fort) and were repulsed by some 700 British Indian troops.[11] It has been stated that: "They [the rebels] never reached the fort and their crushing defeat on this occasion marked the last rebel attempt on the capital."[12] Following the defeat of the rebellion in 1915 the British-brokered 1920 Treaty of Sib was implemented which conferred control of the economically more active coast to the Sultan, whilst the tribes and the Imamate were given wide leeway to autonomously govern most of the country's barren interior. Sultan Said bin Taimur came to power in 1932 and strong relations between him, his country and Britain ensued for nearly 40 years until he was deposed by his son, Qaboos in a palace coup in 1970.

Following the Omani-British Treaty of Friendship, Commerce and Navigation of 1951 (described as a "a direct descendant of the original 1798 treaty"), Britain once again came to the Sultan's aid firstly by ejecting Saudi forces from the Buraimi Oasis in 1955 utilising the British-raised and Trucial States-based Trucial Oman Scouts (TOS), followed by decisive military assistance during the Imamate-instigated Jebel Akhdar rebellion of 1957.[13] Full spectrum support was provided via personnel or units from the TOS, the British officers of the Sultan's military forces and for the first time regular mainland British military units. These included the Life Guards, the Royal Marines and the Cameronians (Scottish infantry) Regiment which would later be Crown Prince Qaboos's unit for his short, but formative career as a British army officer.[14] The Imamate rebellion leaders retreated to the summit of the Jebel Akhdar (Green Mountain) in late 1957 and were only eventually dislodged by large-scale RAF bombing and a final assault by two squadrons of the SAS, recently arrived direct from Malayan Emergency duties, alongside other British (including TOS) and Omani troops in 1959.[15] The insurgent leaders escaped to Dammam in Saudi Arabia, the rebellion was effectively over and the Sultan, with British help, was unchallenged for supremacy over the whole of the Muscat and Omani territory.

Relations with Britain were further formalised at this time after visits by the British Under-Secretary for War, Julian Amery in 1957 and followed by the contemporary Chief of the Imperial General Staff (CIGS), General Sir Gerald Templer of Malayan Emergency fame (known as the 'Tiger' of Malaya) as part of a regional tour.[16] After initial negotiations led by Amery in January 1958 the result was the 'Exchange of Letters' between the Government of the UK and the Sultan of Muscat and Oman on his annual visit to the UK and dated 25th July 1958.[17] As part of the agreement, the UK government agreed to pay a large annual stipend towards the running and reorganisation, modernisation and expansion of the existing Muscat Armed Forces into the newly designated SAF, to the tune of £271,000, and supplied personnel to run it in the form initially of 23 seconded army officers across the rank spectrum from Colonel to Captain.[18] These included the highly experienced Second World War veteran Colonel David Smiley who was the first designated CSAF.[19] A key part of the 1958 arrangements was the extension of the lease for its Masirah Island base facilities for use by the RAF, and management and security arrangements put in place for RAF Salalah in Dhofar province going into the future.

Dhofar War Origins

Britain's ongoing and constant support for Sultan Said bin Taimur helped the Sultan to maintain his power and he effectively ruled according to his wishes. Educated in British India, after taking over the reins of power from his father Taimur, who abdicated in 1932, Said oversaw a regime which was conservative at its most charitable, and was considered by many as verging on the tyrannical at worst.[20] Subjects of the Omani Sultan were largely prevented from travelling abroad, objects or items of the modern world such as public music, radios, newspapers, and even sunglasses were systematically banned with no access to these possible within Oman for its population.[21] Worse still, even when oil revenue came on stream in 1967, very limited funds were directed to the economic or social development of the country in areas such as infrastructure, health and education, it was so limited that by the mid-1960s Oman existed in a seriously retrograde or virtually 'medieval' state of development where the result was an infant mortality rate – abhorrent as it is to modern sensibilities and expectations – of over 70 percent.[22] With Britain's annual £1.5 million contribution, local Zakat tax revenues raised on produce such as fishing, and through drastically controlling any public expenditure Said had managed to gradually get the sovereign finances of the state of Muscat and Oman under control. This was quite an achievement after the gross mismanagement by his father's administration and a legacy of debt primarily to wealthy Muscat-based traders which he inherited. To further boost the privy purse, Gwadar port, a final vestige of the old Omani Empire, was additionally sold to an eager Pakistan in 1958 for £3 million.[23] With this financial windfall, allied to oil revenues of £8 million in 1967, rising to over £40 million by the beginning of the 1970s, such austerity could not merely be written off by observers as 'frugality', and even his close Muscat-based British advisors began to doubt his ability, or more importantly his intention, to progress his country out of such a negative developmental situation.[24]

The situation for the population was even worse in Dhofar. Sultan Said moved permanently from the capital Muscat to his palace in Salalah in Dhofar province in 1958 and continued to run the country via his British advisors based in Muscat, with Dhofar effectively being run as a private estate of fiefdom.[25] Sultan Said also kept numerous slaves at his palace in Salalah and, although he chose to take a Dhofari woman named Mizoon from one of the more powerful and 'aristocratic' tribes (daughter of Sheikh Ahmed of the Bait Ma'asheni tribe which exercised considerable control over large sections of Eastern Dhofar) as his wife he clearly neither liked nor trusted Dhofaris in general. As an illustration of this near contempt held for Dhofaris by the ruler, the Sultan's CSAF, Brigadier

Corran Purdon recounted in his biographical publication titled *'List the Bugle'* Sultan Said's comment to him that, "If you are out walking and meet a Dhofari and a snake, tread on the Dhofari."[26]

Allied to his apparent or rather barely-concealed contempt for his Dhofari subjects, the level of general development was even lower in the province than the rest of Oman. Jim White describes how there was but a single primary school in Dhofar for educating the youth of the province, no medical facilities for the entire Dhofari population at all and neither electricity nor running water for either public services or private dwellings.[27] Compared to the capital city of the UK which remained the Sultan's primary backer, this difference in living standards was to nothing short of extreme. The severe lack of social and economic development remained a key feature despite the oil wealth generated from the latter half of the 1960s. Alongside heavy-handed control of movement out of the country of subjects, and oppressive, and on the surface almost vindictive, taxation and judicial systems (with import taxes for Dhofaris 300% higher than rest of the country, and daily taxes imposed on fishermen and on animal stock for herders), all such factors contributed towards a somewhat hopeless situation for the Dhofari population and morphed into growing resentment and growing unrest in the country.[28] Whilst on the surface an appallingly neglectful system of governance, it has been suggested that Sultan Said was actually undertaking projects and policies to help his country the best way he deemed possible; with almost overwhelming problems and very limited resources. Alston and Laing state: "The Sultan [Said bin Taimur] was not necessarily the cynical and uninterested Ruler he has sometimes been made out to be. He was strongly influenced by his wish to sustain Oman as a tribally-organised society, and by his long-practiced financial prudence," with Cummins adding that, "When it came to developing the country's infrastructure… Sultan Said moved cautiously," avoiding loans and careful to avoid fiscal deficits.[29] Quoting Sultan Said himself, Alston and Laing add to this viewpoint by describing how:

"Certain conditions in Oman are inherited from the past and are not really my fault, and if I do not have the funds to change these conditions, where change is desired, that is still not my fault. If, however, I do have the means and do not improve my people and my country than I should be ashamed." By 1970 many believed that that was exactly the situation, and that he [Sultan Said] should indeed be ashamed.[30]

The Jebel Akhdar rebellion was primarily centred on the issue of authority and control of the country's interior and the competing Imamate and Sultanic power blocs. In contrast, one of the main catalysts for the fermenting of nationalist

The Dhofar War: Background, and Literature Representation   13

grievances and eventually the Dhofar War itself was the experience gained by expatriate Omani workers from Dhofar province. Those who managed to circumvent strict border controls often found employment outside the country, with many taking jobs in the burgeoning new and swiftly developing oil industries or growing security sectors (armed or police forces) in other Gulf countries such as in the TOS in the Trucial states.[31] With their social horizons severely limited in Oman, the almost 'Disney-like' development of social and economic infrastructure in their host countries brought home the true scale of the disparities which existed between their countries and the social and economic conditions of the respective populations. Alongside the mixing with personnel belonging to various dissident groups (including supporters of the Imamate leaders) and further stoked by the message emanating from the Arab Nationalist Movement and championed by President Gamal Abdel Nasser's Egypt, the steps from mere discontent to an active, armed insurgency were few.[32] Although preceded by long-simmering discontent with Sultan Said's rule which sparked the 1957 Imamate rebellion, despite a fatal attack on an oil company vehicle and the destruction of an RAF vehicle (by landmine) from RAF Salalah in 1963, the situation was not yet critical and was deemed to be manageable.[33] The situation then escalated with the first recorded fatal incident of the Dhofari rebellion in 1965, where, "The DLF campaign to liberate Dhofar began after the First Congress, on 9 June 1965, with the ambush of a Government patrol north-west of the Thamrait Road, in which Said al-Ruwai, the first DLF victim, was killed."[34] This raised the stakes and the threat assessment, with the action being perpetrated by followers of Mohammed Bin Nufl, Omani exiles who formed the DLF in the early 1960s.[35] Several DLF founding members had worked abroad in the Gulf region and had witnessed the exponential development in infrastructure, wealth and social development due to oil; something which was not apparent in their native Dhofar. New activist organisations were established in the early years of the 1960s inspired by the Movement of Arab Nationalists (MAN) and the Pan-Arabist message being broadcast throughout the Middle Eastern region by the staunchly anti-Western 'Imperialist' Egyptian regime through the ideas of 'Nasserism'. Groups such as the Dhufari Charitable Association (DCA) and Dhufari Soldiers Association (DSO) were formed and added to the combined growing pro-nationalist and anti-Sultan sentiment in the province.[36] The DSO included Dhofaris serving in the militaries of the Trucial States, Qatar and Bahrain. These men were well-trained by their British-officered units for Arabian physical and social environment-specific general military taskings including anti-insurgency operations, and therefore possessed useful skill sets potentially available to organisations fomenting armed rebellion. It has been stated that many of them were watching closely what was developing in their home province and as a result of the developing situation decided to act towards deposing the incumbent Sultan.[37] Having deserted, or sometimes even whilst on leave, individuals acted with their DLF colleagues to agitate within Dhofar, disrupting oil operations, mining roads and damaging oil company assets.

In response to the rapidly deteriorating security situation, Sultan Said eventually ordered the incumbent CSAF, Colonel Tony Lewis to deploy the SAF to Dhofar, something that had never occurred previously, with the initial deployment of the Northern Frontier Regiment (NFR) in December 1964, followed by their comrades in the Muscat Regiment (MR) in May 1965. With no roads and basic and often old or obsolete equipment and vehicles, it took approximately two weeks to travel the over 500 miles – overland as there were no roads – to reach Salalah. Lewis described the difficulty of his tasking as follows:

> I was therefore faced with a problem far greater than any military staff college could invent. I had been asked to move a force by an unknown route across 600 miles of desert to a country also unknown to us, as big as Wales but of worse terrain. I was to search out a rebel force that lived in the inhospitable jebel country north of the Salalah plain about whom I knew nothing.[38]

In addition, this action was undertaken with old, inaccurate maps which added to the extreme difficulty of the tasking from a command perspective. The one-month single company 'emergency' NFR deployment, designed to 'fly the flag' of the Sultan's authority in Dhofar Province was uneventful. Hunting insurgents was like trying to 'find a needle in a haystack' with less than 2,000 insurgents in an area highlighted by Lewis as being the approximate size of Wales in the UK.[39] After this unexciting month-long tour which took place without incident, the NFR contingent returned to its home base in northern Oman. This largely deterrence-postured operation was followed by several months of relative quiet in Dhofar, then by an increased-size deployment of two companies of the Muscat Regiment (MR) in May 1965.[40] The MR's deployment was more active, signifying an increase in insurgent activity and capability. This led to, from the DLF's perspective, the official start of the Dhofar War on 9 June 1965 after their 'First Congress' or whole organisation meeting, and its subsequent successful attack on an oil company lorry where they killed the driver.[41] Unlike their NFR colleagues' tour, the MR actually engaged militarily with insurgent groupings and also suffered the SAF's first casualty of the insurgency, albeit from an accident as opposed to combat or insurgent hostilities.[42]

The Sultanate's military forces were very limited at the time of these deployments. Alongside a few dated aircraft and a single naval vessel, the primary military capability was provided by the two single-battalion regiments that deployed in 1964 and 1965. In 1965, the DR had been raised to increase the Sultan's overall military capability but was not yet fully formed or operationally capable. Likewise, the resident Dhofar Force (DF) was essentially a private bodyguard unit for the Sultan in Salalah and did not have either the remit or capability to take on the insurgent threat. Importantly, the DF was also completely separate and not part of the SAF, and therefore not under the command of the CSAF. The Pakistani contract commander and officer corps reported directly to the Sultan. With such limited resources the SAF had to maintain order in Oman and control and protect its borders at over twenty separate military outposts throughout the Sultanate.[43] Freeing up the manpower to monitor, deter, then fight an insurgency in Dhofar alongside such core commitments was neither desirable nor practical. All the way up to 1970 the SAF could only put some 600 men in Dhofar at any one time to fight the insurgents, being made up of one reinforced battalion of the single-battalion-sized regiments, whilst "In contrast, from their sanctuary in the PDRY, the PFLOAG could deploy up to 1,800 personnel."[44] These consisted of both full-time fighters and militia forces, and the single SAF battalion had to deter, track (or even find), and if necessarily engage such forces in the extensive Dhofar operational area.

The largely Nationalist and social development-oriented grievances which gave rise to the original DLF and the motivations of its leadership were later displaced by Marxist hardliners led by Muhammad Al Ghassani. The UK's Aden departure in November 1967 and the establishment of the Marxist People's Republic of Southern Yemen (PRSY) was the catalyst for a change in ideological outlook of the DLF with significant support and contact with the regime via its base at Hauf in PRSY territory. The original DLF subsequently morphed into the more ambitiously named and larger-scoped Popular Front for the Liberation of the Occupied Arabian Gulf (PFLOAG). The general revolutionary atmosphere and specific successful Marxist state takeover in Aden as the backdrop to the Dhofar insurgency resulted in a complete takeover of the PFLOAG's leadership by Communist hardliners and the purging of the old nationalist figureheads by 1970.

The name of the organisation changed once again to the PFLOAG (Popular Front for the Liberation of Oman and the Arabian Gulf) in late 1971 when Britain had relinquished control of its territories/protectorates in the Gulf area and exited East of Suez. The political 'own goal' and resulting chaotic British withdrawal from Aden in 1967 and the formation of the Marxist National Liberation Front (NLF)-governed (considered by Britain as a paramilitary terrorist group) Southern Yemeni State became one of the key drivers of the developing intensity of the burgeoning insurgency over the border in Dhofar.[45]

Table 1: Evolution of the Dhofari Insurgent Organisation.

Name of Primary Dhofar Insurgent Group	Origins
Dhofar Liberation Front (DLF)	Formed in 1965 under leadership of Musallim bin Nufl and Yusuf bin Alawi bin Abdulla – the former had previously been in the service of Sultan Said
Popular Front for the Liberation of the Occupied Arabian Gulf (PFLOAG)	Formed in 1968 as a result of the insurgent's Second Congress held in the Wadi Hamrin. Old nationalist leadership displaced by Marxist hardliners by 1970
Popular Front for the Liberation of Oman and the Arabian Gulf (PFLOAG)	Formed in December 1971 due to the amalgamation of the original PFLOAG and the sister northern Oman insurgent organisation the National Democratic Front for the Liberation of the Occupied Arabian Gulf (NDFLOAG)
Popular Front for the Liberation of Oman (PFLO)	Formed in July 1974 as the insurgency was failing and the wider revolutionary aims of a Marxist utopia in Arabia had been sidelined to a specific Oman-based aim

As a result, the insurgents were allowed continued access to a secure base at Hauf located near to the Omani border with the PRSY, and access to Yemeni material and other assistance. With the subsequent formation of the People's Democratic Republic of Yemen (PDRY) in 1970, because of the Marxist nature of the PRSY and later PDRY, wider Communist bloc support became available. This came originally from a China intent on securing "its new ideological role of communist expansion and world revolution", then later primarily the USSR (and via other bloc satellite countries such as Cuba and North Korea) and sympathetic revolutionary administrations or groups in Egypt, Saudi Arabia, and Iraq.[46]

Added to this were the repressive measures employed by the Sultan's forces at his insistence. These included well-capping to deny much-needed water for both humans and precious livestock. It also included house or crop burnings to destroy settlements or deny food stocks allied to mass detentions. All of such activities, as might be expected, turned many 'waverers', 'fence-sitters', or more neutral Dhofaris against the Sultan and his perhaps justifiably perceived oppressive rule.[47] This was in tandem with his refusal to act on the advice of his COIN-experienced British advisors to institute an amnesty programme in a similar vein to that introduced with some success in Malaya. As such, "the only tool to be employed by the SAF against the insurgents was repression", and, alongside ignoring pleas to put in place a fast-track and expansive programme of infrastructure and social development, this only served to intensify the downward spiral of the insurgency for the government side.[48] The rebellion was not suppressed in a decisive and timely manner in the early months and years when the insurgents were more vulnerable in terms of numbers, organisation and capability. Far from effectively dealing with the situation, with a more radical, Communist ideology now in the ascendant and the backing of the great powers of the Communist bloc in place, it only added fuel to the fire. The stage was, therefore, set for a decade-long drawn-out, destructive and expensive conflict that would not officially end until the end of 1975.

History and Principals of Counterinsurgency

In order to view the Dhofar campaign in context, an appreciation of the history and principals of COIN is required, as are definitions of the subject for the purposes of this book. Historically, guerrilla warfare was seen in terms of military conflict and the tactics employed often by the 'weak' over the 'strong' from ancient Chinese times and the writings of Sun Tzu.[49] Ian Beckett describes the development of such irregular modes of warfare into revolutionary guerrilla warfare encompassing subversion, propaganda and military action into a concerted effort to seek power and overthrow the status quo: "More properly, therefore, modern revolutionary guerrilla warfare might be termed insurgency."[50] David Galula clarifies further by stating that "Whereas in conventional war, either side can initiate the conflict, only one – the insurgent – can initiate a revolutionary war, for counterinsurgency is only an effect of insurgency."[51] COIN can, therefore, be seen as merely a response to the actions of the insurgent. Commenting on the development of the concept of insurgency, Beckett states further that:

> In the immediate post-war world, insurgency was most often motivated primarily by ideology, whether communism or nationalism, or a combination of both. Initially, it was also more likely to occur in the kind of rural environment in which guerrillas had traditionally best thrived and which offered the best opportunity to convert a guerrilla or insurgent force into a more conventional military force capable of taking on the authorities on their own terms. Indeed, insurgency was but a means to a particular end, guerrilla tactics being employed strategically to achieve a political goal.[52]

This statement sums up closely the scenario which developed in Dhofar and reflects the situation that morphed into a 10-year-long insurgency in the province.

There is also a requirement to define the terms of reference for this book. Whilst referring to other cases outside the general sphere, it concentrates on comparisons, where required, of the Dhofar COIN campaign with post-1945

British COIN operations and authors who have written on these specific subjects, collectively referred to as 'Classical COIN'. The main case studies of comparison are the British COIN operations carried out in Palestine (1945–1948), the Malayan Emergency (1947–1960), Kenya (Mau Mau Uprising 1952–1960) the Cypriot Insurgency (1955–1959), Brunei/Borneo (1962–1966) and the Aden Emergency (1963–1967); with the long-running insurgency in Northern Ireland (1969–1999) also referenced. Classical and/or British-specific COIN authors of note include contemporaries or participants of such operations including Robert Thompson, David Galula, Julian Paget, and Frank Kitson.[53] Although this book centres around the ideas of such classical era writers, comment from later (termed neo-classical) subject scholars such as Ian Beckett, Thomas Mockaitis, John Nagl and David Kilcullen is also included for comparison and context.[54] Also included to add both scholarly depth and to provide a more contemporary perspective are writers who put forward what might be termed an alternative or 'revisionist' COIN perspective, including John Newsinger, David French, Douglas Porch, and Paul Dixon for example.[55] The issues surrounding this complex subject hold very few 'black and white' truths and there are few definites or certainties, so every point of view should be fully considered.

Specific Themes

Categorisation of the Dhofar COIN Campaign

As might be expected, the Dhofar War literature is very limited compared to that of COIN in general. Whilst clearly a COIN undertaking, it is not clear from previous works how to categorize the Dhofar War within the overall history of anti-insurgency operations. The classical school of COIN essentially collectively roadmaps the best principals and methods for success as experienced through history and especially though the British experience and overall COIN record. The eventual successful conclusion of the Dhofar War has previously been put down to hard-won lessons learned from past campaigns and distilled into the literature of the classical school as highlighted by Marc DeVore when he states:

> It was only natural that the British officers commanding Oman's armed forces turned to past precedents once the situation in Dhofar began to degenerate from 1964 onwards… Although the enemies and terrain differed from one theatre to the next, these campaigns provided British soldiers with unparalleled experience in fighting irregular opponents.[56]

Whilst by no means a unanimously accepted point of view, the success, and the reasons put forward for the success of the Dhofar War have been utilised

The Dhofar War: Background, and Literature Representation 19

to identify a distinctive British way of conducting COIN as a method for success in contemporary and even in future campaigns.[57] What is not apparent in previous works is a clear discussion on how applicable such comparisons are between the Dhofar operation and examples from the classical school of COIN including the key post-Second World War British campaigns as highlighted within this book. As a result, this book therefore argues that although in many important respects the Dhofar War was very similar to previous UK COIN campaigns, it was actually a more unique case and was undertaken in a singular set of circumstances which are never likely be repeated again.[58] Despite this, some general lessons on current and future conduct can also be drawn from its eventual success. Aspects of similarity with previous British campaigns include the common global Cold War or decolonisation background narrative, as well as that of the UK withdrawal East of Suez and from the Gulf Area from the late 1960s. Strong similarities are also apparent in terms of the type of terrain in which the COIN campaign was being prosecuted, the classification of enemy being fought and the typical mode of combat. Also similar are the eventual implementation of well-honed 'hearts and minds'-related initiatives and the utilisation of indigenous security forces to provide intelligence and partake in combat operations.

Writers, however, differ on both the motivation for Britain's involvement in Oman and the Dhofar War as well as the overall conduct of the campaign. Writers such as Fred Halliday and Francis Owtram further the general view that Britain was a 'colonial oppressor' in terms of its historical involvement in Oman and in the Dhofar War also; and Britain's motivations exploitative towards the country overall. In terms of history, Owtram states that "[Due to British policy and actions] The position of a Sultan in Muscat became an onerous one, without freedom of manoeuvre in either external or internal affairs. The Sultans had no illusions about their independence and neither did Western powers other than the British."[59] Running counter to this is the argument that Britain was actually involved in the war out of a strategic security interest but was also simply honouring 200 years of close trade, diplomatic and military ties and a high level of bilateral historical cooperation. Indeed Wendell Phillips states that: "The British [during the Jebel Akhdar operation and aftermath; but equally relevant to the Dhofar campaigns] were not attempting to hold onto something for themselves, for they do not now and never have in the past possessed one square foot of the Kingdom of Oman".[60] Indeed such assistance can be viewed as a natural progression or result of the fact that the friendship between the two countries should, "Endure till the end of time or the sun and moon cease in their revolving careers," as stated in the text of one of the later treaties between the Sultan of Muscat and the (English) East India company.[61]

This book argues that Britain's motivation was based on calculations of self-interest, but was far from the Marxist-type view of colonial exploitation as put forward by some writers.

The conduct of the war can be described variously as being, from a positive perspective, either an exemplary example of a COIN campaign or one which was at least run in a professional and competent manner therefore still enabling a COIN win. Running counter to this is the view that the campaign was actually poorly run. So much so that it resulted in the campaign lasting much longer than need have been and costing more in terms of lives, funds and general disruption; and even nearly ending in defeat for the SAF and the Sultan's regime. Halliday alludes to Britain supporting an oppressive and tyrannical Sultan, whilst later revisionist writers are often highly critical of the conduct of the Dhofar campaign; (not only in terms of the competence of its execution but of the brutality of its conduct and Britain's involvement) which, if widely publicised, would have had little to no chance of ever being condoned by either Parliament or the British people more generally.[62]

In terms of historical timelines, the Dhofar campaign has traditionally been divided into two separate phases; the first pre-1970 and the second post-1970 (pre- and post-coup).[63] The first phase is generally described as being poorly-run and conducted and the second very well-orchestrated and executed. This is somewhat of an arbitrary division and not one which stands up fully to closer analysis, especially since the campaign was close to being lost as late as 1971, and a more subtle or appropriate explanation is required.[64]

One can see therefore, that there are varied historical interpretations of the British COIN record, the comparisons with previous UK COIN campaigns, as well as the motivations behind British involvement, the conduct of the war, and when the campaign was morphed into a winning campaign from one that was essentially being lost. This book aims to clarify such aspects and present the argument that although the Dhofar COIN campaign was not conducted in the glare of the media and along modern politically correct lines, it was ultimately professionally run. It was done so within the bounds of extremely difficult circumstances and was ultimately a grand strategic success. This book also clarifies where the Dhofar War fits into the wider body of COIN (especially classical COIN) writings and whether, and to what extent, it was similar to other post-Second World War British campaigns or was a unique, standalone example of the genre.

Classification of Dhofar COIN Campaign Success
Previous historical works are divided in their treatment of the Dhofar War as a complete success or an ideal type of COIN campaign, and the view that it

was anything but. The perception that the Dhofar War was an ideal example of the art of COIN is highlighted by DeVore when he states, "The British-led campaign in Oman's Dhofar province between 1963 and 1975 is generally considered a 'textbook' counterinsurgency," which "supplanted the Malayan Emergency as the counterinsurgency case study taught at the United Kingdom's Junior Command and Staff Course."[65] In terms of success the Dhofar campaign has, from a historical perspective been lauded as the foremost example of British COIN operations with writers such as John Charters stating that "[The Dhofar War] was a carefully orchestrated campaign that by 1975 had yielded Britain's most clear-cut counter-insurgency victory since Malaya."[66] In more general terms, COIN experts have also even described the execution of the Dhofar War as a kind of pinnacle of its genre; indeed Beckett states, "In short the Dhofar experience represents a model campaign in every way."[67] Opposing such views is the more critical outlook that the campaign was poorly run by willing, but often amateuristic or sub-standard British (loan and contract) officers within the SAF. These were, in turn, backed by an at best distracted government, military and civil service; and at worst disinterested, parsimonious and at times duplicitous British state.[68] This narrative is backed up by the view that the war was effectively at a stalemate at least by 1969 and could possibly have even been lost in 1970 or 1971. Up to this point, the SAF did not hold a permanent presence on the jebel as they did not have the logistical capability to do so. On an annual basis, come the monsoon-like 'Khareef' season, any areas held on the jebel would be abandoned with the troops heading back to the plain and the insurgency simply re-occupying lost territory without even the need to fight. Geraint Hughes describes how government forces effectively surrendered the jebel to the insurgents and later the whole of Dhofar bar the coastal plain by 1970.[69] DeVore further highlights that the state of the campaign was so dire by 1970 despite the best efforts of the British that British officers were actually reporting back to London in 1970 that as a worst case scenario the whole of Dhofar might even be lost to the insurgent forces by 1971.[70] This rot had been firmly established with the loss of Rakhyut in 1969 and capture (and subsequent public 'execution' of some) of the Sultan's garrison there in the August of that year.[71] There is also present a third explanatory narrative, which is the more analytical approach to dividing the Dhofar COIN campaign into two parts; pre-1970 and post-1970, with the former often seen as unsuccessful, and the latter (post-coup and accession of Sultan Qaboos) period as the successful phase of the campaign. This narrative, although more nuanced, still does not provide a sufficient explanation which will be addressed via a different explanatory narrative. In terms of the level of success of the Dhofar COIN campaign, previous historical writings also do not properly explain who were the 'winners' and the 'losers' in the campaign, and to what extent they were such. James Worrall highlights that the literature on the Dhofar War is often blinkered on focussing on the success or otherwise of tactics of the campaign.[72] To remedy this approach, this book examines and clarifies the above thread of inquiry from a more strategically-focussed perspective with regards to the various actors involved in the conflict.

Extent to Which Dhofar COIN Campaign Can Be Considered 'British'
For over two hundred years prior to the Dhofar War, Britain had a long history of influence in (Muscat and) Oman. This influence ranged from the historical military and financial assistance provided by the British Indian Colonial administration based in Calcutta (then later New Delhi) and latterly by the British government itself. These included the Canning Award/Zanzibar subsidy to the expansion of assistance from the late 1950s with the series of 'Exchange of Letters' agreements and amendments and arguably even more significantly so, later in the early 1970s. This significant influence translates into the Dhofar War specifically. To date in the historical literature there exist several distinct narratives to explain, account for or quantify the scale of the British role or influence on the Dhofar campaign and its eventual successful conclusion for the Sultan's regime; and therefore whether it can be considered a 'British' campaign. These range from the UK being on the periphery of the campaign or eventual victory or it being technically not a British campaign at all, to a perspective that considers it was a situation of complete such control from the start of the conflict. This book errs on the side of the latter; that it was in reality undoubtedly primarily a British-controlled-run and won-campaign. This book, in addition, also puts forward a more subtly distinct explanation to add to the debate; that of a progressively shifting or 'sliding' scale of Britain's influence on the Dhofar COIN campaign.[73] In effect this viewpoint states that although overall the Dhofar COIN operation should be considered a British campaign, much evidence exists to suggest the reality is actually more nuanced and that the view as put forward in a majority of the literature of whichever persuasion is often too broad-brushed or focussed on the actual outcome of the campaign.

Within the literature there are several distinct viewpoints on how 'British' the Dhofar COIN campaign was in terms of influence, control and physical execution. On the one hand is the view that the campaign was, by either direct or indirect means, effectively both run and won by Britain.[74] The scope of this particular viewpoint varies from the assertion that Britain ran the campaign and won it in all respects, to a more considered outlook.[75] This narrative acknowledges the UK's key role but also that there were both other important actors as well as explanations for how the war was conducted and victory finally attained. Both ends of this 'orthodox' historical view spectrum generally put forward the idea and assessment, however, that, for the most part, the prime mover in organising, fighting and eventually winning the campaign was Britain.

Another historical perspective present is that of writers who are highly critical of Britain's role in Oman from a historical perspective and in the Dhofar campaign in particular. The spectrum ranges from the largely ideologically opposed such as Halliday and Outram to those primarily critical of the practicalities of the UK actions such as John Newsinger, Douglas Porch and Abdel Takriti. The ideologically opposed perspective purports that the entire Dhofar COIN campaign was essentially a wholly British-run affair with little other influence. This influence was borne essentially from the UK's imperialist policies. This kept Oman in a state of colonial dependency and that the Sultan was essentially a puppet to serve Britain's strategic interests, where "No one involved doubted that in the early 1970s the Sultan's whole war depended on British support at the highest level."[76] Within the more critical (of the UK's role) practical historical interpretations can be found the view that Britain was in charge of the campaign and conducted it largely badly and with a level of violence and morally questionable conduct akin to colonial-era campaigns and previous UK COIN operations.[77] The overall effect, however, is that all such differing or disparate scholarly views boil down to the same basic tenet; that the Dhofar COIN campaign was an almost wholly British-dominated affair, albeit for often very different reasons. Also represented in the body of work on the Dhofar War is the view that it was not really a British campaign at all. It often portrays the COIN campaign as an Omani or an international coalition ranged against the insurgents merely assisted by Britain at most and therefore negating the view that the UK had the key role in the war.[78] This view highlights the significant role and level of control of the Sultan and the pre-eminent role of the SAF and the Sultan himself in the sovereign prosecution of the campaign. As Hughes highlights, "Nonetheless, the sultans were not passive actors and British advice was not always heeded," and British CSAFs were on occasions overruled or deferred to the Sultan's wishes.[79] From 1973 military forces from Jordan and Iran were also introduced into the conflict on the government side. Far from Britain or the SAS winning the war single-handedly, this fact points to a further narrative as to who was responsible for eventual victory in 1975. DeVore, for instance states that:

> Between 1968 and 1973, British assistance did not win the [Dhofar] war, but certainly prevented it from being lost. Victory was only possible once British and Omani diplomacy had managed to construct an informal alliance [or 'coalition of the willing'] among the Middle East's monarchies.[80]

James Goode highlights that the strategic importance of the Iranians in particular in defeating the enemy and bringing the war to a close in 1975 was not just key but absolutely decisive, where "His [the Shah's] troops tipped the balance in favour of the sultan's forces, contributing to a speedy end to the insurrection, for which Iran earned the lasting gratitude of the sultan."[81] This view is even echoed by military figures such as Major General Ken Perkins (CSAF 1975–1977) who stated, "Iranian support undoubtedly tipped the scales; without it the war would have dragged into a stalemate as the SAF alone had insufficient troops to achieve a clear decision."[82] Going further even than this perspective is the minority view that Britain was merely a peripheral actor in the saga and the conduct of the war and eventual victory was predominantly due to internal Omani leadership factors. Essentially this view suggests that the wise leadership and strategic acumen of the new Sultan Qaboos forged all elements of Omani society together, including the SAF, to defeat the common enemy.[83] The collective view of previous commentators is therefore essentially split between two extremes and the view that the Dhofar COIN campaign was an almost entirely British-run and led affair and the polar opposite counterview. The latter viewpoint reflects the view that the reality of the situation was much more complicated, with other important actors or allies involved or that Britain was actually not the main actor at all and was, in a way, even peripheral to the whole campaign. What is missing, and what this book aims to provide is an explanation that demonstrates how the influence and roles of the different actors changed or shifted over the course of the campaign.

What, therefore, was the case at the start of the COIN campaign in 1965 was very different to that which existed at the time of eventual victory some 10 years later in 1975. This is where the 'sliding scale' of influence narrative contributes, as it provides a more nuanced and accurate narrative of the nature and extent of British influence in the campaign.[84] Even the main traditional war viewpoint neglects to clarify fully the overarching extent of the British operational role and the weight attributed to the strategic leverage and influence exerted by the UK. As Alston and Laing comment, "The conduct of the Dhofar War was an international effort… [but] The bulk of the tactical and strategic leadership was however British, and this was the principal British contribution to the war."[85] This book does both accept and emphasise that the Sultans of Oman had a significant degree of actual control over the war. It took, however, British strategic planning and leadership as well as control of all major command aspects to amalgamate all advantages and turn around a failing campaign to eventually result in a decisive victory and a rare COIN win. As Benest states, "the insurgency was in the process of being lost up until 1970, was turned by Graham and then won by Creasey/Fletcher and after them Ken Perkins. John Graham set the scene for what remains the most successful counterinsurgency in modern history."[86]

Part I

The Dhofar War: A Classical British COIN Campaign?

The Dhofar War in many ways strongly resembles the characteristics of classical British COIN campaigns; indeed from many perspectives it is almost indistinguishable. Whilst displaying stark similarities, the Dhofar campaign also exhibits, although fewer in number, certain highly significant and key differences which actually set it apart from the British classical COIN narrative. Through these few, yet key differences, it can be seen that the Dhofar campaign actually displayed certain unique characteristics. Whilst it should, therefore, be included both in the overall narrative of classical British COIN and in all studies on the subject, it should ultimately be classified separately. The Dhofar War was in many ways actually a standalone or unique case.

The Dhofar War is notable for its absence from some key COIN-related historical publications, therefore the status and classification of the campaign within the subject literature requires clarification.[1] To this end, and to clarify the extent of the war's credentials as a classical British COIN campaign, definitions of insurgency, classical COIN and British classical COIN are required for the reader. Whether the Dhofar operation can be specifically considered a classical British COIN campaign is then addressed in the subsequent chapters of Section 1. As such, the Dhofar campaign is compared with key elements of the main UK COIN operations carried out since 1944/5 as well as further afield from both background and strategic as well as campaign-specific perspectives. By doing so, it is clarified whether the Dhofar campaign can be considered part of the same general classical narrative regarding UK COIN (or the 'British Way of Counterinsurgency') and an archetypal example of a British COIN campaign, or conversely as a standalone or unique example of the genre.[2]

Insurgency, Counterinsurgency and the Dhofar Case

There is a clear distinction between guerrilla warfare and insurgency. The former can be described as the largely tactical recourse actions of the weak over the strong, or irregular troops supporting conventional military forces and acting as 'partisans'.[3] As such it is a descriptive phrase to cover the wide spectrum of irregular military tactics throughout history carried out by non-regular forces and used to distinguish them from regular military units and tactics. Such methods of warfare were, however, relatively underutilised until the 20th Century and especially from the 1920s onwards. From this time, however, the old-style guerrilla warfare became politicised or 'revolutionary' in its application; but also in overall intent as can be observed in the case of the Russian Civil War which began during the turmoil of the First World War.[4]

A more sophisticated approach overall, insurgency can therefore be described as an integrated politico-military strategy to overthrow the government or status quo in a territory.[5] As a result, political elements and social and economic, psychological, propaganda and subversion aspects were amalgamated with traditional irregular or guerrilla fighting tactics. This was undertaken in an attempt to subvert and overthrow the governing status quo in countries in an overall higher level strategic approach.[6] "More properly, therefore, modern revolutionary guerrilla warfare might be termed insurgency" which, post-1945 has centred mainly on ideology; again largely a consequence of the Russian revolutions and emergence of the USSR and its Marxist-centred theories.[7] As such, there is a clear differentiation between the basic tactics of the guerrilla fighters and the overarching strategy of insurgency; it being "…a means to a particular end [with] guerrilla tactics being employed strategically to achieve a political goal" and usually occurring over a protracted period of time.[8] As a result of such developments and the evolution of insurgency:

> In response to guerilla warfare, insurgency and terrorism, armed forces [of states] have developed counter-measures to defeat such challenges and prevent their resurgence, often mirroring the [general] development of guerrilla warfare and insurgency.[9]

The activity of counterinsurgency or COIN, therefore, is the state's response to the type and circumstances of an insurgency which threatens the stability or survival of the incumbent governing or power structure status quo.

The insurgency in Dhofar was borne primarily of dissatisfaction with the lot of the Dhofari population from the long-standing reactionary, repressive and neglectful rule of Sultan Said bin Taimur.[10] The privations of the Imamate struggle and subsequent Djebel War, allied to the Sultan's autocratic, often petty and largely paranoid rule and lack of any significant social or economic development in Oman resulted in widespread discontent. Action such as tight control of movements in and out of the country, arbitrary bans on many actions and items such as smoking or music in public, newspapers, sunglasses and even the risk of arrest if not carrying a lit lamp through the streets of Muscat after sunset all added to the growing dissatisfaction with Sultan Said's rule. The legitimate grievances of the Omani population were multiplied in Dhofar. This was reinforced through the previously highlighted eye-opening experiences of expatriate Dhofar workers abroad. Those fortunate Dhofaris who managed to exit the country's strict border regime and were working in neighbouring wealthy Gulf countries saw first-hand the vast wealth disparities of their home to the rest of the region which helped facilitate the initial insurgency. As such, the insurgency was political in nature, aiming to remove a perceived oppressive ruler and change the status quo of governance within the province to improve their lot. With the adoption of guerrilla-style tactics, the Dhofar uprising falls within the definition of insurgency and the subsequent State of (Muscat and) Oman's actions can therefore be properly classified as COIN responses. Whilst starting as a small-scale internal policing action by the SAF against a limited-scope rebellion by a motley band of nationalists, the response developed along with the character and scale of the insurgency. As the insurgency later developed into a fully-fledged Marxist-inspired uprising involving both non-, and external state actors, the Sultan's response resultantly grew in scale and complexity. What began as an initial limited company-level Omani military expedition in 1964 to quell the disturbances as initiated by the then CSAF, Colonel Tony Lewis developed into a country-wide (and cross-border on occasion) COIN campaign eventually involving over 15,000 security personnel from several nations under later CSAFs; Brigadier Corran Purdon, Brigadier John Graham, Major General Timothy Creasey, and finally Major General Ken Perkins.

The Classical School of Counterinsurgency, Classical British COIN and the Dhofar Campaign

The classical school of COIN revolves around two main factors; that of historical timeframe and the motivation of the insurgents themselves. In terms of timeframe, "The term 'classical counter-insurgency' describes the theory of counter-revolutionary warfare developed in response to the so-called wars of national liberation from 1944 to about 1982."[11] Pre-Second World War, unconventional warfare actions such as counter-guerrilla or pacification operations are conversely often referred to in the British case merely as 'Imperial policing' actions.[12] In terms of motivation or purpose the classical school describes the relevant revolutionary or separatist insurgent movements as seeking to gain control of a state, or at least part of its territory.[13] As Michael Crawshaw states: "The common thread in classical insurgency is the attempt to change a government by violent means," and this violence was usually directed against a "colonial or occupying power, or an indigenous government [or ruler] viewed as oppressive" by a segment of the population.[14]

The classical school of COIN is a body of work/theory in the literature centred principally, though not exclusively, on the numerous and high-profile British COIN campaigns of the post-Second World War period, and principally up until the late 1960s. The school of thought is represented, amongst others, by the various contemporaneous works of writers such as Robert Thompson, Julian Paget, Frank Kitson and David Galula.[15] Following these original classical theorists are a group which collectively may be termed 'neo-classicists' such as Thomas Mockaitis, Rod Thornton, David Charters, John Pimlott, David Kilcullen, John Nagl, and Ian Beckett. Such later writers reflect on the key earlier campaigns but also often include later examples including the Dhofar War itself and the early period of the Northern Ireland conflict as well as key non-British classical-era campaigns such as those conducted by French, Portuguese or US forces. In the UK case, in the immediate post-war era the British armed forces faced resourceful and relentless opponents in Palestine up until 1948, and "From 1948–60 British forces were also involved in three [simultaneous] major COIN campaigns – Malaya (1948–60), Kenya (1952–60) and Cyprus (1955–59)."[16] The UK was further compelled to mount a whole series of military operations during the early and mid-1960s in order to cover her retreat from Empire or deal with the fallout from insurgencies affecting newly-independent states. These included non-COIN operations in Jamaica (1960), Guyana (from 1962), and in the Cameroons/Swaziland.[17] Also undertaken were the post-independence quelling of mutinies in Tanganyika, Uganda and Kenya, plus the Suez operation (1956) and assistance to Kuwait (1961).[18] Further, such operations also additionally included the Borneo Confrontation (1962–1966) and the Aden Emergency (1963–1967) as well as the early years of the Northern Ireland 'troubles'.[19]

The British classical COIN tradition, whilst being central to the development of the larger classical school in the campaigns previously highlighted, exhibits several broad defining characteristics or principles which help set it apart from other, non-UK classical-era campaigns. These arguably include the relatively limited sized of these overall campaigns, significant levels of restraint being employed, and general overall COIN campaign success. The Malayan and Kenyan campaigns aside, all other UK COIN campaigns were very limited in terms of size and of British forces committed which illustrates the principal of general moderation and restraint by the UK authorities in such matters. This is also borne out in the numbers of casualties sustained by both sides in these campaigns and the fact that despite use of modern air power and other forms of support to the troops on the ground they were mainly limited size, platoon or company level infantry-oriented operations. Restraint is illustrated in that significant aerial bombing, as employed in Vietnam for instance, was largely avoided as was the use of controversial weapons such as napalm. This caveat remains true even though its use was considered in Oman and the Sultan's government wished to employ it, with the proposal illustratively being rejected by British seconded officers.[20] Whilst revisionist writers often challenge this categorisation, and it being a concept which does not have universal acceptance, the oft-deployed term for this approach is the application of 'minimum use of force' to achieve aims. Historically, it derives from the common law tradition of restraint utilised by British security forces in the standard Imperial policing model; unlike the approach often seen in several other non-British classical-era campaigns.[21]

Although what might be termed 'oppressive measures' were certainly widely utilised in many UK COIN campaigns (including mass deportation or forced resettlement, and the use of capital punishment for infractions such as weapon carrying etc. during imposed states of emergency), the British tradition was underlined by a key and central understanding that insurgency was neither only, or even primarily a military issue or problem.[22] Although the armed forces were utilised as required, political and social factors were treated as equally important and were often considered to provide the most effective weapons with which to both counter, and ultimately prevail in an insurgency. The prevailing view was, therefore, that "Unrest must be dealt with through a combination of reform [e.g. winning 'hearts and minds'] and police measures."[23] 'Hearts and minds'-oriented campaigns on various scales were implemented from Malaya onwards. Political and land reform (e.g. in Kenya), police primacy (where the military was only used as a backup to the primary policing role of the civilian authorities) and promises of independence were all used as part of a wide-ranging number of non-military tools available to counter insurgencies. Such methods were utilised to help remedy the grievances from which unrest stemmed in conjunction with the restrained use of military force under common law standards of operation. Such factors resulted in campaign and COIN success rates which although far from perfect (and whilst not claiming any "magic formula" for success) were better than the COIN efforts of all other COIN-undertaking nations.[24] Whilst the Palestine, Cyprus and especially Adeni campaigns are unlikely to ever be called outright COIN successes, they avoided the mass civilian casualties as seen in several non-UK classical-era COIN campaigns. In addition, they enabled functioning states to continue after British withdrawal and a return to relative stability in short timeframes, which is indicative of a highly pragmatic approach.[25] The COIN operation in Kenya was, however, a military success and those undertaken in Malaya and Brunei/Borneo were definite campaign wins for the British way of COIN alongside, eventually, that undertaken closer to home in Northern Ireland. Further, the Malayan campaign is often used with some justification as the exemplar British COIN campaign and helped to bestow the UK with a reputation for expertise in the field.

The Marxist, left leaning, or revisionist scholars within the COIN literature often disagree with the existence or level of such traits, with the UK's reputation for humanity or restraint for instance being described as a 'myth' or a COIN success rate which is described as actually very poor.[26] The humanitarian-related criticism is often justifiably levelled at the Kenyan campaign with mass screenings of Kikuyu tribespeople where abuse was widespread and large numbers killed either by military action or by judicial executions.[27] Accusations of torture were apparent in Cyprus and Aden (the latter primarily at a notorious locale known as the 'fingernail factory') especially and in terms of brutality even in the exemplar campaign of Malaya, harsh methods were adopted until in many ways "Malaya resembled a police state".[28] When compared, however, in relative terms to the widespread civilian casualties through reliance on mass firepower, general brutality (and as described in the historical literature in the French case even "adopting policies which were in many eyes little different to those of the Gestapo or SS") and 'heavy-handed' actions of other non-UK classical era campaigns (such as the widespread summary executions by French forces in Algeria) this lends a somewhat moderating perspective to the British record.[29] Overall, from a relative perspective, British COIN can, therefore, be seen to display certain characteristics which highlight the general "relative restraint of British counterinsurgency when compared with its French, Dutch or Portuguese counterparts".[30] In all Mockaitis sums up the situation succinctly when he states that, "While certainly not flawless, the British approach to counterinsurgency has been [both relatively humane and] more successful than that of any other nation," adding that:

> British counter-insurgency operations, however, have generally been conspicuous for the lack of such excesses… The British have usually avoided the French policy of brutality employed during the battle of Algiers and the American reliance on indiscriminate firepower applied in Vietnam.[31]

It is from these historic characteristics and principles of British COIN that the Dhofar campaign approach was derived. Britain never committed large numbers of personnel or funding resources to the Dhofar campaign and the level of casualties for both sides was relatively low; it was small scale and Britain purposely kept it that way. Backing up this perspective, Peterson states that "Dhurfar was a very small war, even in the context of 'small wars.'"[32] In addition, with there being little to no evidence for indiscriminate bombing or use of controversial weapons such as napalm – or examples of "what not to do

The Dhofar War: A Classical British COIN Campaign? 31

[in COIN campaigns]" – the narrative of relative restraint with regards to the conduct of the Dhofar campaign is reinforced within the specific British way of COIN.[33]

For the initial six years of the Dhofar Insurgency there was, however, a level of repression exhibited by British-led forces. Collective punishments were widely administered such as crop burning, livestock shooting, the destruction of dwellings and well-capping.[34] Unpalatable perhaps to modern sensibilities, these were, however, tried and tested methods of non-lethal control and coercion from the Imperial policing era. Similarly, these were a far cry from large-scale and often indiscriminate human, property and environmental collateral damage from saturation aerial bombing or artillery barrages as employed in several non-UK COIN campaigns. The situation was, however, significantly addressed from 1970 onwards during the post-coup era after Sultan Qaboos came to the throne. During the last five years of the war the situation improved immeasurably with a British-instigated 'hearts and minds' campaign, social, economic and governance/political development and even an amnesty for insurgents which was not previously permitted under Sultan Said. In terms of relative success, the Dhofar campaign also fits into the general British COIN mould. Along with relative levels of restraint and humanity the Dhofar campaign was seen as a COIN win and therefore complying with the general traits of the UK's Classical COIN tradition, or the "British way of Counter-Insurgency".[35]

From such perspectives the Dhofar campaign illustrates a strong correspondence with the overall definition of a classical COIN campaign, and further with the broad traits of UK classical-era COIN specifically. Dhofar could perhaps, therefore, in such general terms be viewed as an archetypal or typical British COIN campaign. To properly gauge whether and to what extent the Dhofar campaign can actually be considered a classical UK COIN undertaking, a review of the specific and detailed factors or traits of the latter is required and will be explored in this book in subsequent chapters. Post-Second World War British COIN campaigns exhibited certain backgrounds, circumstances, characteristics, as well as tactics and methods of implementation or prosecution. The following chapters of this book identify the main aspects of UK post-1945 campaigns to ascertain the key elements associated with classical British COIN campaigning and their comparison to the Dhofar case. They demonstrate that although in many key respects the war closely reflected previous classical British campaigns (in addition to the general highlighted traits of British COIN), there are key circumstances of the campaign which set it apart and actually made it a unique case. Ultimately, the Dhofar COIN campaign and its level of success occurred and was undertaken in a singular set of circumstances which, like those of the Malayan Emergency are unlikely to be repeated again.[36]

Historical Literature Focus of the Special Air Service (SAS) Regiment

For a secretive unit of the UK's Special Forces capability, the SAS has had significant public literature exposure. Such coverage would likely be very much more than the unit would like; especially so in modern times from the period of the 1991 Gulf War and the revelations of former unit members. The formation of the unit by the charismatic Lieutenant Colonel David Sterling during the Second World War and their exploits behind enemy lines alongside the Long-Range Desert Group (LRDG) in North Africa are the stuff of legend. One only has to read the memoirs of an 'original' such as Jonny Cooper to be amazed at the shoestring nature of the unit and its unpopularity with the rest of the army status quo.[37] It is also clear that the SAS's formation and operational capability was due largely to the character, establishment connections and sheer drive of its founding father, even though Sterling spent the final two years of the war interred in a prisoner of war camp.

Once the war was over, toleration of unorthodox outfits – however successful – in the British armed forces was reversed and the SAS was disbanded, albeit re-surfacing in 1946 as a territorial army unit. Passed over for active service in the Korean War, the conflict which assured the unit's survival was the Malayan Emergency. Ironically the unit's name was initially changed to the Malayan Scouts (SAS) and only in 1952 was 22 SAS formed as a regular unit of the British army. As the Malayan Emergency was petering out after independence and formation of the state of Malaysia in 1957, the SAS was posted to Oman in 1958 to assist with the Jebel Akhdar campaign, with the Imamate rebels pitted against Sultan Said the ruler of Muscat and Oman. Here, with the CSAF, ex-wartime Special Operations Executive (SOE) officer, Colonel David Smiley in charge, and other familiar faces such as Jonny Cooper now a contract officer in the Sultanate's armed forces, the SAS got its first taste of Oman-style insurgency and performed admirably, especially with the storming of the insurgent stronghold of the Jebel Akhdar in 1959. The memoirs of Smiley and Cooper are required reading for those interested in these conflict and the SAS role.[38]

Essentially, solving a problem for the British government discreetly and at minimal cost, allied to the reputation for hunting down communist terrorists in Malaya, ensured the unit's survival. When the British government needed a discreet solution to the burgeoning insurgency in Oman's Dhofar province, they called on the services of the SAS, which served in Dhofar non-stop for some seven years from 1970. Again, the biographies of General Sir Peter De La Billiere and Major General Tony Jeapes are again required reading for those interested in Operation STORM, the seven-year Arabian sojourn of the SAS, and key instances such as the 1972 Battle of Mirbat.[39] It should also be remembered that this was taking place whilst the regiment was increasingly being utilised of another secret war in Northern Ireland, in which Mark Urban's '*Big Boys Rules*' for example is an eye-opening account.[40] The actions of the SAS in the Falklands War, the Iran Embassy Siege, the Balkans, and the First Gulf War are all well-documented. Once the unit's survival was no longer an issue, however, this sort of exposure was largely considered not just unwelcome publicity, but by shedding light on its methods, it was also a potential threat to the unit's operational capability and even the security of its personnel. Even General De La Billiere, the former Commanding Officer of the unit was not immune, being reportedly banned from the Sterling Lines mess in Hereford for supposedly giving away operation secrets in his biographical book '*Looking for Trouble: SAS to Gulf Command*' although the MOD had reportedly approved the book's text. The point of note is that a large percentage of the coverage of the SAS's activities is at the tactical level via biographical materials. There are other good books, but the wider operational and strategic-level use of these Special Forces troops is much less represented in the wider literature. This book also aims to fill part of that existing 'gap'.

Chapter 3

Background and Strategic Level Similarities

The Dhofar campaign was very similar to other British classical COIN campaigns in terms of its general background and context. Taking post-war UK COIN campaigns in general, key similarities can be observed with the Dhofar case in terms of the global Cold War and the rise of nationalism and decolonisation as unifying background contexts.

Cold War Aspect

All classical British COIN campaigns took place within the Cold War era and (apart from post-millennium operations in Sierra Leone, Afghanistan and Iraq) only two classical-era campaigns actually either started prior to 1948 (Palestine) or finished post-1990 (Northern Ireland).[1] All the remainder, including Malaya, Kenya, Cyprus, Oman (Imamate campaign), Brunei/Borneo and Aden all began and finished within this specific timeframe. This timeframe also included the Dhofar COIN campaign which only ended officially in 1975, although British troops did not leave Oman until 1977 and unrest continued for years after the official ending of the war. Further, several UK COIN campaigns encountered as the combatant opposition, either Communist-controlled or trained forces or Marxist-inspired insurgents. In Malaya the opposition were Communist insurgents labelled 'bandits' or 'terrorists' at the time.[2] These were borne of the remnants of the Malayan People's Japanese Army (MPJA) which was formed via the Malayan Communist Party (MCP) as initially established in 1929.[3] In the early phase of the Borneo campaign it was largely the communist-backed revolutionary insurgents of the North Kalimantan People's Army (NKPA) which were engaged and defeated by British forces when attempting to overrun and supplant the governing status quo in Brunei in late 1962.[4] Likewise, the insurgents in Aden had strong backing and support not just from the pro-Soviet and Egypt-dominated United Arab Republic (UAR) regime officially to 1971, but also eventually from pro-Communist and Egyptian-backed North Yemen.

The Dhofar insurgency and COIN operation began in the mid-1960s and victory by government forces was declared in 1975 making it a clear timeline-related fit for being identified as a classical-era Cold War campaign. Although nationalist in its inception, the Dhofar War eventually became firmly entrenched in the Cold War proxy struggle of the time, with Britain representing the Western world against the proxies initially of Mao's revolutionary China, then, from 1972, the Soviet Union. The background scenario for Britain within the Dhofari COIN campaign would have been somewhat familiar to soldiers and officers who had served in previous UK COIN campaigns. Those who had previously served in Malaya, Brunei/Borneo, and especially in Aden would have understood and have been relatively clear on who the enemy was. In a similar vein, the main backers of the insurgents in PDRY and Dhofar in terms of support, training and weapons were the great Communist powers where:

> Until 1972 China had provided a good deal of support, but it was then persuaded by the Shah [of Iran] to desist, agreeing because of its economic and cultural interest in Iran. Russia then became the dominant supporter, although Libya and Cuba also sent money, supplies and training staff.[5]

The key Communist powers were intent on exporting their revolution around the world, and the Middle East was one of the key ideological battlegrounds as "part of the Kremlin's world-wide campaign against the Western Powers".[6] Further to this, the Cold War and Arab nationalism collided in Aden and wider Yemen with Egypt, which was backed with Soviet aid and hardware, engaged in a costly North Yemeni civil war, President Nasser described this as 'his' Vietnam with approximately 50,000 Egyptian troop casualties, and of these about 10,000 killed.[7] With Egyptian and supported groups destabilising the British-formed Southern Federation (including Aden) this contributed to the eventual untidy and humiliating British 'scuttle' from the territory in 1967.[8] A pro-republican regime was then established by the National Liberation Front (NLF) in Aden and by 1970 the communist-led People's Democratic Republic of Yemen (PDRY) was formed. This development created a situation which allowed the Dhofari rebels to both be supplied with aid and arms by their erstwhile sponsors, and to openly operate from a safe base area in Hauf within sovereign (now Marxist) PDRY territory.[9]

The Cold War background aspect with the underlying theme of battling Communism, proxy warfare (and, for the Western Powers, and especially Britain, in preventing a Middle Eastern version of 'domino theory') also closely relates the Dhofar operation to previous classical British COIN campaigns. This included the actions in the Radfan to the north of Aden against tribesmen where the SAS took several casualties with two men decapitated after being killed by the insurgent tribesman and their heads reportedly subsequently displayed on stakes in a barbaric 'victory' display in enemy-controlled territory.[10] Such

Cold War rivalries accounted for the development of several classical British COIN campaigns, including the 12-year long Malayan Emergency, the initial actions of the Brunei/Borneo Confrontation and the Aden/Southern Federation campaigns. The timeframe of the Cold War also accounts for the duration of all but two of the classical-era UK COIN campaigns. As a causative factor as well as a historical timeframe aspect the Cold War is, therefore, a key factor with regards to classical UK campaigns and the Dhofar case mirrors this strongly.

Rise of Nationalism and Decolonisation

Similar to most classical-era British and other European or USA-conducted COIN campaigns, the Dhofar War was also undertaken with the backdrop of the phenomenon of the decolonisation of large tracts of the world. This was brought about to a large extent by the growth of nationalism and nationalistic-centred grievances within such territories, which reflected the situation in Dhofar Province, albeit against an oppressive external power-backed local ruler as opposed to a colonial power per se. As a result, the initial development of the Dhofar Insurgency in the 1960s reflects the roots of the uprisings in Palestine, Malaya, Kenya and Cyprus which all fall primarily within the rise of nationalism and decolonisation narratives. As such, they were therefore also the raison d'etre of the British COIN campaigns developed to counter such revolts from the late 1940s and beyond. The nationalist/anti-colonial movement was key to the instigation and development of two of the earliest and largest-scale UK COIN campaigns, being that of Malaya and Kenya (Mau Mau) which ran almost concurrently for most of the 1950s. In Cyprus, it was not just a case of the nationalist Insurgents pushing for colonial rule to end, but also to join politically with Greece; an aspiration known as Enosis. The resultant British COIN campaign lasted for four years and involved the deployment of thousands of British troops. In addition, even the 30-year long conflict in Northern Ireland was borne of nationalist-related grievances and although it spanned a large percentage of the Cold War, it was not a conflict which was reliant on the wider Soviet-USA superpower confrontation and ideological stand off to sustain it.

Like the high profile and costly nationalistic-based UK COIN campaigns, the operation in Dhofar was strongly linked to such grievances, which were directed towards Britain via opposition to the UK-backed regime of Sultan Said bin Taimur. Although later developing into a full communist-backed insurgency, the origins of the Dhofar insurgency were primarily centred on nationalistic, social, and economic discontent. Although Oman was never a formal colony of the UK there were very strong links between the two countries for centuries dating back at least to the formal 1798 agreements (and arguably back to the

1600s) and as such Britain exerted a significant level of influence on the rulers and therefore the country as a whole.[11] Britain was historically the key external power in the Middle East and especially in the Gulf Region, and with Sultan Said essentially leaving Oman's foreign affairs to Britain to conduct. During his rule Oman had no UN representative and there was virtually zero foreign diplomatic representation in Muscat which meant the imperialist or 'colony' label was set and expressed through the annual 'Question on Oman' as debated in the General Assembly of the UN.[12] This was pushed by republican Middle Eastern nations to free an Oman in the grip of the colonial power of Britain, and was enthusiastically backed by the wider Communist Bloc.[13] Although Oman was never a formal territory of the UK, this set the Dhofar conflict and COIN campaign firmly within the contemporaneous global nationalist or decolonisation context in terms of causative effect. As such, this makes the Dhofar case similar to other classical UK COIN campaigns.

The Dhofar War can, therefore, be viewed as being very similar to the British classical COIN campaigns of the post-Second World War era from a background or causative perspective. The global Cold War or decolonization narrative is consistent for the case of Dhofar, and also for the British withdrawal East of Suez and the Gulf region in the late 1960s and early 1970s. The classical school of COIN covers both types of insurgencies. It can be observed that Palestine, Malaya, Kenya, Cyprus and Northern Ireland all fall primarily within the nationalist or decolonisation narrative, whereas Brunei/early Borneo, Aden, and Dhofar fall more broadly into the Cold War 'ideology-centred' category[14]. This is, however, a somewhat arbitrary distinction as there is significant crossover between such broad categorisations in the case of the Dhofar campaign and even more so in the case of campaigns such as those undertaken in Brunei/Borneo or Malaya which underlines the key similarity between such UK-run COIN campaigns. Overall, the Dhofar COIN campaign therefore clearly fits with the background circumstances of previous post-Second World War British COIN campaigns.

Reasons for UK COIN Campaign involvement

Although Britain's specific motivations for involvement in its various classical UK COIN campaigns varied from case to case, there are several overarching and recurring themes. These included the maintenance of regional and world stability, Imperial responsibility and creating conditions for an orderly transfer of power to a post-colonial indigenous regime (and the maintenance of close economic and other ties). They also included the necessity of maintaining security, order, and the rule of law or further to uphold Britain's power, prestige and moral authority.[15] Britain's motivation for involvement in Oman and Dhofar, although not a colony as such, was based on similar reasoning. These motivational themes can be attributed to all of the classical British COIN campaigns highlighted in this book. With regards to Cyprus, "In the late 1950s the British Empire was trying to cling on to the Island which remained a strategic location, especially around the time of [the] Suez [Crisis]."[16] In Kenya the insurgency was treated as an internal security operation with law and order and protection of the white settlers being one of the primary motivations for involvement, leading to mass arrests or forced resettlements of supporters of the independence activists Thomas Mboya and Jomo Kenyatta.[17] In Malaya, successful early Cold War Communist global expansion and fears of an Asian 'domino theory-esque' takeover was the prime reason for the dogged COIN campaign that ensued for nearly twelve years.[18] With China in Communist hands and the Korean War underway, the insurgency begun by the MCP was viewed in certain quarters of the British Establishment as part of a worldwide Communist conspiracy orchestrated by the Kremlin.[19] Later, once the main insurgent threat had been curbed, the emphasis in Malaya altered. It changed more towards preparation for independence and an orderly handover to the elected representatives of the government in 1957 with stability and close-remaining economic, military and political ties to the UK the priority for the British government. A wide spectrum of geopolitical and internal security threats can therefore be established as the reasons for Britain's involvement in classical-era COIN campaigns. These range from the survival of the governing status quo to external threat, geopolitical interests, internal and external law and order issues, to stability and continued UK regional influence via cooperative successor administration.

In the case of Dhofar (and Oman in general) Britain's motivations for involvement were very similar to its previous COIN campaigns. Britain wished to maintain its somewhat diminished influence and prestige in the Middle Eastern region, following the 1956 Suez Crisis, the Adeni exit in 1967 and the planned strategic retreat from the region in 1971.[20] Britain's motivations were also pragmatic. Unfettered Gulf oil supply security generally and especially the most important Kuwaiti supply via the Strait of Hormuz was a key determining economic factor. Britain's commitment to the Central Treaty Organization (CENTO) – colloquially known as the 'Baghdad Pact' in the UK – as signed in 1955 between Turkey, Iraq, the UK, Pakistan and Iran was also a key factor. This treaty commitment and the strategic requirement for RAF Masirah for this purpose and as a historically important staging post for personnel and aircraft to service both the Gulf region and East of Suez commitments was a key consideration for intervention; as was the extra RAF presence to potentially counter both the overt and covert Communist threat to the Middle East region.

Regional stability was also an important factor for Britain. With the United States being preoccupied by the expanding commitment to the Vietnam campaign, Britain was acting in its traditional regional power or 'policeman' role. This is illustrated with British Foreign & Commonwealth Office (FCO) officials stating in 1971 that, "The defeat of the rebels in Dhofar would encourage others in the Gulf and elsewhere who are opposed to Communist infiltration. Stability in Oman is important for stability in the rest of the Arabian Peninsula."[21] This would have the effect of helping to prevent the spread of Communism throughout southern Arabia and what amounted to a potential Arabian Peninsula version of 'domino theory' where countries fell to Communist domination like dominoes falling in quick succession.[22]

Unlike the wide-ranging, direct and large-scale intervention of the UK in COIN theatres such as Palestine, Malaya, Kenya and Northern Ireland (and even in Cyprus and Borneo), Britain's assistance in Dhofar/Oman was relatively limited in scale and potentially contributed to the longevity of the insurgency. British support has even been described as parsimonious and short-sighted in the extreme. This was the opinion even of a serving (seconded) CSAF, and the lack of support strained relations with Oman and even contract-employed British personnel working for the Sultan – including Colonel Hugh Oldman – where Brigadier Purdon stated:

> We simply could not convince the British Directorate of Military Operations, nor the Defence Staff that if they gave us what we asked for straight away – very little at that time – we could [quickly] crush the rebellion. They had to support the SAF with far more aid and consequent expense later. The old principle of 'Firm and Timely Action' had to be learned yet again at the expense, as always, of lives and limbs.[23]

Such British reluctance to provide more generous levels of support stemmed partly from the formidable range of other commitments undertaken by the post-National Service era UK armed forces, such as those of a colonial or North Atlantic Treaty Organization (NATO)-related nature. This is before even considering the expense of its significant and costly Bahraini and Adeni commitments and other anti-insurgent or COIN operations. This included the Brunei/early Borneo Confrontation, the early days of the Northern Ireland 'troubles' where up to 11,000 troops were drafted to the province and Britain's wider economic problems and resultant plan to withdraw East of Suez in 1971.[24] Although deemed important, commitment to Dhofar and Oman more generally has to be viewed in context, and in terms of national and military priority; of which it was relatively low. As a result Britain was never over-generous with

Oman in terms of assistance. What was given was strictly limited as "All of it [military aid] came with a price tag ...[and] the Sultan was billed for all British servicemen deployed to Oman," and no promises of indefinite assistance were made.[25] Another reason was Britain's unwillingness to commit more deeply in terms of personnel and resources due to the US experience in South East Asia and the negative social and especially political consequences. The authorities in Britain wished to avoid an open-ended commitment. A possible worst case "mini-Vietnam" scenario would potentially be militarily, economically and politically disastrous as had played out in the US via public opinion and public disorder incidents such as street or university campus riots.[26]

The views of Left-leaning, Marxist-inspired or revisionist scholars often purport that from the beginning, Britain was acting in an exploitative manner in Oman and was effectively a colonial oppressor in terms of its historical involvement. This reasoning is also applied to the Dhofar War with Britain's actions often viewed as forced on Oman via a compliant and subservient ruler primarily in the best interests of Britain itself.[27] Running counter to this 'colonial oppressor' related narrative is the view that Britain was involved in the Dhofar War out of a strategic and geo-political security interest, but was also upholding its tradition of over 200 years of cooperation and friendship since at least 1798 on all levels.[28] This represents a similar situation to previous classical British COIN campaigns, although in the case of Oman and Dhofar, without even being part of Britain's formal colonial structure or Empire. Other examples of such cooperation and support are the 'Exchange of Letters' in 1958 signed between the British government and the ruler of Oman which formalised UK substantial military and financial assistance to Oman.[29] This was closely followed by the involvement of regular British military units in the Jebel Akhdar campaign in 1959 including the Life Guards, Royal Marines, and most importantly the SAS, which was sent to Oman directly from the jungles of Malaya.[30] This led to the end of that insurgency and resulted in the survival and extended power base of the Sultan over the whole of Muscat and Omani territory. Britain was tied financially to Oman as a result of the 'Exchange of Letters', including the obligation to operate Salalah airfield as part of the 99-year leasing deal for the use of Oman's Masirah Island in what became known in UK circles as the 'Salalah hook', which the Sultan was keen to maintain as it suited him and enhanced his position and security at Britain's expense.[31] Although a mutually beneficial arrangement in 1958 it later became more onerous to the British side as time wore on, in part as RAF Salalah had very limited strategic value to Britain and was an easily accessible target for PDRY or insurgent forces with UK service personnel constantly in danger and the political risk this entailed.[32] Alongside the clear benefit gained from RAF Masirah came the relative liability of RAF Salalah from the British perspective.

It can therefore be seen that Britain's motivation for involvement in classical-era COIN campaigns was varied but centred largely around security, prestige, internal and external stability and the rule of law. This was allied to maintaining continued interests and links with the countries concerned and a positive post-empire or colonial relationship after formal British withdrawal. It can be seen further that, although not a colony like Aden, involvement in Oman and Dhofar was based on similar reasoning. Britain undoubtedly acted in self-interest in all cases. Oman was, however, a special case in that the UK was never legally or obliged by treaty to prop up the country or her independent rulers, but did so via the British Foreign Office through a mixture of strategic necessity and paternalistic obligation over a period of nearly 200 years. This situation is clearly one at odds with that set forth by Marxist-leaning or revisionist narratives. This status is encapsulated in the wording of the 1800 treaty between the British Government and the Sultan of Muscat which expressed that the friendship between the two countries should "Endure till the end of time or the sun and moon cease in their revolving careers".[33]

Chapter 4

Campaign-Specific Aspects Similarities

The similarities between Dhofar and previous classical UK COIN campaigns are not just apparent from a general background or a strategic-level perspective but also from a specific campaign or operational level standpoint. To enable a comparison such characteristics are grouped along two general themes; those of the general conduct of the war, and key related campaign-specific factors.

General Conduct

The conduct of the Dhofar War is largely described in the two main narrative camps within the subject writings as being on one hand an exemplary example of a COIN campaign or at least generally professional and competent and leading to a rare COIN 'win' via a "textbook counterinsurgency [campaign]".[1] Running counter to this is the view that the war was actually poorly managed. This resulted in the campaign lasting much longer than need have been and costing more in terms of lives, funds and general disruption. In addition is the view that it was also more akin to a brutal colonial war of a previous era (where "the pattern of British counterinsurgency… sought to intimidate the population through tactics of violence"), and far from even being effective in this respect it nearly actually ended in defeat for the SAF and the Sultan's regime.[2] The latter view is succinctly summed up by John Newsinger who stated UK support for Sultan Said's despotism, "which continued under successive governments… remains one of the most unsavoury episodes in post-war British foreign policy".[3]

Operational Conduct Effectiveness

Although resulting in a positive outcome, it can be argued that the Dhofar campaign should have been won by British-led Omani COIN forces much earlier. A campaign that lasted too long and cost more in lives and resources than was potentially necessary is a trait that can legitimately be similarly levelled at other British COIN undertakings. This would include those campaigns which could be considered clear overall COIN losses, such as in Palestine and

Aden. In the Dhofar campaign mould, however, this accusation can also even be levelled at the more successful classical British undertakings such as in Kenya and especially in Malaya. The latter, although mooted as one of Britain's most successful COIN campaigns still took over a decade (12 years in total) to win. It also cost hundreds of millions of pounds before even considering the over 1800 British and Malayan security forces lives lost during its execution.[4] Additionally, in terms of timeframe, the Dhofar COIN campaign itself was to last over a decade, a timescale mirrored closely by both the (much larger) Malayan and Kenyan campaigns. Even the significantly smaller-scale Djebel War of the late 1950s was only concluded successfully after three years with direct British assistance. This included relatively powerful and well-equipped British army units and airpower from regional RAF bases in Aden, Sharjah and Masirah, which could boast the powerful and highly capable RAF Hunter jet fighter aircraft.[5]

Despite the small-scale and relatively primitive insurgent organisation of the mid-1960s the insurgency was not 'nipped in the bud' early and as a result was eventually to last over 11 years. As contemporary CSAF, Brigadier Corran Purdon stated: "[if the required helicopters and field artillery had been received] a year earlier [in 1968] and we might have militarily won the war… final victory was not to come until 1974."[6] In contrast to large-scale early commitments to theatres such as Palestine, Malaya, Kenya and Cyprus, relative prevarication by the British government with regards to Oman and Dhofar specifically meant that by 1967, a swift end to the rebellion had become an ever more distant prospect. Resultingly, and similarly to previous UK COIN campaigns, a longer, more costly operation was necessary to quell the insurgency. With the creation of the communist PDRY in 1970, Soviet and Chinese weapons, training and support meant that the insurgents quickly developed into a well-organised and equipped fighting corps. This now well-equipped organisation was often able to 'outgun' the SAF utilising automatic weapons (when the SAF were using old British army Enfield bolt action rifles) and later had at their disposal heavy machine guns (e.g. Shpagin 12.7mm), Katyusha rockets and even surface-to-air (SAM) missiles.[7] By 1971 there was even the very real possibility that the campaign and therefore Dhofar province could be lost, as recognized among the UK military hierarchy and the Commander of British forces Gulf based in Bahrain.[8] Despite the rapid post-coup expansion of the SAF from approximately 3000 men to over 10,000 in less than two years, the SAF could not by this point even hold a permanent presence on the Jebel, could not therefore count on the support of the Jebalis, and it could be described that a stalemate situation had developed as early as 1970.[9] The initial, localised uprising was not dealt with swiftly and efficiently and had been allowed, by 1968, to develop into a full-blown Marxist insurgency.

Some writers have alluded to a stark change in fortunes for the SAF following the July 1970 coup which resulted in Sultan Qaboos taking the throne, but this interpretation is only partially correct.[10] The campaign was actually to endure significantly more failure before any measurable level of success was experienced. The 1971 plan to take the offensive on the Jebel known as Operation JAGUAR was the brainchild of the then CSAF, Brigadier John Graham and was far from an immediate success. SAF initiatives such as the raising of the tribal militia Firqa units, although important later in the campaign, were not successful from an operational perspective initially. Despite all the encouraging changes in the SAF and the CSAF's aggressively positive overall campaign strategy, government forces only 'turned the corner' and started winning the COIN campaign from late 1972.[11]

The decade-long Dhofar campaign, therefore, mirrored closely previous UK COIN operations from a general conduct perspective in that they tended to be not hugely effective in their early stages. As such they were unable to bring a swift resolution or solution to insurgencies (or at all) in terms of operational conduct, leading generally to longer than potentially necessary campaigns. Whilst the case for any insurgency that is allowed to develop in the first place and proliferate unchecked, the latter situation actually led to several campaign losses endured by Britain including Palestine and in Aden/Southern Federation. A further 'semi-loss' was also endured in Cyprus where the island was no longer part of the British Empire, but the Sovereign Base Areas were, however, retained 'in perpetuity'. Even the shortest previous British COIN campaign win (Djebel War) took approximately three years to bring to a positive and final conclusion. A similar end result took some eight years to achieve in Kenya, up to twelve years in the case of Malaya, and three decades in the extreme case of Northern Ireland.

Morality of Campaign Involvement and of Overall Conduct – Level of Force or 'Brutality' Utilised

Additionally, there is the literature narrative that Britain was involved in an immoral undertaking in Dhofar.[12] With Oman in the late 1960s existing at the level of a virtual 'medieval-like' state, the view puts forward the idea that Britain was consciously complicit in propping up a reactionary regime for their own interests with an oppressive 'puppet-style' ruler.[13] British officers who served with the SAF often sympathised with the Dhofari point of view when they saw the conditions on the ground of the Jebalis and the Sultan's seemingly callous attitude toward his subjects.[14] In addition, even though the COIN campaign was conducted in relative secrecy, knowledge of the MOD practice of seconding officers to the SAF was known and even called into question in the (then non-televised) UK Parliament.[15]

When compared to Britain's previous classical COIN campaigns, criticisms are also highly apparent, highlighting the similarities with the Dhofar case. Whether it be the colonial administration government being propped up against the will of the collective inhabitants (e.g. Palestine) or the colonial regime suppressing the nationalistic will or desire of the people (e.g. Cyprus) there are clear similarities. This also included appropriating land from the rightful indigenous inhabitants and keeping the population in a level of servitude (e.g. Kenya) with greater or lesser levels of brutality or oppression instigated. In all cases, however, British forces were involved in determined efforts to both support and maintain the governance status quo of the country or territory concerned against insurgent activity.

The rights and wrongs can be debated at length in the above cases. Like in Dhofar or wider Oman cases, in the example of the Malayan Emergency and later Brunei revolt/early Borneo Confrontation, the continuance of the status quo was very much at stake. As such, from the perspective of the UK, this justified the COIN campaigns undertaken. This was due to the fact that, "By late 1969, British Officers serving in Oman were reporting to London that the [overall] situation in Dhofar was very bad and if allowed to go unchecked, control of the country might not be maintained for another year."[16] This situation stimulated continued and greater commitment by Britain towards Oman in terms of military, diplomatic and financial support and was a key factor in the planning and eventual launching of the pivotal July 1970 coup which brought Sultan Said's only son, Qaboos, to power. In terms of morality of involvement, the similarities of the Dhofar War with previous UK COIN campaigns are clear. This is especially the case from the perspective of forcefully maintaining the status quo where necessary, where it was often to the aspirational or material detriment of the COIN territory's inhabitants.

Marxist-oriented and revisionist scholars often highlight the brutality of the Dhofar COIN campaign, with it termed an "all-out [British] attack on the population who supported the revolution".[17] Certainly earlier in the campaign, with a high level of secrecy both engendered and forced and very limited press coverage to potentially sway public opinion, Sultan Said's enthusiasm for the SAF to conduct collective punishments was indulged. These included crop or dwelling burnings on villages deemed disloyal or collaborating with the insurgents. British officers such as Korean War veteran and staunch anti-communist Colonel Mike Harvey were complicit in this type of activity, and it was widespread throughout the early campaign stages, as he "hated Communists and his tactics were described as ruthless by many officers".[18] Food denial was a tactic also liberally employed. This was achieved through routine crop burnings (including the use of air-delivered 'home-made' incendiary bombs), the shooting of livestock, control of food movements in and out of towns such as Salalah, and eventually via the cross-jebel barriers erected such as the Hornbeam Line.[19] To deter waverers or potential supporters of the insurgents, the bodies of dead Adoo were often displayed in towns, as after the battle of Mirbat in 1972 when insurgent corpses were displayed publicly in Salalah town square. In addition, as a measure of the extent of the oppressive actions contemplated, although it was not eventually actually utilised in theatre, the SAF purchase, and use of napalm was even seriously considered. This was requested by the Omani authorities via the then SAF Colonel Tim Landon, one of the Sultan's closest advisors and ex-regular British officer. This request was not for use in a defoliant role as was the primary application in Vietnam, but for direct use on enemy combatants.[20]

As a result of such actions, the Dhofar War could be argued to be high on a scale of brutality and therefore displaying similar characteristics to the previous classical British COIN campaigns or those carried out for example in Vietnam, Algeria, Indochina, Guinea, Mozambique and Rhodesia by other COIN-undertaking nations. In Kenya there were widespread judicial executions utilising 'mobile' gallows equipment in the numerous detention camps set up during the Mau Mau Emergency, and the Aden campaign was marred by accounts of beatings and torture by British troops.[21] In Malaya the practice of British soldiers removing the heads of dead insurgents supposedly for intelligence or Special Branch identification purposes was apparent.[22] This was undertaken for the practical purpose of avoiding having to carry whole, and heavy bodies through thick jungle for miles on end, and the public display of insurgent corpses (for instance tied to the bonnets of government vehicles) was widely used as a motivational psyops tactic against the population as a warning against collaboration.[23] Accusations of brutality against British troops were also widespread in both Cyprus and Aden. The UK was seemingly seeking to intimidate the population through tactics of violence in the former. The UK also refused to cooperate with independent inquiries into the matter in the latter. In addition, UK authorities operated a detention facility known as the 'fingernail factory' which allegedly utilised torture and beatings and sensory deprivation techniques which were subsequently also later utilised in Northern Ireland against terrorist suspects.[24]

It can therefore be seen that although Marxist-oriented (or 'left-leaning') revisionist scholars in some ways rightly put forward the view that the operational conduct of the Dhofar COIN campaign was especially brutal and somehow immoral, when compared, however, it was often relatively similar in such terms to previous British and especially some notable non-UK COIN campaigns such as in Algeria involving French forces.[25] In addition, one of the general hallmarks of British COIN campaigns often identified is, even amongst the violence or conflict, their relative humanity and restraint.[26] The use of 'minimum necessary force' might be a more accurate description of measures used as opposed to the 'minimum force' moniker *per se* in both Dhofar and other post-1945 British COIN campaigns thereby highlighting key similarities in this respect.

In terms of conduct, the Dhofar COIN campaign was, like its UK COIN forebears, not particularly effective in the early years which helped the war last for over a decade with all associated – and often multiplied – costs. That Britain was engaged in brutal or oppressive methods is clear but can also be seen to be relatively similar to previous UK and non-British classical COIN campaigns which were 'of their time' and carried out in the context of prevailing social attitudes and tolerances. Modern Western sensibilities may never be reconciled to this view, but there was at the same time, however, ample evidence that restraint was employed at all levels to achieve such aims by British and UK-controlled forces.[27] From all such conduct-related angles, the Dhofar War therefore clearly closely resembles previous classical British COIN operations.

Classification of Insurgent (Conflict Causation and Insurgent Motivation)

As with previous classical UK COIN campaigns, the origins of the Dhofar War and therefore the specific source of motivation of the insurgents clearly impacted the classification of the type of enemy being fought. The Dhofar campaign morphed over time, but started as purely a nationalist-related uprising. At the core of the original nationalist rebellion under Musallim Bin Nufl's Dhofar Liberation Front (DLF) in the province was the dissatisfaction of Dhofaris with their lot in the early 1960s under Sultan Said's rule. Dissatisfaction with the incumbent ruler or regime was also the prime motivational factor behind the insurgencies in Palestine, Cyprus, Kenya and Aden. In the Dhofar insurgency this nationalist perspective was systematically hijacked by radical Marxist elements within the DLF to change the ideological direction of the insurgency to one of a Marxist-based struggle. After the old DLF leadership was ousted by the new ideologues the previous nationalist-inspired insurgent was progressively replaced with one fighting for a revolutionary Marxist-based ideology. This situation reflected that which British forces also encountered, for example in large-scale and over a twelve-year period in Malaya, and later also in the Brunei revolt/early Borneo campaign.

In terms of causative insurgent ideology Peterson states, "Oman (Dhufar) was an irredentist insurgency that eventually became a Marxist movement."[28] It can be seen as a nationalist struggle which developed and morphed into a full-scale Communist insurgency as the ideologically-driven leadership elements grew in power. This enabled the new leadership elements to eventually usurp control from the previously dominant nationalistic-based leadership. Being, therefore, nationalist and/or Communist in terms of motivation is similar to all of previous British classical COIN campaigns. The Malayan Emergency was predominantly a communist insurgency fomented via the Malayan Communist Party (MCP), and the Brunei/early Borneo Campaign featured a mixture of nationalist and Communist Indonesian-supported and trained insurgents initially in the operation; followed later by the large-scale involvement of regular Indonesian forces.[29] The Palestine, Cypriot, Kenyan, and to a certain extent Aden insurgencies were predominantly nationalist or anti-colonial and not primarily Cold War ideologically-inspired in nature. The Dhofar COIN effort was therefore pitted against a nationalist uprising against a "despotic ruler" or perceived oppressive form of governance.[30] This situation was similar to the insurgencies in Palestine, Cyprus, Kenya and Aden, and based on real or perceived wrongs imposed by a ruling power with a view to righting these and/or removing the occupying power; in these cases Britain. Similarly to the Malayan campaign, the Dhofari nationalist uprising was not dealt with successfully in its early stages where it may have been stopped in its tracks at a relatively modest, if proactive cost. Again, like Malaya, it subsequently morphed into a full-blown Marxist-inspired and communist-led and supported insurgency backed by outside powers such as China and the USSR, eventually lasting over 10 years. It is clear, therefore, that the Dhofar campaign was waged against insurgents of similar ideological orientation as those encountered in previous classical UK COIN efforts. This only varies in that Dhofar actually covered both ends of the causative spectrum and therefore the motivations of the insurgents Britain fought against. This made it simultaneously both similar and, in addition, unique in this respect.

Location of Campaign (Urban vs. Rural Setting) and Resultant Level of Success

Although with exceptions such as Northern Ireland, most successful post-Second World War British COIN campaigns were undertaken primarily in rural settings. The British rural-based COIN wins include the Malayan, Kenyan, Djebel War, and Brunei/early Borneo campaigns. By contrast the main COIN losses for the UK were primarily urban-based of which Palestine, Aden and arguably Cyprus were key examples. From this perspective, therefore, the predominantly rural and successful British Dhofar campaign closely corresponds to the location of previous successful UK COIN actions.

Rural insurgencies in the immediate post-1945 world were the norm and the Dhofar COIN campaign was similarly waged primarily in one of the isolated and sparsely populated mountainous region of the country in the Jebel Al Qamar (easternmost range), the Jebel Al Qara (centre) and the Jebel Samhan (west) and away from towns; including even the regional capital, Salalah.[31] There was also insurgent activity in the North of Oman and in the vicinity of Muscat prior to the 1970 coup, with the main insurgent action being in the rural Dhofar Province. In the north, the main focus was predominantly towards the border with the Trucial States (later the UAE) or in the Musandam Peninsula; the latter necessitating Operation INTRADON by the SAS in 1970 to stabilise the situation in the territory and reassert Sultanate authority.[32]

There are clear similarities therefore between the successful Dhofar example and the largest, most lengthy and arguably most successful classical British COIN campaigns of Malaya and Kenya (as well as Brunei/early Borneo and specifically in the Radfan sector of the Aden campaign) which occurred, like in the case of Dhofar, in rural areas. Unsurprisingly, this was a situation which also holds true for many of the non-British classical-era COIN campaigns such as those carried out by France or Portugal in Africa.[33] The Malayan COIN campaign took place primarily in the country's tropical forested areas and later the insurgent food-producing jungle gardens and 'New Villages' and not in the government-controlled cities.[34] The Mau Mau rebellion was pitched against the 12–15,000 insurgent fighting forces or Land Freedom Army (LFA) and took place in the 1,500 square miles of thick rural forest and undergrowth areas of the Kikuyu tribal reserves and prohibited areas of the Aberdare mountain range and Mount Kenya.[35] As such, most British COIN campaigns such as in Malaya, Kenya, Oman (Djebel) and Brunei/early Borneo were carried out in rural-based or difficult terrain such as mountains or jungles which afforded good cover to insurgents. This had the effect that COIN operations to either contain or root out insurgents were considerably more difficult.[36] The Dhofar case mirrored these difficulties including the mountains of the Jebel which were a boon to the insurgents. It aided them in conducting limited guerrilla-style ambushes on government troops and providing thick, seasonal mist cover for camel supply trains from the insurgent western supply depots to units stationed in the east. They were equally a hindrance in terms of mobility, logistics and for the operational effectiveness of the SAF; especially in the Khareef monsoon period between June and October each year which effectively created fixed fighting seasons for the leaders of each side to consider carefully for their respective war strategies.[37] Another factor was the porous border with the PDRY which hampered the SAF in their prosecution of the COIN campaign but created natural cover and an open route for the insurgents to retreat to their safe haven located across the border at Hauf.[38]

All other classical British COIN campaigns cited had a largely urban focus which differed considerably from the COIN campaign in Dhofar. Such predominantly urban-based campaigns resulted largely in less successful COIN undertakings; being either losses or half-losses at best. British COIN forces operating in Jerusalem, Nicosia and Limassol in Cyprus or Little Aden, Crater or Sheik Othman in Aden colony or indeed Belfast in Northern Ireland would, therefore, have seen little comparison in terms of the operational area or battlefield with COIN forces in Kenya, Malaya, Brunei/early Borneo, the Radfan or on the Jebel in Dhofar. The Dhofar insurgency and COIN campaign, therefore, share similarities with several of the larger classical British COIN campaigns in terms of the correlation between the rural location and difficult terrain and whether the COIN campaign was successful.[39]

Scale of Insurgency

All classical British COIN campaigns were relatively and comparatively limited in scope. This can be observed both in a geographical sense and in the scale of fighting and associated operations. Such factors include geographical scale, numbers of troops involved, and overall level of resultant casualties. The Dhofar campaign displays very similar traits to its forebears. As such, it can therefore be seen to be from this perspective very similar to previous classical UK COIN campaigns, which again contributed significantly towards its eventual success.

Area of Operations
The Dhofar campaign was undertaken in the relatively small land area of the province with the insurgents located primarily on the even smaller-again jebel or mountainous areas of the region.[40] This offered a relatively limited area to conduct a COIN campaign with the advantage of only one hostile international border (PDRY) to contend with. The relatively small size of COIN operational area is similar for most of Britain's classical COIN campaigns including the mainly urban-based operations in Palestine, Aden, and Cyprus as well as the rural-oriented operations in Brunei/Borneo. The scale of operational area was significantly larger in Kenya which took place mainly in the Aberdare forested highland regions. It was larger still in the case of Malaya where the COIN operations took place primarily in the extensive swamp and large jungle areas of the country. Even these largest of British COIN operations were conducted in relatively much smaller physical areas than the French campaigns for example

in Indochina and Algeria. This was even more so in the case of Vietnam for US forces where "the Americans were fighting a guerrilla war of considerably vaster proportions than that waged by the British in Malaya".[41] This comparison puts the British experience somewhat into perspective and gives an indication as to why the UK was relatively successful. They did this through electing to undertake involvement in more manageable and potentially 'winnable' COIN operations, and largely avoiding either operational or strategic 'overreach'.[42]

Relative Scale of Combatant Forces
Whilst not definitive in themselves, the comparison of numbers of COIN forces and opposing insurgents in Britain's classical COIN campaigns are indicative of the relatively small historic scale of such undertakings. The numbers of troops deployed by the UK to Oman varied between approximately 100 to 500.[43] By contrast the SAF deployed about 10,000 troops in Dhofar by 1974 (pre-coup the figure was only 3000 men) and the Adoo Insurgents had approximately 2,000 active fighters and 3,000 part-time militia at its peak in 1968–69.[44] In this respect the Dhofar campaign closely mirrors the relatively limited size of all classical British COIN campaigns; including even the significantly larger variants seen in Malaya and Kenya. In Britain's largest COIN campaign in Malaya, the MRLA consisted of just 8000 insurgents.[45] Pitted against these were the British COIN forces amounting to 40,000 with a home guard of 200,000.[46] In Kenya, the Mau Mau LFA insurgents numbered a maximum of 15,000 against 10,000 British-controlled troops and 21,000 police officers.[47] These examples were by far the larger of the British COIN operations and in the more typical smaller British classical COIN campaigns such as Cyprus the fighting wing of EOKA was only some 300 strong, pitted against a few thousand troops and up to 4900 police officers.[48] By way of indicative contrast, there were over 800,000 French troops serving in Algeria by 1959 and some 240,000 Viet Cong and North Vietnamese forces were pitched at their peak against some 1.6 million combined US and South Vietnamese forces (Army of the Republic of Vietnam or ARVN).[49]

Relative Scale of Casualties
The number of casualties in British classical COIN campaigns is also indicative of their limited general scale. This is especially the case when compared to French or US campaigns in the classical COIN era. Within the larger and more extensive or long-running British COIN campaigns, approximately 600 members of the security forces were killed in the Kenyan COIN operation and some 11,500 insurgents.[50] In Malaya approximately 6,400 insurgents were killed in the 'Emergency' versus over 1800 security forces personnel.[51] On a smaller scale

in the case of Aden/South Arabia under 200 British security forces personnel were killed between 1962 and 1967.[52] Likewise with the Cyprus Emergency the figures were by comparison only some 150 security services personnel killed by the insurgents (and c. 90 insurgents by the security forces) and in Borneo the figure was only 114 British and Commonwealth forces killed up to the end of the confrontation in 1966.[53] In the drawn-out and three decade-long conflict in Northern Ireland there was a high casualty rate for the security forces throughout the extended duration of the campaign, largely in the army and Royal Ulster Constabulary (RUC). This included over 100 British military personnel killed in a single year (1972), which included those who died on the UK mainland such as in the bombing of the paratrooper barracks in Aldershot in February of that year.[54] Fewer British military personnel were killed in the entire decade of the 1980s (96 individuals) than in that single year of 'the troubles' and the campaign in Northern Ireland government.[55] 1972 was also the year which was arguably the height of the Dhofar conflict, therefore hinting towards where the priority for resources lay for the UK government. The Northern Ireland COIN campaign was an extended state commitment which took place on UK soil and involved thousands of British troops and (RUC) paramilitary-style police. In contrast to this scenario, during the Dhofar War there were only ever up to 1,000 British soldiers serving in Oman at the deployment's maximum extent (from 1971 to 1974).[56] During the same period only some 21 UK servicemen were killed, and only 35 personnel killed in total overall over 11 years (which included 13 soldiers of 22 SAS Regiment) which gives an indication of the extremely limited scale of the Dhofar theatre.[57] There were approximately 1000 Iranian casualties with an estimated 500 killed in action and a similar number of non-British SAF casualties.[58] Compared to the heavy French COIN casualties suffered in Algeria or Indochina (including the over 7000 French troops killed or wounded at the battle of Dien Bien Phu in 1954 alone) or the over 58,000 US soldiers killed in Vietnam, the classical British COIN campaigns were all similar in that they were mainly relatively small operations involving limited military assets which were comparably less costly in terms of 'blood and treasure' to prosecute on multiple fronts.[59] The limited scale of the Dhofar COIN campaign in terms of casualties was, therefore, similar to a majority of the smaller scale classical British COIN campaigns. The Dhofar operation was even small in comparison with most of these cases leading Peterson to state that "Dhurfar (sic) was a very small war, even in the context of 'small wars'" affording it unique status.[60]

Use of Indigenous Forces in Unconventional Roles

Similar to several other previous post-war British COIN campaigns, UK forces involved in Dhofar utilised indigenous forces in unconventional roles; primarily working alongside British Special Forces. Although not the only British SF unit in existence, the SAS has seen more action and achieved greater operational success in post-Second World War COIN campaigns than any other unit.

The SAS in various guises served throughout the Malayan Emergency and in the Omani Jebel Akhdar Campaign. The unit also served in the Indonesian Confrontation – included 'Claret' secret cross-border operations to gain intelligence, deter, but also to "kill any enemy" in key contested areas as required – and in Aden, Northern Ireland, and later Afghanistan and Iraq.[61] In several of these campaigns, British SF utilised the skills and knowledge of local tribes, and the establishment of the Firqa units in Dhofar was a historically tried and tested UK COIN approach. Several examples are apparent in the historical record of the raising, training and deploying of unconventional, special or para-military indigenous units using local tribes and/or Surrendered Enemy Personnel (SEP). One of the most important of these was the formation of the 'pseudo' or 'counter gangs' utilised by the British military in COIN operations for deep forest penetration patrols in Kenya during the Mau Mau campaign.[62] In a development inspired by the then Captain Frank Kitson when seconded to the Kenyan Police Intelligence department, small units were formed where British officers and troops led operations disguised as insurgents. These were undertaken alongside loyal Kikuyu or SEPs to seek and destroy enemy units utilising "cunning rather than by massive manoeuvres".[63] So successful was this tactic, that the general approach was also used by British forces in Cyprus. Here, undercover detachments known as 'Q' units were formed to locate and track insurgents. It was on such operations that Corporal Labalaba, the later hero of Mirbat, won his British Empire Medal (BEM). The theories behind the development of the 'Q' units and the general approach of utilising disguised British SF soldiers was also employed elsewhere. They were utilised to implement small-team 'Keeni-Meeni' operations to find and engage insurgents and terrorist 'assassins' or 'Cairo Grenadiers' during the Aden COIN campaign due largely to the issue that, "The problem with destroying enemy armed groups and their supporters therefore consists very largely of finding them."[64] Undercover, disguised troops were also a mainstay for decades in the Northern Ireland 'troubles'. SAS soldiers routinely operated in civilian clothes, and contributed personnel to even more specialised and highly secretive SF surveillance units such as the Mobile Reconnaissance Force (MRF) as established by then Brigadier Frank Kitson, the Field (or Force) Research Unit (FRU), and 14 Intelligence

Company (14 Company.).⁶⁵ These were primarily intelligence-gathering units but also contributed to the 41 Republican terrorists killed in the 'troubles' up to the late 1980s.⁶⁶ In addition, indigenous tracking units were also utilised in both Malaya and Borneo; often working alongside and assisting British SF to seek out or provide reconnaissance on or engage enemy forces.⁶⁷ Dyak tribesmen from Borneo were even brought 'cross-theatre' into Malaya from as early as 1948 for such purposes and their finely-honed tracking skills were invaluable in terms of locating insurgent trails and camps.⁶⁸ Vital for intelligence-gathering, in Borneo, British SF personnel lived closely in jungle areas with tribal members of the Ibans, Dyak, Murut and Kalabit peoples who helped to provide information UK forces could not generate themselves. As the former CO of 22 SAS, General Sir Peter De La Billiere stated in his biography, "As in Malaya, we found that the natives themselves were by far the best source of intelligence … We depended on them."⁶⁹ With such a widespread use of indigenous forces in previous classical-era British COIN campaigns it is perhaps unsurprising that this 'tried and tested' approach was recycled in Dhofar when the need presented itself, albeit only in the post-coup era from 1970 onwards. This is when the SAS were permitted to operate on Omani soil to introduce a familiar 'hearts and minds'-style campaign to revitalise the flagging overall COIN effort. In Dhofar, the initial raising and subsequent training and operational deployment of the Firqa units by and with British SF personnel was a classic and effective SAS 'hearts and minds'-related technique which contributed significantly to the insurgent defeat.⁷⁰

Such a task was not straight forward as the Dhofari tribesmen tended to possess a strong independent streak and could not be easily 'tamed' for military service. Their loyalties were also suspect from the British perspective, which is illustrated by the fact that many undertook military training in the Trucial Oman Scouts in the 1950s and 1960s then promptly disappeared whilst on leave often taking their skills to Oman's various insurgent groupings.⁷¹ The SAS, however, with their experience in employing indigenous irregular forces in other British classical COIN campaigns, were able to turn the irregular Firqa into "first-rate" soldiers through their dedicated efforts and highly committed approach.⁷² The Firqa were effectively utilised as scouts, trackers and as guides for SAF operations, but also as home guard units to police 'sanitised' tribal areas.⁷³ By mid-1974 there were approximately 1000 members of the Firqa units and up to 1200 by the end of the war and COIN campaign which illustrates the scale of the undertaking.⁷⁴ In addition to Firqa forces, from 1969 British Intelligence services also supplied arms and money to, and later UK Special Forces personnel trained, engaged and directed, exiled Mahra tribesman. This was undertaken to utilise their skills as an unconventional militia force from their tribal areas which historically spanned the much newer-imposed borders of Oman and the PDRY. Exiled Mahra were encouraged to foment their own brand of cross-border insurgency. This had the benefit for British authorities of being a relatively cost-effective and deniable proxy force conducting destabilising operations in South Yemen/PDRY. The Mahra operation began in earnest in 1972 and was known as Operation DHIB.[75] The Dhofar experience with regards to use of indigenous forces in unconventional roles often differed from the COIN campaigns of other countries where local military forces were raised, but largely for conventional purposes. Although 'turned' insurgents utilised in specialist units were only used on a limited scale by other COIN-conducting nations, it was a staple of several UK COIN successes and Dhofar was no exception.[76]

COIN Experience of Campaign Leadership

The Dhofar War arguably saw the high point of the British army's historical COIN experience. It represented the culmination of three decades of accumulated UK wartime combat and especially irregular warfare or COIN experience of its leaders. All such UK COIN operations, including Dhofar, were to benefit from the unique and cumulative operational experience gained from unconventional Second World War operations from the case of Palestine onwards. This was especially so during the concurrent operations in the late 1940s to the late 1960s covering not only Palestine, but Malaya, Cyprus, Omani Jebel Akhdar Campaign, Borneo, and the early years of the Northern Ireland 'troubles'. This illustrates the similarity between such campaigns in this respect. Dhofar, however, probably represented the pinnacle of British COIN experience for the leaders whose careers covered these conflicts. Like the other campaigns covered, Dhofar also contributed to useful COIN experience which later filtered through to the generational Northern Ireland conflict. This is a situation unlikely ever to be repeated despite long campaigns in Afghanistan and Iraq which were largely unconventional or COIN-based. The situation therefore makes the Dhofar COIN campaign notable for being both a continuation of such common traits but also making it a unique example in this respect.

From Palestine onwards, all British COIN campaigns benefitted from the accumulated anti-insurgent operational experience of both the senior officers commanding operations as well as the more junior officers, Non-Commissioned Officers (NCOs) and troops executing them on the ground.[77] In Dhofar there was apparent a general implementation of hard-won experience by veterans of the earlier British campaigns.

There are numerous examples of this large, accumulated reserve of unconventional military and especially COIN experience to draw from. This

Table 2: COIN and Warfare Experience of Key Commanders Relating to the Dhofar War.

CSAF Name	Tenure	Warfare/COIN Experience
Col. David Smiley	1958–1961 (pre-Dhofar War)	Second World War SAS and Special Operations Executive experience. Irregular warfare operational experience in Albania and Thailand, Omani Jebel Akhdar Campaign
Col. Hugh Oldman	1961–1964 (pre-Dhofar War)	Second World War (MC winner) North Africa campaign, Sudan Defence Force, Aden Protectorate Levies
Col. Tony Lewis	1964–1967	Second World War Commando operations, Omani Jebel Akhdar Campaign. Initial wartime CSAF
Brig. Corran Purdon	1967–1970	Second World War Commando operations (MC won). Post-war COIN campaigns including: Palestine Emergency, Malayan Emergency, Cyprus Emergency
Brig. John Graham	1970–1972	Second World War, Palestine Emergency, Cyprus Emergency
Maj-Gen. Timothy Creasey	1972–1975	Second World War service in both British Indian army and regular British Army, Kenyan and Aden Emergencies
Maj-Gen. Ken Perkins	1975–1977	Palestine Emergency, Korean War, Suez Crisis, Malayan Emergency (Distinguished Flying Cross – DFC – won)
Commander, Dhofar Brigade Name	**Tenure**	**Warfare/COIN Experience**
Col. Mike Harvey	1971–1972	Army and Air Force (RAF Regiment) service in Second World War. Korean War veteran (MC won), formerly CO of Northern Frontier Regiment in Dhofar War (from 1967)
Brig. Jack Fletcher	1972–1974 (died 1976)	Platoon Commander in Malayan Emergency, Company Commander in British Guiana Crisis, CO of Queen's Regiment in Northern Ireland 'troubles' in 1969
Brig. John Akehurst	1974–1976	Malayan Emergency (Mentioned in Despatches)

is especially the case when considering the Dhofar example and the ethics and approach imbued to the SAF through its leaders. In terms of senior officers, the first CSAF, Colonel David Smiley, was an SAS and Special Operations Executive (SOE) veteran with experience of irregular operations in Albania for instance. The SOE was the organisation set up by then Prime Minister Winston

Churchill during the Second World War to 'set Europe ablaze' and undertake all manner of sabotage and other covert activities to hamper the German war effort alongside conventional military actions. Brigadier Corran Purdon won the Military Cross (MC) at the famed St. Nazaire raid (Operation CHARIOT) in May 1942 during the Second World War as an army Commando where he was injured, captured and sent to a prisoner of war camp. This raid, along with other such actions contributed to the issuing of Adolf Hitler's notorious (and illegal – as established at the Nuremberg Trials after the war) 'Commando Order' as announced by the German High Military Command on the 18th of October 1942 where commandos, even if in military uniform or attempting surrender, would be summarily executed. Some of the first to be executed under this order were British soldiers taking part in Operation FRESHMAN in October 1942, the first attempt to disable the 'heavy water' plant at Telemark in Norway. Having survived wartime commando service, Purdon later saw action in the Palestine, Malayan, and Cypriot COIN campaigns and commanded the Royal Ulster Rifles regiment contingent in the Borneo campaign prior to bringing this experience to the role of CSAF in what was arguably the most challenging period of the war from a command perspective.[78] Purdon's successor, Brigadier John Graham saw action in both Palestine and Cyprus, Major General Tim Creasey in the Kenyan Mau Mau and Aden campaigns; latterly as a battalion commander with the Royal Anglian regiment. The final Dhofar Wartime CSAF, Major General Ken Perkins was decorated Distinguished Flying Cross (DFC) and awarded the prestigious Member of the British Empire (MBE) honour as a result of his COIN-related actions in the Malayan campaign, primarily as an army helicopter pilot.[79] Between them, the result was a succession of commanders of the military forces of the Sultanate with unparalleled both wartime and irregular warfare leadership and combat experience which was invaluable for the challenges of the Dhofar campaign.

The CSAFs had arguably the most accumulated irregular command experience, but most of the British SAF staff and regimental fighting officers from the UK armed forces who were deployed to Oman to assist the COIN effort could often boast COIN experience in their careers. Some even had considerable experience spanning many years of post-Empire campaigning. The later Commanders of Dhofar Brigade were also highly experienced soldiers. Names such as Karate black-belt Colonel Mike Harvey spring to mind who had been a 'Glorious Gloster' in the Korean War. During the hostilities, the 1st Battalion of the Gloucester Regiment played a key role in the Battle of Imjin River in 1951, with some 650 men ranged against an entire Chinese division.[80] After fighting to the last round, nearly all officers and men of the regiment were either killed or captured by their Chinese adversaries. Harvey as a Major commanded

D Company, the remnants of which were the only company of the regiment which made it back to allied lines after the battle, and was awarded the Military Cross (MC) for his leadership and personal bravery.[81] This experience was to fuel his anti-Communist zeal in his commanding roles in Dhofar some 20 years later. Of central importance also was the COIN and regional-specific experience of the SAS soldiers and officers who planned and (primarily) implemented the 'hearts and minds' approach in Dhofar after the July 1970 coup. Lieutenant Colonel John Watts and later Lieutenant Colonel Peter De La Billiere for instance were 'old hands' at COIN. Both officers had 'cut their teeth' in unconventional warfare through service in Malaya and in the Djebel campaign in Oman in the 1950s and as part of this had personally commanded covert COIN operations at various levels. De La Billiere subsequently also commanded SAS units in the Radfan/Aden campaign, had run 'Claret' cross-border raids in Borneo against Indonesian (or Indonesian-backed) forces as a Major, as well as having an unofficial yet vital facilitator or 'fixer' role in the covert deployment of British mercenaries in support of ousted Royalist forces in North Yemen in the mid-1960s.[82] As such, there was not much these commanders had not seen or done with regards to the playbook of anti-insurgent operations, and could bring all this accumulated knowledge to the Dhofari theatre.

Like previous classical UK COIN campaigns, this situation culminated in Omani government forces having at their disposal a formidable set of leaders with widespread operational combat and COIN experience leading to:

> [The Dhofar COIN campaign being considered] a classic of its type, in which every principle of counter-insurgency operations built up over the last fifty years in campaigns around the world by the British and other armies… was employed.[83]

The Dhofar campaign outcome was the culmination and pinnacle of decades of accumulated experience of its British military officers and especially its senior leaders in undertaking both conventional and COIN warfare. Such hard-won experience and lessons learned and implemented from the Second World War onwards was utilised to prepare and deploy the SAF against their highly capable insurgent enemies in Dhofar. The unconventional warfare experience gained in the Palestine, Cyprus, Kenya, Oman (Djebel War), Brunei/early Borneo and Aden theatres were put to good use by such leaders to contribute towards overall victory in the Dhofar campaign.

Relative Secrecy & COIN Success

The Dhofar War was a success partly due to the relative secrecy surrounding the decade-long campaign. This success due to relative secrecy was also common to several other UK COIN undertakings including in Malaya and Kenya. Similarly, where relative secrecy was lacking it often led to a less effective COIN campaign. It variously sometimes resulted in a stalemate, mixed result or even a loss as in the cases of Palestine, Cyprus and Aden/Southern Arabia or a drawn out and costly campaign as the 30-year Operation BANNER in Northern Ireland illustrates. The Dhofar COIN campaign was almost unknown outside of military and political circles in the UK, and even (the then non-televised) debate in Parliament on the subject was very limited. Despite occasional press coverage which did actually highlight the involvement of UK personnel in Oman and loan arrangements, information on the precise role of British forces was scant, partly because it was not officially British-run as was the case with previous campaigns, with UK officers just commanding foreign forces. This was also the case because UK forces and indeed seconded or 'loan service' military personnel were involved in multiple other engagements, campaigns, or wars throughout the contemporary period, so Dhofar was largely lost in the general 'noise'. This was the case despite the efforts of writers such as then journalist and later distinguished academic, Professor Fred Halliday who was covertly infiltrated into Dhofar by the insurgents to accompany operations and put forward their perspective to the media. Dhofar was just another small war being undertaken rather reluctantly by British forces in some far-flung part of the world to add to the list and coverage, and therefore public knowledge – and indeed interest – was virtually non-existent prior to 1970, and extremely limited thereafter.[84] The involvement of UK forces in Oman was virtually unknown to the British people from the start (and at least until 1970). This was especially the case in terms of the expansive, large-scale and politically sensitive role of British SF in Oman and Dhofar from 1970. As such, it was stated in official documents that: "it would of course, be important in terms of parliamentary and public opinion here and opinion in the Arab world generally, that the presence of SAS personnel in the Sultanate should not, if possible, be revealed."[85] Whereas other British support-related deployments such as Loan Service or seconded personnel or members of the RAF and Royal Artillery were to a certain extent public knowledge, the role of the SAS was not, and for good reason. This secrecy or 'deniability' had the effect of giving UK politicians and military (both seconded and contract) commanders greater leeway and flexibility in action than was the case often elsewhere as:

Another advantage of both wars in Oman was their general obscurity. Vietnam is the most famous example of how the war effort was affected by adverse publicity and extensive television coverage but Britain faced similar problems in Aden and Northern Ireland.[86]

This situation enabled decisions to be made at all levels which may have been potentially vetoed in other campaigns largely due to the effect of public opinion, and helped to secure eventual military victory. This was a common trait observed across Britain's other more successful classical COIN campaigns despite some notable exceptions due to the fact that these were mainly conducted in a generally benign media environment, and rules of engagement in operations that were often more relaxed. This in turn allowed more firm or direct action against insurgents with less potential political risk.[87] This was especially the case with the large-scale post-war COIN campaigns carried out in remote and often largely inaccessible rural areas within Malaya and Kenya. For reasons of practicality, these attracted significantly less public, international press or political interest than those which occurred in Palestine, Cyprus or Aden for instance.

The Palestine Emergency campaign was significantly affected by adverse media coverage. The local media were vehemently anti-UK in outlook and these sentiments were allowed to be spread through the defence of a relatively free press in the British-run territory. The situation was arguably even more serious in the Cyprus Emergency where a traditionally protected free press utilised this privilege to "…engage freely in sedition, falsehood and slander" and support the insurgent position, much to the detriment of the campaign against EOKA forces.[88] The greater reticence or political interference in military decision-making or actions due to such pressures can be observed, for instance, in Aden. A key example of this was the situation that developed surrounding the Crater district incident in July 1967, which had a significant negative impact on operational effectiveness. This was due to the fact that "the drama in South Arabia, and in particular Aden itself, was unfolding under the glare of the British and international press corps", and the resultant overly-cautious politically-motivated order not to re-enter Crater district in Aden in 1967 (after the killing of 22 soldiers, until the Argyl and Sutherland Highlanders re-entered the area on 4th July) left soldiers "bitter and frustrated".[89] In this case, only the bold, determined, and 'out front' military response borne of stoic personal leadership undertaken by Lieutenant Colonel Colin Mitchell of the Argyll and Sutherland Highlanders that saved the day. His actions brought the situation under control after the police mutinies and subsequent killing of over 20 British soldiers. Although many contemporaries, including his superiors contrarily considered his actions strategically foolish and naïve, this tough stance brought the Crater 'no go' area firmly back under British control, essentially saved the day, and made the Argylls "the heroes of the British public".[90] All this occurred whilst the local and London-based UK military and civilian leadership dithered and poured fuel on the fire through the unwillingness to take hard decisions with the world's press watching, and the authorities acting like "ostriches, with their heads so deep in the sand" on the reality of the combustible situation in the colony.[91] The result was that, despite the short-lived success of the Argylls in restoring order in Aden's Crater district, the odds against success were slim. Citing the example of insurgent 'grenadiers' Lieutenant Colonel Mitchell stated:

> We were like foxhounds waiting for the huntsman to get a shovel and dig out the earth. But the occupants were not game little foxes, they were murderers planning more murder – and they were getting off scot-free in the middle of a British colony while the Egyptian Intelligence Service paid them to be murderers and exalted them as freedom fighters.[92]

The Dhofar campaign, therefore, did not suffer the same negative publicity, international condemnation and hostile media coverage which was the case in several previous UK campaigns; many resulting in COIN losses or mixed results as opposed to wins. From the perspective of a correlation between secrecy or lack of media coverage and the ability to successfully prosecute a COIN campaign, Dhofar had much in common with previous classical-era anti-insurgent undertakings.

Domestic Political Backdrop (UK) & Effects on COIN Operations

The state and nature of then contemporary British politics has a significant effect on all the classical COIN campaigns, and Dhofar was no exception. This was especially the case via the different outlooks exhibited by either Conservative or Labour-led British governments. It is perhaps interesting to observe that the biggest capitulations of British COIN campaigns post-1945 were conducted whilst Labour governments were in power. Contrary to this, the more successful overlapping classical British COIN campaigns in the 1950s were prosecuted by Conservative-led governments which were in power from 1951 to 1964.[93] Another seldom-mentioned action was the covert campaign in North Yemen to support Royalist insurgents against Egyptian and Yemeni Republican forces. This campaign was not an official British action as such. It was, however, implemented primarily by ex-regular British officers by request and (deniable) tacit approval of Ministers of the Conservative government in 1963, with later CO of 22 SAS, Peter De La Billiere also present in an 'unofficial' liaison capacity.[94] In contrast, until 1970 the incumbent Labour government had, over the course of Parliamentary sessions both released a Defence White Paper announcing the intention to quit Aden early and prevaricated on the loss of Crater in 1967 which created the circumstances for the "sorry tale" of the murder of 22 soldiers by mutineers and insurgents wielding terrorist methods in a demonstrable "Loss of political will".[95] As a result of such issues, in all the classical British COIN campaigns covered, the armed forces were often placed in either difficult or even almost impossible situations to deliver results by home-country politicians who often did not have the experience, knowledge, and appreciation of the military aspects to fully comprehend either the operational or strategic picture. From Palestine to Aden the vagaries of domestic politics, changes of governments of different persuasions, and the inevitable changes in policies from foreign policy to that of defence spending all had impacts, and Dhofar was no different.

The lack of apparent will of the Labour government under Harold Wilson (Oct 1964 – Jun 1970) to further expand the assistance offered to the Omani authorities in the Dhofar conflict is in stark contrast to the instigation of the 1970 coup which occurred within weeks of the new Conservative Heath Government coming to power. The relatively parsimonious attitude of the British government with regards to material support for the Sultan was certainly crossbench in nature. The fact remains, however, that Sultan Said was both deposed in a coup and elements of 22 SAS Regiment were operating in Oman a little over a month from the date a Conservative government took power in the UK in 1970.[96] Following the coup, tangible British support for the new Sultan was increased substantially to the great benefit of the contemporary CSAF, Brigadier John Graham, who resultingly stated:

> The result of the 1970 UK election turned out to be a boon for Oman and for us [as the seconded and contract British personnel alike] in her service. Had Labour remained in office the course of events in Oman would not have been so happy for both countries as they have.[97]

This support included loaned British army instructors and crucially, eventually two full SAS squadrons. The latter were utilised initially for bodyguard and infantry unit training duties, which involved both VIP protection and the training of the core of an Omani bodyguard unit for the new Sultan, and the tactical training and marksmanship of northern-Oman-based SAF units preparing for Dhofar deployment.[98] Key subsequent roles included the training of irregular Firqa forces, intelligence gathering and analysis and 'hearts and minds'-related population-centric initiatives; all of which were key to both revitalising and propelling the campaign towards victory.

Although the Dhofar campaign was not technically a wholly British COIN campaign as such, the seconded British officer-run armed forces of the Sultan were frustrated by lack of clear political goals and were underfunded; a situation noticeably similar to previous classical British COIN campaigns such as in Palestine and especially in Aden. This situation also mirrored to a certain extent the status in several other non-UK classical-era campaigns. These included the out of kilter status of contemporary civil-military relations and – with shades of the more recent Afghan and Iraqi campaigns of the 2000s – consequently overly controlling US civilian administrations during the Vietnam War which led to "high level amateurishness [at both the strategic and operational levels]".[99] Another key example was the lack of overall strategic leadership shown by French and Portuguese governments during their respective COIN campaigns in Asia and primarily Africa which directly contributed to coup attempts against the domestic governments in both countries in 1961 and 1974 respectively.[100]

The stark changes in fortune in the Dhofar campaign began from the accession of Sultan Qaboos to the throne and this was enabled in a highly significant way by UK government policies and actions. By the time the Labour party regained power in February 1974 the pattern of British support and involvement was well-established and traction towards a hard-fought victory already in place alongside diversified campaign allies. The win in Dhofar was a significant feather in the cap of Harold Wilson's government in 1975, but the hard decisions and practical activity that set the course of victory was arguably put in place by Edward Heath's Conservative government from 1970 to 1974.

It can therefore be seen that viewed from numerous aspects, the characteristics of the Dhofar campaign closely resemble those of many of the previous classical British COIN campaigns from conduct of the war, to scale of involvement and casualties, and the effect of domestic UK politics. There are, however, several key aspects of the Dhofar campaign which are different from those generally observed in other classical British campaigns. Fundamental differences, including technical dissimilarities can also be identified which suggests the Dhofar campaign actually to be an atypical UK COIN campaign.

Part II

Campaign Differences

Chapter 5

Background and Strategic Level Differences

Despite the numerous similarities as covered in Chapter 4, there were, however, several key differences between the Dhofar War and that of previous classical-era British COIN campaigns. The focus of this chapter is these fundamental differences which cumulatively suggest the Dhofar campaign to actually be an atypical COIN campaign in comparison, therefore making it effectively unique within the annals of British anti-insurgent operations.

Lack of British Political Control of COIN-related Territory

Despite the protestations and propaganda of the insurgents, Britain was not, unlike in other classical British COIN campaigns, either the purported imperialist oppressor or colonial overlord in Oman.[1] With all the UK campaigns discussed previously the areas where the COIN operations were undertaken were officially British administered, usually by the UK Foreign or Colonial Office. This meant all the arms of the state were in place to support the COIN forces such as the local military forces, the police (especially its Special Branch capability), intelligence services and judiciary. This was a situation which General Harold Briggs and General Gerald Templer as Director of Operations and High Commissioner respectively used so effectively with the great state-centred powers afforded to them during the Malayan campaign. Ex-soldier and classical-era writer Julian Paget describes what was developed in Malaya:

> A system based on the triumvirate of 'civil, military, and police' at all levels came into being as part of the Briggs Plan. This was developed into an extremely efficient machine, which [also] became the model for the [organisational approach in the] Kenya and Cyprus Emergencies.[2]

In the Dhofar campaign case this situation was fundamentally different, despite disagreement between scholars on the subject.[3] At worst the Dhofar War could be described as a version of a proxy campaign to support the Omani Sultan-centred ruling status quo, the like of which was a common political-military feature observed throughout the Cold War era.[4] Britain's seconded and privately contracted advisors effectively conducted Oman's foreign relations on behalf of the Sultan in conjunction with the contract military officers and private UK companies involved in the procurement of military supplies.[5] Oman was always, however, a sovereign country with its own ruler and government organisation, Britain never formally being either in control of the country as a colony or wholly in charge of the prosecution of the COIN campaign. This is a fundamentally different situation to all other previous classical British COIN campaigns in the sense that Britain effectively managed the campaign but did not completely run it or own it. The situation was instead more a case of a cost-effective and somewhat detached consultant-like role. Here, Britain achieved its objectives as economically as possible in terms of money and lives, in a more deniable fashion, and with more limited political risk. This situation is a clear departure from the typical British classical campaign narrative, and from this perspective, sets the Dhofar case apart.

Lack of Primary Anti-British Focus of Insurgent Campaign

The classical UK COIN campaigns highlighted so far in this book all display an anti-British focus by default. This can be similarly observed in the cases of Palestine, Malaya, Kenya, Cyprus, Brunei/early Borneo, Aden and even in Northern Ireland.[6] Anti-British focus was, however, more nuanced in the case of Dhofar, as can be seen from insurgent propaganda through different media such as Radio Cairo and Radio Aden.[7] Although insurgent propaganda linked the campaign to a supposed British Imperialist role not just in Oman but rather the whole of the Gulf, the focus of the Insurgency was primarily against the Sultan of Oman and not towards the UK *per se*. Radio propaganda use was widespread by both sides, and even though illiteracy rates were high in Oman, written printed propaganda was also widely utilised both in Oman and abroad in the global information battle for influence and strategic messaging.[8] The pro-insurgent and revolution Gulf Committee was set up in 1971 in Britain, France and Germany as an ideological propaganda mouthpiece for PFLOAG and other similar organisations. It stated in 1972 that "Oman has always been the key to Imperialist stability in the Gulf and while pretending the state is independent, Britain has shored up its tyrannical sultan since the 1820s."[9]

The insurgency developed due to the poor levels of social and economic development in (Oman and) Dhofar and Sultan Said's reactionary and repressive rule which both alienated and kept inhabitants in a state of feudal, medieval-level development.[10] Due to the tangible British support for the Sultan's regime, Britain was heavily criticised in insurgent propaganda, especially after the morphing of the original DLF into a Marxist-controlled organisation. Dhofar and Oman were never, however, British or a formally-controlled territory of the UK which was the key focus for previous COIN campaigns from Palestine onwards. Although Britain exercised considerable influence via Oman's Sultans, it was an independent country with its own armed forces, security apparatus and government. Although for the most part British-officer-led, the struggle was for most of the campaign between the insurgents and the SAF itself on behalf of the ruler and government of Oman and not with UK forces. This was a situation even more clear prior to the upgrade in Britain's support to the Sultan post-1970 coup (which became even more blurred with the subsequent deployment of British troops to assist Oman officially in support and not combat roles). This general narrative is at odds with that espoused by scholars such as Halliday, Outram, Davidson and Newsinger.[11] The general view of such scholars is that the British were essentially calling the shots and the struggle was against imperialist/colonialist control and a 'puppet' regime under the Sultan as illustrated through the various committee actions in the United Nations (UN) on the subject.[12]

The UK's traditional colonial presence and role in the Gulf was widely resented and from this narrow perspective it clearly fits with the anti-British focus faced in previous classical UK COIN campaigns. Dhofar was fundamentally however, not an insurgency against a British administration, regime or colonial empire as in most other UK COIN campaign cases. The primary focus of the insurgency was against the rule of Sultan Said – and later also his son, Qaboos – and was anti-British by default only in the sense that it backed the largely unpopular Sultan. The Sultan's regime was most certainly British-backed and supported, but this is a key and fundamental difference from previous UK COIN campaigns in general and clearly sets the Dhofar case apart.

Chapter 6

Campaign-Specific Aspects Differences

Quality of Insurgent Opposition

Several classical-era British COIN campaigns featured insurgent opponents who were not generally first-rate or professional-level fighting units as compared to those fielded by the UK. In Dhofar, however, the Adoo were eventually to present a formidable enemy which resulted in widespread respect from the British officers of the SAF and UK units posted to Oman.

This is a clear difference from the circumstances encountered with previous British COIN campaigns. There are exceptions to this general premise such as the "fanatical" and highly effective Jewish units encountered during the Palestine COIN campaign and the "skilled and sophisticated insurgents" of the Cypriot EOKA underground units led by Colonel Grivas which were so effective against UK COIN forces.[1] A motivated and effective enemy had also been encountered previously in Oman during the earlier Djebel War of 1957–59, with high ground covered effectively by "well-sited angry men with guns" on the Jebel Akhdar, eventually requiring two squadrons of Malayan COIN-hardened SAS troops plus British regular units such as elements of the Household Division (as well as Trucial Oman Scouts and elements of the Muscat and Northern Frontier Regiments) to dislodge them.[2]

The majority of insurgents Britain fought COIN campaigns against were, however, often far less organised, trained or equipped than British COIN forces. Examples include the poorly equipped and ill-disciplined Mau Mau Land Freedom Army (LFA) combatants; the semi-trained communist and Indonesian-backed rebels and insurgents in Brunei/the early Borneo campaign; 'bandits' as the main insurgent force in Malaya; and the Egyptian-trained National Liberation Front (NLF) agitators (labelled as 'inept' and 'incompetent') in Aden.[3] Such irregular and at best semi-trained insurgents were no real match for combat-hardened and often multi-theatre COIN experienced British units and personnel. These could boast thorough training and were equipped with modern weapons and artillery and aircraft support. These ideologically-committed but in practical terms essentially 'amateur' insurgent groupings countered such capability shortfalls by utilising urban anonymity or difficult rural terrain as a form of protection and force multiplier.[4] Defeating in battle was not necessarily the issue for full-time, professional and well-trained UK COIN forces. It was often more a battle against difficult terrain, lack of intelligence and locating the enemy to engage and potentially destroy them as, "The [primary] problem of destroying enemy armed groups and their supporters consists largely of finding them".[5] Whether it was differentiating Jewish insurgents from the general population in Palestine, EOKA personnel in Cyprus or the extreme difficulty in tracking down insurgents in the Kenyan forests or the dense and remote Malayan or Borneo jungles, this was a problem consistently encountered in all of Britain's classical COIN campaigns.[6]

In Dhofar elements of harsh terrain and environment were all similarly in place and were as much a boon for insurgent forces as they were a hindrance for the British-led SAF. In Dhofar, the Insurgents, in a situation unlike many previous COIN opponents, were an effective small scale, well-trained and organised enemy who operated with both energy and enthusiasm to compound the difficulties for British-run Omani COIN forces. From indoctrination at schools in Hauf in the Communist-controlled PDRY to training courses in either Russia or Peking (now Beijing) in Mao's new revolutionary China, they were motivated and ideologically committed.[7] They also benefitted from foreign Communist advisor training via Chinese and Soviet advisors (as well as from other Communist bloc countries such as Cuba and North Korea, and also from Egypt, Saudi Arabia, and Iraq) in PDRY territory, and were resultingly both committed and tactically astute.[8] Combined with intimate knowledge of the terrain and the seasonal climatic conditions, this made the Adoo a formidable enemy. Many British officers, including high-ranking commanders, learned to respect the abilities of their enemy and often held them in high regard.[9] In addition to this is the fact that Adoo forces were "lavishly equipped" by their Communist sponsors with the latest Soviet bloc weaponry not only in substantial terms but also in campaign-level quantities.[10] This resulted in a situation where the insurgents were often considered tactically the equal of the SAF.[11] As the final wartime Dhofar brigade commander Brigadier John Akehurst recalled, "with anything like fair odds [the Adoo] would usually come off best in contact with the SAF."[12]

The British-officered SAF forces were therefore pitted against insurgents of a much higher calibre and with higher levels of training and equipment than those insurgents typically encountered in previous classical British COIN campaigns. This clearly sets the Dhofar War apart in this respect. This aspect of the fighting ability of the Adoo is in stark contrast to the perception of other insurgent groups encountered. These include the contempt often held for the "Communist terrorist" or bandit groups encountered in Malaya, the backward and 'savage' Mau Mau fighters in Kenya or the 'cowardly' and often indiscriminate Jewish 'terrorists' in Palestine which had the effect of turning the initially sympathetic attitude of British troops serving there against the Jewish settler population in general.[13]

Low-Tech Nature of the Dhofar War

Continuing the atypical theme, as compared to Britain's previous campaigns, the Dhofar conflict was very low-tech in its COIN conduct, especially in the early years, which sets it apart. This was the case from the start of the war in the mid-1960s and all throughout the reign of Sultan Said. This situation effectively endured right up until the final two years of the conflict. The situation was then significantly reversed through large-scale Iranian troop deployments and military hardware and technology introduced to the campaign battlefield. Despite this, for the most part the Dhofar campaign was in a similar vein to the Palestine and Malayan emergencies as well as the Kenyan and Cypriot COIN campaigns as effectively being a limited-scale infantry undertaking. The fighting was carried out by small units in difficult or hazardous terrain by the combatants on the ground.[14] What makes the Dhofar War stand out in this respect is the extreme extent of the low-tech nature of the operation for most of its duration as compared to previous British COIN campaigns. The SAF were disadvantaged throughout much of the Dhofar War, but especially up to 1970, with obsolete kit. This included Second World War vintage bolt-action rifles, a lack of modern battlefield equipment (such as zero helicopter casualty evacuation capability and extremely limited in-country military medical provision) and was plagued with shortages of even the most basic field kit such as uniforms and mountain-suitable boots or other footwear.[15] What was essentially a relatively small-scale infantry-based operational profile was reinforced by artillery when possible and bolstered by air capability in the form of basic transport aircraft. It would not be until 1969, or some four years into the war, that helicopters and strike aircraft became available to support operations in Dhofar. From this time, the highly capable ground-attack BAC Strikemaster aircraft entered service and six Augusta Bell helicopters were finally ordered, with De Havilland DHC-4 Caribous available from late 1970. Such additional aircraft represented very useful new capabilities for Omani COIN forces, but remained relatively outdated in terms of technology and were numerically too few to make sufficient and timely inroads into a slowly stagnating campaign. As such it was the case that for the critical initial four years of the war SAF forces operated at a significant disadvantage compared to the situation encountered in previous UK COIN campaigns.

The shortcomings were stark when compared to the even relatively limited availability of military technology or combat equipment available to support British forces in COIN campaigns such as in Malaya, Kenya or the operational constraints of Northern Ireland for example; and ironically even previously in Oman during the Djebel War of the late 1950s. During the latter, troops were on hand and available from the Trucial states and (Muscat and) Oman as well as the UK, plus substantial RAF bomber and jet fighter support from bases such as RAF Khormaksar (Aden), RAF Sharjah (Trucial States) and RAF Masirah (Oman) to draw from. Even British forces in Aden could, prior to withdrawal in 1967, call upon both large-scale RAF forces and Royal Navy warship support as required.[16] Several squadrons of strike aircraft were ready on hand in the territory to support offensive operations in the Radfan region or operations against insurgents in urban areas, including Hawker Hunter FGA9 aircraft (armed with cannons, rockets and bombs), Shackleton MR3s and numerous types of transport aircraft available and operating out of RAF Khormaksar.[17] Such low-tech operations in Dhofar can be likewise be also negatively compared to contemporaneous non-UK COIN campaigns. These included the COIN actions of France and the USA and even with the forces of (relatively economically undeveloped) Portugal in its almost concurrent African campaigns where naval forces, heavy bomber aircraft and helicopters were readily available in numbers sufficient to effectively support operations.[18]

Following the arrival in Dhofar of the initial Iranian contingents in 1972, numerous modern fast jets and heavy-lift capable Chinook helicopters for example subsequently became available to support the SAF for the first time in the war. Prior to this and for the first eight years of the conflict the luxury of such resources to support the small-scale infantry operations did not exist. This situation contrasts with the relative sophistication of the weaponry increasingly available to the Insurgents; especially from when major backing was forthcoming from the communist PDRY after Britain's 1967 Adeni exit. Generously equipped by their sponsors in the form of revolutionary Communist China then the USSR, the insurgents had access to automatic rifles, Shpagin large-calibre machine guns, and Katyusha rockets (a direct hit from which "could knock a rock-built sangar clean off the hill") which helped them successfully engage the SAF.[19] Towards the end of the war the insurgents even had access to sophisticated surface-to-air missiles (SAMs); with which they managed to down several COIN force aircraft.[20]

Although increasing levels of war-fighting technology were utilised in the Dhofar campaign after the 1970 coup it remained a relatively low-tech affair. British units with hi-tech equipment for the time such as the Green Archer mortar locating radar system then became available. There was also increased military expenditure, expansion and investment which was further boosted from 1972 when the first Iranian contingents arrived, but despite this, the COIN campaign was, in war-fighting technology terms, effectively a poorly funded and equipped small-scale infantry-level fought campaign. Its biggest asset was actually the experience and skill of the seconded or contract British officers leading such units and the stoicism and determination of the largely Baluchi or Omani soldiers.[21] Although increased levels of more sophisticated battlefield technology were introduced from 1970, for a vast majority of the campaign such equipment and technology was simply not available. Even when it was, the extreme topographical and other physical environmental factors such as the Khareef monsoon period hampered its full operational potential. As Peterson states:

> Although the war in Dhurfar [eventually] made good use of helicopters and other aircraft, advanced communications and even Iranian naval vessels providing heavy calibre Naval Gunfire Support in the end, it was won mainly on the ground in small [infantry-based] contacts.[22]

Like its earlier counterparts, the Dhofar Campaign was for the most part a small-unit scale infantry operation in the hands of the skills and leadership of junior British officers in the field. The main difference was that the military technology available to support such operations was extremely limited or even completely absent for nearly all of the campaign. In 1964 there was an almost complete lack of such support for the modest original SAF force despatched by road from Muscat to Dhofar by then CSAF, Colonel Tony Lewis. Although this situation improved slowly over the course of the campaign, even rudimentary levels of battlefield technology such as helicopters were not introduced until after the 1970 coup; but even then, the scale of introduction was not substantial until the arrival of Iranian forces from 1972. For the first eight years of the war up until 1973, therefore, the level of technology was even lower than previous classical-era UK COIN campaigns and overall was possibly the lowest-tech of any COIN operations undertaken by British forces.[23] This arguably makes the Dhofar campaign unique in UK COIN history.

Scope & Extent of SAS-Implemented 'Hearts and Minds' Campaign

As compared to previous classical British COIN campaigns, 'hearts and minds'-type activities in Dhofar were implemented at a relatively late stage in the proceedings yet to a more comprehensive level in relative terms probably than ever seen previously. The scope of implementation of the 'hearts and minds' campaign was in addition more comprehensive than undertaken in previous UK COIN campaigns. Britain effectively engaged in large-scale state-building activities and development as part of its COIN approach. This set the foundations for a functioning, inclusive state able to stand on its own feet militarily, economically and diplomatically, and to protect itself and fight an insurgency on home soil.

Ex-CO of 22 SAS, Colonel (later Major-General) Tony Jeapes alluded to the fact that the Dhofar campaign was a product of half a century of development of doctrine and approach from the experience of British forces in a multitude of irregular campaigns.[24] The Dhofar campaign however, did not employ the standard 'hearts and minds'-related COIN operational plans and tactics seen in the previous classical British COIN campaigns until post-1970 and some five years into the campaign. This was much later than the exemplar of 'hearts and minds' activities in Malaya and Kenya for example. In the former, the Briggs Plan was implemented only two years after the onset of the emergency. This included a 'stick and carrot' approach to winning over the population plus the forced resettlement of the squatter Chinese population to protected 'New Villages' where access to food and movement in and out was strictly controlled to separate insurgents from their either sympathetic or coerced support base.[25] A policy of 'villagisation' of Mau Mau squatters was also undertaken within two years of the campaign start in Kenya and was modelled on the resettlement policy undertaken in Malaya.[26] Efforts, therefore, to separate insurgents from the population occurred much later in Dhofar than in the two largest (and most successful prior to Dhofar) British classical COIN campaigns. The equivalent action in Dhofar was the establishment of a permanent SAF presence on the Jebel and the development of governmental support centres via Civil Action Teams (CATs). These served to re-establish civil authority, provide security and win over the population with both goods and services the insurgents could, or would not provide.[27] This did not occur until Operation JAGUAR in 1971 with the establishment of the centre at White City, an action spearheaded by SAS troops and their Firqa local militia protégés. This was the first government stronghold on the Jebel and proved to be a turning point in the campaign and a base from which other 'hearts and minds'-type activities could be launched. These activities included Operations CAPRICORN and CIVET which were the protected movement of livestock to enable them to be sold at market. Providing such income to the impoverished Jebali communities and bringing them into the sphere of government influence was considered one of the most successful elements of the 'hearts and minds' campaign in Dhofar up to that time.[28] Although the breakthrough in government policy and 'hearts and minds' activities with the establishment of White City was the start of a relatively quick expansion of such centres it did not even begin until some seven years after the start of the insurgency. This was significantly later than in other and similar duration classical UK campaigns.

Post-1970 coup, many of the 'hearts and minds'-related elements of previous British classical COIN campaigns were brought to bear when tried and tested activities became a major priority and the key recommendations of the then CO of 22 SAS, Lieutenant Colonel John Watt's original 'Five Point Plan' were adopted for the war.[29] As such:

> Under Qaboos [therefore], a more familiar pattern of counter-insurgency then began, guided by the SAS-composed BATT [British Army Training Team] and by various seconded or contract British officers attached to the SAF.[30]

The SAS detachment in Oman was tasked with several roles. These varied from Royal bodyguard training to raising local militia, civil, medical and agricultural projects to intelligence gathering and psyops operations; all of which contributed greatly to the eventual successful conclusion of the campaign.[31] Sultan Said had not allowed the SAS to operate in Oman during the early years of the insurgency and practically zero ' hearts and minds'-related activities were employed until Qaboos came to power. Aspects of the change in approach are summarised by Peterson, including the centrality of Intelligence within the overall COIN effort, appropriate use of SF troops and successful creation and use of local militia forces.[32] The raising of the Firqa units was a central platform of the strategy, aided by the implementation of an amnesty programme as in previous classical UK COIN campaigns such as in Malaya. Prior to the coup which toppled him, Sultan Said refused to consider plans put forward by British officers to offer selective amnesty for insurgents.[33] This general attitude to the campaign is summed up in Sultan Said's orders to Brigadier Graham on arrival in his new post of CSAF in 1970, "These people on the Jebel are very bad. Brigadier, I want you to kill them all."[34] Many individual elements in Dhofar's 'hearts and minds' campaign were, therefore, similar to previous classical British COIN campaigns but due to virtually nil such programmes being possible until after the coup in 1970, such initiatives were utilised considerably later in Dhofar than previously.

As well as timing, the 'hearts and minds' activities in Oman are distinguishable from other British classical COIN campaigns in terms of scope. Whilst there was never the scale seen of mass deportations of potential insurgents or the resettlement of hundreds of thousands of settlers as in the Malayan Emergency, for example, the breadth of activities was more diverse and wide-ranging in Dhofar. This is apparent at the tactical as well as governmental strategic level due largely to the lack of development on all fronts in Oman and especially within Dhofar. A sustained effort to bring rudimentary development to the jebel was undertaken where there was literally zero public infrastructure before, including education and healthcare provision. Allied to this, the 'wealth' of the population of the jebel was invested in their herds of animals so assisting the transportation and sale of livestock was a priority. This can be observed in the SAS-devised Operation TAURUS where cattle were transported from the jebel to Salalah to be sold, therefore providing income to the Jebalis and resultingly providing a stake in the status quo.[35] Innovative SAS assistance was further implemented in terms of veterinary services and improving the Jebali livestock though the transportation of prime breeding bulls from the SAS's home base town of Hereford to Dhofar to improve the bloodlines of the local rather sorry-looking but hardy Jebali cattle.[36] If this was not obscure and detail-oriented enough in terms of British support efforts, the SAS also assisted the Jebalis with implementing more effective agricultural practices. This was achieved via the establishment of a first-of-type exhibition or demonstration farm on the Jebel in conjunction with agricultural-scientific support in the guise of soil quality evaluation and expert recommendations for the population on what specific crops were viable in the local conditions.[37] SAS soldiers were obviously not agricultural experts, but with UK-based support, including laboratory facilities, such efforts were all undertaken to win the 'hearts' or gratitude of the population for the government side. Such a concerted effort in these fields was unmatched in terms of scope in previous UK COIN campaigns. It was, however, not just at this tactical support level that British 'hearts and minds' activities went over and above previous campaign efforts.

All previous British classical COIN campaign 'hearts and minds' schemes featured the implementation of significant political or social concessions to woo the population's support back to the side of the governing status quo. In Malaya this took the form of the promise of independence and moves towards the establishment of an inclusive multi-ethnic state. Here, the ethnic Chinese – who provided most of the personnel for the insurgent ranks – would have a stake in society. The promise of independence also moderated the opposition to British influence in Cyprus, as it eventually did also in Kenya and to a certain extent in Aden. In Kenya, a systematic policy of land reform was instigated via the Swynnerton Plan and the historic ban, for example, on native Africans growing coffee was lifted to both pacify and give the Kikuyu an economic stake in society and means of subsistence.[38] In Dhofar social concession-type developments implemented were more fundamental and wider in scope largely because there was an almost complete lack of pre-existing state apparatus. As a result, the British 'hearts and minds' role was far more expansive and effectively became an accelerated state-building effort to secure the state and the support of the people; especially in Dhofar. Immediately after the coup a colloquially named yet very powerful 'Interim Advisory Council' (IAC) was formed by the Sultan's Military Secretary or Minister of Defence, Briton Colonel Oldman to keep the country functioning on behalf of an inexperienced new Sultan. British advice and action was vital to both protect and help grow and nurture the "tender plant" of the administration and to push forward not only on military expansion, training and procurement but also on economic, social and governance issues.[39] Britain basically secured the survival of, and helped develop the new Omani administration and initiated the widespread and large-scale economic development and social programmes which directly and indirectly benefitted the people of Dhofar especially.

Britain's pre-coup assistance in this field through noted soldier, diplomat and explorer Hugh Boustead as a seconded development advisor achieved only modest success due in part to Sultan Said's efforts to slow down or block the programme.[40] Large-scale tangible results were only discernible once Sultan Qaboos came to power and, on the advice of British authorities, money was pumped into civil development as well as towards military necessities; supported by an increase in the national budget from 68.5 million Riyals in 1973 to 325 million Riyals in 1975.[41] The 'hearts and minds' campaign implemented CATs as run largely by SAS personnel, administered such plans and by 1973 such successful yet ad hoc activities were cemented through British support and advice to the administration to enable a standalone Ministry of Development to be established to further institutionalise such efforts. Former Gurkha and Muscat Regiment officer, Lieutenant Colonel Martin Robb became a lead for civil development in Dhofar from 1974, and was appointed the designated head of the Dhofar section of the newly created national governmental Civil Aid Department from early 1975. He later held a seat on the cross-departmental Dhofar Development Committee (which also included the Commander, Dhofar Brigade and Head of Dhofar Intelligence and Firqa Forces) which further institutionalised the civil development effort.[42] The British-instigated and nurtured civil aid programme resulted in the establishment of over 50 new water wells, the construction of over 20 government support centres on the Jebel, and nearly 40 schools in Dhofar during the war in Dhofar alone.[43] This was achieved alongside the introduction of a much-needed 'flying doctor' service which covered even the most remote parts of Dhofar, as well as agricultural and road-building programmes.[44] The civil aid programme via the CATs, the SAS, and the senior British leadership of the SAF was to help ensure the survival of the ruling Omani status quo and the support of the people and their disengagement from the insurgent cause due to many of the initial grievances against the regime being finally addressed.

As per previous classical British COIN campaigns although 'hearts and minds' activities were vital, in Dhofar such efforts were not implemented and developed until at least five years into the war. This was not just relatively later than in comparable UK classical campaigns but was also much more comprehensive in terms of fundamental scope than in previous COIN undertakings. It was by necessity a concentrated version as it was only implemented late in the proceedings with regards to the war's timeline. This was unlike in previous operations where the colonial government or British-supported administration was at least developed and functioning, in Oman this was not the case. Britain had to manage and accelerate nothing less than a comprehensive state-building programme in terms of bolstering military capability, social and economic development as well as governmental organisation and development. Such a programme of assistance also included helping to secure outside recognition of the country and regime through British diplomatic lobbying via the Arab League and UN, with Ambassador Donald Hawley stating:

> [With British administrative and lobbying assistance] applications had been made to both the Arab League and the United Nations for membership, but even Sayyid Tarik [Prime Minister] who was an optimist on this point did not regard it as likely that the application would be successful in 1971. In the event, however, they were and Oman was admitted to the Arab League in September and the United Nations on 7th October 1971.[45]

Additionally, as with other 'hearts and minds' campaigns, the ultimate aim in Dhofar was to both woo and compel the population to support the government side whilst at the same time alienating the insurgents from their support base to enable their defeat. From the civil development perspective it was more skewed towards the archetypal 'velvet glove'-esque or 'open hand of friendship' rather than the 'closed fist' of military action approach and was calculated to win over the support of the Jebalis (as well as the wider Dhofari population) to the government side and the status quo.[46] As such, this approach was key to the war effort. More broadly, the 'woo and compel' overall aim was largely achieved by 1975 in Dhofar through the wide-ranging and expansive British-inspired and implemented 'hearts and minds' campaign which arguably went significantly further in terms of scope than in any of the previous UK COIN engagements. As such, the Dhofar COIN undertaking was atypical of the UK's classical operations. Considering this aspect, it may as a result instead be better termed a 'classical-plus' campaign. This is especially the case when considering the relatively short timeframe in which it was achieved; a situation unique in the annals of British COIN.

Multinational Coalition Required to Win

Alongside local British-controlled or officered forces, previous classical-era British COIN campaigns were usually carried out and concluded, successfully or otherwise, by British Crown or controlled security forces without the assistance or substantial help of foreign allies. The Dhofar campaign broke this mould. It presented a situation where sovereign UK forces were operating alongside British-officered SAF units, Jordanian troops and a large Iranian force which included land, air and sea-borne assets making it unique in the UK's historical COIN narrative. Exceptions include the Rhodesian, Australian and New Zealander troops fighting in Malaya as part of the 28th Commonwealth Infantry Brigade (which accounted for one of the seven brigades operating in the country by 1955), and the Australian and New Zealand troops committed to the Borneo confrontation, but these were considered substantially 'British' in nature due to the Commonwealth or former British Empire connection.[47] In most cases, however, it was largely UK forces alongside the British-controlled or officered local government security forces which constituted the prosecuting forces in previous British COIN campaigns. This mirrored closely the situation prior to 1973 in the case of the Dhofar conflict, with British-officered Omani and (primarily) Baluchi troops conducting the campaign. By 1970 it was clear the SAF were unable to defeat the insurgents and at best a situation of stalemate developed. At worst it increasingly looked as if the war in Dhofar might even potentially be lost to the insurgents if nothing was changed. As a result, more radical operational thinking was required, indeed Marc Devore states that: "By late 1969, British officers serving in Oman were reporting to London that the situation in Dhofar was very bad and if allowed to go unchecked, control of the country might not be maintained for another year".[48]

After the accession of Sultan Qaboos, determined efforts were put in place to turn around the unsatisfactory military stalemate situation. One of the avenues both explored and subsequently exploited fully was the expansion of SAF capability by bringing in foreign allied forces to assist the military campaign. As a result of the growing links and personal relationship between the Sultan of Oman and the Shah of Iran which began at the Persepolis celebration in Iran in 1971, practical Iranian assistance to Sultan Qaboos's cause was not long to materialise.[49] This steady build-up of links was continued via the new Iranian ambassador in Muscat and through much behind-the-scenes diplomacy by military staff between the Omani, Iranian and Jordanian administrations, initially by Brigadier Graham, and later continued by Major General Creasey.[50] This bilateral diplomacy in turn led to the deployment in support of the SAF of Jordanian Special Forces and Combat Engineer units and eventually to an entire Iranian Battle group by 1973 which comprised Special Forces troops, vital heavy lift helicopter capability and some 3,000 men in total.[51] This led to a significant change in the composition of the overall Dhofar COIN forces through a process of internationalisation, where "[by 1973] Iranian combat units actually spearheaded many of the critical late-campaign offensives and Jordanian engineers and SF fortified and defended critical locales."[52] Infantry from the UAE in the form of the Abu Dhabi Defence Force (ADDF) were also made available. Originally this unit was intended to deploy for front-line operations but was later deployed to Northern Oman with a reduced scope of 'internal security' duties only, but this allowed the release of two Oman Gendarmerie (OG) squadrons from static security taskings for forward deployment in Dhofar.[53] In addition to regional support, Oman was able to procure military support supplies from further afield. Claymore anti-personnel mines as well as Tube Launched, Optically Tracked, Wire-Guided (TOW) anti-tank missile systems were purchased from the USA in conjunction with a support package consisting of missile projectiles and US army training instructors.[54]

By early 1975 of the 11,000 plus troops serving in Dhofar only approximately 1000 were British regular forces, with these outnumbered almost 4:1 by foreign (mainly Iranian and Jordanian) troops.[55] This situation is a clear departure from previous classical British COIN campaigns and again highlights the unique nature of the Dhofar War. It presented a situation where it could be considered that "Oman's triumph in Dhofar was actually an international victory" as opposed to an operation conducted solely (or even in a majority) by British forces themselves.[56]

Campaign Outcome

The Dhofar War was eventually a clear military and political win for Britain, which was at odds with most of the previous classical UK COIN campaigns. The overall outcomes of the COIN campaigns in Palestine and Aden have been described as bona fide disasters for Britain, with that of Cyprus not far behind, where in the former case "hundreds of British and other lives have been sacrificed and damage to the tune of millions of pounds has been done".[57] Britain was humiliatingly forced to exit both Palestine and Aden/Southern Arabia which drew widespread criticism, including even from within the UK's own political ranks for the country's apparent "scuttle" from the colony.[58] Combining the disastrous Suez campaign in 1956 and the inability to stop the Unilateral Declaration of Independence (UDI) by Rhodesia in 1965, Britain can be considered to have suffered a significant loss of international prestige during the 1950s and 1960s. In the case of Cyprus, although the sovereign base areas were retained after independence, the UK was vilified in the UN and was effectively outmanoeuvred and forced out as the long-standing colonial power by as few as 300 insurgents in a relatively small operating area (the overall size of the retained areas was relatively small, being only some 120 square miles out of the island's total land mass of 3,572 square miles), and by a politically-savvy Archbishop with a skill for public relations and media manipulation. Here "He [Archbishop Makarios] succeeded in winning over the Greek government, and then used them to arouse world public opinion [against Britain] through the United Nations."[59] The Kenyan Mau Mau campaign was technically a military win for British forces but political control of the territory was lost (although to a relatively pro-UK government) only a few years after the end of the rebellion as the country gained its independence in 1964. Even though independence was granted actually during the campaign (and therefore also British control of the territory's tin and rubber resources), only Malaya, and to a lesser extent, Brunei/Borneo, was the stand-out COIN success. It endured for many years as the model case study of an exemplar COIN campaign, establishing the UK's unconventional warfare expertise reputation and resultant level of influence and latent power. As such, the Brunei/Borneo case provided an outcome where:

> The political significance of the campaign in Borneo was that it preserved the independence of Malaysia and almost certainly prevented the spread of Communism into Indonesia, with far-reaching consequences for the rest of South-East Asia.[60]

Although undertaken in low key circumstances, the Dhofar campaign helped boost Britain's prestige. It achieved this through a positive outcome to counter the numerous diplomatic and military setbacks and humiliations endured on the international scene since 1945, and helped maintain Britain's reputation as both a regional and world power. The win also helped to safeguard the UK economy through securing uninterrupted oil supplies from the Gulf region. During the Cold War years the UK also needed to check Communist great power influence and encroachment in the Gulf region post-1971 and its own military withdrawal 'East of Suez'. Although many were careful to emphasise it was a 'win' for Oman, it remained an effective military victory for Britain against a determined enemy with both tangible and ideological superpower support during the Cold War.[61] This situation is a departure from the outcomes of previous UK COIN campaigns which were often either mixed outcome (military wins but political defeats) or disastrous losses.

As can be seen, the Dhofar War was very similar in a large number of respects to previous classical British COIN campaigns. From similar general geopolitical backgrounds to specifics such as the relatively small scale, predominantly rural location of the Dhofar campaign, to the range of COIN tactics employed and the general conduct of the campaign, the similarities are many and compelling. This is also reflected in the writings and conclusions of key classical and neo-classical COIN commentators and authors. Their influence in understanding the concept of classical British COIN and the consistent threads or DNA-strands that run through all such campaigns is key and enduring. Indeed it has been stated with strong justification that, "The 1960s theorists cast a long shadow."[62] The Dhofar War can be seen on one level as very much an extension of classical British COIN campaigns in numerous different ways. Whilst certainly not without universal agreement, this effect can be observed where "the view has taken root [in UK military circles] that the Dhofar insurgency was vanquished by proven tactics, organisational tools and procedures elaborated during prior counterinsurgencies in Malaya, Kenya and Borneo."[63]

When viewed more critically it is clear, however, that the Dhofar campaign, far from being a mere clone of previous classical UK COIN campaigns, actually displayed several technical, key, or indeed fundamental differences which sets it apart. In several key ways the Dhofar campaign was unique and was a specific product of its time and set of equally singular circumstances. With the exception of the Brunei/early Borneo campaign and the final three years of the Malayan Emergency and unlike previous classical British actions, the Dhofar War was waged in conjunction with a separate sovereign partner with Britain never directly or wholly in control of the anti-insurgent operation *per se*. In addition, in terms of COIN opposition, the insurgents of the Dhofar rebellion were much more capable and were generally much better trained and equipped than often seen in previous classical British campaigns. The Dhofari insurgents benefitted from Cold War competition-grade proxy training and support from the main world Communist powers even if the overall level of campaign technology was lower than in probably any other UK classical COIN campaign. In addition, the 'hearts and minds' campaign initiated in Dhofar was of greater scope and implemented later than in previous locations. It ultimately took a coalition of the military forces of several sovereign international partners (where British forces were in the large minority) to prosecute the campaign to an eventual and successful conclusion. Perhaps the most significant difference when compared to past classical British COIN campaigns was that the Dhofar operation was a resounding win in the end. This compared to a generally overall fairly "dismal" track record in terms of success.[64] The outcome of the Dhofar COIN campaign would in addition, compare favourably to other contemporary non-British classical-era campaigns which in the main ended in either military or political defeats. Examples include those conducted in Vietnam by the USA,

Indochina and Algeria for the French and Mozambique, Guinea and Angola for the Portuguese as well as in Rhodesia for example. As a result, though by no means perfect, Dhofar was a stand-out example of success.

The significance of the British-run Dhofar COIN campaign outcome is highlighted in the COIN literature. It has been said that, "The successful campaign in Dhofar was one of only a few instances where an active Marxist insurgency was defeated by a Western-backed power during the Cold War", and that it was "probably the best counterinsurgency campaign ever fought".[65] The Dhofar campaign was, therefore, a significant and noteworthy departure from the outcomes or levels of success of previous classical British COIN campaigns as well as more contemporary non-UK COIN campaigns conducted around the world.[66]

The issue of success is a key criterion with which to determine how typical the Dhofar operation was when compared to previous classical British COIN campaigns. Whilst Dhofar can be compared favourably to previous British classical COIN campaigns in terms of the end result, the concept of success is more nuanced. Despite the outcome, the Dhofar campaign was not necessarily a paragon of success or of possessing ideal COIN attributes. To determine if the Dhofar COIN campaign was truly successful when compared to previous British COIN undertakings, what is required is a more in-depth survey into notions of success.

Part III

The Dhofar War: Typical in Terms of Success?

Britain is often labelled in the COIN literature as having both a wide experience and discernible level of expertise when conducting such campaigns.[1] The UK conducted numerous COIN campaigns during the classical era, starting with the Palestine Emergency and leading to almost simultaneous COIN operations of varying scales in Malaya, Kenya, Cyprus and Oman itself (Djebel War) in the 1950s. This was followed in the 1960s by concurrent COIN operations in Brunei/Borneo and Aden; with simultaneous operations in Dhofar and Northern Ireland swiftly following. This record of intervention was a large-scale commitment by the UK but within the literature there is, however, a disputed level of success for such campaigns and the Dhofar campaign is no exception.

The literature pertaining to British COIN is both split and relatively flawed on the issue of success of UK COIN. It is generally divided between polar opposite success or failure narratives. On the one hand, the UK is often lauded as the leading expert in matters of COIN and having an impressive success rate (and even the best classical-era COIN record of any nation) such as the view that "the British Army remains the most successful and practiced exponent of counter-insurgency since 1945."[2] On the other hand, the counter-narrative often put forward by revisionist scholars is that the outcomes of the various campaigns were invariably poor; being represented mainly by losses, important defeats or 'half-losses'.[3] The overall view of this perspective can be summed up by the comment that British COIN has been typified by a generally "dismal track record".[4] The more nuanced approach is to consider the British record of success in COIN as actually 'mixed' or indeed average from an absolute perspective, although at the same time – and importantly – with a relatively better record than most other classical-era COIN-undertaking nations. The Dhofar campaign did itself end in victory for the SAF, the Omani authorities and allies. The overall win, however, belies many poor aspects of the campaign which cannot be described as wholly successful.

The Dhofar campaign was an overall success in relative terms. It was an important COIN win in the vein of the Malayan Emergency outcome, and as such was also relatively successful compared to several other UK campaigns and non-UK campaigns of the classical era. It was also, however, anything but text book, ideal or successful from an absolute perspective e.g. from a tactical or campaign prosecution viewpoint.[5] Further, in disagreement with the stance of much of the polarised subject narratives, the more nuanced opinion of this book is that the Dhofar operation fits into the general actuality of mixed levels of success of British COIN since 1945. It was, therefore, typical because it was not a complete success and was significantly flawed. This book, however, further puts forward the idea that the Dhofar campaign was as such a rare COIN win and, allied to its overall strategic significance, was not just typical in its mixed level of success with regards to other classical British COIN campaigns. With hindsight it was actually more successful than could be appreciated even at the announcement of victory in 1975. As a particularly rare success against communist or communist-backed insurgents during the Cold War superpower stand-off, historically it should be considered in the very highest echelon of British COIN campaigns in terms of success.[6] This factor clearly sets the Dhofar example apart from its predecessor campaigns.

The Dhofar campaign can be considered as neither a total success nor a failure, but an amalgam of both. To establish the extent of how much Dhofar reflects other classical British COIN campaigns in terms of success, firstly a general definition of success is established. Secondly the actual level of success of UK COIN is then clarified from a historical perspective. As such, the Dhofar campaign is then contrasted to these to demonstrate how typical it can be considered from this aspect, utilising broad categories and metrics with regards to relative or absolute success. For the purposes of this book, relative success will be defined primarily as a COIN 'win' or COIN forces which physically or militarily prevailed over insurgencies and is a key metric reflected in the COIN literature.[7] In addition to this, the achievement of strategic goals, the different types of cost incurred by COIN forces, the gaining of other benefits from the COIN campaign plus demonstrable benefit for the host nation or state involved is used to assess the position. In terms of absolute success, the actual military performance of Dhofar COIN forces (pre- and post-1970), military structural/operational organisation and the campaign costs incurred by Britain and its key campaign allies is used to determine this section's conclusions.

Success in COIN (General)

Historically, the level of success for the COIN forces of nations taking part in such actions is relatively poor with the incumbents tending to be reactive in posture and insurgents holding the initiative.[8] Of the more than 70 COIN campaigns undertaken worldwide from 1945–2010, only 21 resulted in a win for

The Dhofar War: Typical in Terms of Success? 87

the COIN forces.⁹ This is where, "COIN forces militarily prevailed or had the better of a mixed outcome in a conflict", including classical-era British campaigns conducted in Malaya, Kenya, and Northern Ireland.¹⁰ Whilst quality of COIN forces, support levels, insurgency circumstances and scale all have a mitigating effect on such statistics, the fact that COIN operations have, historically, very often been unsuccessful means that any success should be lauded as a general exception, rather than the rule. In Oman, Britain successfully avoided the often-disastrous effects of a campaign loss and both managed and conducted a campaign that actually resulted in a rare COIN win, especially against Marxist/Communist-backed insurgents. On this level it can be classified as a significant relative success. The campaign did not, however, result in swift success or a win either in the years prior to, or immediately after 1970 and the many costs were cumulatively high all round. The view that Dhofar was somehow a 'textbook' or 'model' campaign in terms of success needs to be qualified to assess its similarity to past campaigns.¹¹

British COIN record & Success Definitions (Relative vs. Absolute Success)

Britain has often been lauded by writers as being historically successful at prosecuting COIN campaigns. The British case is often highlighted as being one of general competence or even expertise in the field of undertaking COIN operations, and of a general historical trend of success. Newsinger, for instance, states that:

> ...the major counterinsurgency campaigns that the British state had waged in Palestine, Malaya, Kenya, Cyprus, South Yemen, Dhofar and Northern Ireland since 1945 had produced a largely celebratory literature. The general argument of this literature was that Britain's campaigns had been conducted with considerable success.¹²

British COIN Record & Success

The oft-cited success which helped forge such a reputation is that of the Malayan Emergency. Here, a predominantly British-controlled force utilised a half century of non-conventional warfare experience to quell a large-scale Communist uprising. In conjunction with concerted 'hearts and minds' activities, large-scale population resettlement methods, amnesty programmes and finely tuned kinetic COIN methods, Britain managed to achieve one of the most successful COIN feats of the modern era.¹³ Even though as part of the campaign early independence for the country was offered to galvanise support for the COIN campaign, British COIN efforts enabled an end to the large-scale emergency to be achieved. The campaign facilitated the defeat of a committed, numerous and well-resourced enemy during the volatile, paranoid, and newly nuclearised early years of the Cold War. In addition, Britain also undertook several other COIN campaigns in the post-Second World War era spread throughout the globe. The UK record shows several examples of additional successful COIN actions including the Kenyan 'Mau Mau' campaign, the Djebel War in Oman, Brunei/early Borneo and the decades-long, ('generational' in terms of time frame), and costly, but ultimately fruitful campaign in Northern Ireland.[14]

Table 3: Classical-Era British COIN Win/Loss Record.

Campaign Name	Dates	Win/Loss	Outcome Comments
*Palestine Emergency	1944–48	Loss	Situation led to complete withdrawal of UK forces and political administration from mandate
*Malayan Emergency	1948–60	Win	12-year conflict/Malayan independence 1957 actually during COIN campaign
*Kenya 'Mau Mau' Uprising	1952–60	Win	Led directly to Kenyan independence in 1964. Accusations of widespread abuse/brutality by British-controlled forces
*Cyprus Emergency	1955–59	Loss/Mixed Result	Mixed result – favouring insurgents. Britain lost control of whole island bar the retained sovereign base areas
*Oman (Imamate Uprising)	1957–59	Win	A technical win, but rebel leaders escaped/survived and continued struggle
Borneo Confrontation (early)	1962–66	Win	Initial Brunei-specific insurgency plus pre-direct Indonesian forces intervention stage in Borneo generally
*Aden Emergency	1963–67	Loss	Led to both early and complete withdrawal of UK forces and political administration
*Oman (Dhofar Rebellion)	1964–75	Win	10-year war undertaken to enable eventual win. Rare victory over Communist insurgency
*Northern Ireland	1969–99	Win	An eventual COIN win, but a cross-generational 30-year plus duration and large financial and human cost UK-wide

*Source: Christopher, P., Clarke, C., Grill, B., and Dunigan, M., *Paths to Victory – Detailed Insurgency Case studies*, (Santa Monica: Rand Corporation, 2013)

Historical COIN experts often promote the idea that Britain had a very good record of success when considering post-Second World War COIN. Key writers of this ilk praise Britain's overall record and conduct with regards to COIN operations. They also highlight that they were often also certainly better conducted, more humane (lacking violent excesses) and ended with results surpassing those campaigns conducted by other countries. These include the French in Southeast Asia and Algeria, the Dutch in Indonesia, the Portuguese in several African campaigns (such as Guinea, Mozambique, and Angola); also included are the Rhodesians (now Zimbabwe) within their own borders or US forces in Vietnam for example. Compared to such examples, Mockaitis states that:

> British counter-insurgency operations, however, have generally been conspicuous for the lack of such excesses... The British have usually avoided the French policy of brutality employed during the battle of Algiers and the American reliance on indiscriminate firepower applied in Vietnam.[15]

In terms of end result indicators, further comparables include the large-scale French COIN losses in Indochina and Algeria for instance and those (running into the tens of thousands) suffered by the USA in Vietnam.[16] Although these campaigns were mostly of a significantly larger scale (and often very differing circumstances) to even Britain's largest scale campaign in Malaya, the indicative relative win to loss ratio of the UK is, however, notable.[17] Writers are, however, divided on whether Britain was actually so successful at this enterprise as such statistics indicate. More critical (neo-classical, revisionist or Marxist-leaning) writers state such views are a distortion of reality and actually Britain's record is a poor one in absolute terms; mostly comprising either outright or semi-losses or unconvincing COIN performances.[18] At the more positive end of such a negative scale would be, for example, the Cyprus COIN campaign. Here, the end result was actually independence, but also the retention of the sovereign base areas or permanent geological 'aircraft carriers' in the Mediterranean and the prevention of Enosis with mainland Greece was a part-strategic success.[19] The loss of control by Britain, however, of most of the strategically-situated island was a political defeat which overall meant a mixed outcome but one that favoured the insurgents thus a 'loss'. In Kenya, the COIN campaign was won from a purely military perspective and transfer of sovereignty was made to a relatively pro-British government post-independence. It still, however, eventually resulted in the loss of one of Britain's most prized overseas colonies in 1964, and only some four years after the COIN campaign ended.[20] Even with the classic success story of Malaya, this was not necessarily the wholesale victory often portrayed.[21] Although an eventual military COIN success, the campaign took over a decade to finally win. Another key compromise to ensure support and ultimately victory was the early granting of independence and loss of another prized territory and control of its natural resources for instance. In this sense, although a win for Britain, the Malayan COIN campaign can be seen as more of a "pyrrhic victory".[22]

For even the more successful British COIN campaigns there remain accusations of "ham-fisted counterinsurgency tactics" and general poor application of the past lessons of other British COIN campaigns which therefore question the conduct of such undertakings.[23] Worse still, the COIN campaigns in Palestine and Aden/South Yemen were severe and "important defeats" which significantly tarnished Britain's wider COIN record.[24] Britain's prestige and world power status was eroded by its inability to successfully manage the Palestine mandate, eventually effectively being forced to hand control over to the UN in what is described as a complete defeat.[25] In Aden, the UK was unable to either defeat insurgent forces or find an effective political solution where control was maintained over the territory and importantly Britain's largest military base areas outside the UK, and in a key, globally significant strategic region. Britain was effectively forced to exit both Palestine and Aden/South Yemen in humiliating blows to its status as both the historic and key contemporary regional power. With a relatively long list of such losses, half-losses or pyrrhic victories, Douglas Porch states that, "In short, were Britain's post-1945 won-lost (COIN) record that of a football team, the coach would most assuredly be searching for alternative employment."[26]

Before the Dhofar War, only Malaya, and the early stages of Brunei/Borneo and to a lesser extent the Mau Mau campaign in Kenya can realistically be considered stand-out COIN successes for Britain. In addition, it has been stated that the Dhofar COIN operation was "a carefully orchestrated campaign that by 1975 had yielded Britain's most [or only] clear-cut counter-insurgency victory since Malaya".[27] As such, the Malayan campaign was utilised by the British Army on its curriculum at its Staff College based in Camberley and presented to the senior officer students effectively as the case study of how to best conduct a COIN campaign until displaced by the even more impressive Dhofar example.[28] Despite clearly documented examples of absolute failure, in the post-imperial period Britain enjoyed considerable relative success against insurgents in several theatres which was at odds with a majority of classical-era campaigns of other nations.[29] These campaigns also resulted in accumulated levels of experience and a general set of principles resulting in Britain being the most successful exponent of COIN in the classical era. This situation can be summed up by the statement that, "While certainly not flawless, the British approach to counterinsurgency has arguably been more successful than that of any other nation."[30]

Britain's COIN success can be adequately explained by neither of the main polarised viewpoints as apparent and portrayed in the wider COIN literature;

a situation applicable equally to the Dhofar campaign. It was in absolute terms a highly mixed record, and neither the overwhelming success of the UK's much vaunted or supposed expertise at COIN or the relatively weak win to loss record (marred by poor COIN techniques and accusations of brutality) as levelled by some.[31] The overall record was actually something in-between the two main narratives but Britain's success as compared to other classical era COIN-undertaking nations was, however, relatively high. This was due in part, however, to the poor outcomes of most of those campaigns; as Newsinger puts it, "The emphasis here is very much on the word comparative."[32] In other words, the point made is that the other non-UK COIN campaigns were so badly conducted and had such poor outcomes that even the relatively poor UK efforts are made to look rather good.

Chapter 7

A Military Success?

To enable an appraisal of success of the Dhofar COIN campaign, several categories are considered. Although these concentrate primarily on elements of success for Britain, those for Oman and the other main coalition allies who joined in the latter stages of the war are also in part considered. Such categories include whether the campaign was an actual military success; the performance of COIN forces; the achievement of strategic goals; an assessment of campaign costs; and the other tangible benefits gained by the COIN participant nations.

Dhofar Campaign Result (Relative Success)

The Dhofar campaign was eventually a win for Oman and for the UK government. When victory was declared in December 1975, the SAF and its allies had militarily defeated a highly capable enemy. Further, this was an enemy which had received both ideological and large-scale tangible equipment and training support and provision via the two leading communist powers in the world and their wider communist bloc proxies, including Cuba, and East Germany. Britain had helped banish the spectre of the Palestine and Suez Crisis failures and the indifferent at best and disastrous at worst campaigns which followed, especially in Cyprus and Aden/South Arabia. Whilst these examples were not all complete military defeats in the conventional sense, such campaigns were unable to convert military performance or capability into an overall politico-military COIN win. In terms of a military victory being achieved, the Dhofar campaign was more akin to the Malayan, Kenyan, Djebel, Brunei/early Borneo and Northern Ireland COIN campaigns. All were overall COIN wins achieved in difficult circumstances and over varying periods of time from a relatively short campaign such as the sub-three-year Djebel War to 12 years in Malaya and upwards of 30 years in the case of Northern Ireland. As such, in relative terms, Britain's COIN record, including the campaign win in Dhofar compares very favourably with that achieved by other classical era COIN undertaking nations. Out of just 21 COIN wins achieved globally from 1945, Britain can claim ownership of five, and arguably six overall.[1] This is quite an achievement given the significant and numerous COIN losses listed for both Britain and other nations in the classical COIN era.

The Dhofar War was, therefore, one of the success stories of UK COIN as it resulted in a clear and decisive military victory. The campaign was very much a success in relative terms both as compared to previous UK COIN operations and those undertaken by other COIN-conducting nations in the classical era. It was, however, not necessarily representative in terms of overall British COIN purely from the 'success' perspective. This is because several UK campaigns cannot be considered military wins or successes as such and this record was additionally marred by numerous absolute-level failures. From this perspective the level of success in Dhofar can therefore be seen to be atypical in terms of Britain's overall COIN record.

Elements of Failure & Poor Pre-1970 Military Performance (Absolute Success)

Up to the time of the July 1970 coup, the SAF had failed to deliver victory against the insurgents. This situation led to a campaign which, despite resulting in overall eventual victory, would last for years longer than potentially should have been the case. This reflects similar situations in previous classical UK COIN campaigns in general and specifically in the Malayan and Kenyan cases. Here, regular UK and British-led colonial forces numbering in the tens of thousands failed to quickly defeat semi-trained Communist Insurgents or essentially forces comprising poorly equipped and trained tribespeople. In the approximately five years of the Dhofar COIN campaign leading up until the 1970 coup, the professional armed forces of the state of Muscat and Oman were unable to militarily defeat the small numbers of Dhofari rebels of the DLF/PFLOAG. This was despite their experienced and competent British commanders from the CSAF to the company commander level, and early superior numerical advantage. As a result the Dhofar COIN campaign morphed into a protracted war of attrition and the longest-running COIN campaign in post-war British history bar Malaya and Northern Ireland.

Sultan Said had been ruler of Muscat and Oman since early 1932. This had been the status quo since his debt-laden father, Sultan Taimur had been effectively forced to abdicate via British government pressure and persuasion, from where he settled into a life of exile in India.[2] Via the same backers who effectively put him in power, Sultan Said ruled as an absolute monarch within his economically and socially backward (even 'medieval-like') territory, and had been secure in his position from any challengers through continued British assistance.[3] The most serious of these challenges to his authority was the Imamate rebellion

(1954–1959). This episode culminated in the Jebel Akhdar campaign in 1959, with the Sultan's position saved by a combined force of Omani, Trucial Oman Scouts (from the neighbouring Trucial States), and regular British units. These included Royal Air Force assets from Aden as well as SF in the form of the SAS, freshly redeployed from a protracted jungle fighting campaign in Malaya. Post-Jebel Akhdar campaign, the Sultan's position was further boosted by the support afforded by the 1958 'Exchange of Letters'. This was a signed declaration between the UK government and the administration of the Sultan of Muscat and Oman which laid out the arrangements for a formalisation of Britain's financial and other security-related assistance to the Sultanate. The result of the agreement was that Britain covered a vast majority of all costs relating to the reorganisation of the Sultan's existing Muscat Armed Forces into the new, and expanded Sultan's Armed Forces (SAF). Not only financial in nature, the agreements also provided an ongoing training and leadership provision. Serving British officers were loaned or 'seconded' to Oman to lead the new SAF, including the organisation's most senior commander. The first CSAF provided under this arrangement was ex-SAS and SOE member Colonel David Smiley in 1958. This was followed in 1961 by the appointment of Colonel Hugh Oldman. Both officers possessed extensive wartime command and fighting experience with colonial or non-ethnically British forces. Oldman's successor from May 1964 was Colonel Tony Lewis, another highly experienced and decorated officer with wartime commando, and therefore irregular warfare experience.[4] Colonel Lewis was the first designated CSAF to take part in what became the Dhofar COIN campaign, and it was he – after receiving his instructions from the Sultan – who issued the order for the SAF to deploy to Dhofar to counter the growing insurgency threat in the province. This initial deployment heralded the start of the numerous problems encountered by the SAF and the subsequent lack of success achieved.

The SAF was initially deployed to Dhofar to deal with the local strife instigated by an individual named Mussalim bin Nufl, who was a Sheikh of one of the houses of the influential Bait Kathir tribe.[5] Aggrieved at being sacked from a job in the Sultan's workshops in Salalah, Bin Nufl then took it upon himself to initiate a vendetta campaign against his former employer.[6] Up until this point the SAF was not even permitted to operate in the Sultan's private estate of Dhofar and was confined to the north of the country.[7] The Sultan's immediate security was provided by his personal slaves, local guards known as askars and locally by a private army known as the Dhofar Force and which was administered separately from the SAF and over which the CSAF had no authority. Lewis received his orders from Brigadier Pat Waterfield, the Sultan's Military Secretary who, in an unconventional arrangement, only spoke to the Sultan in Salalah once per week via radio to receive his ministerial-level instructions.[8] With the Sultan's order to deploy, SAF forces had to travel to and operate in Dhofar from November 1964 having never served in the region before, with no maps, and with the NFR company taking several days to arrive in Salalah by desert track. Colonel Lewis commented:

> I was therefore faced with a problem far greater than any military staff college could invent. I had been asked to move a force by an unknown route across 600 miles of desert to a country also unknown to us, as big as Wales but of worse terrain. I was to search out a rebel force that lived in the inhospitable jebel country north of the Salalah plain about whom I knew nothing.[9]

The first problem pertaining to a lack of military success was that the company-strength Dhofar Force could not effectively contain a small-scale uprising inspired by a slighted local sheikh and the SAF force was likewise completely unprepared for the task at hand.[10] The local-level origins of the troubles were to cloud the judgement of the Sultan. He was convinced that he was facing a local tribal insurrection that could be contained and defeated. This he believed was a similar case to the Imamate rebellion of the 1950s where patronage, pledges of allegiance, his British 'contract' (or technically mercenary personnel), and above all, liberally-distributed money to ensure the loyalty of both individuals and tribes were the key factors that ended the uprising.

The initial tour of the NFR was rather a 'non-event'. No contacts with the Adoo insurgents were reported. As a result, the NFR was ordered back to its barracks in Northern Oman after just four weeks of deployment following what was assumed to be a relatively successful operation to deter the insurgent groupings from further activity.[11] The security situation in Dhofar then remained relatively quiet for a period of six months and some believed the 'flash-in-the-pan' uprising had petered out. This assumption was jolted back to the actual reality of the situation by the capture of a dhow sailing vessel off the coast of Iraq by the Shah of Iran's navy in mid-1965. Along with the dhow itself were a number of ethnic Dhofari dissidents, and a large number of weapons, ammunition and anti-vehicle mines. The captured dissidents were interrogated by the Sultan's authorities, and alongside the wealth of intelligence gained from seized documentation, Colonel Lewis concluded that, "We had a nationalist rebellion on our hands... supported by Saudi Arabia and Iraq who were prepared to provide training, money and military equipment to the [Dhofari] rebels."[12]

With the failure of the resident Dhofar Force to quell the disturbances, the assumed deterrent effect of the SAF deployment was rapidly reappraised and plans put in place to deal with the new situation that presented itself. As a result of the developing situation, two companies of the MR were deployed to Dhofar in May 1965, where they physically engaged with the Adoo and also suffered the SAF's first casualty in the province.[13] After some successful operations, elements of the regiment returned to barracks in Northern Oman as the imminent Khareef ended the possible 'fighting season'. The growing capability and confidence of the insurgent forces was evident after the monsoon season had passed in October. This became clear when they undertook their first major operations in late 1965 against the Sultan's forces and Dhofar-based oil infrastructure. Included in this was a well-planned attack on the civilian midway camp where the insurgents killed the depot manager, which presented clear indications of significant and determined external material support for the Adoo originating from the territory of Saudi Arabia.[14] By this time the SAF only really fully-controlled the Salalah Plain and northern desert areas bordering Saudi territory. In a short time period the western coastal area and the jebel mountainous region were increasingly under Adoo control and they could operate freely with no challenge. As a result, the advantage was firmly with the resident insurgents. These were tribesmen who knew the terrain and climatic nuances intimately, unlike the outsider SAF forces who were effectively considered foreign or 'alien' intruders in their territory.[15]

Due to absolute-level campaign failures it was at this time that a stalemate situation developed and the stage was, therefore, set for an extended conflict with no swift resolution in sight.[16] The SAF controlled the Salalah plain and the insurgents the mountain areas; with forays onto the jebel by the SAF only temporary and always resulting in a withdrawal when the Khareef mists and liquefied muddy conditions returned from July each year. This was an operational approach that was not to substantially change until 1971 and the Brigadier Graham-devised Operation JAGUAR. In early 1966 the SAF also suffered its first deaths due to enemy action, with a British officer and four soldiers of the NFR killed during a SAF operation in the Wadi Naheez.[17] The increasingly confident insurgents also subsequently almost achieved their goal of escaping the oppression of Sultan Said. They did this by successfully infiltrating the DF and conducting an assassination attempt at a guard of honour review at its permanent barracks north of Salalah in April 1966.[18] This event was followed in the May by the first insurgent attack using a rocket-launcher, which caused several SAF deaths. This incident brought home the realisation that the insurgents now clearly had access to sophisticated weaponry, were trained effectively on how to operate these weapon systems and were turning them successfully against the SAF. Not even a combined 1966 Irish Guards, SAS, and naval operation to disrupt the insurgent base located at Hauf near the Omani border was completely successful. Operation FATE as it was called, involved an amphibious landing of the troops from one of the Royal Navy's most sophisticated vessels, HMS *Fearless* (a steam-powered Landing Platform Dock (LPD).[19] Even though some 22 insurgents were apprehended by the soldiers and the town's use as a rebel base was halted, this proved to be only a temporary state of affairs and Hauf remained arguably the insurgents' most important base until the end of the war in 1975.[20]

Neither the SAF in Dhofar or regular British forces from the Southern Federation/Adeni side of the border could, therefore, completely halt the insurgency or put an end to the uprising. The insurgency would, as a result, escalate quickly and additionally change character from a nationalist rebellion into an even more effective Marxist-inspired uprising which would persist for over a decade. As a result it would claim many more lives and cost far more in money and suffering than if it had been quelled effectively by the SAF in 1965 with the significant resources, men, and will in hand at the time. The reasons for this are varied but can be distilled down to some key factors including a lack of sufficient numbers of SAF soldiers allied to a deficit in the necessary equipment (from both numerical and quality perspectives) to fight an insurgency against a superior-equipped enemy. Allied to these challenges was the lack of understanding of fighting insurgencies, or acceptance of good professional advice from his experienced British officers on the strategies necessary to defeat the insurgency by Sultan Said himself.[21].

The extent of such issues harking back to 1964 allied to events subsequently running away from the Sultan's control were so severe that by 1970 the situation was deteriorating at an alarming rate. A situation of military stalemate had been brought about where the SAF was clearly unable to defeat the insurgents outright, with the SAF effectively confined to the Salalah plain or northern desert areas and not holding any permanent military presence or a single base or stronghold on the Jebel. All throughout this period, the insurgents were continually becoming better trained and more combat experienced. The equipment inventories of the Adoo and therefore resultant combat capability were also enhanced via modern weaponry sourced from the USSR and wider Communist bloc. As early as 1970, Omani COIN forces had therefore effectively ceded control to the Adoo of the entire province of Dhofar save the Salalah coastal plain and northern deserts. Due to this, a number of seconded and contract British officers were expressing the opinion that the war and control of the whole province could potentially be lost to the insurgent forces as early as 1971.[22] What started out as a seemingly successful initial deployment by the SAF in 1964 not been capitalised on sufficiently and quickly enough to prevent the spread of the wider insurgency. This contributed to the ability of the insurgent organisation to grow, arm and train with the fortuitous aid of the newly independent PDRY and both China and the USSR. By 1970 a situation had developed where the SAF could not win outright; but neither could the insurgents, so a situation of attritional warfare arose. Each side was entrenched in largely static areas of control, and these only shifted temporarily during each fighting season with the insurgents regaining any lost territory during the Khareef monsoon when the SAF retreated back to the Salalah Plain. The insurgents could justifiably claim the ascendancy in this case.

Similar to the early phases of previous classical UK COIN actions in Malaya and Kenya for instance, pre-1970 the SAF was not able to convert its relative military superiority in terms of numbers, training and equipment into an advantage strong enough to compensate for the challenges set against them. These included the unfamiliar and harsh terrain and a lack of intelligence, both of which contributed to preventing an early defeat of the insurgents in Dhofar. Military shortcomings and missed opportunities were to have severe repercussions by allowing the insurgents time to train, expand, equip and develop into an effective enemy and should be considered a stark absolute-level campaign failure. The battle lines were drawn and the opposing commanders were compelled to adjust their war strategies accordingly.

The Oversold Impact of the 1970 Coup & Inability of the SAF to Demonstrate War-winning Performance Up Until 1972

Far from being a model campaign or textbook example of how to conduct a COIN operation, from the beginning, therefore, the Dhofar COIN strategy was failing and the SAF seemingly did not have the capability to reverse the situation.[23] Many of the key lessons learned at great cost from previous classical UK COIN operations were not, or could not be, implemented by the CSAF and his officers for a number of reasons; chiefly the policies and attitudes of the incumbent Sultan.[24] The situation was one of both potential and looming disaster for the SAF, Oman and the region as a whole without drastic actions to attempt to recover the situation. This came in the form of the July 1970 coup which brought Sultan Qaboos to power. The coup was a key occurrence in the campaign but it was far from the central trigger event which heralded the change from stalemate and near loss to one of success. It must be remembered that victory would not be declared until 1975 and a further five long – and costly – campaigning years into the future.

The UK authorities had become increasingly concerned with the way the Dhofar campaign was progressing through regular updates from the Bahrain-based Political Resident (PRPG), the Muscat-based Consulate-General and via the CSAF. Unofficial opinion was also solicited from more junior officers, especially seconded officers re-joining their UK regimental chain of command. They were reporting that the military situation was steadily deteriorating, and the spectre of defeat to the communist insurgents and a wider communist putsch on the Arabian Peninsula a real possibility.[25] Although official archival records remain scarce and contemporary accounts by participants lacking in 'culpability-related' detail and Britain's overall role in the coup; elements of the literature are, however, justifiably forthright in their attribution of Britain's accountability. Relatively recent revelations, such as (posthumously) by Brigadier John Graham that he was ordered not just to help Qaboos escape if the coup was unsuccessful but to stop the coup from failing, if necessary utilising the SAF which was under his direct command.[26] What is clear is that as a result of the arrangements put in place and their subsequent implementation by SAF personnel, the Sultan's Salalah palace was raided on 23rd July and after a brief firefight Sultan Said was persuaded to surrender and sign a declaration of abdication in favour of his son, Qaboos. Whilst being complicit in the execution of the coup itself, at the same time Britain also provided subsequent medical treatment in Bahrain and safe passage via RAF aircraft to the UK. This enabled the Sultan to be able to retire in comfort and safety in London's Dorchester Hotel up until his death by heart attack two years later and burial in the Muslim section of Brookwood Cemetery in Woking.[27] The impression left is of a rather reluctant, but in the end deemed, strategically-necessary action, to preserve vital interests using the minimum of force as a mark of respect to a long-time ally of the UK.[28]

Although the July 1970 coup was to have far-reaching effects in terms of campaign effectiveness, there was no direct or instant turnaround in the military situation allied to a quick defeat of the Adoo insurgents. As such this narrative runs counter to some writers of a clear pre- and post-1970 division of the Dhofar COIN operation and a direct post-1970 renaissance of the campaign due to the coup following the poor SAF COIN performance noted up until 1970.[29] With the SAS subsequently deployed *en masse*, the building of intelligence capability, the training of the Firqa and the implementation of an effective 'hearts and minds' campaign was possible. Allied to a general expansion of the SAF, both the optimism and the capability of Oman's COIN forces significantly increased. With the removal of the unpopular Sultan Said and the installation of his half-Dhofari son, Qaboos, the new era was off to a good start from a public relations perspective. It was, however, also solidly backed up by tangible actions. These included the reversal of a number of his father's repressive laws and the introduction of a comprehensive civil aid programme. These actions resulted in the reversal of many of the trigger issues for the initial insurgency. These included the restrictions on travel and general lack of civil development/

amenities with only three schools in the whole of Oman (all in Muscat); and especially in Dhofar where there was "…[an] obsession with regulations, usually by outright prohibition of even the most minor comforts of day-to-day existence".[30] With the raising of the locally-connected Firqa units by the SAS in tandem with a new, yet long-advocated-for amnesty programme, the number of SEPs deserting the insurgents increased dramatically. From 1 January 1971 to 1 March 1972 420 SEPs abandoned the insurgent cause (with many of them joining the Firqa units) with 1,591 SEPs in total up to that point.[31]

The coup was undoubtedly a key turning point in the war, but it was not the most important change-inducing factor. The coup represented a break from the ineffective leadership of Sultan Said and his underfunding of the campaign, and with the new Sultan Qaboos at the helm, the situation did change rapidly. New and substantial social and economic development plans were swiftly implemented, allied to the removal of many of the fundamentals of discontent which bred the initial nationalist rebellion. Overall campaign success was not, however, to come quickly with the long-awaited large-scale SAF Jebel-based offensives Operations JAGUAR and LEOPARD failing to reach the aims of their architects and the unrelenting growth of the strength and capability of the Adoo. The fact remains that the coup occurred five years into the war, and the war did not subsequently end until 1975, or another five years of hard campaigning. Although it certainly helped change the trajectory of the war the coup did not win it. Notably, even at the announcement of victory in 1975 the insurgency was not completely eliminated. British and Iranian troops remained deployed in theatre post-1975 and further SAF deaths from combat with remaining insurgent groupings occurred on several occasions.[32] The coup was no instant remedy and at best it can be described as a change of the fundamentals which led to a progressive improvement in the campaign's conduct.

Continuing Deficient SAF Performance to 1972

Despite a significant growth in numbers and capability post-coup, there were many continuing problems (as well as other newer issues which became apparent) which contributed to ongoing poor performance by the SAF and a continuing failure to end the insurgency. Central to these issues were those involved in the establishment and subsequent deployment of the tribal and SEP-constituted Firqa. This was despite the proven expertise of their dedicated SAS handlers and trainers. Whilst to prove their worth later in the campaign, the Firqa were inherently disorganised, fragmented, ill-disciplined and difficult to control, and were somewhat generously described by one SAS commander as "little rascals".[33] They also often had selfish motivations which extended to power politics over their own tribal areas and frequently acted principally according to the prospect of financial gain.[34] An example was the Firqat Salahudin, the initial raised multi-tribal unit which had to be disbanded and split up as an inter-tribal unit as it could not work together and which effectively resulted in a state of mutiny.[35] The poor general performance and ill-discipline of the Firqa involved in Operation JAGUAR in 1971 reportedly infuriated the then CO of 22 SAS, Lieutenant Colonel John Watts.[36] He attributed their performance as part of JAGUAR as contributing to its failure, just before he was due to be redeployed back to the UK thus denying him a success. He resented the fact that his men expended so much training and support effort on the Firqa and risked their lives operating with them, but the argumentative tribesman could not deliver what was asked of them on the ground.

The long-planned and much anticipated post-coup offensives conceived by the CSAF, Brigadier Graham to turn the tide of the campaign after COIN forces had been on the back foot for several years were also not the success either hoped for or expected. The large-scale SAF, and Firqa-undertaken (with discreet yet large scale support – including direct combat – from the SAS) Operations JAGUAR and Operation LEOPARD were designed to establish the first permanent SAF presence on the Jebel. The initial permanent base area was to be at Jibjat/White City alongside the creation of small Adoo-blocking bases on the Jebel. Although the operations started positively and the immediate desired end states were eventually achieved, performance by the Firqa for example was poor and they did not lead to the hoped for swift compounding of success and quick roll-back of the insurgents from the Jebel with resulting defeat. As a result, the impact of these operations to the overall campaign was minor and they were therefore considered relative disappointments from a theatre perspective.[37] The 'divide and conquer' strategy via the construction of blocking lines across the jebel was also an initial disappointment. The much-hoped-for initiative of the Leopard Line of 1971 (initially constructed during Operation LEOPARD) was actually abandoned in due course by the SAF so the immediate coup period and subsequent two years of campaigning was somewhat of a 'false start'. Much was hoped for after long months of planning whilst hemmed in on the Salalah Plain, then the large scale break out onto the Jebel with greatly expanded and newly trained forces. These did not reach their full operational potential so were considered disappointing overall. Resultingly, any 'high hopes' stemming from the great improvements in governance and especially to the SAF in the post-coup era for a relatively swift defeat of the Adoo were dashed.

Brigadier Graham's 'divide and conquer' strategy was not initially a success and with the abandonment of the initial Leopard Line only started to show success with the constructions of the Hornbeam Line from late 1972, out of the remnants of the previous line construction. The new line was much more successful in denying passage and logistical support across the jebel from the PDRY and Sherishitti Caves to Adoo units in the east. This strategy of dividing up the Jebel into controllable segments was later reinforced under his successor CSAFs with the Damavand Line in 1974. The later culmination of his strategy, in conjunction with substantially increased British military aid, the failure of the insurgents to capture Taqa and the high-profile Adoo defeat at the Battle of Mirbat in July 1972 actually represented what might be termed the military turning point of the war; not the 1970 coup.[38] 1972 was the turning point only, and did not represent the defeat of the insurgents. They were bloodied after Mirbat but not defeated, and they would continue the fight effectively for over three more years. It would take the substantial combined military inputs of Jordan and Iran from late 1972 to bring the necessary momentum to this welcome, although very late turning point after some seven years of hostilities. Approaching three years since Qaboos' accession and literature-described key campaign turning point towards success, it could be argued that military failure and poor SAF performance should be seen as the overwhelming campaign narrative at least until mid-1972.[39] The 1970 coup should resultingly not be viewed as the fundamental turning point in the war. It was certainly important, but did not have the required campaign-level effects required to achieve a swift defeat of the insurgents.

This situation at this point in the war cannot, therefore, be described as an unmitigated success. From the start of the undertaking up to at least mid-1972 the Dhofar COIN campaign could be described as being relatively poorly conducted with a lacklustre performance in terms of required outcomes. As such, in reality, there was arguably a continuance of the previously outlined poor pre-1970 SAF performance. With tangible success not apparent until late 1972 and victory not declared until 1975, this fundamentally challenges the narrative that the operation was a textbook or model insurgency campaign. Even when Sultan Said was removed in the 1970 coup and British assistance was belatedly increased, the tide of battle only changed towards the end of 1972 or start of 1973. This is when the Hornbeam Line and associated post-divide eastern sector clearance strategy had started to reap dividends in addition to the success of the Sarfait and Mirbat operations. Prior to this there was even a period of time (up until 1971) when it was feared that COIN forces could actually be defeated, with the commander of British Forces in the Gulf Major-General Roly Gibbs even describing in July 1970 that Dhofar could be lost to the insurgent forces if the Sultan was not removed.[40]

Failure derived from Military Structural and Operational Organisation:

SAF Manning & Equipment Issues

In 1965, the CSAF, Colonel Tony Lewis considered the force under his command a well-trained, albeit small army. Competently trained and exercised by his predecessor (Colonel Hugh Oldman), Lewis stated, "My immediate impression [on assuming command] was one of satisfaction. I realised I had been fortunate to take over a force which was highly operational [and] efficient," and which was "streamlined in every way for war".[41] Despite Colonel Lewis' apparent satisfaction with the state of the SAF forces under his command, there were many challenges which reduced the effectiveness of the initial military response to the insurgency. The SAF in its contemporary form was effectively set up to only deal with limited, and standard, internal security taskings in northern Oman. It was not culturally or practically prepared for engagement in a burgeoning insurgency over 500 miles from home. Changing this scenario was neither a swift nor a straightforward process.

At the time the SAF consisted of small numbers of aircraft and a single naval boom and its fighting ability primarily rested with two regiments of foot consisting of the Muscal Regiment and the Northern Frontier Regiment. A brand-new infantry unit named the Desert Regiment (DR) was initially raised in 1965 but was not fully operational until late 1968. In addition, the specialist Dhofar Force was completely separate from the SAF. In terms of numbers available, the SAF had to operate over 20 separate military posts including the border region with the Trucial States in its primary internal security role, and troop numbers to attend to any required large-scale additional deployments were scarce.[42] The initial NFR deployment in 1964 was only company-strength (four platoons plus support elements of approximately 150 soldiers in total), with the subsequent MR deployment in May 1965 doubling in size.[43] With the vastness of the Dhofar operating area, the SAF simply did not have enough men to deal with the insurgency and its other roles. As such, "In addition, throughout the 1965–1970 period, the SAF never deployed more than one reinforced battalion to fight the insurgents in Dhofar. In contrast, from their sanctuary in the PDRY, the PFLOAG could deploy up to 1800 personnel [both full-time fighters and militia]."[44]

Although relatively well-trained by its British officers, equipment-wise the situation was not quite so good. As Colonel Lewis described:

> The Military Secretary controlled the purse strings and, as at that time the total national revenue was in the region of £1.25 million compared to £4,000 million now, we didn't have Bucks Fizz for breakfast. Every penny

had to be properly spent and the use of the money balanced between such choices as new weapons, pay for soldiers, clothing and equipment, [and] improvements to military posts and so on.[45]

Essentially, the SAF suffered an overall general poor quality of equipment. This included old Second World War-era (bolt-action) Lee Enfield rifles for the infantry which was by then a far cry from the resources the Adoo could call on.[46] Against this obsolete equipment the insurgents were supplied with modern Soviet weaponry with which to engage COIN forces. This took the form of the Communist standard – but devastatingly effective – AK-47 'Kalashnikov' assault rifle with its large 7.62mm round.[47] Far from just more effective automatic rifles against the SAF's bolt-action equivalent, the insurgents had access to Rocket-Propelled Grenades (RPGs), heavy machine guns, 82–107mm rockets, and modern mortars, leaving the SAF largely out-gunned in most aspects.[48] Unlike well-equipped British and UK-controlled forces set against relatively poorly trained and armed insurgents groupings in previous classical British campaigns, this negative operational situation was compounded by the reluctance of Sultan Said to purchase modern weapons and helicopters as requested by his then CSAF, Brigadier Corran Purdon.[49] Towards the latter stages of the conflict, the Insurgents even fielded sophisticated Surface-to-Air Missile (SAM) systems (SAM-7s) and scored several successes against COIN force aircraft.[50]

In terms of numbers, the SAF was only substantially and quickly increased in size after the 1970 coup. In less than two years the size of the SAF was more than tripled to over 10,000 men which helped even the odds when deployed against the 2,000 contemporary full-time front-line insurgents and 4000 supporting militiamen of PFLOAG.[51] Although the British SAS and other UK regular unit elements were deployed to Dhofar from 1970, apart from the seconded officers attached to the SAF this meant for the initial six years of the COIN campaign there were insufficient troop numbers to defeat the insurgents. With the post-coup SAF and regular British forces expansion the situation was improved substantially. In part, however, due to the large operating area, the increase in size and spread of insurgent units and the effective logistical set up via PDRY, it was still considered by civil servants and senior British officers that the COIN campaign could even be lost in 1971.[52] Such expansion could still therefore be considered inadequate. With further British reluctance to commit regular British army combat units this situation was only resolved with upwards of some 5,000 Jordanian and Iranian troops committed to the campaign from 1973.[53] It was only at this juncture in the COIN campaign that the issue of insufficient SAF numbers was effectively reversed and a comprehensive strategy of offensive operations could be implemented by the command and start to bear fruit. This was assisted by the provision of Iranian warships, fighter jets and heavy lift helicopter capability which substantially bolstered the SAFs extremely limited arsenal.

It can be seen, therefore, that at least until 1970, and more realistically up until 1973, the Sultan's military organisation was ill-equipped in terms of manpower, equipment and weaponry to fight and win the conflict in Dhofar province. This was a significant factor in relatively poor SAF performance and its inability to defeat the insurgents early in the campaign. As such, this situation cannot be described as a textbook or ideal COIN response and reflects a failure of adequate threat realisation and subsequent planning and preparation. The historical record should reflect that British commanders and their political masters shoulder their share of the blame. Responsibility, however, lies largely on the side of the Sultan for such negative campaign outcomes to 1970, and through a process of inertia up until 1973.

Strategy and Tactics

Although partly driven by numbers available and the other commitments of the force, the overall strategy of the SAF also helped to ensure the initial uprising was not thwarted effectively. The inability in terms of capability or lack of will of the SAF to energetically establish itself on the jebel in the early days of the COIN campaign set the scene for the conflict for the next half decade.[54] By the time the second SAF deployment to Dhofar by the Muscat Regiment was reduced to one company by August 1965, the pattern was already set. The SAF controlled the Salalah plain only with the jebel areas effectively dominated by the Adoo; a situation that was not fully reversed until 1975.[55] An early permanent presence on the jebel would have shown greater direct military intent than the mere ability to move soldiers from the north to Dhofar as undertaken in the first SAF deployment in 1964. This could have reinforced government and SAF power and credibility. It would have demonstrated a willingness to engage formally with the Dhofari population but also to engage militarily with the insurgents who at that point had unfettered jebel access. This would have proven to average Dhofaris who just wanted the basic human requirement of security – from anywhere or anyone – that the SAF was a "…horse worth backing".[56]

Another aspect of campaign-negative strategy was the lack of any concerted 'hearts and minds' activities until after the 1970 coup. The initial reliance on the liberal use of repressive measures and collective punishments such as the burning of crops or dwellings in an attempt to control the Jebali population helped to turn the people away even more from the now perceived 'oppressive' government side. Far from being welcomed with open arms by the Jebali population as liberators, the SAF was often seen as a distant, foreign, and alien oppressor force in their lands.[57]

Colonel Lewis strongly recommended the use the 'hearts and minds'-related measures to the Sultan to engage the Jebalis as part of a 'sticks and carrots' approach to reward or punish as appropriate to discourage insurgent interaction.[58] Such measures had been used effectively in previous British COIN campaigns in Kenya and Malaya, through forced resettlement programmes, and in the rural Radfan region as part of the overall Aden COIN campaign. Non-lethal tactics such as food denial were also proven and successful anti-insurgent approaches. If the locals had limited food supplies, there was even less for the insurgents to beg, borrow or purchase from the villagers and then the hungry insurgent was a less effective military asset.[59] In many ways this was a logical and effective approach, with Lewis for example highlighting how, after the combined SAS and Irish Guards raid on Hauf and the 'biting' of the collective punishments, "The rebels had no resupply since early 1966 and the Jebali's themselves were under severe restrictions of movement and lacked food."[60] Such actions, however, also led to much of the previously neutral population turning their support to the insurgent side. An example of SAF commanders undertaking such actions was the NFR's CO from 1967, the then Lieutenant Colonel Mike Harvey. Harvey was a Korean War veteran who witnessed many of his regiment killed by Communists. Largely because of this experience Harvey was staunchly anti-Communist and implemented Sultan Said's hard-line policies (including destroying the water resources of jebel communities who gave support to the Insurgents) with zeal.[61] Allied to related factors such as the 'outsider' SAF force not having more than a temporary foothold on the mountainous Jebel areas each year, it is perhaps obvious who, due to such oppressive actions, the Jebali inhabitants considered the enemy and who, conversely, were better representing their best interests or security needs.

Sultan Said himself also played a major and direct part in the early failures of the campaign, which was to help elongate and expand the rebellion in his feudal Dhofari territory, by ignoring the sensible professional advice of his CSAFs. The incumbent CSAF, Colonel Tony Lewis' strong recommendation to introduce early elements of a 'hearts and minds' strategy fell on deaf ears. Lewis explained to the Sultan in precise detail how the previous Malayan and Kenyan COIN campaigns had been much boosted and the insurgents eventually defeated through the non-kinetic means of leniency through a programme of amnesty, which brought former insurgents over to the government side whilst depleting their ranks.[62] The Sultan was in no mood to compromise. His mind was made up and he was set only on the "hard-line" elements of his CSAF's approach.⁶³ With no amnesty programme introduced until after the 1970 coup, Lewis described how:

> Throughout the remainder of my time in Oman I persisted with this idea [of introducing a Malaya-like amnesty programme] but to no good. Given a favourable answer I am sure that we could have brought the Dhofar trouble to an end there and then instead of eight years later.⁶⁴

Sultan Said also hampered the vital asset of intelligence throughout the Dhofar War until his removal. Intelligence as a feature of COIN was a key element in the success or otherwise of all previous classical-era British COIN campaigns. The poor collection, processing and utilisation of intelligence-related information from the start of such campaigns was a key element in failure, with Palestine, Aden, and arguably Cyprus being notable examples.⁶⁵ Key amongst intelligence-related capability was the Special Branch (SB) capability of the civilian police force. The Malayan campaign was in part a success due to a robust SB organisation which worked in tandem with military intelligence assets as part of the joined-up approach championed by General Templer. Where failure was the outcome, this could, in part, be blamed on poor SB resources. The Cypriot and Aden COIN campaigns were lost in part due to the successful attritional approach of the insurgents against less well-defended civilian police assets via widespread counter-surveillance, help from a generally anti-British in terms of sentiment population, and a deliberate and systematic programme of targeting SB officers for assassination which had the overall effect of reducing the effectiveness of the organisation. As a result, the British authorities introduced countermeasures including the formation of 'Q' Units in Cyprus and the formation of SAS 'Keenie Meenie' squads in Aden which were aimed at reducing the capacity of the insurgent organisations to carry out such assassinations.⁶⁶ When first deployed to Dhofar, the SAF was specifically denied the ability to bring any intelligence officer into 'his' province by order of the Sultan, with the explanation given that he alone would provide his CSAF with any intelligence-related information he required for operations.⁶⁷ Even though Lewis subsequently covertly inserted Force Intelligence Officer Captain Bob Brown into Dhofar, this attitude to intelligence was pervasive. Sultan Said later insisted on the sacking of the same officer (then promoted and with the title of chief Dhofar Intelligence Officer). It is apparent that the Sultan did not trust him, his methods, or the extensive alternative human intelligence network Brown skilfully crafted in the province. As a result of the loss of Brown in his intelligence role, Brigadier Purdon described in his memoirs how he was effectively blind in Dhofar after this point in terms of reliable intelligence at a vital stage in the campaign.[68]

Despite their key role in his victory against the imamate rebels at the end of the 1950s which kept him in power, Sultan Said refused to let the British SAS operate inside Oman or Dhofar. The unit's unique and specialised skill sets which facilitated a campaign victory against the Sultan's previous enemies within the country were not, therefore, utilised in Oman until after the 1970 coup. To put this into perspective this was not until some five years after the official start of the insurgency in Dhofar and some halfway through the war's duration. After the change of ruler, the SAS were quickly deployed. As they had done successfully in Malaya, Brunei/Borneo and later in Northern Ireland, the SAS set to work producing vital information such as an enemy Order of Battle (ORBAT). They addressed this through the development of an embryonic intelligence organisation which rapidly improved the intelligence picture and enhanced the effectiveness of the SAF going forward. Blocking their utilisation and unique capabilities earlier – even in an advisory capacity – contributed to the delay of vital COIN-winning activities which in turn led to the extended length of the overall insurgency.

The Sultan's reluctance to provide sufficient funding to properly develop, arm, equip, and even clothe the SAF also had a negative effect on operational capability from the outset of the campaign. The SAF was run on a tight budget and unit equipment was often outdated or poor quality. Additionally, the lack of numbers to undertake internal security duties as well as deploy to Dhofar was only begun to be addressed in 1965 with the raising of the Desert Regiment (DR). This third SAF unit had to be formed initially by poaching personnel from the existing two battalions. Progress was so slow that by the time Colonel Lewis was replaced by Brigadier Corran Purdon as CSAF in 1967 the new unit was neither combat-ready nor prepared for a Dhofar deployment.[69] Lewis also alludes to the "very tenuous and unsatisfactory medical system" in the country, supporting military operations with no surgeons in Dhofar and lack of evacuation facilities for casualties.[70] This was an issue which Brigadier Purdon was to constantly wrestle with throughout his tenure. He spend much of his time trying to persuade the Sultan and his (British) Military Secretary to purchase helicopters in part to avoid the reality of casualties having to be man-handled off the jebel or taken off strapped to a mule, whilst they 'bled out'.[71] Helicopters would have also transformed the logistical capabilities of the SAF with regards to troops and supplies within theatre. Alongside helicopters, Brigadier Purdon found himself advocating for the purchase of new artillery, and although eventually such equipment was reluctantly agreed to and ordered it was only available for operational use by the next CSAF, Brigadier Graham.

A Military Success? 109

This seemingly almost negligent attitude of the Sultan with regards to funding his military and the campaign more widely was a reinforcing factor in failure. Whilst this factor highlights the impact on the SAF itself, it also alludes to the resulting time and opportunity therefore given to the insurgents to receive sophisticated arms and professional training from Communist instructors and become a more efficient fighting force.[72] This meant that not giving the SAF the tools to fight effectively resulted in ineffective campaigning which failed to capitalise on a relatively weak insurgent organisation for the initial two years of the war up until 1967. The opportunity to end the insurgency early was, therefore, missed.

The consequences of the failures deriving from structural and operational organisational issues were significant. Factors such as SAF manning and equipment, strategy, and tactics combined with numerous Sultan-centric failures (especially in the initial phase of the campaign) were to have a profound effect in terms of longevity and cost for all concerned. The combined effect of all these factors was to deny the opportunity for an early win for the SAF against the insurgents. It also lost any hope of gaining the support of the Jebali population which was instead subsequently the end state achieved by the insurgents through a combination of threats, ideological appeal, or simply by domination through the "regime of terror which PFLOAG introduced".[73] The lack of numerical superiority or the ability to fully cover or saturate the area of operations hampered the campaign. Likewise, the failure to quickly quell the unrest and the delayed (and then even slow) expansion to a third SAF battalion and introduction of battlefield essentials such as helicopters and modern artillery until 1969 was very much a missed opportunity.[74] More correctly it was the failure to convert a series of opportunities to defeat the insurgency in its early stages which resulted in an extended, decade-long campaign. Once these opportunities were not taken then other events such as the formation of the PDRY and the morphing of the original nationalist insurgency into a Marxist one took place. This meant that far from the conflict being successfully contained it actually grew, evolved, and expanded to something completely out of the control of the SAF and incumbent Sultan. From this perspective the campaign cannot be described as either textbook or model in its conduct and the term 'progressive failure' springs instead to mind.

In relative terms from both a UK and international perspective the Dhofar COIN campaign was a military success and a rare Cold War win against Marxist insurgents. The relatively poorly equipped and manned SAF failed to quell the insurgency in the early period of the conflict, which helped it morph into a decade-long insurgency. This situation mirrors similar failures in other ultimately successful classical-era British campaigns such as in the Malayan

Emergency, the Mau Mau campaign in Kenya and the even longer campaign in Northern Ireland. Even the much-vaunted 1970 coup, the improvements then implemented within the SAF, and extra British assistance failed to stem the insurgency; with the campaign on a losing trajectory to potentially even be lost by 1971. Only the crushing blow for the insurgents (facilitated largely by the SAS) at the Battle of Mirbat in mid-1972 and the gathering positive campaign momentum allied to the arrival of the Jordanian and Iranian troops turned the tide of the conflict in favour of the government forces.

Chapter 8

A Strategic Counterinsurgency Success?

Dhofar Campaign vs. Classical UK COIN Campaigns

As with several previous classical-era British COIN campaigns, the key primary strategic aims in Dhofar were achieved. For only the third time in history a communist-backed insurrection had been beaten and the 'historical inevitability' of successful Communist-inspired revolution and expansion was dealt an important blow.[1] Oman's governing status quo as well as regional stability was ensured and the British influence and economic interests were maintained via the new Sultan, installed following the July 1970 coup.

In Malaya, the threat of communist takeover was thwarted and the insurgency crushed, albeit over a 12-year period. This helped prevent a much-feared uncontrolled Southeast Asian Cold War 'domino effect' process at the same time as the pivotal French losses to Communist forces in Indochina. The COIN win in Malaya helped to maintain regional stability, as well as guaranteeing the survival of the status quo and continued British access to raw materials such as rubber and tin and access to the Malayan market. The Djebel War COIN win enabled the survival of an ally in the form of a younger Sultan Said and therefore the governing status quo in Muscat. It also enabled continued British access to potentially lucrative oil concessions and to the CENTO and both Middle and Far East staging post-vital facilities on Oman's Masirah Island. This action also contributed to the general stability in the immediate region and enabled Britain to maintain its interests in the Trucial States as well as in Oman. Similarly the COIN win in the Brunei/early Borneo campaign set the ground for an acceptance and subsequent survival of an embryonic Malaysian state from insurgents and their outside-state backers as well as maintaining the UK-backed ruling status quo in Brunei. Likewise, in Northern Ireland, although it took in the region of thirty years to achieve, with patience and resolve the British authorities achieved the maintenance of the UK domestic political union and the end of the insurgency through military, then primarily via political means. Regional and local stability was also achieved in Kenya as a result of a bitter COIN campaign, but, like Malaya, it resulted in the loss of the territory from British direct control and therefore can to a certain extent be considered a strategic loss. In other campaigns such as in Palestine, Aden, or even Cyprus the level of achievement of strategic goals was arguably either much less successful from this perspective or can even be considered complete strategic-level failures.

In the case of Dhofar, firstly, British actions halted the spread of communist insurgency in the Arabian Peninsula during the Cold War-period. Due to the Dhofari insurgent defeat, Oman and its allies all also gained a higher state of regional geo-strategic stability. The 1968 establishment of the PDRY aside, this was achieved through the thwarting of further regional communist influence. As a result, an Arabian Peninsula version of 'domino effect' and a hostile Omani Communist takeover was avoided which, in turn secured the Omani half of the Strait of Hormuz which was so vital for transporting the world oil supplies.[2] Further, due to the Dhofar COIN win the vital flow of oil to Britain and the world's other advanced economies was safeguarded, which can be considered an important strategic success.[3]

The strategic aim of regional stability was also achieved for Britain's allies in the Dhofar COIN campaign. In a similar manner to Malaya, Kenya, Cyprus and Brunei/Borneo, the viability and integrity of the Omani state was secured from outside influence or incursion. Dhofar was successfully pacified, and any major territorial or status quo leadership threat to Oman was removed. For both Jordan and Iran, from a global and regional perspective the British-led and managed Dhofar campaign helped thwart Communist influence in the Middle Eastern area. Had this not taken place, the situation would potentially have been a threat to their own national stability with communist anti-monarchical nationalistic rhetoric gaining regional traction and Soviet proxy forces attempting to turn the Gulf into a Soviet 'lake'.[4] For Iran especially, involvement also ensured the safety and control of the Strait of Hormuz, allowing its own oil to be exported to the rest of the world with the opposite side of the waterway i.e. the Musandam Peninsula remaining under a friendly government's control. Iranian oil contributed significantly to the two thirds of the global oil requirement supplied by the Gulf (including 30% of the contemporary US oil requirement, 70% of Europe's, and 90% of that of Japan), and all had to be transported via this key maritime throughfare.[5] Being on the winning side was also a significant feather in the cap of King Hussein of Jordan and Iran's Shah Mohammad Reza. This was similar to the kudos and prestige gained by Britain for its involvement in such a rare COIN victory, especially a campaign against communist-backed forces.[6] This, in turn, reinforced the perception of strength and stability of the two monarchs who both presided over countries or administrations with relatively limited histories of legitimacy, and a level of potential vulnerability due to existing poor governance structures.[7] This was especially important in a region then beset with tensions due to the expansion of Arab nationalism

Dhofar landscape showing the Khareef monsoon mists which develop annually between June and October. (© S. Quick 2022)

The Towering – and inhospitable – Jebel (mountain) landscape in Dhofar. (© S. Quick 2022)

A Jebali tribesman from the Central Region of Dhofar (holding a Lee Enfield Second World War vintage rifle). (© *S. Pass 1974*)

Dhofar Operational Headquarters of the Sultan's Armed Forces (SAF) Muscat Regiment. (© *S. Pass 1974*)

Salalah Palace in Dhofar Province, site of the coup which brought the 29-year old Sultan Qaboos to power in 1970. (© S. Quick 2022)

The restored Wali's Fort at Mirbat (view from sea). (© S. Quick 2022)

The Dhofar Gendarmerie-manned Mirbat Fort, site of the fierce SAS-led resistance to the large-scale oncoming insurgent attack at the Battle of Mirbat (19th July 1972). View from the perspective of the advancing Insurgents. (© S. Quick 2022)

The 'gun pit' at Mirbat Fort, where SAS troopers fired the sole (Second World War-vintage) 25-pounder artillery piece at the lines of advancing insurgents on 'open sights' (at short, often point-blank range). Sergeant Talaiasi Labalaba and Trooper Thomas Tobin of the SAS both died of wounds sustained at the gun pit. (© S. Quick 2022)

View of the Town of Mirbat and the Wali's Fort from Mirbat Fort showing the almost complete absence of cover and the distance run by Sergeant Talaiasi Labalaba – under constant enemy fire – to take over the gun position to prevent the fort from being overrun by the advancing insurgents. (© *S. Quick 2022*)

British Royal Air Force (RAF) Wessex helicopter and deployed UK troops operating on the Dhofari Jebel. (© *S. Pass 1974*)

British soldier firing a 105mm artillery piece in 'Gun Alley' in the vicinity of Mughsayl, Dhofar. (© S. Pass 1974)

Baluchi SAF troops (from Northern Frontier Regiment) manning a mortar position at Reef Base on the 30-mile long Hornbeam Line ('Reef' was the largest base constructed on the Hornbeam Line). (© S. Pass 1974)

British-piloted Sultan of Oman Air Force (SOAF) Skyvan aircraft – the workhorse of the Omani air force and utilised for transporting equipment throughout the Dhofar theatre. (© S. Pass 1974)

British troops being transported from Mughsayl (coastal origin of the Hornbeam Line) in Dhofar province to RAF Salalah. (© S. Pass 1974)

British-piloted SOAF Augusta Bell 205 'Huey' helicopter supplying UK troops (Royal Engineers) on the jebel. (© S. Pass 1974)

Bayt Al Falaj Fort ('House of Water' or 'House of the Water Channel' in Arabic language) near Muscat. Historic Headquarters of the British Commander, Sultan's Armed Forces (CSAF) both before, and throughout the Dhofar War. The fort has housed the Sultan's Armed Forces Museum since 1988. (© S. Quick 2019)

and related largely anti-monarchical views of such nationalists alongside the radical views of communist or Marxist regimes such as the PDRY, as well as the "Radical Arab regimes in Iraq, Syria and Libya".[8]

For Britain itself, the achieved strategic aim of regional stability resulted in halting the spread of communist influence into the Arabian Peninsula at the border with the PDRY. This created a recognised 'hard' international barrier and salvaged Britain's failure to retain the strategic military facilities in Aden or prevent the emergence of a Communist state in its former colony. This regionally stabilising effect also had the result of securing the continued viability and sovereign status of not just Oman but also of the recently-independent (1971) small Gulf territories such as Bahrain and Qatar and the newly established Federation of Trucial States (known as the UAE) as part of Britain's strategic East of Suez withdrawal programme. Britain was therefore also able to conduct its planned 'East of Suez' withdrawal without the region descending into Communist-fuelled chaos whilst at the same time maintaining its strategically important military staging-post facilities at RAF Masirah in Omani territory. This was in direct contrast to the previous calamitous withdrawals from both Palestine and Aden and the resulting loss of international prestige.[9] Britain, therefore, avoided a melt-down in the general stability of the region upon withdrawal as would have been the case if a communist takeover in Oman had allowed the Gulf monarchies to be undermined and potentially also overthrown.[10] Despite the volatility associated with the 1967 and 1973 Arab-Israeli Wars, in the greater Cold War proxy power game the COIN win in Dhofar helped to achieve a level of stability for the region as a whole by limiting the spread of communist influence, proxy war, or physical regime takeovers.

In addition, Britain was able to achieve its key strategic objectives whilst utilising its diplomatic skill and leverage to successfully avoid provoking the PDRY so far as to facilitate open warfare between it, Oman and possibly also even the UK. It also achieved this whilst still proactively, forcefully, and successfully eroding insurgent capability on several fronts. Britain's measured diplomatic counsel via advisors such as the incumbent CSAF and local British diplomatic representatives tempered the full extent of the response ordered by a 'bristling' Sultan Qaboos who was essentially spoiling for a fight on cross-border issues which affected issues of sovereignty. These included the Sultan of Oman's Air Force (SOAF) attacks on the insurgent stronghold of Hauf, and the penetration of SAS-trained Mahra tribesmen deep into PDRY territory to conduct sabotage operations.[11] Sultan Qaboos's strong desire for cross-border reprisals against targets in the PDRY "put him at odds" with many diplomatic, military and other government figures from his British sponsors.[12] This was due to fears of the potential for any localised conflict spreading and Britain being dragged into direct conflict with another sovereign state. Britain was therefore in a position that in order to achieve its wider strategic objectives, it had to both appease and reign in their ally the Sultan of Oman, which took both skill, patience, and determination, and some diplomatic brinkmanship to achieve. Britain also had to create the 'facts on the ground' which would cause the attrition of the enemy forces, but to conduct the activity in a diplomatically acceptable way – to observers in the outside world at least – so as to avoid provoking or causing more support or sympathy for the PDRY position. This was an outcome not always so successfully achieved in previous COIN campaigns. In Palestine and Aden for example, Britain failed on all such fronts and was forced to exit in humiliating circumstances having lost control of strategically important territory. This was especially the case in Aden. The hasty departure from its 120-year-old territory and the UK's largest overseas military bases was described a humiliating "scuttle".[13] Similarly in Cyprus, although Britain did retain the sovereign base areas, it was forced to give up the control of the remainder of this key strategic eastern Mediterranean territory. This was due to numerous military, political, and public diplomacy failures. Key amongst these was the inability to kinetically defeat the EOKA forces led by Colonel Georgios Grivas and being 'out-strategised' by the politics and public relations-savvy Archbishop Makarios, which cumulatively resulted in a near total loss of support of the local inhabitants for the UK as the long-time colonial power.[14]

The Dhofar War was, therefore, a major achievement in many respects for Britain and its allies and an undoubted geo-strategic success. In this respect it echoed previous classical UK COIN campaigns in terms of contributing to the thwarting of both regional and global communist bloc expansion and potential subsequent domination. This contrasts starkly with the strategic failures of French and US policies and COIN campaigns in Southeast Asia for example. In addition, the enduring flow of vital Gulf oil supplies was achieved whilst simultaneously undertaking a strategic general military and political withdrawal from the region in the early 1970s. As a result, the UK-led campaign also contributed in a significant manner to securing the general stability of the region. This also directly benefitted Britain's key regional allies of Oman, Jordan and Iran in strategic terms.

Chapter 9

A Cost-Effective Campaign?

UK Perspective

Overall, the British government achieved its key strategic aims whilst adhering to the generally frugal attitude towards the cost or length of the support given to Oman.[1] Britain also managed to achieve such aims without committing overly large direct military resources to the Dhofar campaign. Despite some negative factors, such as a greater overall expense than was necessary and gradual loss of influence in Oman in several key areas, the UK achieved its strategic objectives at relatively modest cost.

When the Dhofar campaign began in earnest in the mid-1960s, Britain was already involved in COIN operations in Brunei/Borneo and in Aden/Southern Federation. The UK needed to achieve its strategic aims including encouraging both Omani and regional Gulf stability, and the general resistance to communist infiltration. Allied to this was the need to ensure access to vital strategic oil supplies whilst at the same time avoiding a protracted large-scale commitment or the campaign being subject to substantial 'mission creep'. Chief among these concerns from the British perspective was the much-feared 'mini-Vietnam' scenario, where for instance, "It would be important to ensure that a decision to send SAS personnel to the Sultanate does not become an open-ended commitment."[2] In accordance with the 1958 'Exchange of Letters' Britain also only provided relatively limited financial assistance and a small number of seconded regimental and staff officers. This limited assistance scenario was especially the case when viewed in the context of contemporary era operations such as that in Aden (including in the mountainous Radfan region near the North Yemen border) or even the much larger-scale deployment of regular British military units involved in Palestine, Malaya, Cyprus, Kenya, Borneo and Northern Ireland. By a further degree of contrast, Dhofar and indeed all the above campaigns were far smaller in cost as compared to the vast resources and hundreds of thousands of military personnel committed by the United States to the Vietnam War or to the Indochina and Algerian campaigns by France.[3] Additionally, in terms of the desire to minimise the financial impact of backing the Sultanate, UK assistance to Oman was largely not aid as such. Perhaps surprisingly, British support including supplies, loaned military personnel and direct troop support provision was actually largely invoiced in full to the Sultanate. From a financial perspective, this further limited Britain's liability in the overall venture, as "All of it [Britain's aid to Oman] came with a price tag. Initially, the Sultan was charged for every bit of aid received, including equipment provided from existing British Army stores."[4] This scenario meant that, at least in the five years up until the major campaign changes resulting from the 1970 coup, Britain was able to prosecute the Dhofar COIN campaign in a relatively inexpensive manner.

Due in part to this conscious and generally thrifty aid-related policy allied to one of limited engagement, the relatively limited scale of cost to the UK was also prevalent in terms of campaign casualties. Although the Dhofar COIN campaign was conducted in circumstances (until at least 1970, and to 1975 and beyond regarding SAS involvement) kept secret from the general public, high British military casualties would likely have been leaked at some point to the press and would therefore have been politically unacceptable at any level. As highlighted in Section 1 of this book, between 1971 and 1974 during the conflict phase which saw the greatest numbers of British troops as well as regular British military units serving in Dhofar, there were only some 21 British military personnel killed.[5] This is a very modest casualty rate when compared to the 1,845 members of the security forces killed in the Malayan Emergency or even the 590 killed in the Mau Mau campaign in Kenya.[6] In Northern Ireland, the length and tempo of the conflict was reflected in a low attrition rate in terms of deaths. Despite this, there were still nearly 1000 security forces fatalities up to the late 1990s, with over 100 soldiers killed in 1972 alone, including those who perished in the February bombing of the Parachute Regiment's barracks in Aldershot on the UK mainland.[7] The Dhofar War casualties were extremely modest when compared to the Northern Ireland campaign and other British COIN actions. This is further put into perspective when compared to some contemporary non-British COIN campaigns. Although such a comparison must be caveated by stating clearly that Dhofar was completely different in terms of scale of conflict such as operational combat area and numbers of personnel involved, the casualty figures for Dhofar indicatively are quite often on a different scale of magnitude. Examples of this include the large casualty rates sustained by French military forces of the Fourth Republic in Indochina (now Vietnam, Laos, and Cambodia) and later US casualties in the same region. These included over 7,000 French forces killed and wounded just at the infamous battle of Dien Bien Phu (March-May 1954) which hastened the withdrawal of French forces from Indochina and deepening US involvement, or the nearly 60,000 personnel killed in action subsequently sustained in the Vietnam War by US forces.[8] By consciously limiting the scale of UK commitment to support the

Sultanate in the Dhofar War, like for most previous COIN ventures, Britain successfully therefore avoided the deeper involvement and larger numbers of casualties suffered elsewhere.

Although the cost-effective attributes of the Dhofar campaign were clear, there were also far fewer positive factors relating to the issue of cost which can be observed. Due to the inability/failure to win the Dhofar COIN campaign early (and its subsequent extension by many unnecessary and potentially avoidable years), although relatively low per se, greater numbers of lives and economic resources were expended in pursuit of firstly avoiding defeat and secondly of achieving final victory. As a matter of policy, Britain's approach to the war in Dhofar was also to support the Sultan of Oman in his campaign, but to do so with the minimum of economic and military commitment and expenditure. The UK ended up, however, not only committing substantial military and economic resources to the military campaign but effectively implementing a comprehensive state-building approach as part of the overall war strategy. This helped to facilitate the fast-forward nature of Omani development to bring the country and its institutions into something resembling a modern state to enable the Sultanate to better protect itself. This was at odds with the initial general British government policy throughout the war of avoiding an open-ended financial or military commitment. This policy approach was in place due largely to other large-scale commitments which accounted for large proportions of Britain's military and economic resources. These included the British commitments to the Borneo Confrontation up to 1966, and the security commitments in Aden and wider Southern Federation up to the 1967 withdrawal date. Domestic economic reasons also played a key part in the decision-making process. Due largely to domestic economic issues, and the lengthy 'Sterling Crisis' which resulted in a balance of payments emergency, a 'run' on the pound and currency devaluation in 1967, the UK looked to trim its overseas commitments to try and balance the books. Defence was a key target for Roy Jenkins (who took over the Chancellor of the Exchequer role after James Callaghan resigned after devaluation), and executing a landmark almost total military withdrawal East of Suez for 1971 was deemed part of the solution. With this economic situation as a backdrop, the British government had no desire to increase military forces or commitments abroad, and especially out of the priority Cold War NATO areas. This would have countered both the letter and spirit of the strategic withdrawal plan 'East of Suez' as announced in 1968.

Despite this, due in part to not committing sufficient resources early on in the campaign, Britain was drawn in further and failed to keep its involvement in Oman and the Dhofar War at 'arm's length'. As a result, the aspiration to keep the commitment as minimal as possible from the terms of the original 1958

Exchange of Letters and essentially to prop up the Omani ruling status quo as cheaply as possible for Britain's strategic benefit, was not fulfilled. In many ways this can be considered a failure. From a military perspective Britain deemed it necessary to amend the terms of the 1958 agreement to actually provide more loan service officers. Additionally, from 1970 the SAS were committed to Oman in its largest deployment since the Second World War. Eventually two squadrons were deployed to Oman as well as the CO of the Regiment being in the field of operations for extended periods of time. This was no small commitment given the other duties and responsibilities of the regiment, allied to their ongoing covert role in Northern Ireland theatre. In addition to the SAS, a Field Surgical Team (FST) was deployed to Dhofar, as well as elements of the Royal Engineers. The latter was sent to undertake civil development construction works as well as undertaking military engineering tasks such as the later building of the Hornbeam Line and minelaying and disposal. Royal Artillery personnel were also deployed for the protection of the then increasingly exposed and vulnerable RAF Salalah, a situation that remained until at least 1972 as illustrated by the Adoo's attack on the base (including hitting the officers' mess whilst a barbeque was underway) on the 9th June anniversary of the war's official start.[9] Other increases in military commitment included the deployment of army and Royal Marine training teams to the Sultanate from Cyprus and the UK mainland (and from Bahrain up to British withdrawal in 1971) to train the SAF, and the provision of specialist personnel to set up the new training wing at Ghalla for the embryonic Omani officer training programme.[10]

Overall, this was a substantial commitment given the British military's worldwide commitments. This was especially the case when considering the contemporary situation and ever-widening military commitments necessary in Northern Ireland which peaked at 22,000 troops from 1971–72.[11] Britain went out of its way to provide support to Oman, even though this provision was potentially detrimental to its own security concerns or requirements; especially if it didn't directly 'cost' any extra to the Exchequer. The both extended and large-scale deployment of the SAS in either one or two squadron formations (the latter accounting for approximately half of the regiment's full manpower) and releasing almost the whole British Army ring-fenced 'war stock' of ammunition to Oman are key examples.[12] The failure to completely contain elements of larger and more extensive commitment than originally envisaged as well as rising associated costs is also illustrated by the fact that British forces did not leave Oman immediately after hostilities ended. Some units stayed in theatre for significantly greater periods. These included a squadron of British Army Engineers which only returned home once Operation TENABLE (the name for the engineering support operation of the British Army in Dhofar) ended in late 1977, and a twelve-man SAS unit which remained in theatre until 1978.[13] These war-related direct British troop support provisions therefore remained in place for up to three years after Sultan Qaboos declared the war's end and victory over the insurgents in December 1975. This shows both a commitment to Oman, but also a form of 'mission creep' and a much greater extended liability than initially envisaged.

Alongside this extra military commitment, due to the failed development of a comprehensive intelligence-gathering and interpretation organisation since 1965, the UK loaned members of the British Secret Intelligence Service (SIS, otherwise known as MI6) to set up the nucleus of an internal intelligence service in Oman. This was initially named the Oman Intelligence Service (OIS) and, alongside the specialist intelligence-related capabilities and in-theatre actions of the SAS, significantly improved the intelligence picture in both Dhofar for the war specifically and wider Oman more generally.[14] As an integral part of the wider post-coup British support package provided to the Sultanate, SAS Regiment experts were deployed to develop the original civilian Civil Action Teams (CATs) programme which started a concerted civil development programme in Dhofar. This was part of the wider, non-kinetic 'hearts and minds' element of the war. This also showed the flexibility and broad expertise provided by the SAS from 1970, as they were instrumental in not only core military or intelligence-related efforts but also civilian developmental projects. Perhaps more surprisingly still, the SAS operational remit in Dhofar also covered agricultural and veterinary support. Not the usual role of elite Special Forces troops, the SAS organised experts to help improve the Jebali agricultural practices, yields, and animal health and the establishment of a demonstration farms. Efforts were made to improve the Jebali animal stocks via bulls flown in from the regiment's UK-based home town of Hereford, as Jebali cattle were the traditional source of Jebali wealth, prestige and economic survival. Improving the bloodline of their prized cattle was a relatively simple and cost-effective way to help the Jebalis. The SAS were even instrumental in organising a large-scale drive of cattle from the mountains of the Jebel to the plain so the tribesmen could sell their animals to the government in Operation TAURUS.[15] All this was done in the name of gaining the 'hearts' of the Jebali population, or to at least make them realise where their best economic interests lay in the longer term.

Far from succeeding in keeping a hands-off policy of limited engagement and avoiding a large-scale or open-ended commitment, due to the dire circumstances of the campaign, Britain therefore had to increase support to post-coup Oman for an all-encompassing state-building effort to avoid the loss of the COIN campaign and enable an eventual win. This building up capability due to the complete absence of sufficient military, intelligence, social and economic development was a situation unlike Britain's previous COIN campaigns. Although facing different challenges in every campaign example, there was already an existence of at least rudimentary government, military organisation and developmental progress. In other words Britain did not have to haul the other host nations of COIN campaigns such as Malaya, Kenya and Cyprus out of almost "medieval" backwardness and virtually without many of the accepted features of a sovereign state, to be able to undertake an effective COIN campaign.[16] Alongside providing the military leadership for the Sultan's military and various capabilities for the SAS as well as the wider British military support, the state building aspect was arguably Britain's most important contribution to the Dhofar War.

Although relatively modest, the casualties derived from the Dhofar campaign began to mount and, due to mistakes which helped lengthen the overall campaign, these were higher than perhaps should have been the case. From January 1971 up until April 1974 Britain lost 21 men (seconded and contract) killed in Oman.[17] If the campaign had progressed more successfully with more extensive or even decisive British input in a timelier manner and the insurgents dealt with effectively earlier in the war, these casualties could potentially have been prevented or at least reduced. It would perhaps have also prevented the 12 deaths suffered by the elite SAS regiment between 1970 to 1976 which would not have been an insignificant loss to a relatively small and highly specialised unit with long training timelines, specific skill sets, and abilities that were also required in the UK and in contemporary Northern Ireland in particular.[18] These overall figures also do not include the British wounded casualties which occurred from combat, training or other reasons. These amounted to 27 between 1971 and 1974, including the eight largely lower leg injuries incurred from the Adoo recoilless gun projectile attack on the officers' mess of RAF Salalah on 9th June 1972 whilst a barbeque was being held.[19]

Other negative impacts and therefore costs due to the failure of the early campaign and immediate post-coup period include the general decline of Britain's influence in Oman.[20] Britain had gone from a historical position of controlling influence with the "last remaining princely state of the Raj" of Muscat and Oman and its client ruling dynasty to a much lesser role.[21] From the time of the coup in July 1970, in a very short period of time Oman achieved full Arab League and UN membership, had permitted the establishment of several foreign embassies in Muscat and both created and deployed an embryonic diplomatic corps to the world's key capitals. This was a long way from Britain having previously been effectively handed almost total responsibility by Sultan Said for controlling the Sultanate's external and foreign affairs.[22] This impacted further with loss of influence in terms of government contracts, with British companies previously the almost exclusive destination for such civil development or military-related work agreements. A measure of influence continued post-coup and after the war with orders for Jaguar military aircraft and Rapier air defence systems, but the almost complete dominance of Britain in this respect was no longer the case. The new Sultan undertook military procurement from countries other than the UK. As mentioned previously, he purchased mines and TOW anti-tank missiles from the USA (two), converted to fast patrol gunboats from the Netherlands for example, as well as purchasing stocks of weapons and military equipment from Iran, Jordan, Abu Dhabi, Qatar and Saudi Arabia.[23] Civil development contracts were also distributed more widely. Whereas they had almost been the exclusive preserve of the UK, counties such as West Germany and the USA secured large scale agreements which led UK Ambassador Donald Hawley to report in 1972 that British firms were struggling to gain major Omani government contracts.[24] This situation illustrates that the wider war had brought potential changes and the new Sultan had a freer hand and was exercising it, often to Britain's detriment.[25] The eventual outcome of this evolving programme of assistance was that by helping Oman to become more self-reliant and helping the country to help itself, Britain inadvertently was losing its overarching influence. Britain was not only losing influence in relation to the COIN campaign itself, but also its historical position of influence with the Sultanate as the almost exclusive political, economic, and military partner to the Omani sultans.

Other COIN Allies Perspective

Despite the many benefits of the UK-managed COIN campaign win (in terms of domestic, internal and regional stability, maintenance of the ruling status quo and a level of prestige for those nations involved), the prolonging of the conflict longer than was ideal, possibly or indeed necessarily had the effect of increasing the costs to those nations. Such costs involved ran from the economic to other measurement yardsticks such as casualties sustained. These were the practical results or negative outcomes of wider initial campaign failure, which marred the overall view of the British-led campaign. Oman also paid a significant price for the drawn-out COIN campaign in Dhofar due especially to the earlier failures of the SAF alongside British assistance to bring the insurgency to a halt. The SAF suffered 42 men killed and 93 wounded from the start of the conflict up until October 1971 (a significant number from a force only approximately 3,000 strong as late as 1970) with many more following up to the war's end.[26] With the protracted nature of the campaign this figure kept steadily rising. Even though the successful final Sherishitti Caves (Adoo's main western supply base area in Dhofar) action in 1975 was heralded as the end of the COIN campaign and victory was declared, the insurgency was not completely eliminated. Although a majority of the remaining insurgents fled over the border to the safe haven of the PDRY, numbers remained in both Dhofar and the rest of Oman and carried on a low-level campaign of insurgency. Indeed the final SAF casualty suffered due to insurgent activity was not to come until some four years after victory was declared by Sultan Qaboos in 1975.[27]

In addition to SAF casualties, the Dhofar COIN campaign caused large-scale civilian and citizen casualties; including those of the Dhofari insurgents. It is estimated that the insurgents lost over 500 killed and over 200 wounded (confirmed) from 1965 to 1975 (with over 150 confirmed killed during the pre-coup period from 1967 to 1970 alone), and up to ten thousand Jebali civilians are estimated to have lost their lives during the war, with the real figure likely to be substantially higher.[28] Civilians were killed due to insurgent and COIN force actions alike, and as in any conflict were the real victims of the Dhofar War. Civilian casualty figures are only based on estimates and the true death toll may never be known. These can be considered the forgotten or 'silent' victims of the war. The excesses of the Communist apparatchiks through murder and torture of the Jebali inhabitants accounted for many of these lives.[29] Their excesses were undertaken to force acceptance of their Marxist-based doctrine or in retaliation for assisting their enemies. These could have been stopped or at least reduced earlier had the performance of COIN forces been more successful from the outset of the insurgency in 1965, instead of the inhabitants living in constant fear for at least seven years of the decade long war.[30]

From an economic perspective the Dhofar War was near-disastrous for Oman. Due to the inability to quell the insurgency in the mid-1960s and the poor execution and results of the campaign at least until 1972, the prosecution of the war was consuming ever greater levels of precious state funds. Despite the increase in oil income from the late 1960s the situation was damaging economic and social development by diverting scarce resources away from such vital national priorities. Although similar issues of enforced longevity of campaigns were seen in the Kenyan and Northern Ireland cases for example, the host nations in these cases were far more economically developed and were therefore better able to afford or absorb such elongated periods of expenditure. The ever-increasing cost of the war in Dhofar was consuming 50% of total Omani GDP by the early 1970s and, due to this in conjunction with the resource-intense civil development programme simultaneously underway, Oman was at several points on the brink of bankruptcy.[31] The country was actually near to complete economic collapse by 1975 due to the financial pressure exerted by the COIN campaign and the costs involved in military expansion and operations, despite Britain agreeing to cover up to 50% of seconded personnel costs by 1973.[32] This situation was only partially relieved through the benefits of Oman's oil income. This benefit was intensified in 1974 due to the effects of the 1973 Arab-Israeli War and subsequent oil crisis which increased the Sultanate's oil income by a factor of four during 1974 to over 200 million Riyals.[33] Without this funding boost, Oman would possibly have faced bankruptcy, with second and third order effects being potential withdrawal from Dhofar or potential large-scale intervention by Britain, the USA, or other allies. This would have been required to prop up the regime and military effort, and plans were actually in place after withdrawal East of Suez from 1971 onwards to deploy a full British battalion battle group as required to the Sultanate to avert the potential collapse of Oman's governing status quo.[34] This was not a desired solution from the British perspective so all efforts were concentrated on preventing this outcome. Aside from military contingencies, other efforts to contain the situation included financial actions. As a result of mismanagement and inexperience in general over financial affairs, Britain had to broker a substantial loan to the Sultanate. This was a commercial loan organised via the British Bank of the Middle East (BBME). In addition to the monetary aspect, a Bank of England official was also seconded to the Omani government as a senior advisor to try and help keep the house finances and therefore critical war effort expenditure both available and under control.[35]

The commitments (both diplomatically and militarily) for both Jordan and Iran were likely also much more costly than first envisioned by the respective leaders. In terms of timeframe of commitment, both Jordanian and Iranian forces arrived in Oman by 1973. There was to be no swift and glorious victory for these forces and their leaders, King Hussain of Jordan and Shah Mohammad Reza Pahlavi of Iran, once deployed in support of the SAF. The reality was hard and costly fighting for nearly three years until the ceasefire and Omani proclamation of victory in December 1975. These commitments were not just for the deployment of fighting soldiers but the logistics to support them. In total Jordan committed some 800 troops to the COIN campaign, but this was significantly exceeded by the eventual commitment of over 3000 (and upwards of 5,000 rotated in total) Iranian military forces deployed as part of the Imperial Iranian Battle Group (IIBG).[36] In terms of material support, prior to the commitment of large numbers of military forces the Iranians provided large amounts of much needed war supplies delivered via an initial sixty C130 transport aircraft sorties to Oman in August 1972.[37] In addition, the Jordanian King gifted 12 new 25-pounder artillery pieces and some 31 Hawker Hunter jet fighter aircraft to bolster the SOAF arsenal in 1975 – a highly capable aircraft and a mainstay of contemporary regional air forces in Iraq, Jordan, Qatar, Kuwait, Lebanon, and Saudi Arabia for example – and initially provided pilots to fly them as well.[38] Such commitments were both expensive and represented a level of national risk in terms of military capability on hand to deal with unexpected contemporary regional conflicts, with an example being the 1973 'Yom Kippur' Arab-Israeli War. They were, however, intended only as relatively short-term support measures to bolster an ally. Even when the war came to an end in December 1975, the commitments did not actually end immediately. The final Jordanian forces (engineers) did not depart from Oman until some two years after the 1975 declaration of victory, in May 1977.[39] Iranian forces remained deployed to Oman even longer than the SAS (who finally left in 1978 after eight years in theatre). The Artesh finally departed only during the final throes of the Iranian Revolution in 1979.[40]

In addition, both Iran and Jordan also suffered significant numbers of casualties during the war. In a relative sense, although Jordan bore numerous casualties, those suffered by Iran were greater than all the rest of the COIN allies combined.[41] Iran suffered upwards of 1000 military personnel killed and wounded during the Dhofar War in just over two years of campaign involvement.[42] This also significantly outnumbered those casualties suffered by Britain which amounted to only 35 killed personnel in total over the ten years of fighting.[43] The differences with regards to casualty rates is quite dramatic. As such it alludes to the fact that Iran suffered a higher battlefield casualty rate than any nation involved in the Dhofar conflict except Oman (as a population, primarily Dhofari – not just SAF) itself.[44] Add to this the loss of expensive, multi-million dollar items of equipment in action such as fighter jets and helicopters to either insurgent small arms fire or towards the end of the campaign to sophisticated insurgent SAM-7 missiles and the high cost of the Dhofar campaign to all countries – but especially to Iran – is clear.[45]

Overall, for a COIN win and for a rare victory against Communist insurgents in the Cold War period, the Dhofar campaign can be viewed as being relatively cost-efficient per se. It can also be considered relatively cost-efficient for the UK in relation to its previous campaigns, with fewer resources committed to achieve the overall win. Multiple strategic aims were successfully achieved, and those objectives influencing regional stability also benefitted Oman, Iran and Jordan. The campaign, however, did last much longer than should ideally have been the case. The cost in terms of manpower and 'blood and treasure' would have been less if better conducted from the beginning of hostilities in the mid-1960s. From this perspective it was similar to all other British campaigns, especially those conducted in Malaya, Kenya and Northern Ireland, which were all lengthy undertakings where COIN efforts were slow to take positive effect. Britain had to expend more resources in Oman than initially envisaged or desirable. This was a situation likewise applicable to all of Oman's other key COIN allies.

Chapter 10

Other Evidence of Success – Continuing UK influence in Oman post-campaign

Military & Economic links

The COIN campaign win in Dhofar also led to Britain's other main achievement, which was its continuing influence in Oman. This reflected several similar situations in countries following the conclusion of previous classical-era British campaigns. Britain earned the deep gratitude of Sultan Qaboos, and despite the 1971 departure of the long-standing influential figure of the Bahrain-based Political Resident (PRPG) and the Muscat-based Consul-General (and eventually of Britain from both RAF stations in Salalah and on Masirah Island), so the UK's influence in Oman going forward resultingly remained strong.[1] Cooperative, professional and friendly relations were continued post-conflict with Oman and these both substantial and deep links have continued up to the modern day. British seconded and contract personnel remaining attached to the Omani armed forces up to the rank of Brigadier.[2] This situation is reminiscent of the Malayan, Kenyan and Cypriot campaigns where economic, military and diplomatic ties flourished post-conflict. Military bases remained for example in Cyprus and in Singapore (after expulsion from the Federation of Malaysia in 1965) up until 1971 and 'East of Suez'-related British withdrawal. This was the case even in Aden. Despite a brutal and (for the British) disastrous COIN campaign capped off with a humiliating withdrawal, cordial, professional links remained with the new (previously 'terrorist') NLF-run government. Even after the insurgency and the British departure, ex-RAF pilots initially still remained contracted directly to the new South Arabian (later PDRY) air force and British company Airwork was contracted to run the engineering and maintenance support of both the country's air force and naval assets up to 1970.[3] Airwork, which also had a key role to play in the Dhofar War, maintained a presence in Southern Yemen in one guise or another for ad hoc aeronautical or maritime engineering services for a further 20-year plus period after the Aden COIN campaign and only ceased work in the territory in 1984.[4]

The Sultan was undoubtedly grateful for British support during the Dhofar War. As a sign of this gratitude, contracts were awarded to UK companies, thereby providing a distinct economic benefit for Britain.[5] With the Muscat-based Ambassador and his staff also discreetly lobbying in the background, large civilian development services and export contracts were awarded to UK companies. Some of the biggest contracts awarded were for military equipment procurement such as the Rapier air defence system and Jaguar fighter-bomber aircraft, with additional orders placed for Jaguars and new 'prestige' equipment items such as Scorpion and Challenger tanks following in the 1980s.[6] These benefitted the directly-contracted British companies such as Taylor Woodrow and Cable & Wireless, as well as the British exchequer via taxation; a form of 'payback' for the government and its diplomatic representatives for all the lobbying undertaken on behalf of these firms.[7] The 1975 fiscal year saw an over 90% rise in British exports to Oman over the previous twelve month period, which is testament to the preferential treatment of UK firms due to wartime services and support provided which resulted in the survival of the Sultanate's ruling status quo.[8]

The British financial benefit gained as a result of the Dhofar War was not only limited to companies. Individuals also benefitted. Perhaps the best-known example of personal benefit accrued from the Dhofar War was the case of British citizen Timothy Landon. Landon was the son of an army officer and his Canadian wife and joined the British army to serve as an officer. He later served in the SAF under Sultan Said as both a seconded and later under Qaboos as a directly employed contract officer. As a reported classmate of Sultan Qaboos at Sandhurst in the early 1960s, Landon became a high-ranking advisor to his Sandhurst batchmate after the 1970 coup where he earned the not altogether complementary title of the "White Sultan" and eventually rose to the rank of Brigadier-General in the SAF as a contract, or directly employed officer to the Omani military.[9] For his support and 'services rendered' prior, during and after the July 1970 coup, Landon also received a fixed income of Oman's oil revenue via Sultan Qaboos and substantial additional commissions through his association and myriad business deals with Oman and on behalf of or with Sultan Qaboos from real estate to art. These included the purchase of art and property in the UK and Europe for Qaboos worth millions of pounds for which he was awarded commission or a 'finder's fee'. Such financial arrangements enabled him to subsequently purchase stately homes, shooting estates, and even a whole village in Hampshire in England with the proceeds, the latter coming complete with a country pub where years later Prince Harry would have his Stag (Bachelor) Party.[10] Through his large Omani-sourced accrued wealth, Landon worked his way into influential positions in both UK and Omani circles, married an Austrian Princess and even received an honorary Knighthood from HM Queen Elizabeth.[11] Landon utilised his privileged position in Oman and with its ruler to eventually amass a substantial fortune. He reportedly accrued wealth of over £500 million as an arms and oil broker making him one of the wealthiest individuals in the UK, and even reportedly received a yearly birthday gift of £1 million from Sultan Qaboos up to the former's death in 2007.[12]

Although the Landon case is somewhat of an outlier, or atypical in its prominence, it does illustrate the fact that some individuals from the UK gained substantially from the Dhofar War and Oman more generally. As such, there was certainly a less palatable or indeed less honourable side to the involvement of Britons from an individual or case by case basis, despite, in the Landon example, him being held in obvious high regard by Sultan Qaboos. Most Britons acted in an entirely 'above board' manner, but others certainly profited handsomely from their involvement, taking literally the old saying 'all's fair in love and war'.

Continued Influence of British Military Personnel

Perhaps more significant even than the above economic or financial aspects was the continued influence of seconded serving, then retired (previously often seconded officers in the Dhofar War) British military personnel in top positions of authority in the Omani government and military. This was to an extent unique even as compared to the transitional security arrangements involving UK military personnel in several other countries post-COIN campaign and/ or post-independence of even the more successful of British COIN campaigns with Malaya or Kenya the prime examples. This ensured a significant level of leverage for the UK on Omani policy and actions in the spheres of security and military affairs, even though dealing with a fully independent, sovereign government with its own seat in the UN. 'Oman-isation' of the Sultanate's armed forces or the replacement of expatriate – in this case largely British – military officer-level personnel with Omani citizens, only really started in earnest in the early 1980s.[13] Prior to this, British officers remained dominant especially in the highest grade roles, with an example being the appointment of the by then Brigadier Peter Thwaites as the Omani Chairman of the Joint Staff in 1976. He, in turn, was replaced by the then General Sir Tim Creasey in 1981 as the re-titled Chief of the Defence Staff who therefore took on his second stint in charge of the Armed Forces of Oman as a loaned serving British army officer.[14] A key example of this continuance of top-level military influence, despite the almost complete 'Oman-isation' of the SAF by the late 1980s, was the, again, seconded British military officer Air Marshall Sir Erik Bennett. He held the position of Commander, SOAF until 1990 when the branch was retitled the Royal Air Force of Oman (RAFO) with an Omani officer in the lead role.[15] In circumstances probably unique in world terms, this ensured direct or indirect

British influence at the highest levels of another nation's military hierarchy. The result was that for well over a decade after the Dhofar War, the British government arguably exercised a form of direct leverage over both Omani and to a certain extent also Arabian Peninsula military and security-related affairs via its imbedded senior officers.

UK Military Training Benefits

UK Military personnel/units (general)
Britain also gained important military training benefits from the war. Due to the fact that upwards of 1,000 regular British forces personnel were stationed in Oman at its peak, with troop and unit rotations thousands of individuals collectively (from the SAS, Royal Artillery, Royal Engineers, RAF (including RAF Regiment), Intelligence Corps, Medical Corps and Royal Navy for instance) therefore saw service in a war zone, often involving kinetic combat operations.[16] Such live training opportunities for British military personnel were a relatively rare occurrence post-1967. This was the date of the withdrawal from the major base areas of Aden and an insurgency, and by this time also most of the old Imperial possessions were self-governing with less scope for foreign military service or operations. British soldiers would more likely have found themselves stationed in West Germany with large numbers of personnel and equipment located statically in the Western sectors during the Cold War. Active, war-zone operations were useful from a training perspective as such unit and individual experience gained in the large-scale campaigns of Malaya and Kenya was (especially by 1970) becoming dated and passing into the realms of regimental history as opposed to being current and practiced operational knowledge. From an individual perspective, Ian Gardiner describes how, as a young Royal Marines Captain he was exposed to combat and was able to hone his tactical command and his leadership skills to a more demanding location, cultural, and linguistic extent than he was ever likely to experience in the British military; in many ways a kind of 'finishing school' for a military – especially infantry – officer. He stated that this experience was to directly benefit him – and similarly many junior RM officers who served in Oman – for service in the later Falklands campaign in 1982 and throughout his later career.[17] Another example was the then Flight Lieutenant Graham 'Jock' Stirrup who volunteered for Dhofar service as a loaned or seconded officer with SOAF from 1973–1975 and gained valuable combat experience as a Strikemaster pilot.[18] Far from hampering his career as was often the prevailing view in RAF circles, Stirrup later rose to become the UK's Chief of Defence Staff (CDS), serving in this role from 2006 to 2010.

Senior Officers/Leaders

In terms of leadership benefits contemporary senior officers also benefitted. Like the experiences of the British commanders gained in previous COIN campaigns in Palestine, Malaya, Kenya and Cyprus, the senior officers seconded to Oman also acquired professional command experience on a war-footing and would take this experience back to the UK armed forces. Brigadier Purdon, Brigadier Graham and Major General Creasey experienced brigade-plus size command involving tri-service joint operations to different degrees and complexities. The multi-national commands headed by the CSAFs consisted also of Baluchi, Omani, and even Jordanian and Iranian troops and all this during live, wartime conditions. After Dhofar command, Major General Creasey was later to serve in Northern Ireland during the height of the troubles as General Officer Commanding (GOC) for two years from 1977 to 1979.[19] Such live training opportunities were also provided to individual British loaned officers, but also to seconded British units who benefitted at the regimental level as well as foreign forces. The significant troop formations deployed by Jordan and Iran under SAF command also received a similar level of operational experience and benefit, which was a key reason as to why they were sent by their respective leaders. British units such as the SAS, the Royal Engineers, and Royal Artillery all therefore achieved valuable unit-wide operational experience and training in a combat zone. The SAS even entered Northern Ireland on an emergency tour in strength in 1976 soon after the drawdown and large-scale British withdrawal from Oman post victory in December of the previous year. The often two-squadron deployment of the Regiment in Dhofar was very rare and not even replicated during the height of the Iraqi campaign (2nd Gulf War) as part of Task Force Black and Task Force Knight, where single squadron deployments were the standard.[20]

The spread of military benefits gained from involvement in the Dhofar War was not just limited to UK forces, but to campaign allies too. Key amongst these were both Jordan and Iran who also significantly benefitted from the training opportunities presented by the Dhofar War. Jordanian forces consisting primarily of engineers, pilots and Special Forces troops numbered about 800 at their height in 1975 with the latter the largest contingent at 555 men in total.[21] Not only was this politically important support for Oman and a welcomed boost to fighting troops to support the SAF, the deployment of Jordanian military units and personnel provided useful 'live' training; especially relevant with hostilities with Israel then a consistent potential threat to national security. In addition, Iranian engineers constructed large-scale military engineering projects such as the Damavand Line, and the air force became well practiced in logistical movements of equipment and troops as well as in fighter/bomber live combat missions. The Iranian navy was also able to conduct live naval bombardment operations from the Arabian Sea into targets in Dhofar with the opportunity to utilise the theatre as a live weapon proving-ground, for instance for their then newly-acquired Italian-made 'Sea Killer' surface-to-surface missile.[22] The largest scale training benefit, however, was for the army and Special Forces units where troops were regularly rotated every three months to give maximum training and combat experience.[23] By the time the Iranian forces eventually left Oman in 1979, over 15,000 soldiers had been rotated through Oman's live wartime operational zone.[24] This gave all ranks valuable training and live operational experience to complement their internally US-sponsored training and organisation.[25]

UK Reputational Enhancement Through COIN Win

In addition to the above factors, although conducted in a very low-key manner and in the main well away from the media and public (even after the 1970 coup when there was more officially sanctioned publicity), the campaign win in Dhofar helped bolster Britain's credibility. Its reputation as a both capable and influential military power was boosted to allies and enemies alike, both in the region's as well as the wider world. This was especially the case after the damage inflicted on the UK's international reputation by the disastrous Aden COIN campaign and humiliating withdrawal, to add to the reputational damage done to Britain by the Palestine debacle some two decades earlier in 1948, with incidents such as the Suez Crisis in between. War-winning assistance in Dhofar was undertaken in a discreet manner but those that needed to know 'got' the message. In narrative terms, the Cold War Superpowers to the relatively fragile new states of the Gulf formerly under British protection (such as the UAE and Bahrain) and even potential enemies such as the Marxist PDRY were sent a clear message. The higher decision-making echelons of military and government in these countries were all able to witness British resolve and capability to maintain the governing status quo in a key ally and fight to do so if necessary in a model example of how to counter Communist insurrection.[26] In a sense similar to Britain's stoic COIN campaign and eventual win in Malaya, despite the fall of China to a Marxist regime and the ideological spill over into the Korean War, the win in Dhofar proved Communist forces and insurgencies could actually be beaten. In short, the campaign win boosted Britain's reputation, and gave others hope that communist insurgency was not always necessarily a death knell for the governing status quo, and could be beaten if tackled in the right way.[27] Britain had clearly shown how this could be done.

Britain ended the Second World War as a victor. It cemented its place in the contemporaneous world order via the 'reward' of one of the hugely influential five permanent seats on the UN Security Council and via developing a strategic nuclear weapons capability. Despite this, however, the UK's actual and perceived world power standing was in relatively swift decline. This was seen in absolute terms via the Suez Crisis in 1956 and the swift loss of empire during the 1950s and 1960s, and in relative terms due to the emergence of the two superpowers. In a bipolar Cold War world Britain was no longer a hegemon or superpower as she had once been despite the victory in the Second World War, and was effectively 'broken' economically. As a leading member of NATO and the West and a colonial power, Britain still had superpower outlay in terms of military expenditure which further deteriorated its economic position. The extensive costs of wartime military operations did not end on VE (Victory in Europe) Day, with large-scale operations undertaken from 1945–46 to re-establish European colonial control in Asia (e.g. Indochina and Malaya) from nationalist and or Communist movements after the defeat of the Japanese occupiers.[28] Large-scale military (COIN) operations were also undertaken in Palestine up to 1948 and then in Malaya for a full twelve years up until 1960. Concurrently Britain was prosecuting COIN campaigns in both Kenya and Cyprus as well as the ill-fated invasion of the Suez Canal in October 1956. With the Kenyan, Cyprus and Malayan Emergencies still underway, Britain also carried out a military intervention in Oman to end the Imamate Rebellion at the end of the 1950s. Britain later intervened in Brunei/Borneo from 1963–1966 and was fighting an insurgency in Aden which ended in humiliating departure in 1967 as well as undertaking smaller operations, for instance in British Guiana and Jamaica in the Caribbean region.[29] The loss of Cyprus, Kenya and Aden allied to the international embarrassment of Rhodesia's 1956 Unilateral Declaration of Independence (UDI) seriously damaged Britain's international 'power' reputation. The COIN win in Oman helped reverse this trend. The 1975 win enabled Britain to reap the much-needed reputational boost from both a power and military competence perspective through a COIN victory which was a rare feat in the Cold War era.[30]

Britain had managed to achieve in Dhofar a victory against insurgents which other imperial or world power nations had failed to achieve. Although such campaigns were generally on a significantly larger scale than most of Britain's COIN campaigns it was unmatched at the time. The French had been defeated firstly in Indochina and later in Algeria; the latter campaign even contributed towards an attempted coup d'état in France itself in 1961.[31] In the same year the Portuguese were militarily forced out of their Goa Indian enclave which they had ruled since the 16th Century. The largely conscript Portuguese forces were not technically defeated in military terms in costly (in terms of money and lives) but later COIN campaigns fought simultaneously in Guinea, Mozambique and Angola were lost from a political perspective by Portugal, and were subsequently the backdrop to the Carnation Revolution and successful military coup in the country in 1974 which ousted the government of Estado Novo.[32] Likewise the Rhodesians and Dutch for example, also undertook unsuccessful COIN campaigns despite their relative wealth and ample military resources. Similarly in 1975, in the same year the US forces withdrew after a humiliating campaign loss in South Vietnam, Britain discreetly toasted the successful defeat of the Communist insurgents in Dhofar.[33] It must be re-iterated that the Dhofar War was an extremely limited COIN campaign in terms of size as compared to such non-UK campaigns and even when compared to most previous British COIN operations. It was, nonetheless, not only a rare military victory against insurgents per se but especially those of a Communist bent, but also an important diplomatic win, and contributed to securing Britain's regional and world strategic interests in the area in multiple ways.

Benefits to 'Host' Nation (Oman)

With some clear exceptions such as Palestine or Aden, despite vicious and sustained COIN campaigns against determined insurgents, most territories following British departure after such campaigns were left in stable overall conditions. In general, this enabled relatively peaceful governmental and social and economic development after hostilities had ended. In this key respect Oman/Dhofar was no different. Malaya became fully independent in 1957 actually during the emergency and in the midst of the associated COIN campaign. The status quo survived and Britain continued the campaign for a further three years. This was undertaken in part to ensure the survival and stability of the new government and good relations with it after departure. With the military defeat of the Mau Mau insurgents via the COIN campaign by 1960, Kenya was put on a trajectory for independence by late 1963 in a state of relative stability with the Kenyatta administration taking over the governing mantle. In Cyprus, Enosis (the aspiration to achieve political union with Greece) was avoided and apart from continuing tensions between the ethnic Greek and Turkish populations on the island (which later led to the unilateral division of the island in 1974) the island was left in a relative state of stability immediately post-conflict in 1959. Further, the Northern Borneo territories including Brunei either gained independence or were successfully integrated into a stable new Malaysian Federation which, apart from expulsion of Singapore in 1965, endures to this day as the stable and prosperous state of Malaysia.

Stability

Like for the host nations of other classical British COIN campaigns, one of the key benefits of the Dhofar War campaign for Oman was continued stability and viability.

Oman's governing status quo had prevailed, and the country had avoided the descent into a full-scale civil war and potential provincial Communist domination. Oman had also emerged from the campaign territorially intact. The COIN win also reinforced both Sultan Qaboos' own, and his country's legitimacy in the eyes of not just Oman's population, but of the entire Gulf region and indeed the world. This was achieved in part via Arab League and UN membership from 1971. The Sultanate had, therefore, taken great developmental leaps on multiple fronts under Sultan Qaboos and "from [being an] an isolated country under Sai'id, to a small and respected participant of the global community".[34] The Sultanate had emerged from widespread accusations of merely being a British 'puppet state' and onto the international stage with reinforced internal and external legitimacy, therefore moving from a long-held state of British 'protection' to one of capable international actor.[35]

Military Development

British training and leadership for indigenous COIN forces such as Malayan and Kenyan Home Guard units (which went on to form the nucleus of post-COIN and post-independence national military forces) created many benefits for the host nations. After five years of relatively ineffective COIN campaigning due in part to the influence of Sultan Said, post-1970 Britain's input directly benefitted Oman from a military perspective. In the British-backed coup his son, Qaboos took power in 1970, and alongside a recently-introduced new national currency implemented by the British Bank of the Middle East (BBME), within the next few months the country had 're-branded' to the extent of not only implementing a new official name but also a brand new national flag.[36] The influx of British assistance helped to stabilise the dire situation the government forces faced after five years of Sultan Said's ultimate control over the campaign, and saw the expansion and improvement of the SAF. This not only enabled the war to be won in Dhofar but raised the profile of what was the key and most – and arguably the only – effective national organisation under the Sultan's authority until that point.

Alongside the expansion of the SAF from approximately 3,000 men to over 10,000, the organisation enjoyed direct British training support and the provision of specialist British units such as the SAS itself, a Field Surgical Tean (FST), Royal Engineers, and a Royal Artillery 'cracker battery' and a loaned Wessex helicopter detachment.[37] A key component of the British capability provision to the Sultanate was the raising, and subsequent leading of the Firqa units by the SAS. These indigenous militia consisted largely of Surrendered Enemy Personnel (SEPs) who were trained and utilised with a view to defeating their former insurgent comrades-in-arms. Despite many developmental problems the Firqa were to prove vital to breaking the morale of the insurgents. As such, they were subsequently crucial in helping to turn the tide of the war away from the upper hand long-enjoyed by the Adoo, and firmly back to the government side.[38] All such developments on the military front helped towards developing a more effective Sultanate military capability in the form of the SAF. As a result, it could simultaneously effectively take on the much expanded, well-trained and equipped PFLOAG forces in Dhofar as well as carrying out its widespread security duties across the entirety of Omani territory.[39] Post-war these developments provided the basis for ongoing security for Oman going forward to what is now "generally recognised in modern times as one of the best equipped and organised militaries on the Arabian Peninsula".[40]

Omani Internal Governance Benefits
This external re-alignment of perception of status and tangible levels or organisation was also mirrored in terms of internal governance in Oman. Although the country remained a top-down governing absolute monarchy, post-coup there was a concerted effort to develop and put in place the organisation of governmental bureaucracy essential for the functioning of a modern state. The former Sultan's brother, Tariq returned to Oman at his nephew's request as Prime Minister soon after the 1970 coup and was tasked to develop the governmental infrastructure and oversee the formation of a new government.[41] Under his authority new government departments were established. These largely had Sultanate nationals installed as Ministers to showcase to the outside world the important legitimising narrative of Omanis running Oman by themselves.[42]

The issue of internal state policing was also developed. Until 1970 civilian policing in Oman was undertaken by the paramilitary Oman Gendarmerie (OG) only, and a new national police force called the Royal Oman Police (ROP) was subsequently established, taking on all policing-related functions of the OG by 1972.[43] A similar story is apparent with the development of an internal state security and intelligence apparatus. This organisation was initially called the Oman Intelligence Service (OIS) and set up and directed initially by officers of Britain's SIS; it then developed into the suitably opaquely titled Oman Research Department (ORD) in 1974. This gave the Omani state an effective civilian intelligence capability for the first time.[44]

Whilst many teething problems were encountered in setting up and developing such organisations, infrastructure, and individual governmental departments, it still represented clear evidence of Omani progress in these spheres. What previously had been a country run exclusively by a reclusive Sultan remote from the capital city in his palace in Salalah changed radically. The resulting government organisation, hand in hand with the expanded and further capability-enhanced armed forces, propelled Oman from a developmental backwater to budding new state.

Social and Economic Benefit
Oman benefitted militarily from the COIN campaign win but also from a social and economic perspective. Improvements made in Dhofar and Oman as a result of the war can, therefore, be considered a great success for the UK-run campaign. As Beckett states, "In Oman, the reforms begun in 1970 have been extended to produce the infrastructure of a modern state with improved communications, industry and medical and educational facilities"[45]

Although not a primary planned outcome of the Dhofari COIN campaign, the province as well as greater Oman did experience benefits in terms of economic expansion. Although oil exploitation and therefore income had begun under the reign of his father, this was expanded under Qaboos' rule. It was a vital necessity to help pay for the expansion and operation of the SAF to conduct the war, as well as the necessary social and infrastructure development of the country post-1970. Oil revenues, alongside the military and economic aid of Britain and Oman's other allies was one of the key factors in achieving eventual victory, as the cost of prosecuting the war ballooned to over 50% of the Sultanate's GDP by 1971.[46] This was partially offset by the fact that oil revenue was 40 times that of the country in 1969 over that enjoyed in the early 1960s, and became a much lesser issue financially following the 1973 oil crisis and the resultant almost stratospheric increase in international crude oil prices which boosted Omani coffers.[47] The Sultanate's total government budget effectively quadrupled from 65.5 to 240 million Riyals in a single year from 1973 to 1974.[48] By 1975, this figure had further dramatically increased to 325 million Riyals), and this increase in national income, alongside the practical benefits of the British-devised and executed 'hearts and minds' campaign enabled a large programme of investment in the country.[49] As a result of the oil crisis bounty, the government was able to implement a fast-track scheme of development. This included building schools, hospitals and other infrastructure projects such as roads and port facilities from Dhofar to Muscat propelling the country forward in a short time frame from a state of almost 'medieval' backwardness and lack of civil development to modern nation state status.[50]

In addition, the repressive laws imposed on his subjects in Oman and Dhofar specifically by Sultan Said over decades of rule were either relaxed or removed.[51]

These included the restrictions on movement, and from the long-instigated rules banning "wicked Western imports" such as transistor radios or cameras.[52] All such state-building activities initiated during the Dhofar War helped pacify the discontent of the Jebalis and to at least reduce or in many ways negate (or at least reduce) many of the fundamental reasons why the original nationalist-led insurgency first developed, For Oman, this has fortunately acted as a continuing source of stability up to the modern era, for instance helping to offset or avoid some of the worst potential outcomes of the 2011 Arab Spring.[53]

The Dhofar COIN campaign was an overall success or a 'win'. As such, in relative terms it reflected a majority of post-Second World War UK COIN campaigns in this respect and a level of success higher than all other classical-era COIN protagonist nations.[54] Despite its problems the campaign ended in 1975 with a resounding win for the UK, Oman and COIN allies and a defeat for the insurgents. In absolute terms, it was a long way, however, from being an idealised COIN campaign.[55] In this respect it was also similar to most previous British COIN campaign 'wins' in being less successful from an operational level perspective than the outcome and Britain's perceived COIN reputation would suggest. The Dhofar Campaign can even be viewed as harbouring many and significant actual failures which were apparent from the start of the campaign in 1964 and were not fully rectified even after the 1970 coup.

From a military perspective, the Dhofar COIN operation has been described in the literature as representing a model campaign in every way.[56] For Britain, the victory in the Dhofar War added to the list of classical-era campaign wins and reinforced its image of military competence and COIN expertise and helped to restore the reputational balance of less successful post-war campaigns. The Dhofar undertaking succeeded where nearly all other classical-era COIN undertaking nations failed in their own campaigns. In contrast, it was also achieved only a few short months after the loss of the Vietnam War, also highlighting the campaign's importance in the Cold War era.[57] From a strategic aims perspective, Britain contributed to Gulf regional stability and contributed to the psychological impact on both the region and the world that Communist insurgencies could be stopped. Britain helped ensure the continued pro-Western administration of the strategically vital Strait of Hormuz and therefore the free-flow of oil and continued Western economic prosperity for a relatively limited cost.[58] Like in the cases of several of the other British COIN campaigns referenced in this book, the Dhofar War enabled the host country to maintain viability as a platform for continued stability after independence. Britain also benefited from the enduring goodwill of the Omani Sultan. This scenario was both expressed through and translated practically into continuing economic and government-level links such as large-scale military contracts through to the continued deployment of seconded advisors for years after the Dhofar War ended. For Britain, the Dhofar COIN campaign also represented a transition from a wholly immersive colonial or imperial policing model of COIN to a more distanced or hands-off consultancy-type approach. This was unique at the time to Oman and a less costly model which was to be successfully adopted later in later campaigns such as Sierra Leone.[59] In addition to other benefits such as training for UK military units and leaders also apparent, as well as for Oman and its other allies, on the surface the Dhofar campaign can be viewed as a great all-round success for all the participants on the Omani side of the conflict.

Although victory in the Dhofar War was notably achieved in the same year as the US loss in another contemporary Cold War conflict against communist forces it was far from an almost-role model example of COIN.[60] It can conversely be viewed as being a failure in many ways. This began with Colonel Tony Lewis' abortive initial expedition to Dhofar in 1965 and continued all the way through to the final push on the insurgent's key Sherishitti Caves complex in Western Dhofar some ten years later. Such elements of failure helped it endure for nearly a decade as was the case similarly in Malaya, Kenya and (even more so) in Northern Ireland. These include the failures of the prosecuting COIN forces, those stemming from the military structural and operational organisation of the SAF and the anti-insurgent coalition as well as the costs incurred by the same. The forces were well led by experienced British officers, but they could only achieve so much with the inertia of lack of investment in the SAF for example. Operationally, the resistance and therefore failure of Sultan Said to invest the proceeds of his country's new-found oil wealth (it has been said he kept the proceeds in cash under his bed) contributed to an underfunded and ill-equipped SAF which allowed the insurgents to consolidate and contributed to a longer and more costly campaign all-round.[61] In addition, although it was a key event, a further five years after the 1970 coup would elapse before the COIN win was achieved with all the attendant cost in 'blood and treasure' for all COIN forces. This fact is a overall clear indicator of elements of significant campaign failure.

Despite the drawbacks and notable examples of absolute-level failure in the campaign, it did ultimately result in a win. It was a victory for Britain, the Sultan and allies and an extremely rare one against communist/communist-backed insurgents. This backs the assertion that British COIN operations were generally more successfully conducted than those campaigns conducted by other classical-era COIN-undertaking nations.[62] More impressive was the fact that this was achieved despite the limited resources available. It can therefore be considered that the Dhofar campaign was actually Britain's most clear-cut counter-insurgency victory since Malaya; even likely surpassing the latter in terms of overall success.[63] The victory was a timely boost to the West as well as the non-Communist or 'free' world in general, with the Dhofar operation being also perhaps with the benefit of hindsight a more significant strategic level victory than even appreciated at the time.[64]

The main conclusion of this section is therefore that the Dhofar campaign was neither text book nor ideal in terms of operational or absolute success. In the end, however, the result of the campaign reflected the generally successful narrative of British post-war COIN. It can therefore be considered a success in relative terms and, therefore, atypical when compared to the overall UK COIN record. As highlighted, however, it retains 'one-off' characteristics so in terms of success should ultimately be regarded as distinct from its campaign forebears and *Sui Generis* or unique in nature.[65]

Part IV

A Truly British Counter-insurgency Action?

In the classical COIN era Britain undertook numerous campaigns ranging from the large-scale (as in Malaya) to the relatively limited (as in Cyprus). Although experiencing what amounted to effective campaign losses in Palestine and Aden for example, British forces are credited with a relatively respectable campaign success ratio. All such campaigns were undertaken in contemporary current or ex-British territories by UK government-controlled forces. In the case of Dhofar this was fundamentally different. When viewed more widely however, the overall British influence on the campaign and the similarities to previous UK COIN actions was so great it can arguably be considered an overwhelmingly British COIN undertakings. This should not, however, lead to the conclusion that from a British influence perspective that Dhofar was that Dhofar was just a mere clone of previous British campaigns. The Dhofar COIN action were still substantially different in its level of British control or influence to almost all other previous classical-era campaigns, displaying unique characteristics.

As such, the final section of this book puts forward the argument that the Dhofar campaign was, overall, a British COIN campaign in the classical mould but with substantial caveats which still make it unique. It covers the credible argument that the campaign was fundamentally different from previous UK COIN offerings so cannot be viewed as typical. There is also the more nuanced view that Britain's control and influence waned over time and therefore was not static. In many ways this illustrates the declining level of British influence and control over the Dhofar campaign; especially in its latter stages. As such, despite the many differences identified with previous UK COIN actions which make the Dhofar operation distinctly non-typical, the level of British influence is so cumulatively strong that it should be considered a fundamentally UK COIN campaign.

To enable this, the level of UK military campaign control is assessed as well as the often-overlooked influence of the Omani Sultans themselves. The changing narrative of Britain's influence is also be explored to provide a more nuanced explanation of UK influence over the campaign. The level of overall Britishness' is clarified via the evolution of the political and economic relations between

Oman and the UK and its impact in British influence over Dhofar and the conflict. These include treaty history, direct UK support to Oman, the 1970 coup, diplomatic assistance as well as British governance and state-building influence and impact. Also considered is British influence over COIN campaign strategy, and command and control of the SAF, and UK influence over Dhofar COIN operations themselves (both from a training and war-fighting perspective).

From personnel to equipment, strategic and tactical planning and execution Britain's influence over the Dhofar COIN campaign was central. Evidence suggests, however, that the situation is not as one-sided as put forward in certain quarters of the literature, and the influence of other nations should be fully considered, as well as the Omani Sultans.[1] Essentially it is a question of scale of influence. From one perspective it can be said that one of Britain's key roles was to stop the war being lost in the first place.[2] This was strived for to avoid all the attendant risks of an insurgent victory in Dhofar. Associated with this were the potentially dire outcomes not only for wider Oman, but for the UK-protected Gulf Monarchies and for general stability in the Arabian Peninsula. Alternatively, there is the view that Britain's input was less substantial or crucial to the overall victory. This narrative misses the point somewhat, and a more nuanced and useful approach is to view Britain's role and influence over both Oman and the Dhofar War not in terms of a static phenomenon, but one that changed and evolved over time. What began as a purely British-led effort with the initial SAF deployments ordered by Colonel Lewis developed over time.[3] The earlier stages of the campaign, which could not be won by UK assistance alone, eventually changed into the form of an international coalition involving substantial military forces from both Jordan and Iran as well as financial and wider military aid from multiple Gulf countries.[4] This enabled the overall British-engineered campaign strategy to be implemented, as well as the final tactical push at Sherishitti to be successfully conducted and victory finally declared in 1975.

The Dhofar campaign cannot be described as wholly British in the sense that the UK did not supply the required materials of war, carry out the majority of fighting (and did not sustain the highest levels of casualties) to ensure victory as was the case in Malaya and in the UK's other key classical-era campaigns. Britain's relative numerical and tangible influence in several key areas of the Dhofar COIN campaign (and in Oman itself) actually diminished over time.[5] In terms, however, of command, strategy and the execution of the campaign as well as large-scale state-building efforts, such key influence did not diminish. Britain's role in this respect was decisive and remained so from the start of the campaign to its conclusion in 1975. The Dhofar War was to all intents and purposes a British-run campaign, yet still remained different or unique as compared to its previous COIN undertakings.

Despite the strong evidence to the contrary there are, however, some valid arguments that Britain's influence was not the overriding and critical factor in undertaking and winning the Dhofar COIN campaign. A review of such influences is appropriate.

Factors Negating British Influence

Military Influence

During the first half of the Dhofar War up to 1970, it can be observed that Britain was Oman's major military partner, but the UK did not technically either run or fight the Dhofar campaign. From the manpower and funding arrangements put in place from the 1958 Exchange of Letters and subsequent agreement enhancements the UK effectively bank-rolled the formation of, and provided the leadership for, the SAF. Unlike in its previous classical-era campaigns the UK, however, never provided large combat forces to fight in Dhofar. Britain, therefore, did not technically fight or win the war from a conventional military perspective. Even within the SAF itself, British personnel were in the vast minority. Several nationalities other than the UK were represented in the leadership and command structure of the SAF and this situation of the influence of other nations was to accelerate; especially from 1973 onwards. As Fred Halliday states:

> While British personnel commanded these revamped forces, other nations also participated. Australians and Rhodesians flew with the SOAF. Pakistan, which had supported the Sultan of Muscat before 1970, had around a hundred officers in Dhofar by the end of 1972. India began to train the navy. Iran, worried by the example of Dhofar, sent helicopter crews and later troops. Jordan supplied intelligence officers and helped to train Omani officers.[6]

Whilst Britain provided the leadership in terms of the key officers of the SAF's combat units, the rank and file of the SAF was almost exclusively Omani and (even more substantially) Baluchi in composition. It was the thousands of these men who actually carried out the fighting on the ground in Dhofar and to whom victory is in many ways justifiably sometimes credited.[7]

Even within the expanded and diversified nature of the Sultan's forces constructed to fight and eventually win the COIN campaign, Britain was never to have large forces involved. This assistance was subsequently to be dwarfed from 1973 onwards by further foreign troop contributions. The balance of military numbers was to significantly change from 1970, and subsequently further from 1973. Up the point of the 1970 coup, the SAF comprised approximately 3000 men, but under Sultan Qaboos and via major assistance from the British government, this number had more than tripled to a figure over 10,000 by the end of 1972.[8] By 1975 this number has expanded further to include some 3000 Iranians troops, over 1,000 largely SAS-trained Dhofari Firqa militiamen, up to 1,000 British regular service personnel and some 800 Jordanians.[9] The British contingent was eventually therefore substantial, but the overall non-SAF fighting force on the side of the Sultan consisted mainly of the troops of outside regional powers, and principally from Iran. At the time of military victory at the Sherishitti Caves complex in 1975 there were nearly four times the numbers of Iranian and Jordanian military personnel fighting on the Sultan's side than those of Britain; with many of the latter being solely employed to protect the RAF personnel required to operate the facilities at RAF Salalah. From a purely numerical perspective, therefore, Britain did not provide anywhere near the largest contingent of combat troops to the Sultan's ultimately victorious coalition.

Although King Hussein of Jordan supplied a battalion of SF troops, engineers, intelligence officers and later some thirty Hawker Hunter jet aircraft as a gift to Sultan Qaboos and Oman, the most significant contribution to the COIN campaign in terms of troops, equipment and operational capability came from Iran.[10] After establishing diplomatic relations, the Shah of Iran invited Sultan Qaboos to the large-scale Persepolis celebrations in late 1971 which celebrated 2,500 years of the Persian Empire and historic ruling dynasty.[11] This event was followed towards the latter stages of 1972 with the establishment of the first Iranian Ambassadorial post in Muscat.[12] This was a significant step, especially when one considers the historically often troubled relationship between Iran and its Arab neighbours. This diplomatic interaction was then followed by the first provision of substantial tangible military aid from Iran to Oman. This took the form of a large-scale airlift involving over 50 transport aircraft loads of supplies via the Imperial Iranian Air force; a both symbolic but also much needed boost to the Omani war supplies chest.[13] Iranian assistance did not end there. At the end of 1972, Iran provided the first contingent of SF troops to the Omani COIN forces. These, and all Iranian units, were well generously supplied from home with a well-developed and large-scale logistical capability and were essentially self-sufficient. The Iranian contingent deployed to Oman was, at its largest extent during the war, in excess of 3000 men, with over 15,000 personnel from across the Iranian fighting services from Special Forces to Navy serving in total through a system of regular rotation of units, which provided much useful combat experience for Iranian Forces across the board..[14] This deployment eventually consisted of a full brigade, which was supported by artillery, SF, fighter jets and other air force assets such as Chinook helicopters. The Iranian contingent eventually took on the title of the Imperial Iranian Brigade (IIBG).

The intervention by Jordanian and Iranian forces was of key importance to the war and when viewed in broader terms does put the British contribution into some perspective. Not only were there more men provided by Iran than Britain to fight or man the numerous and personnel-intensive static positions, such as the dividing lines on the jebel itself including the Hornbeam Line and the Midway Road, but there was the welcome provision of air assets. Chief amongst these for a large-scale operational area with very little metalled road surface (especially in the Jebel) was heavy lift helicopter transportation capability provided by the Chinook helicopters of the Iranian Air Force. This meant large scale battlefield logistical capability was made available to the SAF for the first time in the war. Due to this new capability, supplies such as ammunition or water or troop units – as well as casualties – could be quickly moved around the battlespace, something inconceivable in the early days of the campaign. Previously, casualties had to be evacuated off the Jebel via stretcher or mule train and eventual onward transportation to out-of-country medical facilities. Prior to the deployment of British Field Surgical Teams (FSTs) after the 1970 coup, the nearest such British facilities were either in Aden (to 1967) or Bahrain. By the time, therefore, a serious casualty had been manhandled off the Jebel and transported to suitable medical facilities his chances of survival rapidly diminished. As stated by contemporary CO of the Muscat Regiment Lieutenant Colonel Peter Thwaites:

> The crying need for helicopters was for casualty evacuation… Every officer had tales to tell of these long marches, with stretchers being man-handled down perpendicular slopes while a man's lifeblood dripped slowly away.[15]

In addition to helicopter lift capability, Iranian support also included maritime assets and the provision of naval supply and ship-borne gunfire assistance to aid land forces. Such large-scale tangible military support had been almost completely unavailable to the SAF, and especially so since the withdrawal of British forces from Aden in 1967.

In terms of quality of contribution, the Iranian forces were often heavily criticised in terms of performance, but in the end their contribution purely in terms of numbers, equipment and extra capability told. Negative feedback or reports on Iranian forces included their 'trigger-happy' or 'shoot-first-and-ask-questions-later' mindset. It also included poor standards of field craft (even at the most basic or elementary level), indiscriminate use of firepower, and often poor performance in both field and contact scenarios which resulted in large scale self-inflicted casualties for their own units on numerous occasions.[16] One particular contemporary issue relating to operating with Artesh forces was the general outlook or attitude of the Iranian troops which raised eyebrows especially to the British officers working in or alongside the SAF. One of these officers was a Royal Marine Captain, Ian Gardner, who went so far as to state:

> [They] need not have been incompetent, but unlike the Omanis, you could not teach the Iranians [soldiers or officers] anything; they knew it all. The sublime combination of arrogance and ignorance was a marvel to behold [especially to the deployed British officers].[17]

Despite these drawbacks, the overall, campaign-level Iranian contribution, in terms of the equipment and extra capability they provided was a key factor in the insurgent defeat. Chief among these factors was the relative and absolute numbers of troops provided to boost Omani COIN forces. The sheer weight of Iranian numbers compared to other supporting forces and the combat capability this added to the armoury of successive CSAFs should not be overlooked, a fact backed up by comments from the victorious SAF commander, Major General Ken Perkins. He personally stated that the extra capability brought by available Iranian troop numbers and associated equipment "…tipped the scales" in the war, and that without such provision the conflict would have descended into a longer, even more drawn out military stalemate.[18]

The narrative, therefore, that the Dhofar campaign was, from a military perspective, for all intents and purposes a purely British operation is put firmly into context. The contribution of the Jordanian and especially the Iranian troops was vital to the latter parts of the campaign and for facilitating the final COIN win; indeed it can be observed that many British accounts of the Dhofar conflict deliberately downplay or actually denigrate the key Iranian campaign contribution.[19] From this perspective it could be said that British assistance in all its guises did not actually win the war; but merely set the ground for eventual victory by preventing the war from being lost earlier in the campaign. It could be argued that an international coalition on behalf of Oman actually therefore sealed the victory, thus the Dhofar War can be seen as a wider partnership at its conclusion.[20] This scenario is at odds with the orthodox/traditional view of the Dhofar War being a fundamentally British COIN campaign and therefore effectively a UK-delivered victory.[21] From this perspective the credit should therefore be spread more evenly between the forces allied to the Sultanate's COIN efforts.

Influence of Omani Sultans

Far from being the compliant puppet or 'client' ruler on behalf of Britain and his British advisors maintained for the servicing of the strategic security interests of the UK, the Sultans of Oman were always technically in charge. They were in charge of their own state, and certainly had a central, indeed pivotal role in the conduct and overall success of the war effort.[22] This is illustrated by the comment by Hughes that: "Nonetheless, the sultans were not passive actors and British 'advice' was not always heeded," on occasion with highly negative consequences for the campaign when viewed in wider terms.[23] They were the acknowledged sovereign heads of state and Commanders-in-Chief of their military forces.

With Sultan Said the issues of under-funding for the SAF, the lack of vital equipment and the need for more infantry units to win the war were clearly highlighted to him by his highly experienced British CSAFs.[24] As the ruler, the timetable of expansion and purchase was always the Sultan's own decision, despite British advice sometimes going against his personal wishes. In addition, despite having a Dhofari wife, Sultan Said generally did not display much in the way of fondness for his provincial subjects. Instead, he insisted on the implementation of repressive measures against them as a form of collective punishment for assisting the insurgents. Examples of such included the capping (concreting over) of wells, the burning of houses (indeed sometimes whole villages or settlements) and destroying of crops by aerial incendiaries (Skyvan aircraft dropped drums of AVTUR jet fuel with attached flares) in food denial actions which helped alienate the Dhofaris further and were an effective recruiting tool for the insurgents.[25] Whether it was for reasons of 'face' or pride or some other culturally-related reason, Sultan Said also refused to pardon surrendered insurgents against the strong advice of his British advisors. This was even the case when the clear benefits of 'leniency' as a strategy to win over insurgents to the government side – as successfully implemented in the Malayan COIN campaign – had been explained in detail to him by his commanders.[26] The Sultan was seemingly only interested in the implementation of harsh or oppressive measures against the insurgents with an attitude which if different – as explained by Colonel Lewis as his CSAF – "could have brought the Dhofar trouble to an end there and then instead of [many] years later."[27]

The negative influence of Sultan Said can also be seen in terms of its effect on Dhofar COIN operations. Correspondence between Sultan Said and his officers shows him to have been overly controlling or getting bogged down on trivial campaign aspects. He was also concerned with relatively irrelevant minutiae instead of the broader strategic picture which, overall, affected the efficiency and operation of the campaign. An example of this overly controlling or strategically-unfocussed trait includes correspondence from Sultan Said to Lieutenant Colonel Peter Thwaites, the Commander of the Muscat Regiment. This reveals a preoccupation with minutiae, and not with grand strategy or operational details which were in his remit as Sultan but, for instance, on the movement of single weapons or small amounts of ammunition from the Salalah armoury for military use.[28] Sultan Said also meddled in junior officer or NCO-level decisions such as the arrival dates in Oman of junior seconded officers or even about the distribution of building supplies by the resident SAF battalion in Dhofar.[29] This does not suggest that Sultan Said was either thinking or working at the strategic level. It suggests, on the contrary, that he was a micro-manager who was focussed on low level issues and who did not really trust those around him to do their jobs properly.

From a military operational perspective, from the initial SAF deployment in 1964 the Sultan refused to put his Dhofar Force 'private army' under the SAF, and therefore British seconded officer-run CSAF control. They were not even permitted to be used for static guarding-related duties to release troops for combat duties in the province. Whether he trusted his Pakistani contract officers who commanded the Dhofar Force more than his seconded British officers is an interesting question. Either way, this hampered initial operations for the newly deployed SAF which had no previous experience of the province, unlike the resident Dhofar Force. The permanently resident force lived and breathed Dhofar and its social and geographic nuances on a daily basis and so could have been of invaluable use to the SAF and the overall war effort, especially in the early stages of the insurgency when the Adoo were at their weakest. In addition to this aspect, the Sultan also refused to commission many Omani officers and did not let them command fighting troops which put much greater strain on the limited contract and seconded British officer contingent of the SAF.[30] To many it seemed the Omani officers were just put in place 'for show' and Sultan Said had no real intention of giving them any authority within the chain of command; likely to avoid potential coup issues as had been the case in other Middle Eastern countries during the 1950s, 1960s and 1970s. The Sultan also regularly intervened in other military issues which should have been the remit of SAF officers or at least the CSAF or his senior commanders, and this included intelligence; and related personnel issues. Sultan Said initially refused permission for an intelligence officer to be allowed into his personal fiefdom when the SAF were first deployed to Dhofar. He caveated this decision by stating that he would provide Colonel Lewis as his overall commander with any intelligence information relating to the province that he might need.[31] Another such incident was the sacking of Major Bob Brown who was one of the key intelligence officers in Dhofar, which had far-reaching operational effects. CSAF

Brigadier Corran Purdon asserted that the Sultan did not fully trust Major Brown – or more likely was suspicious of the effective network of informers Brown had set up in the province – and insisted on his dismissal which left him as the commander of the war effort 'blind' in terms of intelligence, especially from the HUMINT (Human Intelligence) perspective.[32] More concerningly perhaps, he further stated, "The lack of good intelligence was to be prevalent during my time and I often wonder if we could have seized an early victory had Bob [Brown] remained; I believe we could have."[33] This illustrates how much of a negative influence Sultan Said was on the wartime intelligence picture in Dhofar, with all the associated second and third order effects in terms of the campaign. Even his most senior commander was subsequently effectively of the opinion that the Sultan's actions probably lengthened the war.

Funding for his military forces and civilian development programmes within Oman was another area where Sultan Said negatively impacted the war effort. No one it seems could persuade Sultan Said to spend the required level of funds on the armed forces or to instigate large enough scale civilian development programmes which may have removed the major causes of Dhofari discontent. This may have headed off the rebellion at an earlier stage. Sultan Said considered the developing insurgency to be simply another tribally-based rebellion which could be managed and defeated in due course as necessary in the mould of the Imamate Rebellion and its leaders (brothers) Ghalib and Talib bin Ali and Sulayman bin Himyar. Like the Imamate uprising, he considered that he could handle the situation utilising his long experience as the ruler and detailed knowledge of his peoples, allied to the liberal distribution of funds where required to lubricate negotiations or 'buy' allies, and failing that the use of military force. The expectation from Sultan Said's perspective was that the Adoo would eventually 'fold' with minimal intervention and that life would quickly get back to normal as it had done in the past. This was not to be the case.

All such factors combined were leading to a situation where British officials believed the Sultan, in Dhofar, "may have written himself a prescription for ultimate defeat".[34] It was this type of intractability on behalf of Sultan Said which helped facilitate the coup in 1970.[35] The Sultan's inflexibility and somewhat naïve assessment of the roots of the rebellion and type of conflict helped lead to a critical situation in both Dhofar and northern Oman with insurgent activity also taking place much closer to the capital. All of this led to his eventual downfall. Eventually the UK government's patience with Sultan Said's administration and its approach to and performance in the war was exhausted and the coup was instigated with both British agreement and input to help salvage the Dhofar COIN campaign.[36]

It was not just Sultan Said who had a sometimes-negative impact on the campaign or frustrated British efforts to defeat the insurgents. Despite having a positive impact in several areas, Sultan Qaboos arguably also had a similarly negative impact at times. On acceding to the throne, Sultan Qaboos provided positive input which assisted the British-officer run campaign. This was achieved – in compliance with British advice – by starting to roll back or rectifying a number of the issues that were either contributory causes or at least facilitators of the insurgency in the first place, or hindered the campaign against the Adoo. Like his father, Qaboos was also not a compliant 'puppet' ruler. As time progressed, he increasingly began to assert his authority in areas such as procurement and even on some operational matters and make his own decisions. This was not always positive and sometimes went against sound and experienced British advice. It has been stated that:

> From the beginning of his reign, the sultan worked to limit British influence over his government. His resistance intensified as Oman enjoyed a windfall of oil wealth beginning in 1973. For better or for worse, Qaboos himself has a significant role in the emergence of Oman in the period 1970–1977.[37]

Although Sultan Qaboos was highly inexperienced in terms of governance and relied heavily on his resident British advisors, he eventually moved to employ his own pick of Arab advisors and courted American contacts to aid his administration and country. Previously, in a similar vein to his father, such close and influential advisors would have been almost exclusively British. The influence of such new advisors on the scene also trickled down into areas crucial to the Dhofar War. Procurement was one such issue, and the new advisors influenced the awarding of both civilian and military contracts and Britain, or British advisors, were increasingly sidelined from major non-military or operational wartime decisions. A key or select group of such advisors are identified collectively as the so-called "Muscat Mafia".[38] The Sultan allowed a cabal of non-British advisors to form around him, often brokered by trusted 'inner circle' advisors such as Tim Landon. The new faces at court were mainly of Arabic origin, but also from the USA, and all such appointments were a threat to British influence over Omani policy in general and over the Sultan specifically. Such new advisors included the politically well-connected Libyan businessmen Omer Barouni and Yahya Omer. The new group of advisors also included the British-educated Saudi banker, Ghassan Shaker, and all became trusted confidants of the Sultan. Collectively, they gained influential and even powerful positions within the Omani governing hierarchy. This included not only influence over procurement and contracting decisions but also diplomatic policy, and their collective sway served to displace much of the courtly and impartial advice of the Sultan's previously largely British advisors which went back decades in his father's rule.³⁹ It was Shaker who later introduced the Sultan to the influential and well-connected Robert B. Anderson. Anderson was formerly a cabinet-level member of Dwight D. Eisenhower's Presidential administration, serving variously as Secretary to the Treasury and Assistant Secretary of Defense, and he became a regular fixture in this new, often secretive, inner circle of advisors to Sultan Qaboos.⁴⁰ The connections provided by such advisors bore fruit for Oman. Britain was the key overall mover behind the scenes to help Oman navigate, and remove the objections of other countries to gain memberships of international organisations early on Qaboos's reign, but Anderson in particular played his part. His connections within the US administration and personal links to King Faisal of Saudi Arabia were key to removing the existing Saudi objections to Oman joining the Arab League and then the UN, and were on a par or perhaps more important in sealing this arrangement than UK efforts in this regard manoeuvring.⁴¹ Through such background contacts and manoeuvring, that Oman became a member of these two important global institutions was not just a 'nice to have'. From a public relations perspective it showcased legitimate Omani independence and that the Omanis were running their own affairs. At the same time it also stymied some of the arguments of the insurgents and their international supporters for exactly the same reason. Oman was not under some sort of Imperial yoke; it was making its own way. Being on the inside (as opposed to outside which was Sultan Said's preference) also helped Oman address issues of perception and strategic messaging. It was also key to win to counter insurgent or supporting nation (PDRY and Egyptian for example) propaganda or influence on important actors and decision-makers within these two key international organisations, which therefore had a direct impact on the evolution of the war and its eventual outcome. From the British perspective, these outcomes were undoubtedly useful in campaign terms, but the sway of such new advisors did represent a level of undermining of its overall historical influence over the Sultans of Oman and its ability to get things 'done' with regards to the ongoing Dhofar campaign.

New cabal of advisors aside, Qaboos also at times disagreed with his key British advisors on the issue of military procurement which ultimately had operational impacts. His insistence on certain actions affected the financial control of Oman's military budget by funnelling resources to expensive and 'non-essential' military projects and therefore away from front line SAF units in Dhofar and the main war effort. Instead of concentrating all available funds (including by this time healthy oil revenues) to the basic, and relatively simple largely infantry-based theatre requirements of the SAF at the coal face in Dhofar, Qaboos wanted to purchase expensive equipment that his British advisors thought an unwise and unnecessary use of limited resources.[42] Two significant examples of this negative trait were the Sultan's insistence on purchasing the British-made Rapier air defence system and the Anglo-French Jaguar ground attack aircraft. Despite their own national allegiance, British advisors considered both Rapier and Jaguar strategically and operationally unnecessary and far too expensive for Oman at that time, given the long-term service contracts and training requirements above and beyond actual unit purchase. Hinting at what was perhaps the real reason for Qaboos's interest in such military hardware, the incumbent CSAF Major General Creasey considering it primarily a "status symbol" purchase, with Qaboos effectively 'keeping up with the Joneses' with his fellow Middle Eastern monarchs on who had the latest and best military kit.[43] In a similar vein, Qaboos also seriously explored the possibility of purchasing Mirage jets from France, highlighting his determination to have prestige fighter jets in his military, and against the practical advice given, eventually forced through the purchase of both Rapier and Jaguar aircraft, later telling the final wartime CSAF, Major General Kenneth Perkins just to 'get on with it'.[44] As alluded to by Major General Creasey, these were arguably essentially 'vanity purchases'. They were, at least in part, aimed to maintain the dignity of the Sultan with his wealthier and more militarily powerful neighbours, lacked operational justification, and placed a large strain on Oman's available resources and questioned Qaboos's economic and military judgement.[45]

Such purchases were part of a "guns and butter approach" of large-scale military expenditure allied to an equally ambitious national infrastructure and social development programme.[46] This was a have-it-all approach funded by increased oil revenues but not backed up by any measure of fiscal experience or prudence. The result, despite the best efforts of British advice to mitigate its effects, eventually brought Oman to the verge of financial and economic collapse in 1975 which put the war effort in jeopardy.[47] These episodes expose some perhaps questionable traits of Qaboos's leadership and judgement or simply a lack of experience. Either way it put the war effort at risk, strained British patience, and required the latter to intervene to shore up Omani finances. It also, however, illustrates Qaboos' willingness to overrule his advisors and rule as he saw fit. It also shows he was gaining confidence in his role as Sultan, and was not afraid to make bold decisions on economic, military and other issues which were key to the war effort. This overspending or arguably financially reckless trait was never fully mitigated. Later, Sultan Qaboos was to undertake a similarly impractical purchase of British Challenger tanks in the years after the war against the advice of his British advisors. Whilst a useful move perhaps in terms of 'defence diplomacy' and giving business to his friends and allies,

Challengers were designed for fighting Warsaw Pact forces on the plains of central Europe and were not for the deserts of the Arabian Peninsula.[48]

From procurement and wider advice on financial issues, Sultan Qaboos also had occasion to disagree with his British military advisors on wartime operational matters. On several of these he overruled his British advisors and arguably jeopardised the war effort. A key example of this trait was the airstrikes ordered against PDRY targets in retaliation for the latter's military attack on the Omani border fort located at Habrut in early May 1972. Qaboos was insistent on a policy of airstrikes to deter further PDRY artillery bombardments and cross-border insertions by Yemeni regular troops. This was in part to even the score, but also to maintain 'face' or honour with his enemies, allies or regional neighbours. UK officials in London, and several of the Sultan's British advisors were against such a move due to the potential not just for Oman but – and probably most important from London's perspective – the UK too to be drawn not only into a prolonged internal insurgency, but potential escalation into conflict between Oman and the PDRY. This would have risked the potential for serious diplomatic repercussions for Britain in the Cold War climate and the volatile contemporary Middle Eastern region as a whole. The campaign would likely have been affected with Arab League and UN intervention pushed by the Soviet bloc which would have meant Oman losing any diplomatic advantage. This scenario would likely have destroyed any practical operational momentum towards Omani victory over the insurgents. It would also have diverted diplomatic and military assets away from the main effort of fighting the war in Dhofar against non-state insurgent actors to a potentially more serious military stand-off with the state forces of the PDRY and possible military engagement by other Soviet state proxies.

Ultimately, although against the direct advice of many of his key advisors and especially British officials, Sultan Qaboos got his way with retaliatory airstrikes. These were launched in the last week of May 1972, primarily against the town of Hauf. This was the 'safe' base area for the Dhofari insurgents located inside PDRY territory and previously untouchable since Britain's military withdrawal from Aden in 1967. Seeing the determination of Qaboos to proceed with the cross-border airstrikes, the UK government could only insist on a compromise brokered by the CSAF, Brigadier John Graham and the British Ambassador to Oman, Donald Hawley, to mitigate the potential political fallout. The 'deal' struck was that no seconded or loaned serving British officers were to take part in the action. The airstrike and artillery bombardment operation, known as Operation AQOOBA (Punishment) was not only undertaken by, but was also even 'ordered' by privately-contracted British officers only.[49] After consultation with Ambassador Hawley, blank pages of standard SAF HQ headed paper were signed by Colonel Colin Maxwell as the Deputy CSAF and importantly also the SAF's senior contract officer. These signed blank pages were then retrospectively completed with specific operational orders for AQOOBA as dictated by the seconded CSAF (Brigadier Graham). The operational plans of the seconded CSAF were then carried out to the letter, although they were officially authorised by another Briton; a contract officer and not one loaned to the Sultanate by the UK. Even though this provided a level of deniability to the British government, the potential for at least a dilution of operational effort in Dhofar and greater international interest, or worse, interference in the COIN campaign was real. This emphasises the reality that Britain did not have the authority or ability to compel, order or even directly influence Qaboos not to proceed on something he had set his mind to. Whilst British influence on the campaign was strong and, in many ways, highly influential, the UK did not 'own' or run the campaign as such. This was ultimately the realm of the Sultan. Sultan Said showed he was in charge on numerous occasions, and the extent of his control can be seen by the negative consequences on the Dhofar campaign via his whims, prejudices and resulting decisions. Although Sultan Qaboos was more supportive to British plans and ideas:

> While he benefitted from British guidance, particularly in the conduct of the campaign against the insurgency in Dhofar, Qaboos's own beliefs, the views of fellow monarchs in the Middle East, and the counsel of his Arab and American advisors were at least as important in influencing his decisions, many of which ran counter to British advice.[50]

In addition to sometimes negative influence on policy, procurement, and even the strategy of the Dhofar COIN campaign, there also exists a narrative that victory in the war was influenced, decisively controlled, or even effectively won exclusively by the hand of the Sultan himself. This minority view asserts that the main reason the war was won was because of the leadership and strategic skills, knowledge and prowess of Sultan Qaboos.[51] The view holds that it was the Sultan's wise leadership and overall strategic outlook that was the key element in the insurgent defeat once Qaboos succeeded to the throne in 1970 and his talents in this field were able to be realised as the Sultanate's leader. It also describes how, having been both the architect and driving force behind liberating his country from the consequences of his father's autocratic, authoritarian, and reactionary rule (which kept the country in a perpetual state of social and economic underdevelopment and essentially in a rather 'dismal' condition) his leadership and abilities were the primary reason for the insurgent defeat in 1975.[52] This view also emphasises how Qaboos's military training and experience, allied to his leadership abilities enabled him to 'out-strategise' the insurgents and bring about their defeat.[53] This is certainly a minority view in the Dhofar War literature and has sycophantic undertones. A more realistic counterview suggests that:

> The official [Omani] version [of events], spelt out in a succession of nicely produced booklets aimed at journalists and other opinion formers for 'guidance' is that Qaboos sprang, fully loaded so to speak, onto the stage, waved a wand … and transformed his country [and proceeded to win the war almost] overnight.[54]

John Beasant and Christopher Ling put forward the opinion that this sort of reporting was simply political "spin" and that such excessive claims throughout Qaboos' reign, quite often designed by the Sultan's Ministry of Information would have embarrassed even the Third Reich's notorious information spin-master, Dr. Josef Goebbels![55] This latter day tendency for revisionism and to various extents rather whitewashed official narratives or similarly sycophantic viewpoints or statements quite unfairly draw attention from (or even negate in the minds of many) the undeniably positive influence of the new 29-year-old Sultan on the social and economic development of the Sultanate and on forging the conditions which allowed the eventual insurgent defeat.[56] In many ways, Qaboos did have a profoundly positive effect on the country and the Dhofar conflict. He brought a very different governing style and set of priorities to the leadership of his country. This development had a decisive effect on the modernisation of the country and included the reversal of many of his father's repressive policies which alienated Dhofaris especially, and a more progressive social agenda. This was no doubt helped by the fact that Qaboos was not an 'outsider' from Northern Oman or Muscat. Qaboos's mother was a Dhofari, and he was born in the province and grew up there. He had never lived in or even ever visited the Sultanate's capital city of Muscat. He was much more 'one of us' from the Dhofari perspective than his father and indeed many others with power or influence. This clarity of purpose exhibited by Sultan Qaboos was strongly allied to the priority to do what it took to support his military commanders. This was done via the allocation of the necessary funds for vital equipment and the expansion of the armed forces as per British-formulated plans, and his agreement to external help such as the vital assistance of the SAS (which was banned under his father) to eventually deal successfully with the insurgency. As a result of this determination Sultan Qaboos was able to announce victory in December 1975. This was quite an extraordinary situation given that the war had been close to defeat for the Sultanate only a few years prior.

Britain's influence on the Dhofar campaign can, therefore, be seen to be very substantial, but not complete by any stretch of the imagination. Although coming at a later stage of the campaign, the important influence of both Jordan and Iran should be fully considered as a counterweight to the traditional UK-centric view of the war. In addition, the not-insubstantial influence of the Sultans of Oman should be added to the weight of argument, from both a positive and negative perspective. This acts to temper the traditional perspectives of virtual British dominance over the entirety of the Dhofar COIN campaign.[57]

Chapter 11

The Changing Nature of the British Role

Whilst the 'for' and 'against' narratives relating to British influence over the Dhofar COIN campaign are collectively dominant and are in many ways highly valid, such views do not provide a complete or accurate explanation of what occurred with regards to overall British influence. Even with large swathes of both credible secondary (largely book) and primary (archival) references to support such narratives the reality is, however, considerably more nuanced. A more balanced view of British influence is that Britain's role evolved significantly over the course of the war. This viewpoint acknowledges that on the one hand, both the pro and anti-British influence narratives are in many ways correct. On the other hand it also puts forward the idea that these are only partly correct as they neglect the bigger picture shift in influence over the campaign's duration.

What started out effectively as a British-led campaign from the early deployments into Dhofar by the SAF under the leadership of Colonel Lewis and could not be won by UK assistance alone, morphed over time into an international coalition.[1] This further enabled the overall British-engineered war strategy to be implemented, as well as the final operations in and around the Sherishitti Caves complex to be successfully conducted and victory finally declared. In conventional terms, therefore, the Dhofar campaign cannot be described as British. This is because the UK did not provide all the necessary supplies or logistical support or even carry out the majority of the kinetic 'fighting' actions to ensure victory as Britain's relative numerical and tangible influence waned over time.[2] With reference to Britain's other classical-era COIN campaigns, the exact opposite was the case in Malaya, Brunei/early Borneo and even in Northern Ireland. In terms, however, of command, strategy and the execution of the campaign as well as – hitherto unseen – in terms of state-building efforts Britain's role remained decisive from the start of the war until its conclusion. Overall, it can be credibly argued that the Dhofar campaign was most influenced by Britain, but the more subtle reality is that this was not, however, a situation that remained static throughout its duration. What started very much as a majority British influenced or controlled COIN campaign was to change over time to a situation where Britain's influence diminished significantly, and can be divided broadly into three time-specific phases.[3]

In phase 1 (1965-70), the war can can be considered largely 'British' in almost all respects. Alongside the general level of cooperation with and influence over Oman by Britain gained through centuries of interaction and at times intervention (such as the 1920 Treaty of Sib and the later Jebel Akhdar Rebellion), the precursor agreements in 1958 known as the 'Exchange of Letters' was the moment Britain's official role in Oman was formalised. Although British Indian troops and their UK officers had been deployed to and served in the Sultanate on numerous occasions, the difference was now that serving personnel – largely officers – were seconded or loaned directly to the Sultan's military. This was both to train and develop the force along professional lines. Not just in terms of personnel, British commitment was also formalised in terms of specified sums of money to be provided by the UK government to Oman as start-up capital as well as ongoing running costs for the newly reorganised and named – or perhaps more accurately 'created' – Sultan's Armed Forces. This commitment is illustrated by the fact that when the SAF was despatched in 1964 to deal with the embryonic Dhofar Insurgency, it did so not only with a loaned serving British officer as the overall force commander, but a large percentage of the regimental field officers of the SAF's combat units were of a similar status.[4] As a result, both the organisational structure and subsequent fighting ability of the SAF was almost wholly a result of the support afforded to the Sultanate by the UK government. This was because Oman simply did not have either the finances or the expertise to undertake the overall task on its own. During this period, the preponderance of British advisors was made more complete because Sultan Said effectively left them to get on with governmental business in Muscat whilst he set up his court on a permanent basis hundreds of miles away in Salalah from 1958. Whilst he directed his (British) Military Secretary and his subordinate CSAF on broad strategic matters from Salalah, day-to-day operational and theatre management of the Dhofar campaign was effectively left up to them. A cohort of other Muscat-based British advisors also effectively ran all aspects of the Sultanate's governance under the same broad arrangements.

During Phase 2 (1970 to late-1972), the Sultan's many negative influences on the military campaign, including his stubborn resistance to sound British advice on issues such as the introduction of an amnesty for insurgents reached the point of no return in British eyes by early 1970. At this point it was the British government that facilitated and ensured the success of the July 1970 palace coup which removed Sultan Said from power with the aim of changing governance to enable a flagging COIN campaign and take the initiative once more against the insurgents.[5] Following the coup, the British government then quickly formed the Interim Advisory Council (IAC). This was an emergency committee of key – largely British – individuals from the governmental, military and business communities. It was handed extraordinary powers to ensure all aspects of governance continued in as seamless a fashion as possible given the upheaval of the coup. This was done to 'hold the fort' whilst Sultan Qaboos cemented his authority and the business of ruling got back to normal and to prevent the new administration failing before it even got started. In addition to this was the central requirement for the military campaign to continue unabated. Part of this was the need to ensure the commanders had all resources necessary to maintain maximum pressure on the insurgents so the latter could not exploit any confusion or lack of focus caused by the change in power structures after the coup. British influence at this point therefore remained both central and key to the execution of the war. In the immediate post-coup era, British advice was to bolster military efforts alongside a wide-ranging civil development programme to work hand in hand to bring the Dhofari, and especially Jebali inhabitants across to the government side in terms of their support.

This was a conscious element of what might be termed a traditional British 'hearts and minds' approach to COIN. It was largely facilitated from the British perspective through the deployment of 22 SAS Regiment to Dhofar and utilising their unique intelligence, training, and covert warfare skill sets to best effect. This was undertaken in conjunction with the deployment of other regular UK military support-related units including the RAF Regiment (airfield defence), Royal Artillery (airfield defence, spotters, technical support), Royal Engineers ('hearts and minds'-related well digging, civil construction projects as well as minefield laying/enemy mine disposal and cross Jebel barrier construction), Intelligence Corps, Veterinary Corps and army and RAF Field Surgical Teams (FSTs). The 'hearts and minds' strategy with UK Special Forces personnel firmly at the core of all related activities was borne of successful similar such programmes undertaken in previous British COIN campaigns such as in Malaya or Brunei/Borneo. The approach was used to either win over support of, or intimidate or compel the general population away from either actively aiding or merely supporting the insurgent cause and back into the government fold in a combined and highly managed 'sticks and carrots' approach.[6] Additional to this was the introduction of a programme of amnesty for insurgents with financial incentives for 'defecting' and bringing across insurgent weaponry which mirrored aspects of eventual British policy and efforts in previous COIN campaigns. Perhaps the classic example of this was the Malayan Insurgency where policy changed from prosecuting SEPs to a *de facto* approach of non-prosecution to encourage more to defect to the government side and weaken the insurgent cause.[7]

In Phase 2, the 1970 Palace Coup and the developments which took place in the days and weeks which followed it clearly point to a situation of near complete British dominance over not only the Dhofar War, but over Oman itself. This can be observed through the British-instigated change of leadership in the country. The British-imposed IAC – as chaired by Briton Colonel Hugh Oldman – and mostly comprising other British personalities from the UK state, Sultan's service or private sector perspectives also effectively ran the country for several weeks until Qaboos's uncle Tariq arrived in Oman to take up the Prime Minister role. The latter IAC grouping included the influential heads of the British Bank of the Middle East (BBME) and the PDO oil company. Throughout Phase 2, there was also clear reliance on both seconded and regular British military personnel and later units to prosecute the COIN operations in Dhofar. Perhaps the ultimate expression of this influence is illustrated by the Battle of Mirbat in July 1972. Here, British and UK-trained and controlled forces decisively defeated the Adoo when the latter attempted a large-scale conventional assault on the town. Such occurrences serve to illustrate the both central and decisive influence of Britain over Oman and the Dhofar campaign up until 1972. Despite this influence, concrete success in the Dhofar campaign certainly did not occur immediately after the coup which brought Sultan Qaboos to the throne. Paramount British influence during Phase 2 did not secure a quick win in the conflict from this high point of influence. Once Sultan Qaboos had 'found his feet' and consolidated his position which included the diversification of the advisors from which he took counsel, the overarching influence, or even control of the UK in Oman and the Dhofar campaign began to diminish. This was in part through the influence on the administration and leadership of Oman of other advisors chosen by Qaboos, from ex-US politician Robert B. Anderson to the previously alluded to Mafia-like grouping which had Qaboos's ear on many policy matters and aspects of high level military procurement.[8] Such individuals eventually took over the functions and role of the IAC and side-lined the position of the Sultan's Uncle, Tariq, whose presence in the Sultanate's administration as Prime Minister was a UK diplomatic initiative to help legitimise, and gain acceptance for the new administration. Being denied the freedom of manoeuvre within the administration and with the Sultan's centralisation of power roles within government Tariq eventually resigned his post and left both the administration and Oman itself before the year was out.[9]

This situation of overarching influence up until 1972 did not last. The virtual monopoly of Britain's influence over the Dhofar campaign changed significantly and in a relatively short time period in Phase 3 of the war (late 1972–75). Although the number of British military personnel was eventually increased to in the region of 1000 individuals and the CSAF and key SAF officers remained British, the relative level of the UK's influence diminished.[10] This was due in part to the long-held view in British government and civil service circles that an open-ended commitment to Oman in the conflict was undesirable. It was considered that any assistance such as the deployment of the SAS in up to two squadron strength, should be short term, so few further assets of large scale or cost were committed to the campaign.[11] The search was, therefore, on for a more equitable solution. The quick 'snowball effect' victory envisaged as stemming from Operation JAGUAR in 1971 did not materialise as had been hoped by British planners. With an ongoing campaign allied to Britain's own economic and military issues, British diplomatic efforts were concentrated on the broadening of relations and ties between Oman and its neighbours to enable extra help for the War effort to be procured.[12] In conjunction with Britain's decreased influence at Court on many non-militarily operational matters due to the increasing sway of non-British advisors from 1972, the balance changed significantly. The long-standing situation of virtual British-only support changed relatively quickly into a perhaps unlikely-looking coalition spanning Europe to the Middle East in which the UK's contribution was quickly overtaken in comparative terms.[13] Through the efforts of British diplomacy, plus an increasingly assertive Sultan, both significant and sizeable support in the form of financial aid or direct military aid was proactively assembled from across the Arabian Peninsula and wider Middle East, especially from Jordan and eventually – and most substantially – from Iran. In terms of the latter, a situation developed where the Iranians at maximum strength deployed over three times as many troops in Oman as compared to Britain, and allied to the addition of the sizeable Jordanian contingent this represented a combined number of troops available for Dhofar operations which in numerical terms was over quadruple that of the British contribution.[14] This was a highly significant change in both relative and absolute troop number contributions to the war effort and facilitated a shift in influence in terms of who did the majority of the fighting and who was responsible for most of the material gains against the insurgents in theatre. This was due in part to the situation that although technically under CSAF's command, the Iranian forces reported to the Shah directly. This situation and the fact that policies such as the regular rotation of Iranian troops were undertaken illustrates the influence of the Shah behind the scenes of COIN force capability; often to the frustration of the British officer formally charged with prosecuting the war.[15]

Despite their many and well-documented drawbacks and negative characteristics, the cumulative mass of Iranian troop numbers and firepower as well as air force assets in theatre (both fighter jets and helicopters) proved pivotal in terms of taking the fight to the insurgents in an effective manner, and an essential factor in achieving the eventual victory.[16] It has been described how, "Only Iran's direct military intervention and the dramatic growth of Oman's financial resources after the 1973 oil crisis provided the resources to conduct large-scale offensive operations."[17] In terms of military numbers and operational capability it could be legitimately argued that the Iranians were perhaps more important from a practical, or 'boots on the ground' perspective in 1975 than Britain in winning the Dhofar War and ending the insurgency. The Jordanian, and especially Iranian, military contributions represented a significant situational change from the British-only funded, trained, supplied, officered and led forces pitched against the Dhofari insurgents in Phase 1 of the campaign. It therefore represented a key reduction in British operational control and influence. This was the case despite the fact that the serving British Army CSAF remained technically in overall command of the new, and more diverse 'international' war effort.

Unlike in all previous classical-era UK COIN campaigns, Britain also did not exercise complete control at the highest level, unlike in all previous classical UK COIN campaigns, as the Sultan remained technically in overall charge of his armed forces and their operational efforts. This was despite the fact that his armed forces were led and administered by British officers at all levels. Although the CSAF and most other senior commanders or regimental commanding officers were seconded British armed forces personnel, the majority of SAF officers at all levels were 'contract' personnel with no direct contractual or legal obligation to the UK government or its armed forces. Such officers worked directly for the Omani government and the SAF as private individuals subject to equally private contractual arrangements. Although largely recruited through a UK company with strong links to the British government, technically they would be classed as mercenaries. The Sultan or his senior non-British advisors therefore had the power to terminate contracts and 'hire and fire' as they saw fit. In addition to this important aspect, steadily over time and via a proactive policy the new, yet now more settled and confident Sultan continued to diversify the background of the close advisors he surrounded himself with towards non-British personnel, which formed a "palace clique" meaning British access to the Sultan on many – especially non-military – issues was reduced.[18] This contributed in part to the many occasions where, for better or worse Qaboos actually elected to overrule his remaining British advisors. This situation further eroded Britain's influence over the new Sultan, in Oman generally and specifically over the ongoing Dhofar COIN campaign.

Additionally, neither Sultan Said or Qaboos were wholly dominated by the UK as was the case throughout its Empire as Oman was never formally British territory and always remained a sovereign entity. Although the UK held considerable sway over the Omani leaders in the past, the situation rapidly changed after the accession of Sultan Qaboos; and especially so after 1971. Previously, through choice and as part of bilateral agreements, however, Sultan

Said effectively sub-contracted the running of much of his affairs to the UK, which was especially the case in relation to external affairs. By choice, the Sultanate had no seat in the UN and as requested by Sultan Said, Britain represented its interests in this forum all the way until October 1971 when Oman was admitted.[19] A month prior to this in September 1971, Oman was also admitted to the Arab League and the first diplomatic missions were set up abroad as well as the first non-UK or Indian embassies in Muscat. All such actions had the effect of enhancing the image of an independent and fully sovereign Oman, no longer under the 'imperialist yoke' of Britain. They also had the effect of diminishing UK influence over Omani affairs and ultimately, therefore, over the Dhofar campaign itself.

After his succession in 1970, Sultan Qaboos was initially highly dependent on UK-provided advice and security to ensure the survival of his new administration, but this also changed over time. As the new Sultan settled into his new role and started to explore his new found power, he started to proactively and progressively push back on the almost complete British influence over his country and the war which he observed.[20] Slowly but surely, as his confidence grew he began to question his advisors more. He took more policy decisions and in general assumed a more assertive leadership role on all aspects of governance and the social and economic development of the Sultanate and the ways in which the country's new found oil wealth was utilised. This more 'hands on' style of governance was also seen in terms of the ongoing war in Dhofar that he inherited. Qaboos was mindful of the experience and advice of his British advisors, but he did not leave virtually all decisions to his commanders as was the general approach of his father. He had input, made decisions and was not shy in overruling such advisors on military procurement issues as well as – on occasion – on operational matters which caused some consternation with British officials.[21] At the time of victory in 1975, the Sultan had not only survived as Oman's leader but had managed to consolidate his power and position. Whilst achieving this he had successfully limited British influence over his administration and pushed through to reality a much-needed large-scale social and infrastructure development programme. Sultan Qaboos also benefitted from the emergence of Oman onto the international diplomatic scene. For the first time the Sultanate had a seat in the Arab League and UN, as well as a diplomatic corps with representatives stationed around the world. This was something verging on unthinkable in 1970 under the previous ruler. It reinforced the international perception of Oman as an independent nation with its ruler at the helm, and a war under the control of a sovereign entity.

Britain's historic economic influence over Oman also began to weaken significantly post-coup in 1970. From Sultan Said being effectively dependent on British funding to run his country and for the war effort, Sultan Qaboos enjoyed increasing oil revenues. This had the unexpected result of effecting a four-fold increase in overall state income due to the 1973 oil crisis which was a timely boost to the war chest for the Dhofar campaign and for overall governance efforts in the realms of social development, for example.[22] The plentiful income now flowing into the state's coffers was not just used for priorities such as the war effort or social development programmes. Despite an expansive war being fought in Omani territory and unlike his relatively frugal father, Qaboos undoubtedly had a flair for spending, and some might even term it 'conspicuous consumption'. Because they had no power to stop it, this often chaffed with his British advisors because they could see that such spending in the middle of a war was not practical, but also from a public relations perspective was both undesirable and sent the 'wrong' message to multiple audiences. Prime examples of this penchant for spending by Qaboos were the building of luxurious new palaces. This included the rebuilding of the historic Al Alam palace in Muscat and later projects such as the large-scale Bait Al Baraka palace complex located outside the capital at Seeb, designed to be the primary residence for the Sultan in Northern Oman.[23] Wartime palace-building expenses aside, the Sultan also overruled his British advisors on expensive procurement issues. Key examples were the previously highlighted purchase of the Rapier Air Defence system and Jaguar aircraft. Qaboos opted to purchase these despite sound advice from his advisors that they were too expensive and not the priority for military expenditure in Dhofar. Prestige is likely the motive behind both the palace building expenditure and a key rationale for the insistence on such military equipment purchases.

By 1973 and phase 3 of the war, Oman was effectively financially and diplomatically free from Britain's overarching influence for the first time since at least 1861. The financial links were to live on however. The British Bank of the Middle East (BBME) provided large loans to see the Qaboos administration through the 1975 'mini' financial crisis brought on by overspending and lack of financial discipline and control by the Sultan and his government.[24] Although the CSAF as a seconded or loan officer provided by the British government delivered overall victory to the Sultanate, he did so as a loyal subordinate to the by now stable, well-established, non-economically dependent and increasingly wealthy administration of Sultan Qaboos. This is a key point which clearly illustrates the 'evening up' of the power relationship between Oman and Britain. In the Qaboos era, Britain worked alongside the Sultan of Oman now as a much more equal partner in the war than had been the case in the past under Sultan Said's rule. The ruler the UK installed in a coup as a pliant replacement for his father was now very much in charge, and was his own man.

Table 4: Britain And Dhofar COIN Campaign – 'Sliding Scale Of Influence' Phases.

Phases	CSAF Tenure	Key Features/Events
PHASE 1 1964–1970	Col. T. Lewis Brig. C. Purdon	Operations from Muscat controlled largely by UK advisors, 'Exchange' of Letters provides funding to form the SAF, and provides its senior and regimental leadership
PHASE 2 1970-late-1972	Brig .J. Graham	British instigated Palace coup (1970) which brings Sultan Qaboos to power Represents 'high point' of British Influence (Interim Advisory Council forms, increase in direct British military support – e.g. SAS deployment – 'Hearts and Minds' campaign initiated and pivotal SAS-facilitated win at Battle of Mirbat in July 1972) Beginning of decline in British influence (Arrival of Tariq as Prime Minister, Arab League and UN memberships gained, and Omani officer training school established)
PHASE 3 late-1972–1975	Maj-Gen T. Creasey Maj-Gen K. Perkins	Further continued decline in British diplomatic and advisor influence Arrival of Jordanian and Iranian troops and equipment from 1972* By 1975, c. 5,000 Omani troops, 1200 Firqa, 3000 Iranians, 800 Jordanians and just c. 1000 UK troops** Majority of offensive operations in Western theatre spearheaded by Iranian troops backed up by Iranian air and sea assets

* J.E. Peterson, *Oman's Insurgencies: The Sultanate's Struggle for Supremacy* (Lebanon: Saqi, 2007) p.482–485
** Marc DeVore, 'The United Kingdom's Last Hot War of the Cold War: Oman 1963–75' *Cold War History*, First article 1–31, (2011) p.20
Stephen Quick, *The Dhofar War: British Covert Campaigning in Arabia 1965–1975* (Exeter: Exeter University Press, 2024) p.8–14

Chapter 12

Evolution of British Political and Economic Influence

For over two hundred years prior to the start of the Dhofar War, Britain enjoyed an expansive history of influence in Muscat and Oman, which later directly affected both its conduct and the campaign's eventual result. This influence ranged from cooperation to intervention when deemed necessary, as well as the historical financial and military assistance provided by the British Indian Colonial administration and latterly by the British government itself. This historical influence included the Canning Award/Zanzibar 'subsidy'. This was the financial arrangement put in place to compensate the Ruler of Muscat when the wealthy territory of Zanzibar was split from his control in 1861. The British government took over the payment of the Zanzibar subsidy from the British Indian Government after Indian independence and it continued to be paid from London until the late 1960s.[1] British economic (and military) assistance to Oman also included the 1958 'Exchange of Letters' financial arrangements and again significantly in the early 1970s in the time period following the coup which brought Sultan Qaboos to the throne. British political and economic influence in Omani affairs and therefore the former's bearing on the Dhofar campaign were key factors. Diplomatic and treaty relations between England and Oman were initiated by the East India Company for the purpose of regulating trade in the 1650s.[2] English, then later British influence rose steadily through an increase in diplomatic interaction to formal treaty; primarily for the purpose of limiting French influence in the Gulf region and within Oman specifically.[3] Due in part to France's Emperor Napoleon Bonaparte's planned, and later eventual conquest of Egypt (and suspected designs on the 'Jewel in the Crown' of India) closer relations flourished in the late 1700s. The Sultans of Oman were also keen on such closer relations with Britain to help offset the rising influence of the Qawasim Sheikhs and Wahhabis in the region. Britain entered into treaty relations with the Omani Sultan in 1798 and later provided him an annual subsidy paid in gold via the Indian government.[4] Later, discontented Imamate forces attacked Muscat and deposed the then Sultan in 1868, a situation which lasted until 1871 when forces under Sayyid Turki killed Imam Azzin and captured Muscat, with the British government brokering the overall surrender to Turki's forces.⁵ This important intervention by British political agent personnel essentially acting as the broker between competing claims for the prize of the Sultan's position acted as the historical forerunners for later, and much more substantial UK assistance to their Sultanic clients.

Britain later provided military assistance to a beleaguered Sultan of Muscat and Oman in 1913 when Imamate forces rebelled, and garrisoned Bait Al Falaj fort in Muscat with British Indian troops to deter further challenges to the Sultan's authority. Britain played an even bigger role in 1915 whilst concurrently embroiled in the horrors of the Western Front in the First World War. Here, 3000 rebels attacked Bait Al Falaj fort but were repulsed by some 700 British Indian Army troops, including the 2nd Rajput Light Infantry and 102nd King Edward's Grenadiers.⁶ Following the subjugation of the 1915 rebellion the British-brokered Treaty of Sib was implemented in 1920. The treaty effectively divided authority within Muscat and Omani territory. The Sultan was allotted full control of the entire Muscat and Omani coast. The independent tribes and the Imamate were given effective control over the country's barren interior but also several key historic towns. The treaty worked at the time because the Sultan could control seaborne trade, and the Imamate and tribes were able to continue their traditional religion-centred existence in their ancestral homelands. The issue only came to the fore when the subject of oil prospecting was added to the agenda and the control of such resources. Just over a decade after the British-brokered Treaty of Sib, Sultan Said bin Taimur then came to power in 1932 and strong relations between him, his country and the UK ensued for nearly 40 years until he was deposed by his erstwhile sponsors via a coup in 1970.

History & Treaty Ties

Following the Omani-British Treaty of Friendship, Commerce and Navigation of 1951, Britain once again came to the Sultan's aid.⁷ The first key instance was the expulsion of Saudi armed police forces from the Abu Dhabi Emirate and Muscat and Oman-controlled villages of the Buraimi Oasis in 1955. This was achieved by deploying the British-officered (and Foreign Office-controlled) Trucial Oman Scouts (TOS) to the poorly demarcated border area, followed by decisive military assistance utilising regular British troops during the Jebel Akhdar rebellion of 1957–59.⁸ With India already independent for a decade, the British support was provided via directly British-controlled personnel or units. These came in the form of a combined force made up of multiple units. The TOS was deployed from the neighbouring Trucial States to Oman in its first true international deployment for a force designed as an internal security force only.⁹ The second element was the contract, and later the seconded officers of the Sultan's military forces supplied as part of the 'Exchange of Letters' agreements under the command of the first CSAF, Colonel David Smiley. The third element was the first use of regular British military units, including variously the 13th/18th Hussars, the Life Guards, Royal Marines and the Cameronians; the latter which would become Qaboos's regiment in the 1960s when serving in the British army.[10] The Imamate forces were pushed back by the Sultan's military units and their allies, and, being outgunned, had no choice but to retreat. They did so up the towering natural monument of the Jebel Akhdar located in the Hajar mountain range (approximately 90 miles north of Muscat) in late 1957. Because of its defensive qualities the Imamate leaders acted with impunity for some two years from their mountain base, and were only eventually removed by large-scale bombing by RAF assets from Aden and the Trucial States and a major assault by the final element of the combined force formed to take on the Imamate forces, the SAS Regiment. Two squadrons of the SAS spearheaded a final assault of the Jebel Akhdar in January 1959, working alongside other regular British, TOS, and Omani troops. The wily insurgent leaders however evaded capture. They escaped to Saudi Arabia and the rebellion was all but over. As a result of this combined – and SAS-led – force the Sultan achieved a decisive victory. He consolidated his power and brought peace in Oman for the first time in years which lasted until the advent of the Dhofar Liberation Front's struggle in the province from 1963.

Such historical British support to Oman was important, but can be described as somewhat 'ad hoc'. Treaty arrangements and periodic military support were valuable, but what might be considered deep practical links were only formalised in 1958, which did have the effect of contributing to the Sultan's defeat of the Imamate rebellion. After precursor negotiations undertaken from the British side by former Special Operations Executive (SOE) officer – and former colleague and friend of the first CSAF, Colonel David Smiley – Julian Amery, an agreement was made with the Sultan of Muscat and Oman. On his annual trip to London, Sultan Said and the British government signed what became known as the 'Exchange of Letters' on 25th July 1958.[11] This agreement was important because upon its signing, Britain was formally bound both financially and via military 'assets' to assist Oman to establish, train, and subsequently build up a modern armed force for the Sultanate. Britain provided 'start up' and longer-term support funding to both reshape and redesignate the Muscat Armed Forces (MAF) into the new Sultan's Armed Forces. As part of the agreement, the British government agreed to pay a large annual stipend (£271,000 per year) towards the running and reorganisation, modernisation and expansion of the existing MAF (which previously consisted only of the Batinah Force, the Muscat Regiment and the Muscat and Oman Field Force) into the newly-designated Sultan's

Armed Forces (SAF) complete with a small new air force.[12] Britain also agreed to supply seconded or loaned regular British army officers to the newly-formed SAF. This initiative included both the commander of the force, and over 20 other officers for headquarters and regimental duties. The officer chosen to lead the force was the former SOE officer and Second World War veteran Colonel David Smiley who was the first designated CSAF with (Colonel) Pat Waterfield moving from the post of Chief of Staff to that of 'Military Secretary'.[13] Apart from being trusted by Amery, the well-connected Smiley had wide experience of irregular warfare in both Albania and Thailand during the Second World War so was a natural choice to lead the newly-organised force which had an insurgency to deal with.[14] The 1958 'Exchange of Letters' also tied Britain to Oman in another mutually beneficial clause. This confirmed that Britain would significantly extend the lease for the RAF facilities on the strategically-important Masirah Island, located off the Omani coast approximately half way between Muscat and Salalah. The agreements also specified ongoing arrangements for the running of RAF Salalah. Negotiated by a wily Sultan Said, in exchange for access to the facilities and location of Masirah Island which he knew the British valued as a transit hub and intelligence-gathering asset, the latter were obliged to maintain RAF Salalah. By this arrangement Britain was obliged to operate, man, and maintain the base in its entirety from airfield and security to air traffic control on an asset which was primarily used by the Sultan's own air force. As such, the arrangement became known as somewhat of a burden in British political and military circles and was given the unofficial designation of the Salalah 'Hook'.

Strategic UK Succession Planning – Crown Prince Qaboos

As his father had been before him, Sultan Qaboos was moulded by the British from early on for a potential leadership role. As was done in many territories across the decades, this was undertaken in part as a strategic 'insurance policy' if his own father proved to be 'unreliable' in relation to British interests, which is essentially what was utilised in 1970. To enable this, and perhaps ironically, with the agreement of Sultan Said, Qaboos was sent to the UK to be schooled in the late 1950s. This British education was not just for the young Qaboos's general benefit, but to prepare him for attendance of the British Army's officer training establishment at Sandhurst, and for the duration of this preparatory time he lived modestly lodged with a family near Bury St. Edmunds.[15] All details related to Qaboos's educational sojourn in the UK were thoroughly arranged by Major Leslie Chauncey. He was a highly experienced soldier-diplomat who was a previous Consul General to Muscat. Respected by Sultan Said, Chauncey was invited to join his service as a private individual and became a trusted advisor to the Sultan. It was "certainly at Chauncey's recommendation that the young prince attend the Royal Military Academy in Sandhurst, Berkshire", and it was he who liaised with his establishment contacts at the UK Foreign Office to find a socially suitable and discreet family for him to both live with and be tutored by, to prepare the young heir for the challenges he would face there.[16] This preparation period of two years under the watchful direction of the Romans family fulfilled its purpose and Qaboos was admitted to Sandhurst in 1960 to undertake the British Army officer commissioning course which he subsequently passed.[17] Qaboos then served in Germany for a year as a regular officer in the British Army's Cameronians Regiment, which was chosen specifically as it had recently served with distinction in the Jebel Akhdar campaign. After being discharged from the British Army, Qaboos undertook a three-month long worldwide educational and sightseeing tour in the style of British aristocrats of the 1700s and 1800s, travelling to Europe, Asia and the USA, and enjoyed a long-awaited meeting with his paternal grandfather and ex-ruler who was living in self-imposed exile in India.[18] This was all undertaken to educate the young prince and heir, but he had still not been permitted ever to visit Muscat, the capital city of his native land. He was accompanied (or rather chaperoned at Sultan Said's request) on this "Grand Tour" by Major Chauncey and his wife, and afterwards returned to the UK where he was posted to local government departments in Bedfordshire and Warwickshire to learn about, and get hands-on experience dealing with aspects of regional, or small state-level management and governance.[19]

The support and organisation as well as bureaucratic flexibility offered by the UK was not all altruistic. Far from it. As with the sons of rulers of British client states or close allies being educated there, it was usually of benefit to the UK in some way. Through education or military training, it was hoped – or indeed calculated – that the end product of this process would be an Anglophile prince who would continue this outlook if, and often, when he came to power in his home country. Anglophile princes around the world were strategically beneficial for Britain, but on another level these individuals could offer alternative figures of governance should the need arise. This ultimate 'insurance policy' was rarely utilised, but in the case of Qaboos it was. When Sultan Said had stretched British patience to breaking point with his conduct regarding the Dhofar War, through the above process there was a potential alternative, which was ultimately 'cashed in' in July 1970. With his UK education combined with his military training and service, Qaboos was seen as a viable alternative, and he was effectively as 'British, and as 'establishment' as someone of foreign extraction could be. By bringing Qaboos to the throne, he would have been expected to both protect British interests and run the Sultanate and prosecute the Dhofar War more how the latter collectively considered it should be.[20] The in-depth coaching, mentoring and essentially preparation of Qaboos for leadership, governance and command was ultimately a success in terms of British interests. It also arguably was one of the key reasons for the success of the Omani COIN campaign against the Dhofari insurgents. If there had been no programme of British mentoring, because of the limited alternatives there may not have been a change in governance in Oman in 1970. If the fresh approach provided by Qaboos had never materialised then the campaign against the insurgents – which was at best a stalemate at the time – may never have been recovered and the war potentially lost. All of this illustrates the key influence of Britain over Oman, its leaders and ultimately over the Dhofar War itself.

Domestic UK Political Influence and Effects

As well as a positive influence on the Dhofar campaign which highlights the integral nature of Britain to both its development and execution from its outset, it can also be argued conversely that the high level of UK influence can also be illustrated through its negative impacts. Whether positive or negative in their outcomes, a true illustration of the extent of British influence can be observed. Of prime importance in this respect was Britain's withdrawal from the Southern Federation and the territory of Aden itself in 1967. After the coup de grace of the 1966 Defence Review the Federalist forces rapidly collapsed as, "The whole federation had been built on British policy, British assurances and British subvention. These were now taken away."[21] Although 1968 was the actual date set for withdrawal and independence, the level of turmoil and eventual collapse caused by British policy necessitated this policy being brought forward to 1967. This resulted in a humiliating "scuttle" with the result being the takeover of the protectorate by NLF forces and subsequent establishment of the socialist PDRY state.[22] Although warned by British Foreign Office officials as having a likely negative influence on the situation in Dhofar, with increased support for the DLF the policy of withdrawal was pushed through by the Labour government of the day.[23] This prediction came to pass and the emergence of the communist PDRY strongly influenced the metamorphosis of the primarily nationalist Dhofari DLF insurgents into the Marxist PFLOAG organisation and handed them unfettered access once more to a safe haven at Hauf with subsequent added (newly-formed) Marxist-state protection and support.[24]

With the withdrawal of the UK's substantial military forces from Aden protectorate, Britain had less military power on hand or the practical ability to intervene in Dhofar if required. The UK therefore had less influence on the development of events in the insurgency which helped extend the conflict which is described as the start "of the rot" in terms of the situation in Dhofar.[25] It also helped extend the timeframe of the insurgency by allowing the insurgents precious time to develop, expand and train and for their communist sponsors from the PDRY and further afield to be able to comprehensively arm them with the latest in Soviet bloc weaponry. By 1975 this even included sophisticated SAM-7 missiles used to deadly effect against the Omani coalition force aircraft on several occasions.[26] This situation was both complemented and exacerbated by Britain also displaying a somewhat reluctant attitude towards the provision of military (and other) aid to Oman to help the war effort. This was the case from the outset of the insurgency in 1964 and remained the overriding policy at least until the issue came to a head in 1970 and the coup against Sultan Said was instigated. As described previously, both Colonel Lewis and Brigadier Purdon were of the opinion that the forces under their command could have defeated the insurgents if they had had better resources at their disposal; which Britain was technically in the position to provide.[27] Extra British governmental support over 'Exchange of Letters' levels and direct action supported by the substantial military resources based at Aden – such as the combined SAS, Irish Guards, and Royal Marines ship-borne raid on Hauf from HMS *Fearless* in 1966 – was possible but a distinct policy of avoiding deeper or long-term commitment or cost in Dhofar was apparent.[28] This was primarily to avoid the UK being dragged into an unwanted "Mini-Vietnam" replica scenario in Dhofar and the Arabian Peninsula with fears of a region-wide "domino effect" of revolution and regime change.[29] This often led to frustrations for the British-army CSAFs in place and charged with conducting the Dhofar campaign. It also, however, frustrated the Omani authorities. This even included Colonel Hugh Oldman who was the British national serving as the Omani Military Secretary. He described the overall British governmental attitude towards assistance to Oman and the war effort as "disgraceful".[30] Even when British assistance was substantially increased when fears started gaining traction of a potential defeat which eventually forced action, this assistance was in effect too little, too late.

Whilst helping to stabilise the new Qaboos regime, the uplift in assistance did not facilitate a wholly successful initial offensive against the Dhofari insurgents in October 1971 via Operations JAGUAR and LEOPARD. These failed to deliver a decisive victory, were actually rather a disappointment, and fell well short of achieving the "grand offensive['s]" initial aims with unopposed SAF freedom of movement on the jebel only secured by mid-1973.[31] With victory not declared until December 1975 there were four more years of hard campaigning to endure after the launch of these large-scale operations when hopes had initially been so high. With greater UK resources committed to the campaign in addition to, and over and above the mainly SAS, Royal Engineers, and Royal Artillery assets deployed post-coup, the situation could have been improved. The objectives of the 1971 offensives potentially could have been achieved without the resulting gloomy outlook of senior officers as to the future prospects of both large-scale offensive operations and the wider campaign in general.[32] This large-scale extra required assistance never actually materialised.

Overall, it is clear that Britain played a pivotal role in the organisation and prosecution of the Dhofar campaign. This was mainly in terms of a positive input but also from the consequences of negative influence factors, especially those arising from the poorly conceived (from a political perspective) Aden withdrawal in 1967. This reinforces, however, the overall importance of Britain's influence and role in the conflict in general. The Dhofar COIN campaign was on the brink of defeat by 1971 and without the concerted efforts of UK personnel (as well as funding and materials) the war may well have been lost by early 1972.[33] It is also clear that the role of Britain and its influence in Oman was on an even wider and deeper scale than just the prosecution of a war for an ally, through the additional unique overarching state-building efforts implemented by the UK.

Economic Influence

The extent of British economic influence in Oman is illustrated by the fact that Oman was effectively financially 'bank-rolled' by Britain from 1861 onwards with the introduction of the Canning Award/Zanzibar subsidy. This was later reinforced through the financial assistance package established via the 1958 'Exchange of Letters', the financial aspects of which ran concurrently with the subsidy until the latter was phased out in the late 1960s. Direct British support was the basis for the formation of the SAF (and creation of the Sultan of Oman's Air Force [SOAF]. It was also the basis for the continuing development and effectiveness of the Omani military, and British officers supplied on extended loan (usually between six months and up to three years for the most senior personnel) by the UK government led the SAF at every juncture from CSAF, through his headquarters staff, to unit company command-level. The level of influence this enabled for the UK over how the Dhofar campaign was conducted is clear. Sultans Said and Qaboos would have both been acutely aware of the reality of the situation and to balance such influence either played the British at their own game such as Sultan Said's built-in 'insurance policy' of the Salalah 'Hook', or Qaboos proactively working to decrease general British influence over his administration.[34]

This underlying current of independence of thought and action and attempting to limit British influence was given a boost in 1964 with the discovery of commercial level oil deposits in Oman. Even though, due in part to this new-found income stream, the British Treasury subsequently ended the old Zanzibar subsidy payment in 1968, this ultimately gave the Omani ruler more options and made him less reliant on the British government for his income. This situation was increased dramatically by the income derived from oil due largely to the effects of the 1973 oil crisis which heavily impacted the world economy and the subsequent rise in global oil prices.[35] This resulted in a four-fold increase in oil income for the Sultanate by the following year (topping 200 million Omani Riyals in 1974) and a further substantial rise by the end of 1975 (increased by another 30% to over 300 million) and gave the Sultan more financial options than in the past.[36] This windfall of extra – and relatively unexpected – income meant there was more in the national pot to spend on all required, or rather desired, developmental projects, and the new Sultan did not hold back. One example is the previously highlighted joint purchase of Jaguar attack aircraft and the Rapier air defence system from Britain in 1974 at the then eye-watering cost of approximately £83 million (approaching £1 billion in today's money adjusted for inflation).[37] Strongly counselled by his British advisors as to the unnecessary nature of the equipment and that it was too expensive for Oman, for better or for worse Sultan Qaboos made up his own mind to proceed with the purchase and commit to the approximately five-year implementation period.[38] He would have been unlikely to be able to make such a bold financial decision – especially against the advice of his British advisors – if Oman's national oil-derived income had not received such a dramatic increase.

In addition to the rise in oil income, Oman also received substantial donations and support from select Middle Eastern neighbours. These, primarily Arabian Peninsula states such as the Kingdom of Saudi Arabia, were able to supply monies where military forces would likely prove be politically unacceptable at the international, but primarily the domestic level.[39] Alongside the windfall oil income, this further armed the Sultan with both the opportunity and the freedom to utilise non-British monies for both procurement and civil development issues. Rather like a lottery winner, Oman had gone from poverty and reliance especially on British aid to an almost embarrassment of riches in a short time period, so Qaboos did not have to sacrifice one priority for the other.[40] As a result, Britain's influence in terms of economic leverage over Oman and the Dhofar campaign can be seen to have substantially reduced in scale over time. Britain's historic economic influence over Oman is, however, clear. Despite a relative reduction in said influence over time, it remained a key factor especially for the initial eight years of the Dhofar conflict. This is a key point, in that for four-fifths of the war Britain was the only option, as there was no other backer or provider to the Sultanate to fight a potentially existential threat.

Indirect UK support

In terms of direct support, pre-1970 Oman was initially heavily reliant on British assistance. From a financial and material perspective this reliance afforded the UK considerable influence over the Sultan as well as the Dhofar campaign itself. Historically, Britain had supplied a stipend to Oman via the British Indian government (and later direct from the British government) and with the 'Exchange of Letters' in 1958 the formal assistance package for the reorganisation of the SAF and introduction of long-term seconded officers from the British armed forces was instigated. In 1960, the original 1958 'Exchange of Letters' agreements were updated. The amendments were instigated following the visit of the Sultan to London and talks with Edward Heath, the then Lord Privy Seal who later became Prime Minister in 1970 and was in charge when the coup was instigated, and who also authorised the deployment of the SAS to Oman for the first time since 1959. The amended agreements would see Britain providing nearly £1 million on an annual basis for the ongoing running costs of the SAF, plus a further £1 million one-off payment towards efforts to restructure the force.[41] UK-derived monies were also pledged to meet the majority of costs for the extended scope of a much widened and much-needed civil-development programme to be used in part to bring tangible development to Dhofar province, and by doing so, to clearly demonstrate the benefits of the central government to the Jebali population.[42] In addition to extra monetary support to facilitate swift expansions of military and civil development plans, Britain quietly expanded the number of seconded military personnel to the Sultanate. It was a modest increase in absolute terms, but given the loaned personnel were military officers or leaders largely in the captain to colonel seniority bracket, in a small military this provided a large influx of extra capacity for the SAF. Numbers of loaned British military personnel were almost doubled from twenty-three to forty; a significant increase with campaign-significant repercussions. In addition, it was also agreed to cover initial SOAF costs which had then recently been established with two loaned RAF officers and Percival Provost aircraft.[43] The expansion of British-supplied funds and military personnel was all undertaken with an eye to improving the effectiveness of the COIN campaign against the insurgents in Dhofar, and represented a substantial and growing commitment.

During the Heath premiership from 1970, British materiel support to Oman was further upgraded. It was expanded to include not just monetary funds, materials, and seconded military personnel on an individual basis but the deployment of British regular units. This was a major step from the British perspective and carried more risk in terms of being potentially dragged into a deeper commitment. First was the covert deployment of the 22nd SAS

Regiment, followed by the discreet – but less covert – mobilisation of more support-related units such as the Royal Artillery utilised primarily to protect Salalah airfield, and the Royal Engineers to undertake both military and civil construction projects, but also with an SAF training role.

Indirect British support did not stop there. Even though Oman paid for most British military support, the cost was high and cumulatively became more of a burden.[44] To relieve the Omani treasury, by 1973 Britain started to subsidise select costs, which included those for the salaries of seconded personnel.[45] Added to the ongoing costs of maintaining RAF Salalah (and maintaining over 200 regular British personnel there to do so) effectively as a sub-contracted project for the benefit of the Sultan's Air Force, this was a both large, and increasing financial burden for the UK.[46] This expenditure should be viewed from an overall strategic cost perspective relating to Oman as well as Britain's wider interests. Whilst not specifically linked to Britain's Dhofar War efforts, the cost of running RAF Salalah was additional to that required for RAF Masirah which was on extended lease from Oman as part of the 1958 'Exchange of Letters' agreements. It was, however, in terms of the condition for use was the continued funding and management of RAF Salalah. RAF Masirah was more costly to run for the UK as it housed over 600 personnel as opposed to the approximately 200 at RAF Salalah.[47] Instead of the small SOAF contingent, RAF facilities, including facilities management, air traffic control services and force protection at RAF Masirah were home to sophisticated RAF aircraft. Hawker Hunter, Victor V-Bombers and Nimrod nuclear submarine hunters plied its runway and in covert warfare and information gathering terms it also housed a powerful radio transmitter, ostensibly for the BBC, which was in reality a cover for listening post facilities operated by Britain's Secret Intelligence Service (SIS/MI6) which covered the Middle and Far East regions.[48]

The funding as provided by the Canning Award/Zanzibar Subsidy and especially the later 'Exchange of Letters' in 1958 and its upgrade amendments in 1960 was a great facilitator of progress in modernising Oman's capabilities. These modernisations applied primarily to the military sphere but also covered civil development projects. From the British side they were certainly expensive, but provided substantial leverage, however, over Oman and its rulers. The main downside for Sultan Said, and later Sultan Qaboos was that they were tied financially to Britain, and their ability to fight an insurgency within their own territory was fully dependent on a foreign backer from the initial SAF deployment under Colonel Tony Lewis in 1964. This situation of almost complete financial reliance would remain in place for many years which limited the Sultans in their decision-making capacity; essentially their 'room to manoeuvre' on many issues. It is arguable that this state of economic dependency was the status

> 'Exchange of Letters between the Government of the United Kingdom of Great Britain and Northern Ireland and the Sultan of Muscat and Oman concerning the Sultan's Armed Forces, Civil Aviation, Royal Air Force facilities and Economic Development in Muscat and Oman, London 25 July 1958' (London: HMSO, Cmnd. 507, Treaty Series No. 28 (1958)).
>
> The Secretary of State for Foreign Affairs to the Sultan of Muscat and Oman, 25 July 1958.
> With reference to the discussions which I have had the pleasure of holding with Your Highness in London, and following upon those which took place in Muscat betwen Your Highness and Mr. Julian Amery in January, 1958, I have the honour to set out below my understanding of the agreement which has been reached between us.
> In pursuance of the common interest of Your Highness and Her Majesty's Government in furthering the progress of the Sultanate of Muscat and Oman, Her Majesty's Government in the United Kingdom have agreed to extend assistance towards the strengthening of Your Highness's Army. Her Majesty's Government will also, at Your Highness's request, make available Regular officers on secondment from the British Army, who will, while serving in the Sultanate, form an integral part of Your Highness's Armed Forces. The terms and conditions of service of these seconded British officers have been agreed with Your Highness. Her Majesty's Government will also provide training facilities for members of Your Highness's Armed Forces and will make advice available on training and other matters as may be required by Your Highness.
> Her Majesty's Government will also assist Your Highness in establishment of an Air Force as an integral part of Your Highness's Armed Forces, and they will make available personnel to this Air Force.
> Your Highness has approved the conclusion of an agreement for the extension of the present arrangements regarding civil aviation and the use by the Royal Air Force of the airfields at Salalah and Masirah.
> We also discussed the economic and development problems of the Sultanate and Her Majesty's Government agreed to assist Your Highness in carrying out a civil development programme which will include the improvement of roads, medical and education facilities and an agricultural research programme
> If Your Highness agrees that the foregoing correctly sets out the agreement reached between us I have the honour to suggest that this letter and Your Highness's reply should be regarded as constituting an Agreement between Your Highness and my Government.
> I have the honour to be, with the highest consideration,
> Your Highness's sincere friend, Selwyn Lloyd.
> London, 25 July 1958.
>
> Your Excellency,
> We have received Your Excellency's letter of to-day's date, setting out the agreement which has been reached in discussions between ourself and Her Majesty's Government in the United Kingdom, and confirm that your letter and this reply should be regarded as constituting an agreement between us and your Government.
> Your sincere friend, Said bin Taimur.

Figure 2: Text of 1958 'Exchange of Letters' Agreement Between British Government and Sultan of Muscat and Oman.
Source: J.E. Peterson, *Oman's Insurgencies: The Sultanate's Struggle for Supremacy* (Lebanon: Saqi, 2007) p.103.
Image © *Oman's Insurgencies: The Sultanate's Struggle for Supremacy* by J. E. Peterson (Saqi Books, 2007)

quo situation up until the onset of oil income allied to the withdrawal of the Canning Award/Zanzibar Subsidy in 1968. More likely in reality it was the case all the way up until the 1973 Oil Crisis and the multi-fold increases in oil prices which boosted the Omani national purse to hitherto unseen levels.[49]

Table 5: Key British Indirect Military Support/Coin Assistance to Oman and the Dhofar War.

Phase	Highlights	Details*
Up to 1960	1958 Exchange of Letters (Jul)	Up to 24 British officers seconded to Omani forces. To consist of: Commander of Omani Forces (CSAF – initially Col. David Smiley) Two regimental commanders Up to 22 other officers and four 'other ranks' £271,000 annually for running costs of Oman's armed forces
	Imamate War/Jebel Akhdar Campaign	£162k capital costs and £68k annual costs for Sultan's Air Force Agreements re: leases and arrangements for RAF Masirah and RAF Salalah British Forces (inc. Trucial Oman Scouts, Royal Marines, 13/18 Hussars) support Sultan's forces against Imamate forces 1958 Similar support (plus 22 SAS, Lifeguards) spearhead/ support SAF in final attack on insurgent positions on Jebel Akhdar to end Imamate rebellion (Jan 1959)
1960–1970	1960 Exchange of Letters 'upgrade' (Aug 1960)	Personnel uplift – Up to 15 x extra junior officers made available to SAF on secondment (in addition to previously agreed personnel) Uplift in monetary contributions to Oman – Over £1 million towards SAF reorganisation costs and c. £900k towards annual/recurrent costs
	Airwork Ltd Contracted	Not UK govt. but closely linked. Serviced and battle prepped all SOAF aircraft and had additional key recruiting role for contract personnel to SAF**
1970 onwards	Post-Coup Uplift	SAS deployed to Oman – Various duties inc. Sultan protection, training Sultan bodyguard, SAF pre-deployment training, Firqa training/formation, Intelligence gathering/set up int. cell, 'Hearts and Minds' campaign (inc. medical support, veterinary support, information services/white propaganda) Royal Engineers, Royal Artillery ('Cracker Battery') and 'Green Archer' mortar location unit for RAF Salalah deployed Intelligence Corps personnel deployed

* J.E. Peterson, *Oman's Insurgencies: The Sultanate's Struggle for Supremacy* (Lebanon: Saqi, 2007) p.102 –p.148
** Keith McCloskey, *Airwork: A History* (Stroud: The History Press, 2012) p. 97–100

Airpower was also a vital element in the SAF's arsenal against the insurgent and was used effectively as required but also served as a deterrent. Informal British influence was additionally very much apparent in this important sphere. Although not always directly British government supplied or supported, the SOAF aircraft were maintained, repaired and armed for combat sorties in Dhofar by the personnel of the privately-owned UK company, Airwork Services Ltd. The company had had strong links to British military, Foreign Office, and wider government circles with air force flight training and aircraft maintenance contracts in many existing or former UK overseas territories.[50] In addition to the key task of keeping the Strikemaster fighter and transport aircraft of SOAF flight and combat-ready the company also had a recruiting role in the Sultanate, acting as the primary agents for the recruitment and contracting of privately employed or 'contract' personnel for the SAF.[51] This method of personnel provision was in contrast to the serving seconded or 'Loan Service Personnel' provided directly by the UK government. There were always substantially more contract officers than seconded, so the potential for indirect influence can be clearly seen. Although a private company, a large measure of 'backdoor' governmental influence was apparent due to the fact that Airwork Ltd. had strong links to the British military and government through domestic flight training contracts and numerous contracts abroad which would have likely only been secured with at least tacit UK governmental support.[52] The Omani Airwork contract was relatively small in terms of its overall business in general and in the Middle East in particular, in contrast for instance to its extensive Saudi contracts. Despite this, the company's somewhat cosy yet unofficial relationship with the government resulted in a relatively high level of indirect UK influence over two key aspects of the war. It afforded the UK both wide-ranging influence and control over contract personnel within the SAF (allied to direct control over loaned personnel) as well as over vital SOAF aerial combat capability primarily within Dhofar Province for the COIN campaign but also throughout the wider Sultanate.[53]

Mixed UK private and British government approved or encouraged tangible military support for Oman gave substantial influence and a measure of control over the Dhofar campaign. Britain was both the key and by far the largest arms exporter to Oman for the entire period of the Dhofar War (bar 1972 alone, when Iran was the largest exporter) and all the way up to at least 1981 when US assistance overtook British arms exports for the first time.[54] This situation, allied to direct government to government assistance, solidified London's influence over Oman. As such it therefore also had a clear knock-on influence on the capability to conduct and the success of the Dhofar campaign in particular.

Civilian & Military UK Advisors to Oman

Civilian Advisors

The Sultan's government and military administration historically involved a high level of British influence which had both an indirect and direct bearing on the Dhofar campaign from military and governmental perspectives. Although primarily due to private individuals of British descent, historic support and considerable influence was exercised by the resident Consul General and in turn the Bahrain-based British Political Resident up until the end of 1971 when the post was abolished. Up to 1970, Brigadier Pat Waterfield, a British citizen and former army officer engaged on a private contract to work directly for the Sultan, held the title of the Omani Military Secretary (effectively 'Minister of Defence').[55] This meant that in effect the second most powerful military actor after the Sultan in Oman was a British foreigner. He was replaced by another old Oman 'hand' Briton Colonel Hugh Oldman, which ensured continuity, and they had command over the both seconded CSAF and the contract officer Deputy CSAF (Colonel, later Brigadier Colin Maxwell). Alongside these military-oriented British personnel were myriad civilian administrators which again shows the almost pervasive British influence over Oman and its ruler. These included the influential and trusted Sultan's Private Secretary Jim Maclean, and Neil Innes, his ex-Royal Navy and Sudan Political Service but perhaps rather grandly titled 'Minister of External Affairs'. Through such personnel British influence strongly affected linkage with the UK authorities and general Dhofar campaign policy. This was undertaken through the well-established contemporary 'old school tie' network where:

> Britain exercised enormous control over the sultan. His defence secretary and chief of intelligence were British army officers, his chief adviser was a former British diplomat, and all but one of his government ministers were British.[56]

This unusual nationality-based and British-dominated advisory set-up to the ruler, allied to the fact that Sultan Said effectively retired to his Salalah Palace in the late 1950s meant the influence of such advisors was substantial. During the early phase of the war, British-seconded CSAF Colonel Lewis operated his British-officered SAF units through receiving orders from the Sultan's Muscat-based British Military Secretary, in an almost completely British chain of command. Brigadier Pat Waterfield, who fulfilled this role only spoke to the Sultan officially once per week to gain his orders via radio broadcast communication over 500 desert-strewn miles away from his Salalah palace.⁵⁷ It is clear to see the potential for Britain to influence, manipulate or even control the Dhofar campaign from Muscat; a situation further reinforced by the presence of the Political Resident and Commander British Forces Bahrain (CBFB) in the region for the initial five to six years of the war up to 1971 and the 'East of Suez' withdrawal. They were direct representatives of the British state, executed regional diplomatic and military policy and were based only a short flight away up the Arabian Peninsula in Bahrain. This was further reinforced through the influence via the presence of the resident British in-country diplomat (originally to 1971 a Consul General, then Ambassador) who was subservient to the Political Resident (to 1971). These diplomats were resident in Muscat – not Salalah – and met with the other British advisors on a weekly if not daily basis of both their professional duties but also as part of the expatriate social circles they moved in. The CSAF and the Military Secretary were two key examples of such advisors. All these British state representatives or ex-British state representatives working either for the UK government or the Sultan essentially had free rein to run affairs in Muscat, with the Sultan permanently based in Salalah. This included military policy as developed at the Muscat-based Bayt Al Falaj SAF Headquarters. In addition to these were other influential British citizens who operated in Oman governing circles, such as the long-time principal personal advisor to the Sultan, Leslie Chauncy who as mentioned was a key figure in Qaboos's training and education.⁵⁸ He was a previous (post-war) UK Consul General to Muscat and returned in a private capacity to serve the Sultan in 1961. Another highly influential Briton who found themselves embroiled in Muscat governing circles was the multi-skilled and high-profile ex-officer, explorer and diplomat Sir Hugh Boustead. He was seconded by the UK government to Sultan Said's administration in the late 1950s as his expert social and economic development advisor.⁵⁹ Combined, all these characters paint a picture of almost complete either direct, or more pervasively, indirect influence of Britain variously over the Omani Sultans, their administrations and therefore policy and actions. By extension, this included the Dhofar War and the Omani COIN campaign.

Commercial business links also provided the UK with significant informal leverage over the Sultanate and its ruler. Although informal, such influence was a key factor affecting Omani defence capability per se, but also its ability to conduct the war in Dhofar. Charles Kendall was a fascinating character and a key player in Oman in terms of Britain's influence. He was not only the owner of London-based Kendall & Sons chandlery or commercial agency, but wore the 'hat' of London-based Omani 'Consul' from the mid-1960s. As Sultan Said had no formal diplomatic corps, and left Britain to represent the Sultanate in the UN, Charles Kendal had the rare honour of being Oman's only official diplomat.⁶⁰ He was given this position, similarly to most other British-descent advisors because Sultan Said trusted him. As an absolute ruler, the Sultan could appoint who he liked to do what he liked and this was the way he did business. In the Kendall case it meant he made a trusted business colleague a diplomat, whilst at the same time this person was negotiating contracts for the purchase of military supplies in the UK. He liaised with the British Ministry of Defence and Foreign Office on Oman's behalf (which to some might look like a conflict of interest) and with Brigadier Waterfield as the Omani Military Secretary, and all with an underlying commercial interest.⁶¹ Charles Kendall was undoubtedly a key factor in Oman gaining the military supplies it needed for the Dhofar War from its outset. This illustrates the importance of Kendall and his firm both to Oman and for Britain to supply the SAF with military equipment such as ammunition, as well as the integral nature of both the company as a private entity and its owner to the close official/governmental relationship between the two countries.⁶² Even more it illustrates that the military capability of Oman for the Dhofar War was highly influenced or even dependent on individual Britons in general, or the wider UK government as an entity.

From a business perspective, in addition to the Charles Kendall factor, UK influence can be further illustrated through finance and banking. Formed in the post-Second World War era in 1948, the British Bank of the Middle East (BBME) was central to the Sultanate in that it held Sultan Said's wealth. Again, as an absolute monarchy, the Sultan's wealth was the Sultanate's wealth and vice versa. As such a private UK bank effectively controlled the financial reserves of the entire Omani state, acting almost like a Bank of England equivalent.⁶³ Although never used to the Sultan's detriment, this gave the BBME very significant influence over both Oman and its ruler, and ensured the bank also had a key role to play in financing the Omani security architecture and by default the Dhofar campaign. Similarly, the oil company PDO (Oman), the UK-controlled and long-term concern in Oman, illustrated the far-reaching level of British influence over the Sultanate, both militarily and financially. PDO (Oman) initially contributed to the historic development of the Omani security architecture by the raising of a military unit to protect its prospecting teams from uncooperative tribal actors when drilling in what was traditionally Imamate territory. This unit was called the Muscat and Oman Field Force (MOFF) which was raised in 1952. In a very British workaround, the unit was paid for by a private British company, it nominally reported to Sultan Said, but was trained and equipped by the UK Ministry of Defence. Its importance is firstly that it enabled PDO (Oman) to prospect, which was in the company's, the Sultan's, and the British government's (potential tax earnings) interest. Secondly, it was important because alongside its main protective duties, the

MOFF become increasingly involved in actions associated with the Imamate Rebellion for the Sultan, and in 1957, it was absorbed into the Sultanate's military forces alongside the new Muscat Regiment and Northern Frontier Regiment and renamed the Oman Regiment (OR).[64] On the economic front, the importance of PDO (Oman) to the Sultanate and the Dhofar War going forward was the company's striking of oil deposits in commercial quantities in 1964, which happened to also be the same year the Sultan's forces were first deployed to Dhofar. The first ever commercial oil export cargo to depart Oman took place in 1967 with Japan as the destination. As a result of this new found income, the British Treasury decided to end the old Zanzibar Subsidy payment to the Sultan. In turn, this meant that with the loss of one key income stream, the Omani Sultan became even more dependent financially on the conduct, commercial decision, and goodwill of two majority British run or owned entities; a bank and an oil company. From a Dhofar War perspective, this additionally meant the life blood of finance available to fight the Sultanate's COIN campaign was both provided (initially the UK government subsidy, then oil from PD (O)), and managed (by BBME) by British-related entities. This was the case continuously throughout the decade-long duration of the war.

Military Advisors
It is clear, therefore, that Britain exercised very considerable direct and indirect influence over the Sultanate's government and economy. This strongly affected government policy, which in turn had a resulting effect on the Dhofar campaign. This situation is even more striking when considering the Military leadership of the SAF, which was tasked with prosecuting the Dhofar War. Historically, the CSAF was always a British seconded officer, and this had been the case since the original 'Exchange of Letters' in 1958 and the deployment of wartime SAS and SOE officer, Colonel David Smiley to take up the role. Throughout the war, therefore, and ultimately at the time of victory and beyond, the most senior officer of the SAF was a serving member of the British Army. Although working directly for the Sultan and under orders to serve him loyally in all respects, he remained part of the British military's chain of command and its political masters so in many ways he had divided loyalties; as did all seconded officers to a degree. In addition, the commander of operational or 'fighting' forces in Dhofar itself was also always a British officer. In the early years of the conflict, the de facto commander of Dhofar forces was the commanding officer of the resident SAF battalion which was rotated every four to six months. When the new regimental CO arrived in Dhofar, he took over this role from his predecessor, and so on. This arrangement continued until January 1971 when the role became a permanent staff position. This is the date when Lieutenant Colonel Teddy Turnhill of the

Desert Regiment (DR) handed over all command responsibilities to the new Senior Officer, HQ Dhofar; Korean War veteran Colonel Mike Harvey.[65] As the whole SAF expanded (as did the forces of the Sultan based in Dhofar) the rank structure was amended. The CSAF was upgraded from Brigadier to Major General, and the Senior Officer, HQ Dhofar billet was upgraded from a Colonel level appointment to one designated for the rank of Brigadier. The first incumbent of this new command was Brigadier Jack Fletcher in 1972. He was followed in mid-1974 by Brigadier John Akehurst who occupied the post until the end of the war in 1975 and beyond before departing Oman in 1976. In addition to the CSAF senior staff officers, and the commander in charge of prosecuting the COIN campaign in Dhofar itself, bar some administrative and medical staff and junior Arab officers, the officers of the individual SAF regiments who fought in Dhofar were nearly all British. These officers were a mix of seconded and contract personnel, but the commanding officer was always an LSP officer. From a military advisor and armed forces chain of command perspective the dominance of British officers is clear. From the Brigadier or Major General level head of the Sultan's military to the most junior captain in one of the SAF's fighting regiments there was intact British control from top to bottom.

In addition to these points was the fact that Sultan Said refused to fully integrate Arab officers into the SAF. This was largely because, and not without historical precedent, he considered such officers more likely to be less reliable and more likely to rebel against his rule and stage a coup. This had occurred in several Middle Eastern countries during his reign including in Egypt where officers led by Gamel Abdel Nasser toppled King Farouk in 1952, promoting a destabilising nationalist and anti-Imperialist agenda which had reverberations around the region. As a result of such actions Middle Eastern monarchies were collectively at risk and Sultan Said had no intention of letting that happen in Oman. He maintained power by working with the region's primary colonial power and by effectively utilising 'mercenaries' who had no interest in power as such. He refused to progress these Arab officers past the rank of Lieutenant and further prevented them from taking postings where they commanded groups or bodies of men, from where a potential coup situation could arise.[66] Although there were a handful of very junior Arab officers in the SAF, its leadership 'backbone' until reforms under Sultan Qaboos consisted almost exclusively of British seconded personnel and primarily ex-UK military officers employed on contract.[67] This began to change after the coup in 1970, with a new British-devised and implemented Omani officer training programme for Arab and Baluch candidates under the most senior contract officer in the SAF, the long-serving DCSAF, Colonel Colin Maxwell. The number of Arab and

Baluch officers trained and serving in the SAF was, however, relatively small, (only counting up to 100 by 1972) therefore had minimal effect at the tactical and even more so at the strategic level of leadership, again emphasising British influence over the campaign.[68]

British officers therefore provided virtually all the key SAF trained officer manpower throughout the war. As well as providing well-trained leaders to effect tactical success, there was arguably a greater impact at the higher operational and strategic level. The impact of such officers was substantially 'outsized' in relation to their raw numbers, as:

> While the UK never had more than a few hundred troops in Oman during the Dhofar War, it has a disproportionate share of influence during the campaign because Britons occupied key decision-making positions within the Sultanate.[69]

This concentration of influence at all levels of warfare, but especially at the operational strategic domains, meant that British personnel had the most significant and important role in prosecuting the war.[70] With the key command positions almost exclusively under seconded British officer control this also gave the UK military and therefore government direct influence and control over the COIN campaign from day one. This influence effectively prevented an early defeat for the Sultanate and likewise largely facilitated the eventual final victory in 1975.

Britain and the July 1970 Coup

The 1970 coup was a key determining factor in the Dhofar conflict and the Sultanate's COIN campaign. It has been stated that:

> It is rare in an insurgency or counterinsurgency to be able to pinpoint the [key or principal] event that turned the tide of the conflict. In the case of Oman however, that point was 23 July 1970, when Sultan Qaboos assumed the mantle of leadership.[71]

This is due to the fact that the whole trajectory of the COIN campaign and war in general changed from this point in time. In many ways the coup can be considered the pivot point that brought a new era of hope for the campaign and ensured both social, economic, and primarily military initiatives were undertaken to turn around a war effort that was teetering on failure by 1970.

The British role in the coup, and therefore its influence over the entire course of the war, was decisive. There was clear discontent in Oman and especially

Dhofar which was the reason for the initial development of the insurgency, but Sultan Said was secure in his position. The insurgents never controlled the extensive Salalah Plain or the regional capital itself, even at the greatest extent of their powers in 1970. Due to there being no Omani officer corps to speak of the only real actor capable of facilitating a change of ruler was Britain. Still not officially acknowledged, it is clear Britain was the prime mover behind the coup. In recent years the 'drip-drip' of interviews or new historical papers have backed up this assertion.[72]

What is also clear is that both military and social development spending increased under the new Sultan Qaboos, with large funds channelled swiftly towards a large-scale SAF expansion. Plans were quickly formulated to rapidly expand the Sultan's military which began almost immediately after the coup. In addition, the long-sought deployment of the SAS was initiated with Sultan Qaboos's blessing to provide security, assist in building the intelligence picture, and aid training. Importantly, the SAS's unique skill sets were also utilised specifically to start the time-honoured strategy of a major 'hearts and minds' effort as part of Operation STORM, implemented to wean the initiative away from the insurgent cause and resultantly to the government side. In a key development, a long-sought-for (by the British) amnesty programme for insurgents was also introduced which helped woo enemy combatants over to the government side and often service in the new indigenous Firqa units. These were units which were being formed, trained and led by their expert SAS handlers through the regiment's long association with irregular warfare and working with indigenous tribal peoples in multiple countries to provide both intelligence-gathering capabilities and form combat-capable militia units. The coup ushered in a new phase of the campaign, providing new hope and capability to back up such sentiments. The British role in bringing Sultan Qaboos to power was decisive. The result of this event and its repercussions enabled the deteriorating COIN campaign to be brought back on track and eventually to facilitate the insurgent defeat.

British Diplomatic Assistance to Oman

Britain's expertise and long history of diplomatic representation assisted the Omani administration and the new Sultan to navigate the necessary diplomatic channels to achieve recognition on the world stage.[73] Britain's first task was to make sure the new Sultan was accepted as the leader of Oman following the clearly non-democratic change of administration in July 1970. This was an urgent requirement both inside and more importantly external to the Sultanate and was key to continuing the fight in Dhofar. Internally, the deposing of Sultan

Said was not announced until three days after the event to prevent potential panic or attempted reversal.[74] In this time the former Sultan was evacuated to Bahrain for medical assistance with British escorts and then on to the UK where he was permitted to live in comfortable exile.[75] There were also stage managed appearances, including a 'triumphant unveiling' to meet his subjects in Muscat just one week after the coup, which was also the first time Qaboos had ever seen his own capital city.[76]

The next stage of British orchestrated attempts to gain external acceptance for both Qaboos and especially Oman was firstly timing of the announcements of his accession, which was coordinated through Britain's diplomatic network to ensure there were no surprises and no significant rejections by other governments to the new ruling reality in Oman. Further, swift diplomatic efforts were directed to restoring Oman's diplomatic profile, both to solidify Qaboos's rule, but also as the best means to create a favourable international opinion on Oman's actions in Dhofar and potentially garner a level of moral and tangible assistance. By choice Sultan Said had previously left his British backers to manage his foreign affairs for him and had effectively 'outsourced' his country's representation at the United Nations through the UK, seeing no benefit to having an independent seat for Oman in the world's foremost international organisation.[77] The UK also helped facilitate the establishment of an initial diplomatic corps and open up Muscat to foreign Ambassadors, where only Britain and India were previously permitted to do so.[78]

When Sultan Said retired to Salalah in 1958, his diplomatic relations were undertaken via the British Consul General via the Bahrain-based Political Resident and ultimately the British Foreign Office. This colonial-esque structure which harked back to the pre-independence British Indian government was not sustainable in the new era, and Britain realised changes were required to assist the wider war effort. As such it took the necessary steps to achieve this, and:

> Under the guidance of his British advisors, the new Sultan [alongside his uncle and new Prime Minister, Tariq] took steps to end Oman's diplomatic isolation – joining the United Nations and the Arab League as well as establishing diplomatic relations with anti-Communist regimes in the region such as Iran and Jordan.[79]

Britain's diplomatic experience helped to facilitate this process and Oman because a member of the Arab League in September 1971, and the UN a few weeks later in the October of the same year.[80] Oman's isolation on the international stage was at an end, and whilst in many ways the process took away the historic leverage Britain exercised over Oman and its rulers, it was nonetheless the former which acted with vigour to raise the Sultanate's diplomatic status. Britain realised it could not help Oman prevail in the Dhofar conflict through the resources available, so changed tack to help the Sultanate open up to the international community to effectively become more self-reliant, and therefore avoiding unwelcome – and politically unacceptable – potential deeper British involvement. This approach subsequently bore fruit. Oman's sovereign UN representation was one of the key factors in the Sultanate being able to prevail in the diplomatic furore surrounding the artillery and air force bombing of Hauf in PDRY territory in 1972. The retaliation, codenamed Operation AQOOBA or 'punishment' was launched after the PDRY destroyed a Sultanate's border fort. Through its UN presence, British support, and the CSAF, Brigadier John Graham writing the Omani's official statement on the matter in the UN, far from being widely condemned, Oman received a positive response from the international community. In this case, Britain and Oman proved 'the pen is often mightier than the sword', and the situation further resulted in pleasingly widespread messages of support for Oman and Sultan Qaboos personally by Islamic nations (even from Saudi Arabia, North Yemen, and Egypt), not just for its bold actions in the PDRY, but also for its vigorous prosecution of a campaign to counter a major source of regional instability.[81] In addition, these widespread messages of diplomatic support were quickly followed by concrete actions such as the nomination and installation of the first Ambassadors from Iran and Jordan to Muscat which then resulted in further tangible military assistance for the Dhofar campaign.[82]

Severe economic problems which came to a head in Britain in 1967 effectively led to the UK decision to withdraw East of Suez.[83] 1967 saw a financial 'run' on the pound, the humiliating requirement to approach the IMF for a large loan and large-scale devaluation of Sterling by the end of the year under Harold Wilson's Labour government. Its tenure also included the "scuttle" from Aden in 1967 which further weakened the British ability to influence events in Oman and Dhofar from a military perspective.[84] Partly as a result of such domestic economic issues there was a concerted effort to proactively spread the responsibility for supporting Oman and reduce the reliance on the UK's single source assistance which was necessarily finite, and which could only be of limited scale due to ongoing economic and political issues in Britain itself. British actions in the diplomatic arena were designed both to help its ally prevail in the war, but also to limit and prevent the expansion of its own, already very large moral and tangible assistance to Oman. The monetary, military and personnel demands on Britain were already very high and Oman was not its only concern, with events in Northern Ireland rapidly descending into another unwelcome permanent and expensive military commitment. Later in the war, this overall approach was taken to further lengths by the UK Labour administration which took power in 1974 as a broad policy change compared to the relatively generous previous Heath conservative government era.[85] British officials facilitated closer ties and bilateral agreements with friendly regional governments, including the United Arab Emirates which resulted in a measure of welcome financial and military aid or assistance; with war-winning links forged with both Jordan and Iran.[86]

Whilst Sultan Qaboos certainly had a role to play in creating external links with such countries such as visiting Iran for the Persepolis celebrations (marking the 2,500th anniversary of the Persian 'Empire') in 1971, the overall approach to forging such external assistance was British by design with key actors being the CSAFs Brigadier Graham, and later Major General Creasey. The liaison undertaken by these two British officers with both London and officials from Jordan and Iran was to yield much in the way of tangible support for the Sultanate which proved to be war-winning in its extent. This began with the sixty C130 planeloads of supplies from Iran delivered as a birthday gift to the Sultan from the Shah in mid-1972, and ended up with Oman benefitting from the deployment of a Special Forces battalion from Jordan and a fully supported infantry brigade of over 3,000 men from Iran.[87] British diplomatic assistance was, therefore, key to both raising the country's international profile and legitimacy, but also in gaining a wide range of both moral and tangible support for Oman to back the Sultanate's campaign in Dhofar.

Governance & State-Building Aspects of UK Influence

British diplomatic influence was not just confined to external relations and brokering support for the Sultan and Dhofar campaign. Britain had a key role in the state-building aspect of the new Oman under Qaboos. This started in earnest from the point of the coup which had a pivotal effect on the development and eventual outcome of the campaign. As the new Sultan Qaboos had near zero governing experience, senior British military, political and business leaders formed a rather understatedly named Interim Advisory Council (IAC) to take control of the Omani government once the coup had dethroned Sultan Said, which belied the power it held for the short time of its existence. The IAC then invited Qaboos' uncle Sayyid Tariq bin Taimur who was living abroad in exile to join the government as the Prime Minister; likely without even consulting the new Sultan.[88] Bringing Tariq into government was a highly 'inclusive' and strategic political act designed to help bring various powerful Omani factions together. This, in turn, was calculated by the British to help give the new administration a clear level of legitimacy, help it both survive and govern effectively, and importantly keep the Omani focus firmly on maintaining the intensity of COIN efforts in Dhofar.

With the Qaboos administration up and running relatively successfully on most fronts, after surviving its first few months Britain's most urgent aspect of governance and state-building was largely done, and the role was now to keep the good ship Qaboos on the 'straight and narrow'. This was not always easy in the following months and years, as Qaboos settled into his role. Becoming more confident in his abilities and wanting to consolidate his power, the inexperienced 29-year-old with no governing experience worked over time to decrease UK-related influence in his court and government and built up a wide-ranging alternative, non-British, group of key advisors. Whilst the military campaign remained almost fully under British influence, the new advisory set up had the desired effect of eventually limiting influence and sidelining Britain and British advisors on many non-direct Dhofar campaign issues relating especially to the economy, social development, and concerningly for Britain also in the realm of procurement.[89] This process was not immediate, and the UK role remained key, however, in preserving, guiding, and nurturing the new Qaboos administration through its most vulnerable period.[90] This, in turn, was crucial for the somewhat teetering war effort because if the new administration had been allowed to implode, or make rash economic or other policy decisions the outcome could have been severe. Happily, stalwart British assistance prevented this from happening, and initially guided the Qaboos administration through the initial two years to be able to achieve the campaign turnaround by the end of 1972 and to be firmly on the path to eventual victory some three years later.

In terms of the evolution of the UK and Omani political and economic relationship, it can therefore be seen that there is substantial evidence to suggest that the Dhofar campaign, whilst influential, was not a completely British-centred campaign. This is due to the many non-UK-related factors playing an important role in the campaign with the role of the Sultan chief amongst these. Closer consideration, however, reveals the centrality of British influence over Oman and the Dhofar Campaign. Britain was the major political and economic backer of Oman both before and during the insurgency, and the COIN campaign would not have been won without this input. The British role is reinforced further when military-related aspects are considered, whether it be leadership provision or the deployment of units such as the SAS to the Dhofar theatre. Combined, these aspects therefore provide a strong justification for the case that the Dhofar War, to all intents and purposes, was a British-run affair.

Chapter 13

British-Linked War Strategy

War Strategy – development and control

From the outset of the Dhofar conflict, the overall campaign strategy was developed and implemented by British personnel, and this advanced planning and military expenditure strategy led directly to the achievement of eventual victory. The key individual charged with theatre-specific strategy development was the British-supplied CSAF. The seconded CSAF was an experienced military professional who had the devolved autonomy from both his British and Sultanic superiors to devise his own theatre strategy. By virtue of the prevailing chain of command there was also a level, albeit capped, of UK military, Ministry of Defence, and therefore British government input.

This strategy was approved via the UK nationals in the political position of Omani Military Secretary (Defence Secretary equivalent) who would gain the Sultan's 'buy-in' to the general strategic approach. This strategy was then executed in-theatre by the seconded (and contract) British officers of the SAF from the mid-1960s, with input from regular officers of the UK armed forces from 1970 when units were deployed to Oman. Dhofar War strategy was therefore largely both devised and carried out by British personnel in one guise or another.

July 1970 is often portrayed as the turning point in the war and the change from the phase of poor performance, due to changes instigated as a result of the coup which brought the new Sultan Qaboos to the throne.[1] One of the most important outcomes of this event was that the SAS was initially deployed to Oman, initially a few men but later in two squadron strength. This was a key element of the attempt by British commanders to implement a 'classical style' or "model" COIN campaign as had been applied elsewhere with more than a modest level of success, including in the Malayan Emergency.[2] One of the key developments was the adoption of the SAS's then commanding officer, Lieutenant Colonel John Watts' plan to turn around the Dhofar campaign from a stagnating potential loss into a win. Watts was a highly experienced Special Forces operator and veteran SAS commander. He also had previous experience of the country with active service in the campaign to recapture the Jebel Akhdar in 1959 during the Imamate rebellion. In a perhaps curiously timed event, Watts was to visit Oman at the behest of the British government prior to the landmark 1970 coup (in March of that year) to review the Dhofar War situation and make recommendations on how to turn the campaign around potentially with SAS help. The result was the Watts 'Five-Point Plan' which formed the basis or blueprint for what developed into Operation STORM, the codename assigned for the SAS operational deployment to Oman.[3] The key recommendations of the plan prioritised the most urgent areas of concern relating to the COIN campaign. The first recommendation was the critical requirement to improve the intelligence picture in Oman. As such, this included the need to both develop and implement an effective intelligence system. This was because there was neither an effective military or civilian intelligence gathering or analysis system in place in early 1970, and there was consequently very little knowledge of Adoo unit command structure, strength and dispositions. The SAS had the experience and skills to achieve this in a relatively short time frame. To wear down insurgent morale and fighting capability the second priority was to encourage defections from the insurgent ranks over to the government side, utilising amnesty, and 'reward' payments for weapons turned in for example. Thirdly, the priority was to implement a veterinary assistance and water-provision programme to show the government wanted to help the Jebalis who lived primarily off the land. This was key, non-military 'hearts and minds'-type activity. The fourth priority was to provide – often extremely basic – medical assistance to the Jebali population which would act alongside the third factor to promote goodwill amongst the population, and would be effective simply because there was literally zero medical support in place for the Jebalis at the time. The fifth priority was to instigate a Psyops programme to spread 'white propaganda' in Dhofar to capitalise on the goodwill elements, counter the disinformation being spread by foreign supporters of the insurgents (for instance via Radio Aden and Radio Cairo wireless stations) and further reinforce the 'positive' government narrative.[4]

These elements would have been familiar to British troops, and especially SAS soldiers who had served in previous UK COIN campaigns. They were tried-and-tested constituent parts of a classical British-style 'hearts and minds' methodology on how to both educate and change the way the Dhofaris thought about the central government, and in effect 'win over' their support. Such elements had all been used before individually or in concert in Britain's previous COIN campaigns with considerable success. In Oman's case this equated to improving the image of the Sultan's administration and the SAF whilst discrediting the insurgents. As such, it was also designed to degrade their ability to fight to eventually win over the loyalty or support of the Jebali population to the government side. The idea was that if the population's support could be 'turned', it would enable a denial of support for the insurgents and deplete the numbers of their fighting ranks through desertion (and recruitment to the government-controlled indigenous Firqa militia units) to enable the Dhofar campaign to be won. To enable what was essentially still a theoretical plan to be activated quickly, the overall Director of the SAS, Brigadier Fergie Semple visited Oman post-coup to see the situation for himself. As a result the original Watts plan was tweaked in minor aspects. To all intents and purposes, however, the essence of the original plan was not subsequently altered in any major way for the remainder of Operation STORM or of the wider COIN campaign.[5] Viewed more broadly, the Watts Plan proposed a strategy that would enable the population to be gradually won over. Not straight away, but incrementally, and with improved intelligence, this would allow the military line to be held and the potential initial defeat of government forces to be avoided. Essentially this was a 'fixer' scheme to bail out a campaign teetering on failure. This 'avoiding defeat' baseline, enhanced by increased numbers of Surrendered Enemy Personnel (SEP) would then progressively enable the Adoo to be weakened, and would then enable the SAF to go fully on the offensive and eventually defeat them. Combined with the SAS's creation of the Firqa indigenous militia capability, this end state was achieved acting in tandem with more conventional warfare aspects.

The SAS role in the Watts Plan in both helping to avoid initial defeat for the Sultanate and in the wider ongoing war effort was pivotal in all respects.

In order to categorise the importance of the SAS to the Dhofar Conflict and Omani COIN effort, it should be stated that the secret SAS deployment was the foundational element of the British Government's strategy to both revive and invigorate the ailing Dhofar campaign. It was something long pushed for by CSAFs, especially former commando Brigadier Corran Purdon, who knew their value in irregular warfare scenarios. Inexplicably barred from operating in Oman by Sultan Said given their key role in defeating the Imamate rebels and storming the Jebel Akhdar, the SAS were not involved in Oman in any official capacity until circumstances relating to Omani governance changed dramatically. Once Sultan Qaboos had taken power in 1970 the British were officially 'invited' (which essentially meant that Qaboos rubber stamped the British proposal) to provide further assistance to the overall COIN campaign, and the SAS were finally deployed for duties in Oman.[6] It is likely that forward elements of the SAS were deployed to Oman within days, if not hours of the successful coup to get to work as outlined in Watt's plan.

Post-coup the SAF was quickly expanded, and the COIN campaign in general received a substantial financial and material boost. Watt's 'Five-Point Plan' was the central tenet of the campaign once the SAS deployment was underway. It was a distilled version of previous well-worn and utilised British COIN experience over several decades. Veterans of either the Malayan Emergency or Kenyan

Mau Mau campaigns would have been familiar with the general approach to win over the inhabitants whilst facilitating the attrition of insurgent numbers and capability.[7] The rudimentary level of civil development undertaken by British-controlled forces in Malaya for instance, was taken further in Dhofar. In Malaya, new, albeit very basic, settlements were constructed for the vulnerable (or collaborationist) ethnically Chinese squatters to both isolate them from the insurgents and attempt to improve their security and material standard of living. In Dhofar, Civil Action Teams (CATs) run initially by SAS troopers undertook well-digging projects, and the construction of shops, mosques, schools, and government centres in coastal settlements and on the Jebel which exhibited the importance attached to such activities from the government. With the expansion in 'hearts and minds'-related activities later in the campaign, such relatively ad hoc yet widespread SAS-led undertakings eventually evolved into a formal government department in 1975 under former Gurkha and second-in-command of the Muscat Regiment Lieutenant Colonel, Martin Robb which was known as the Civil Aid Department (CAD).[8] The Watts Plan recognised that the key to winning the war was the support of the people, and the key to winning over the people was to help their stomachs to be full, their (numerous) medical issues to be addressed and perhaps most importantly their, and their family's security to be guaranteed. The highly effective 'sticks and carrots' approach it promoted was something very familiar to a number of the senior SAF and regular British officers in Oman who had served in previous classical British COIN actions. This included the twelve-year-long Malayan campaign; where distinguished veterans included both Watts as the architect of the new approach in Dhofar, as well as other senior SAS commanders who served in the province including later Generals Tony Jeapes and Peter De La Billiere.[9]

An important aspect of the SAS-devised and implemented 'hearts and minds' strategy in Dhofar was the promotion of the government 'narrative' and use of 'white' propaganda to counter that of the insurgents. Much effort in this area was expended to undermine the Marxist leaders of PFLOAG who had consolidated their grip on power and ousted the original nationalists by 1970. This was achieved by reinforcing the message that the atheist Communists were not acting in the Dhofari's best interests. They were portrayed, with some justification, as outsiders who were anti-Islam, and therefore that their cause could not be trusted. Islam was the cornerstone of the existence of much of the Jebali population, and the insurgents were attempting to force the tribespeople to abandon their religious beliefs. The key slogan penned and implemented by the in-house SAS Psychological Warfare unit was "Islam is our way, Freedom is our aim", and it was specifically designed to break down any support for the righteousness or ideals of the 'heroic' insurgents by emphasising the fundamental incompatibility of their anti-religion Marxist-inspired beliefs with Omani society.[10] This team utilised an innovative range and blend of methods to convey this message to the Dhofari, and importantly the Jebali people. They utilised Sultan of Oman's Air Force (SOAF) assets to drop information leaflets over targeted areas of the Jebel. These were in-house designed, produced locally or in Bahrain, and were often largely pictorial pamphlets tailored to the fact that most people were illiterate and therefore could not read.[11] Wireless broadcasts devised by a dedicated SAS Non-Commissioned Officer (NCO) Psyops were made to the Jebali population via the newly-established Radio Dhofar which was established specifically for this purpose, and message delivery was ensured by the distribution of cheap transistor radios to all corners of the jebel.[12] These were not free, as even a nominal cost endowed them with 'value' or a level of 'prestige' or they would likely be discarded by the inhabitants. Radio Dhofar therefore provided the first public counter-narrative to the years of subversive propaganda and disinformation fed to the Dhofari population via Radio Aden and Radio Cairo and as such was a key, SAS-implemented initiative. Ultimately, such operations as scrupulously formulated and executed by the SAS were deemed both vital and highly effective in sowing the seeds of doubt in the minds of the Jebalis as to where their best interests lay and weakening the insurgent cause.[13]

Such initiatives helped to significantly weaken insurgent morale and led to a situation where the initially small numbers of SEPs defecting to the government side expanded rapidly. By reinforcing the Dhofari population's growing disillusionment and alienation from the increasingly militant, abusive (carrying out torture and executions of 'uncooperative' Jebalis), and Marxist-controlled insurgent organisation, numerous fighters and supporters of the insurgents defected to the government side.[14] Just in the period 1st January 1971 to 1st March 1972, some 420 SEPs abandoned the insurgent cause and came over to the government side – with many of them joining the Firqa units so boosting COIN force numbers also – out of the total 1,591 SEP cases by the war's official end.[15] This situation was further reinforced by the more expansive theatre-wide strategy devised and implemented by Brigadier Graham as the CSAF to 'divide and conquer' the jebel by carving up the territory utilising man-made physical lines made of barbed wire and reinforced either side with minefields to deter access. These were designed to disrupt insurgent communications and supplies from the Hauf safe area in PDRY territory eastward into Dhofar. The main hub in Dhofari territory was the western Sherishitti supply dump and base area, and the disruption of the logistical flow of materials across the border and to the east of Sherishitti would then restrict onward distribution across to the central and eastern jebel regions. In turn this was aimed to slowly squeeze the logistical

194   The Dhofar Conflict

supply of insurgent groupings operating to the north of Salalah, Taqa, and Mirbat to hamper their ability to fight. The use of blocking lines should not be considered a brilliant new plan devised by the CSAF. Although the overall COIN campaign ended in failure, the French had utilised such a theatre strategy with considerable success in Algeria. The Morice Line was completed in Algeria in 1957 and featured electrification, minefields and *in situ* stationed patrol troops and was highly effective in reducing insurgent activity originating from across the border in Tunisia.[16] It was a new approach in the Dhofar theatre however, and was both professionally and enthusiastically implemented by Graham following experience of seeing the effectiveness of the French approach whilst assigned to a NATO role in France.[17] Graham effectively co-opted and utilised the French approach to 'squeeze' the insurgents and put increasing pressure on the organisation, as well as to erode morale all with the aim to curtail their overall fighting ability. After the 'divide' of the engineer-constructed lines, the 'conquer' element would take place. Here, the insurgents would be 'flushed out' of the areas hemmed in by the lines from each sector. Firstly, the eastern and central regions were largely cleared, and operations then moved progressively further west. This Graham-instituted theatre strategy which resulted in the Hornbeam Line was continued with vigour by Major General Tim Creasey when he took over the CSAF role. Under Creasey's watch and via Brigadier Jack Fletcher as his Dhofar Brigade Commander, construction took place of the Iranian-built Damavand Line in the Western theatre, and all such 'divide and conquer' initiatives helped to neuter the operational effectiveness of the insurgents and contributed significantly to their eventual defeat.[18]

Development of Intelligence Capabilities

The acquisition and use of good intelligence and the development of the necessary machinery to sustain it is vital for any successful COIN campaign.[19] A deficit of quality intelligence was an instrumental factor in the COIN failures sustained by Britain in Palestine, Cyprus, and Aden. Conversely, the police and military intelligence infrastructure formed and honed throughout the 12-year-long campaign in Malaya was key to the eventual insurgent defeat. The topic is of specific interest because of the initial acute lack of quality intelligence in both Oman and Dhofar in particular for a large period in the war. From the start of the Dhofar campaign, Sultan Said forbade his then CSAF (Colonel Lewis) to deploy an intelligence officer to the province on the initial required SAF deployment to Dhofar in 1964. Due to his expert knowledge of the province he had an alternative solution. Through his links to the tribes and their leading personalities, his Wali-based system of authority and wide retinue of servants and advisors who had their 'ear to the ground', the Sultan assured his CSAF that he would provide all necessary intelligence himself so SAF intelligence officers in Dhofar were not required.[20] This edict was ignored by the CSAF, Colonel Lewis and the Force Intelligence Officer (the then) Captain Bob Brown was smuggled into the province disguised as a standard NFR regimental officer.[21] The initial situation relating to the 1964 deployment was recovered, but this controlling, almost paranoid attitude towards intelligence was a recurring theme throughout the rule of Sultan Said and hampered the war effort.[22] With the above situation relating to the Sultan, allied to limited resources, the pervasive lack of both intelligence gathering and analysis capabilities also had an effect on the campaign. One of the reasons for the staging of the coup to oust Sultan Said was the NDFLOAG attacks in northern Oman in June 1970, which were the result of significant failures in intelligence. Although successfully contained with most insurgents captured or killed, the attacks indicated how fundamentally weak the intelligence apparatus was in terms of detecting and preventing such subversive activity in Oman and in Dhofar especially and the vulnerability of the Omani ruling status quo.[23] The NDFLOAG episode also highlighted the scale of anti-regime activity in the whole of Oman and not just in Dhofar itself, which was seen by many in the UK as well as in Oman as the 'last straw' with the situation having gone too far therefore necessitating a change in leadership.

Post-coup the SAS provided a substantial uplift in intelligence-gathering and utilisation, an example being the development of the first complete Order of Battle (ORBAT) for the Insurgent organisation. The SAS also both harnessed and maximised the new and clear intelligence-gleaning possibilities of the newly developed Firqa organisation to create the first purpose-formed military intelligence cell in the Sultanate.[24] This SAS-run cell undertook the centralisation of all intelligence sources in a joined-up manner to increase the useability of information gathered. As such it enabled all elements of the archetypal intelligence cycle of activity to be undertaken relating to the full spectrum of collection, collation and analysis, and dissemination of such information to the end users which in Oman and Dhofar specifically would primarily be the SAF command hierarchy.[25] To enable the implementation of such activities alongside BATT (and in equal secret), members of the British Army's Intelligence Corps (IC) were covertly deployed to Dhofar from the post-coup months of 1970 to add an extra layer of specialist expertise to intelligence-related efforts. As part of efforts to develop the human intelligence (HUMINT) capabilities of the fledgeling military intelligence cell, specialist IC interrogators known as the BATT 'Radio Detachment' were drafted in as part of this deployment.[26] Intelligence gained from the debriefing and interrogation of surrendered Adoo fighters was a key string to the bow of the new intelligence cycle capabilities of Omani COIN forces.

At the state level, this process of professionalisation was also pursued. The civilian Office of Information Services (OIS) was founded in the post-Said era to provide a standalone civilian intelligence capability and to support the war in Dhofar and was later renamed the Oman Research Department (ORD) in 1974.[27] The OIS was both set up and mentored by Secret Intelligence Service (SIS/MI6 officers and it had a British officer, former Bomber Command navigator Colonel and later Brigadier. And a future Lord Lieutenant of Orkney) Malcolm Dennison as its head.[28] The SIS/MI6 resources were seconded to the Sultanate to build its overall intelligence capability in a concerted British government effort to rectify the poor intelligence picture in both Oman generally and especially in the Dhofar theatre. This development, alongside the intelligence-gathering and utilisation capabilities of the SAS and Intelligence Corps personnel had a fundamental role in developing both the profile of, and the effectiveness of intelligence utilisation of the Sultan's administration. This, in turn, was a boon to the CSAF and other senior SAF commanders who now had access to important data on which to better develop their overall strategic approach and follow-on operational efforts to the benefit of the COIN effort in general.

Such post-coup developments in the intelligence field were to prove vital. This was in terms of the overall COIN campaign but also from a more immediate perspective in terms of threat. In 1972, the new intelligence apparatus sprang into action to help thwart an immediate threat posed by PFLOAG's northern Oman-based affiliate organisation, the National Democratic Front for the Liberation of the Occupied Arabian Gulf (NDFLOAG). In December 1972, Operation JASON was launched which aimed to dismantle the immediate threat posed to the Sultanate by the organisation, and as a result, via coordinated raids, dozens of suspected members of the organisation were apprehended and taken into custody in northern Oman. Of the upwards of 50 individuals apprehended, among their number were serving military officers, members of the Oman Gendarmerie as well as even the staff driver of the then OIS intelligence service head Malcolm Dennison.[29] Operation JASON was described by British Ambassador Donald Hawley as a very "close run" business.[30] Had the requisite intelligence not been available and the operation not successfully launched, it could have been disastrous for not just the Dhofar campaign but Oman in general. Due to the largely British-instigated intelligence-related efforts via the SAS and SIS, the NDFLOAG cells and their weapons caches were discovered, and their plans in Northern Oman were thwarted. The military ringleaders were then subsequently executed by firing squad, which clearly demonstrated to all the price of disloyalty and treason which acted as a further deterrent.[31]

That the NDFLOAG and its activities in northern Oman were both effectively detected and subsequently largely dismantled was a feather in the cap of British government, and its seconded representatives' efforts to improve the intelligence organisation in Oman. Had British efforts in the intelligence capability sphere not been so determined, the result for Oman at this fragile stage of the COIN campaign could have been terminal for the governing status quo as well as the Sultanate's COIN effort.

It can therefore be seen that from the 1958 'Exchange of Letters' between the British and Omani governments, control at the strategic level was largely British. This was a situation created through the process of pledging the services of British officers to lead the new armed forces of the Sultan and at every level through the military chain of command down to regimental level. The Sultans undoubtedly had their say with regards to military actions and were accommodated, when possible. When such factors became too much of an issue, however, and were negatively affecting the campaign to the level that defeat was a possibility, a British-backed coup changed the Sultanate's leadership to the benefit of the war effort. The CSAF was responsible for theatre strategy, and Brigadier John Graham implemented the 'divide and conquer' approach to engage the insurgent threat. This approach essentially pushed the insurgents west towards the PDRY border, boxing them in to an increasingly diminished area utilising a series of blocking lines. Each line was constructed further to the west and included the 30-mile-long Hornbeam Line, and the later Iranian-built Damavand Line, as well as less substantial obstacles such as the Leopard and Hammer Lines. To support 'their man on the ground', post-coup the British government took the strategic decision to significantly raise military aid to Oman and deploy regular support units. These included the Royal Engineers, Royal Artillery, Intelligence Corps, and finally arguably most importantly (especially in the immediate post-coup era in 1970 up to the end of 1972), the SAS Regiment. These decisions were made to prevent a loss of Oman to a potential communist alternative form of governance, and safeguard the economic importance of the Strait of Hormuz of which one half was Omani-controlled. Allied to this were the historical links between the UK and Oman which spanned back over 200 years and the close cooperation between the Sultanate and initially the British Indian government and then the UK government after Indian independence in 1947.

The British decision to send Special Forces troops to Oman was a strategic-level decision which paid off handsomely. The SAS's unique skill sets, experience and capabilities literally took a losing campaign and helped turn it around in less than two years. Special Forces units are designed to have larger strategic-level effects which outweigh their costs, and traditionally usually keep a low profile. Operation STORM and the often two squadron deployment of the SAS to Oman was secret. Post-coup whilst the UK's governmental information and publicity machine was justifying further British, then later Jordanian and Iranian intervention, the SAS role remained secret, right up until their departure from Oman in 1977 and for several years beyond. The unit's input in creating an Omani military intelligence capability, information/propaganda services to weaken the morale of the Adoo, and their training and leading of the Firqa units was key to the final victory. The task could simply not have been completed without them. That is not to say victory was achieved because of the SAS. The SAS was one critical element, but not the only one. British political and diplomatic support, as well as military and economic aid, were all key factors. The win should be viewed as all such elements or 'instruments of state power' working in concert to achieve the final aim.

Chapter 14

Operational Control, Training & War Fighting

Strategic level decisions or approaches are key to winning in COIN, and the Dhofar War is a very good illustrative case study. Such decisions, from that by the British government to back regime change in Oman and to deploy regular forces to the Sultanate, and Brigadier Graham's winning 'divide and conquer' theatre strategic approach. A Special Forces capability is a strategic level capability. The decision to deploy the SAS to Oman was a strategic level move by the UK authorities. The SAS's subsequent influence was so significant in the Dhofar conflict because it reverberated through all the levels of warfare, from the strategic level down. Strategic level factors are, however, only as good as the operational-level implementation of such plans, and the ground-level tactical execution. Actions at the tactical and operation levels can likewise fundamentally impact at the strategic level, with the Battle of Mirbat in early 1972 being a key example. The UK had a fundamental impact at the operational and tactical levels which arguably makes the war, and the final defeat of the insurgent threat, a largely UK-facilitated outcome.

From the CSAF to the regimental and unit commanding officers, the operational control of the SAF was effectively in the hands of serving UK seconded military personnel. Add to this the fact that second-in-command regimental personnel were usually experienced British officers on private contract to the Omani authorities, and that a former career British army officer was employed as the Military Secretary (effectively Defence Secretary) by the Sultan, and this adds up to a situation where UK officers, and therefore Britain indirectly, had almost complete operational control of the SAF. As such, senior British regimental officers, reporting to the contemporary CSAF, had almost full autonomy to prosecute the COIN campaign on a day-to-day basis whilst deployed in Dhofar. This remained the case until 1971 when the Dhofar theatre was designated as a separate command with a full Colonel initially in charge, and later when numbers of personnel, equipment, units, capability and responsibilities grew even larger with a Brigadier at the helm. This was a far cry from the start of the war when the initial wartime commander of Omani forces was only of Colonel rank. With British personnel at all military levels including the CSAF or overall SAF commander, influence was, therefore, maintained throughout the campaign, with only the Sultan himself and the British Military Secretary more senior in position with regards to Oman's armed forces.[1] As Brigadier Corran Purdon stated, "I was… totally independent. I had no boss, other than the Sultan, who was Commander-in-Chief of his Armed Forces."[2] Especially in the early days of the war, the CSAF and his subordinate commanders were able to fight their own personal war with limited outside interference. As the war progressed, from 1972 Iranian troops began to arrive and Jordanian forces from 1974. Eventually the combined numbers of such troops vastly outnumbered those deployed by the UK. By 1975, Britain's approximately 1,000 (mainly support) military personnel were allied to some 4,000 combined Iranian and Jordanian troops, and not forgetting the now expanded approximately 10,000 military personnel of the SAF consisting of Omani, and an even larger number of Baluchi contract soldiers from Pakistan.[3] Such forces were quickly to take over significant responsibilities in the Dhofar theatre and were by 1975 eventually either patrolling or guarding key locations against enemy actions or were at the forefront of many of the vital offensive operations.[4] Such non-British forces, or a wider coalition of several international partners, have been credited with achieving the eventual insurgent defeat and it is difficult to argue against this from an operational perspective.[5] It was, however, from the operational control perspective stemming from the almost complete British dominance in the SAF chain of command and leadership at every level that the UK operational and tactical level role can be viewed. Along with the CSAF having all foreign forces placed under his command, these combined factors illustrate the British role in achieving the 'win'.

By virtue of the military chain of command and pastoral system in the SAF regimental system, British officers had always overseen internal unit training. As most regimental officers were of UK descent, such training was largely undertaken along British army lines. Despite the language differences (either Arabic or Baluchi), the tactics taught were essentially borne from UK training manuals with standard operating procedures (SOPs) adjusted as required for local conditions. From 1970, this aspect was further reinforced. When the accelerated expansion of the SAF began post-coup, extra professional training expertise was required to build up a capable force which more than tripled in size in less than two years to 10,000 personnel.[6] This came in the form of regular British military personnel or units brought in to cope with the extra training demands to prepare the new troops for Dhofar operations and likely combat. The SAF soldier training regiment based at Ghalla in northern Oman was expanded, and overall training capacity and capability enhanced by visiting resident instructional teams released on rotation from British military units (primarily Royal Marines and British Army) initially from Bahrain, Sharjah, and Cyprus.[7] Attention was also turned to the fledgling non-British officer training requirement. As part of the ambitious and wide-ranging 'Oman-isation' plan put into place and managed by the SAF's Deputy Commander, Colonel Colin Maxwell, a rudimentary officers' training wing was also established at the Ghalla facility in 1971 and was commanded by a British officer.[8] Despite being run with minimal facilities the officer training programme was a positive development. Although undoubtedly positive, the initiative did not impact the war to any great extent as it started late in the conflict in terms of training times for producing Omani and Baluchi SAF officers. It did not take place in time for them to gain experience and be promoted up the chain of command to positions of operational or strategic impact. The programme did, however, help shape the continuing development of indigenous Omani military capability and laid the foundations for an Omani officer corps and later a fully 'Oman-ised' military force. From a minimal number of Arab officers with no permitted command responsibilities, the new training programme resulted in approximately 100 officers of Arab or Baluchi origin being either in the officer training pipeline attending academies abroad or having 'passed out' from Ghalla by 1972.[9] Not only preeminent in terms of command and execution of the Dhofar campaign and the training of SAF soldiery, British seconded or contract officers essentially initiated the entire officer training programme for Oman. This fed into the overall SAF 'Oman-isation' programme which, somewhat ironically would see the eventual replacement of all British officers seconded to the organisation in a relatively short period of time. Related to this, all senior SAF command positions were to become held by Omanis eventually by 1990, with the departure of the long-serving British Air Vice-Marshal Erik Bennett as the seconded commander of the SOAF.[10]

As had been done in previous British COIN campaigns, another key element of UK training input in Oman and the Dhofar COIN campaign was that of the Firqa units. Utilising long regimental experience gained from such campaigns, the Firqa were not only created, but also trained, mentored and initially led into battle by members of the SAS. By the end of the war, the Firqa units comprised approaching 2,000 individuals, with the vast majority of them trained by members of the BATT, and later in the war by former SAS troopers returning to Oman on private contract to the SAF.[11] Despite an abortive start with the dissolution with the multi-tribal Firqat Salahadin which suffered a mutinous outbreak (and was subsequently disbanded) and continued issues relating to reliability and lack of discipline, the Firqa played a key role in the campaign.[12] The Firqa units were largely made up of insurgents who surrendered either by effect of government 'white' propaganda, fears relating to their leaders, the bounty paid for weapons handed in or the amnesty programme instigated post-coup. Many were also 'turned' and became Firqa recruits due to tribal or family links. As such, it was not unknown for there to be both insurgents and Firqa members in the same Jebali families. In addition to this recruitment role the same kinship and family-related factors brought important benefits in terms of intelligence, which, once the SAS-developed intelligence cell was functional, assisted the SAF in both the planning and conduct of operations. Furthermore, the Firqa employed the same well-developed and instinctive martial skills well-suited to their jebel homeland for the SAF as many had shown in their previous incarnations as insurgents, which provided great 'raw' potential for military use. To capitalise on this, the SAS soldiers allocated to the Firqa lived with and worked alongside their steeds. They lived in very basic, if not 'deprived' conditions and moulded their fledgling units with patience and skill. This was no different to the approach their regimental forbears and the unit had undertaken in previous COIN campaigns. Here, such as in Brunei/Borneo and Malaya the SAS had lived 'cheek by jowl' alongside indigenous tribespeople, learning their language, working with their customs and traditions and cultural idiosyncrasies. The SAS provided everything for their Firqa units from training to rations and ammunition and most crucially field leadership. The natural skills of the Jebali tribesmen were honed and disciplined into effective units and then employed to the benefit of the Sultan's administration. Benefitting from training from elite SF soldiers, this was often to a higher standard even than regular SAF troops.[13]

Whilst the Firqa were undoubtedly at times ill-disciplined, irresponsible, generally unreliable, and often selfish in their attitudes (extreme self, or parochial own-tribal interest), this would always be the case compared to professional, let alone Special Forces, soldiers of almost any state. Despite this, the Firqa were ultimately pivotal to the war effort. This was primarily because they created a 'kinship linkage' between the insurgents and government forces, operating in a grey area of loyalties which was difficult for any non-Dhofaris to comprehend. The SAF would unlikely have ever been able to as effectively persuade insurgents to voluntarily join the Firqa or give up valuable intelligence on insurgent positions or plans, which in turn would potentially have a campaign-level impact as the SAS. In all, with the clear British input to their utility, the Firqa were justifiably described by later SAS commander in Dhofar, Lieutenant Colonel Tony Jeapes, as the "most important government department to be created to win the war".[14] British influence therefore relating to the initial raising, and subsequent training and leading of the Firqa units was paramount. Without the SAS's long-proven ability to be able to mould effective indigenous militia units from scratch into multi-role (including combat) detachments, this would have deprived the COIN effort of a vital component. The likely knock-on effect of this would have been a longer war, making the final cost much higher in terms of 'blood and treasure' for both sides. The British strategic-level decision to send the SAS to Oman therefore reaped both tangible and significant operational benefits.

From the CSAF to the fighting regimental unit officers, Dhofar COIN campaign actions were conceived, planned and executed mainly by either seconded or contract British officers. This situation underlines the key position of the UK in the war's prosecution at operational and tactical levels. The CSAF, with senior British officers reporting to him directly, had almost full autonomy to prosecute the Dhofar campaign on a day-to-day basis, with only the Sultan himself and the (British) Military Secretary more senior in position in the SAF chain of authority. Accordingly British influence was maintained throughout the campaign right down to the actions of the most junior regimental officer, which in Dhofar was the army rank of captain.

These captains, who were either seconded from the British army (or equivalent rank from the Royal Marines or RAF) or contract officers, often had to take on more responsibility than their peers in the UK armed forces. In Dhofar, the smallest combat unit usually deployed was a half-company, of approximately 60 soldiers, commanded by a captain.[15] The language issue presented the first set of challenges for these men. It was not just a case of undertaking a standard military Arabic course at the Army School of Languages at Beaconsfield prior to deployment to be able to command such units. After the decision to split the mixed Arab and Baluch soldiers into ethnically separate entities in 1971 there were several Baluch-only language units.[16] The first formed was the Baluch Guard/Frontier Force (FF), followed in due course by the Southern Regiment (KJ) and the Western Frontier Regiment (WFR). These Baluch regiments were not only language specific but deployed constantly to Dhofar with no periodic rest to a northern Oman-based barracks like the Arab regiments. The British officers of these units had an especially challenging existence.

Added to this situation was the general inability to delegate technical tasks as would be the case in western armies, because of the general lack of technical education in terms of mathematics, or general military knowledge of using equipment other than standard rifles. Due to this, combined with the ever-present language issue, half-company to full company support elements such as heavy machine gun, mortar or external air support had to be coordinated by the British officer (usually of captain rank) on the ground. That is not to say the soldiers could not operate the equipment. They often could with skill and could be as brave as anyone else in battle, but could generally not coordinate independently as NCOs, corporals or even private soldiers were trained to do at the basic level in modern western-based armies. The British captain had to coordinate all fire support, including artillery, and call-in airstrikes from Omani air force assets himself, whilst leading any particular tactical action, leading Major General Creasey to comment that: "The fighting capability of any [SAF] sub-unit is [only] as good or bad as the standard of its British officer," adding that local troops in general "lack the education to be able to carry out many essential tasks in combat".[17] This was made more difficult by the language issue, as technical artillery support was largely controlled in English, and it was, even more importantly the standard operating language of SOAF. Strikemaster jet strafing machine gun runs on enemy positions, or diving Sura rocket attacks on dug in insurgent heavy machine gun or mortar positions, were called in and controlled in the English language. Lives depended on this communication process. With rare exceptions, the only individual with the capability to undertake this in a company or half company was the British officer. This led to a situation where such a captain in combat action would not only be leading his men to achieve the military objective but would also be coordinating his own mortars and fire support in either Arabic or Baluchi (pre-1971 he would often have to do this in elements of both languages) whilst also coordinating external support as required such as field artillery or air support in English.[18]

It was fortuitous that the high quality of British officer training, honed over decades if not centuries, produced a well-rounded and both technical and leadership-capable officer product. Added to this, especially in the early war years, even junior officers serving in Dhofar very often had prior experience of COIN campaigns. This included experience gained in Southeast Asia such as that in Brunei or the early Borneo campaign, or the rural combat in the Radfan and town-based urban anti-insurgent actions up to 1967 in Aden or later even Northern Ireland. This overall situation and level of responsibility for junior officers was summed up well by the CSAF from 1967–1969, Brigadier Corran Purdon, who stated about the men charged leading his Arab and Baluch soldiers that: "I greatly admired the splendid young British officers [either seconded or contracted to the SAF] who led them [their local soldiers] from the front", which, in turn, created strong, cohesive units which could perform well in arduous conditions.[19]

Wider SAS Role in Conflict

The SAS also brought a unique addition of skills and experience to Dhofar once officially deployed from 1970 after the July coup which brought Sultan Qaboos to power. Some officials had serious reservations about initially deploying the SAS to Oman and the British government refused to admit to its presence once actually deployed.[20] Their tour was only supposed to be for a limited six-month duration and confined to a single troop then squadron of men (approximately

16 to 64 personnel respectively). With an expansion of role and operational necessities, this grew to a two-squadron deployment for long periods of the war. Unlike for most other British units, the SAS did not leave and return home once victory was announced by Sultan Qaboos in December 1975. To continue their mission and promote stability as well as being on-call for any contingency, the SAS did not depart Oman until the following year, in 1976.[21] The change in size of deployment was also mirrored by that of the Regiment's role. The planned support-only and mentoring and training role did not last long. This quickly morphed into one where SAS soldiers were involved in direct combat alongside their Firqa understudies. The role of the SAS essentially became blurred between training and live combat operations, starting with Operation JAGUAR in October 1971 and the SAF's attempt to go on the offensive and gain a permanent foothold on the Jebel.[22]

Initially under the highly experienced command of Lieutenant Colonel John Watts, and followed by Lieutenant Colonel Peter De La Billiere and later Lieutenant-Colonel Tony Jeapes, the SAS and the reputations of their political masters were in good hands. With combined professional and unconventional warfare experience stretching into decades, including either involvement or combat operations in the Jebel Akhdar, Malayan and Borneo campaigns and the Yemen Civil War, these officers were the right men for the job at hand. 22 SAS Regiment was deployed to Oman within days of the coup under the purposefully bland pseudonym of the 'British Army Training Team' (BATT). The BATT was sent to stop the rot and help turn the campaign around. As a strategic-effect Special Forces capability, the SAS were not initially deployed to engage in combat duties, but merely to act as 'force multipliers'. The combat element did eventually happen, but they were sent initially in a purely support-related capacity to boost Omani military capability. In accordance with circumstances as well as the recently developed (by July 1970) Watts Five-Point Plan, the first role was to prop up the new regime with Sultan Qaboos at the helm. SAS troopers were dispatched to Oman almost immediately after the coup to intensively train and develop a bodyguard unit for the new Sultan. The SAF did not have this capability, and close-quarter urban or rural firearms training was a standard SAS skill set. This was undertaken because Oman, and especially Dhofar, was in a desperate state of social development. Despite the great outpouring of joy and celebration at the deposing of the widely disliked Sultan Said, no amount of tinkering could fix such anti-Sultan-related sentiments overnight. The fear was that once this positivity had subsided and old grievances once more potentially bubbled to the surface, Sultan Qaboos would have similar ire pointed towards him and his life could be in danger.[23] The first priority then was survival of the new administration. The next priority was bolstering SAF capability to fight and win against the insurgents. In a large operating area with small enemy units acting with virtual impunity on the Jebel, information was key. Firstly, the enemy's Order of Battle (ORBAT) was determined.[24] The Adoo ORBAT included the leadership hierarchy, the various units and their compositions, locations, and capabilities, allied to detailed breakdowns of supply routes and equipment and stores dumps.[25] Next, as previously described, the SAS helped to form the first military intelligence cell and re-organised all such assets to improve the intelligence picture on which operational and strategic decisions could then be based. Within the SAS intelligence unit, seconded British Army Intelligence Corps interrogators and Psyops specialists augmented the already vastly improved intelligence picture which had been almost completely lacking until the arrival of the SAS.[26] With the Sultan and ruling administration's safety protected and a much-improved intelligence picture developing, the next priority could be implemented. This was the art well-practiced by the SAS in theatres such as Malaya of developing and implementing 'hearts and minds'-related activities with the aim of winning over the population to the government side and eroding support for, and therefore the effectiveness of the Dhofari insurgents.[27] This followed a broadly two-pronged approach, with the first to win over the population, and the related second aim to encourage desertions from the Adoo to degrade the wider organisation's fighting ability.

On the first front, a priority was civil development and improving the 'lot' of the Jebalis. SAS medical teams started treating basic ailments of the local population, at coastal settlements, and after the 1971 SAF offensives (Operations LEOPARD and JAGUAR) were based at locations on the Jebel. This created goodwill among the people for very little cost with simple antibiotics creating 'miracle' cures and even (the often placebo effect of) Aspirin used to good effect on people who had never experienced any kind of modern medical treatment.[28] The only widespread treatment was that of traditional 'branding' using hot metal to burn the skin, which usually caused more problems with infection or gangrene than the initial ailments.[29] As part of the post-1971 offensive plans, SAS Civil Action Teams (CATs) also followed and helped develop wells and the building of health, educational and government-related buildings on the Jebel to show the government was trying to help the people and improve their lives. The CATs were successful and were the forerunners of the Omani-government funded Dhofar Civil Aid Department which formalised, expanded and continued their good works under Lieutenant Colonel Martin Robb in 1975.[30] By the war's end, the Dhofar Civil Aid Department alongside the activities of the original CATs had constructed over 40 government centres in the province, 50-plus wells, over 30 schools, and had laid down approximately 100 miles of tarmac roads, where prior, the latter had not existed at all.[31]

A government presence and new schools, mosques and wells were all positive developments. As a population, however, which lived off the land (and sea), helping the Jebalis to help themselves economically was also a key pillar of the SAS 'hearts and minds' mission. Not the kind of activity one might associate with elite special forces soldiers, but these developments were vital, nonetheless. Alongside personnel from the Royal Veterinary Corps of the British Army, SAS soldiers provided assistance to locals with their livestock ailments. They even went as far as to fly in prime Hereford Bulls from the regiment's home town in England to invigorate the rather depleted genetic stock of the existing herds.[32] They also organised a 'bull run' herding livestock off the mountains and into Salalah so the government could purchase head of cattle (as part of 'Operation TAURUS') to give the Jebalis a stake in the status quo as well as putting some much needed money in their pockets.[33] In addition, help was given relating to agricultural practices, the best crops to grow for the conditions, and even the establishment of a 'model' farm which doubled as a kind of rudimentary practical agricultural college.[34]

As highlighted previously, one of the key roles of the SAS in the Dhofar conflict was the raising of the local militia Firqa units. The SAS had almost total control and influence over this process until Firqa forces in their entirety were transferred to SAF control in 1972. Even after this date, such units were, however, subsequently still largely led by ex-SAS men contracted to the SAF even after the change of organisational command as they were effectively the only type of soldier able to handle their nuances and get the best performance out of them.[35] One of the key resulting factors was the morphing of the original support-type mission of the SAS to one involving combat. As well as raising, training, and supporting them in every possible way, it was found that the Firqa were only effective in action if also led by SAS soldiers. This meant of the approximately 600 Firqa trained and operational by 1971 (and the 1,800 local militiamen in existence by the end of the war) nearly all were trained and led either by serving, or retired SAS soldiers.[36] As a result, the CSAF had an extremely effective extra operational capability at his disposal. Only the highly trained SAS soldiers could both raise, control and get the best out of these often cantankerous, venous, disorganised, untrustworthy, yet often brave irregular militiamen who were highly 'connected' in both tribal and environmental terms. The role of the SAS in this sphere is alluded to by Dhofar Brigade Commander, Brigadier John Akehurst when commenting on the importance of the Firqa in the overall war effort, stating: "I must reiterate how vitally important the Firqats (*sic*) were in the struggle."[37] The CSAF, Brigadier John Graham, fully backed up this comment in his memoirs and vindicated the SAS efforts by stating: "The creation of the resultant Firqa force was to be a campaign-winning factor of cardinal importance."[38]

The Battle of Mirbat

Nowhere is the evolution of the SAS's support and 'capacity-building' role to one of combat duties illustrated more than the Battle of Mirbat. On 19 July 1972 government forces with a small, embedded SAS detachment initially held out against and later helped to defeat a large insurgent force which attacked the town at dawn. As other publications go into great depth on the details of the event, and the remit of this book is focused on the wider British role in the Dhofar War and counter-insurgency in general, the battle will only be covered in brief here. The battle was so important, however, from an operational and strategic perspective that a brief review is entirely appropriate.

By way of background to the battle, after the high hopes of turning the war around and defeating the insurgents after the 1970 coup, this initial enthusiasm was dampened. The initial Operation LEOPARD and JAGUAR high profile offensives carried out by the SAF to regain a foothold on the Jebel were somewhat of a disappointment in overall terms and the process of re-conquering the Jebel was slow and frustrating. In April 1972, Operation SIMBA was then launched. Here, a helicopter-launched assault was carried out close to the PDRY border to seize the strategically important Sarfait position which held the key to the cross-border insurgent supply routes. It was a bold, "audacious…[and also] strategically compelling" military action, but the Sarfait position itself was very difficult to defend.[39] The secured location subsequently required constant helicopter support and the position was under near constant insurgent attack using heavy calibre weapons, mortars and artillery.[40] It seemed the SAF had 'bitten off more than it could chew' in military terms and resources including of precious manpower and equipment were diverted which could have been better utilised in attacking the enemy elsewhere. Operation SIMBA did not end the war, nor did it defeat the insurgents, and the result was a level of anxiety or disquiet in many British SAF officers. The successful SOAF airstrikes against the Hauf stronghold in the PDRY which followed Operation SIMBA in May 1972 (in retaliation for the destruction of the Sultanate Fort at Habrut on the border) boosted SAF morale but stirred the metaphorical hornets' nest. Whilst not defeated, the insurgents were increasingly pressurised by the cross-Jebel blocking strategy instituted by Brigadier Graham as CSAF. The Adoo's long successful logistical supply routes from west to east were hampered and they suffered mounting casualties. The solution chosen by the insurgents was to attempt a 'spectacular' defeat over government forces, and they chose the isolated seaside town of Mirbat to prove their mettle and continued intent.[41]

In a departure from standard irregular warfare-type 'hit and run' tactics, the insurgents attempted a large-scale conventional assault on the town. They did so at dawn on 19 July, when the town's defenders consisting of some 30 local Askars, 25 Dhofar Gendarmerie soldiers, and the remainder of the Firqat Salahudin (the majority on patrol on the Jebel) were off guard, sleeping, or attending to their personal routines.[42] After killing the lookouts posted on nearby high ground over 200 insurgents attacked the town in coordinated waves, reportedly marching in 'open order' whilst firing their weapons.[43] The main focus of the insurgent attack was the isolated Mirbat Fort which was occupied by Dhofar Gendarmerie soldiers; an image of which you can see on the front cover of this book. The small SAS team was located in what became known as the 'BATT-house' near to the Wali's Fort, closer to the sea and guarding the entrance to the small town's port proper. The scale of the assault was unprecedented in the seven years of the war to date, and the SAS commander, Captain Mile Kealy led his men in a dogged defence of the town. One of the two Fijian SAS men present that day sprinted under fire from the BATT house to the DG Fort to help prevent its fall and ended up firing a Second World War-era artillery piece at zero elevation at the oncoming insurgents. Corporal Talaiasi Labalaba was seriously injured but contributed to the holding back of the attackers until some more support, including Captain Kealy, could arrive. The onslaught continued and only a break in the cloudy monsoon weather allowed British-piloted SOAF jets to operate and attack the insurgents as they advanced which helped to save the day.

The heroics were undoubted, but the words of the commander of the SAS in Dhofar at the time, Lieutenant Colonel Peter De La Billiere ring true that, "To call Mirbat a close-run thing would be a masterpiece of understatement."[44] It was rare strokes of luck firstly that elements of G Squadron SAS happened to be in-country to take over from their B squadron colleagues and could be airlifted to assist at short notice, and secondly that the 'Khareef' monsoon mists cleared to allow the SOAF aircraft (as commanded by Squadron Leader Bill Stoker) to devastate the insurgent ranks.[45] As a result of these fortuitous singularities, allied in no small part to the leadership and bravery of the SAS personnel present, the assault on Mirbat was nothing short of a catastrophe for the insurgents. The Adoo suffered 29 confirmed killed (where bodies were physically recovered) out of approximately 200 attackers (whilst it is estimated as many as 100 insurgents were probably killed) – a significant proportion of their overall fighting strength in the central Jebel sector and beyond.[46] Instead of achieving its aim of inflicting a humiliating public defeat on government forces, the defeat was squarely on the insurgents.[47]

The Battle of Mirbat was a serious setback for the overall insurgent cause and was a major, if not the key, turning point in the war and the SAS should take a significant amount of credit for achieving this.[48] To the CSAF of the time of the battle, Brigadier John Graham, described Mirbat as being the "Bloodiest nose ever suffered by [the insurgents]" and overall campaign success accelerated as a result.⁴⁹ The defeat was not only a military defeat for the insurgents but had a psychological effect on the insurgents and their cause. Post-battle there were recriminations, infighting, 'kangaroo courts' and executions of those held responsible for the shameful perceived outcome and a crisis of confidence in the leadership and the overall cause.⁵⁰ The SAS role was key in terms of the Mirbat detachment and vital G Squadron reinforcements, and the bravery shown was undoubted. On a visit to the Mirbat battlefield on the 50th anniversary of the event on 19 July 2022, the author's impression was of a bleak wasteland with open ground and zero cover for the handful of surprised defenders outside the isolated buildings they occupied. More astonishing was the act of bravery of Corporal Labalaba in his run from the BATT house to the DG Fort. The run was several hundred metres long, with zero cover and the latter half of it on a progressive incline. Many might consider the run near suicidal, and his actions at the DG Fort gun pit were equally brave, but these deeds helped hold off the attackers and eventually carry the day. Surely worthy of more than the posthumous mention in despatches as awarded to that brave soldier.

The SAS suffered multiple casualties that day, including one killed (Corporal Labalaba), and one who died of his wounds later, Trooper Tobin. Overall, however, the SAS-related contribution should not be seen out of context of the overall British-associated input which made the win at the Battle of Mirbat possible, from the SOAF jets under Squadron Leader Stoker (who Lieutenant-Colonel De La Billiere recommended for a bravery award in a letter to Brigadier Graham), to the UK-trained SAF forces and Firqa present who played their part.⁵¹ The SAS, however, played the key part in an action which seriously undermined the offensive capability of the insurgents and helped the overall COIN campaign turn a corner from stalemate to one of increasing success.

It can therefore be seen that in terms of military influence, although Britain still supplied the CSAF and senior regimental commanders of the SAF, the arrival of Jordanian and especially Iranian troops changed the balance. It meant a relative loss of British military superiority or numerical strength in 'on-the-ground' operations, even though the strategic picture was still largely controlled. In absolute numbers, by 1975 the Iranians and Jordanians combined had more than four times the numbers of military personnel in Dhofar than Britain, and it is to the former that the accolade of finally tipping the balance and seizing the final victory often goes.⁵² Even the British CSAF under whose watch the final victory in the Dhofar COIN campaign over the insurgents was achieved echoed this sentiment. The final wartime CSAF, Major General Ken Perkins stated that although Britain should be proud of its contribution in defending Oman and developing the strategy of victory it was ultimately the sheer weight of numbers

Table 6: Key British COIN Training and Warfighting Contributions to Dhofar Campaign.

Factor	Dates (Approx)	Specifics
CSAF	1964–1975 (entire Dhofar COIN campaign)	Every CSAF for the duration of the Dhofar COIN campaign was a serving British military officer
Seconded Military Advisors	1964–1975	All SAF regimental commanding officers were seconded British officers (2i/cs usually ex-regular British officers on contract)
Regular UK Military Units	1970 onwards	Deployment of Royal Engineers, Royal Artillery, Intelligence Corps units to Dhofar primarily in support-related capacities
UK Special Forces	1970 onwards	Formal 22 SAS Regiment deployment to Dhofar took place from 1970. Roles included Sultan bodyguard training, SAF training, intelligence duties and formation/training/leading Firqa units as well as other 'hearts and minds' activities such as medical assistance to Jebalis, veterinary support and information services (white propaganda)
UK Military Training Teams	1970 onwards	Regular British training teams despatched from Cyprus and Bahrain to train SAF units Regular UK personnel set up new SAF officer training Wing at Ghalla
Combat Assistance by Regular UK Forces	1970 onwards	Primarily SAS actions in conjunction with Firqa units. Move from training to support to leading and combat role for SAS detachments
Battle of Mirbat	July 1972	Key role of SAS in battle which was to prove major turning point of the war (aided by SAF and SOAF units) Multiple SAS casualties, but over 100 insurgent casualties overall and a clear (conventional) defeat for the Adoo forces

of extra troops as supplied by the Iranian forces that tipped the balance of the contest in the Omani government's favour.[53] The British CSAF simply did not have enough troops at his disposal to engage and defeat the Adoo and force through the win in the desired timeframe. He further stated that without the Iranian contribution, the war would have "dragged into stalemate" without the possibility of a decisive conclusion or win for the Omani government forces.[54]

In addition to this reduction in military influence, Britain's traditional and for many years' exclusive diplomatic role and associated sway over Oman, its Sultan and latterly the Dhofar COIN campaign also diminished over time. In 1970 Britain can be credited with facilitating the Salalah palace coup; the UK asserted such influence in a stark and decisive way for the last time in Oman.[55]

With the new Sultan quickly 'finding his feet' and gaining confidence he began to assert himself. Sultan Qaboos took over the role of the British-appointed and dominated Interim Advisory Council. He also then acted to both undermine and diminish the influence of his uncle Tariq within the government (who subsequently resigned as a result in 1971) and developed his own set of advisors from the Arab world and even the USA to counterbalance British influence.[56] As a result, over time the role and influence of the UK and British personnel over the internal and external affairs of Oman was progressively and substantially curtailed and limited to specific areas of government business and authority; primarily in the military sphere and the running of the Dhofar War as a result.

This reduction of UK influence over Oman and by default the Dhofar campaign is also apparent in Oman's emergence into the standard Westphalian system of diplomatic relations as first formalised at the Congress of Vienna in 1815.[57] Although facilitated by Britain behind the scenes using its influence to assist the acceptance of Oman into the Arab League then ultimately the UN in 1971, this meant a further reduction of overall influence in Omani affairs. Omani diplomatic missions were established in several countries and Muscat saw the establishment of foreign consuls and embassies which with the exception of India has been the sole and exclusive preserve of Britain for centuries. In addition there was a shift towards engaging diplomatically towards the countries of the Gulf region (including Iran) and North Africa, whereas prior to the events of 1970 Sultan Said had effectively left, or rather 'sub-contracted' the conduct of Oman's external affairs entirely to the UK.[58]

This resulted in the realignment of a quasi-colonial relationship with a European power to engaging fully with its regional neighbours as a country which finally resembled a full and sovereign entity. From an economic perspective, what had also been an almost exclusive bilateral relationship between Britain and (Muscat and) Oman also morphed into a much less exclusive relationship in which the former's influence was diminished. With the discovery of commercial oil deposits, the ending of the Zanzibar Subsidy and latterly the impact on hydrocarbon prices due to the 1973 Arab-Israeli 'Yom Kippur' War and resultant oil crisis, Oman was no longer financially dependent on the UK. The result of this situation was that it gave Sultan Qaboos more leverage to follow his own policies in terms of civil development, military expansion and procurement as well as with regards to the overall governance of his country. By 1973 Oman was well on the way to becoming a relatively wealthy nation and was by this time effectively financially independent of the UK. This reduced much of the historic economic leverage the UK exerted over Oman and diminished Britain's general level of influence over the country and consequently over the war.

Operational Control, Training & War Fighting   213

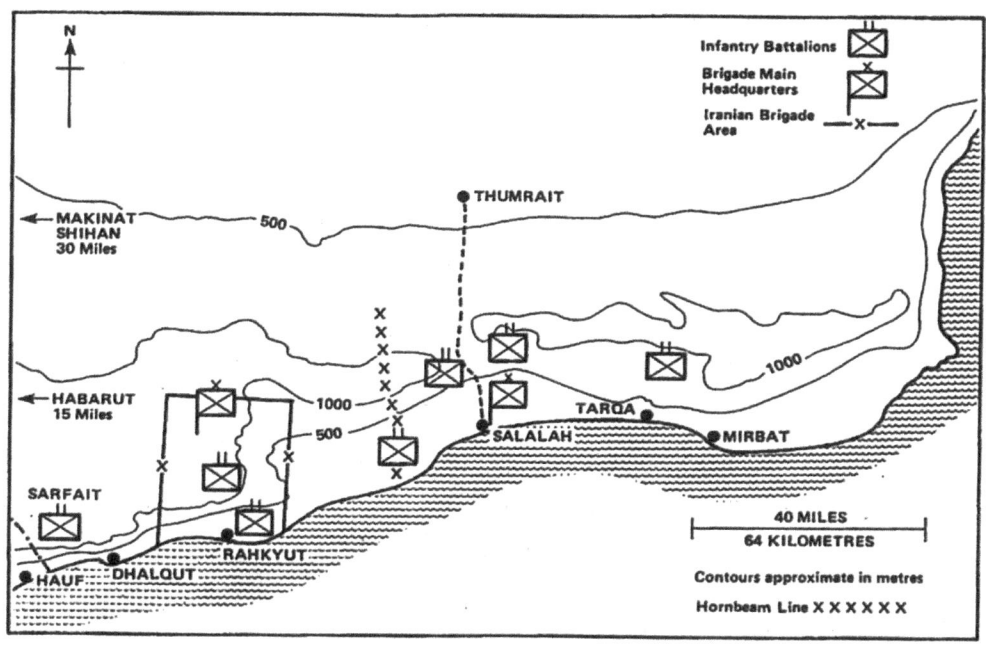

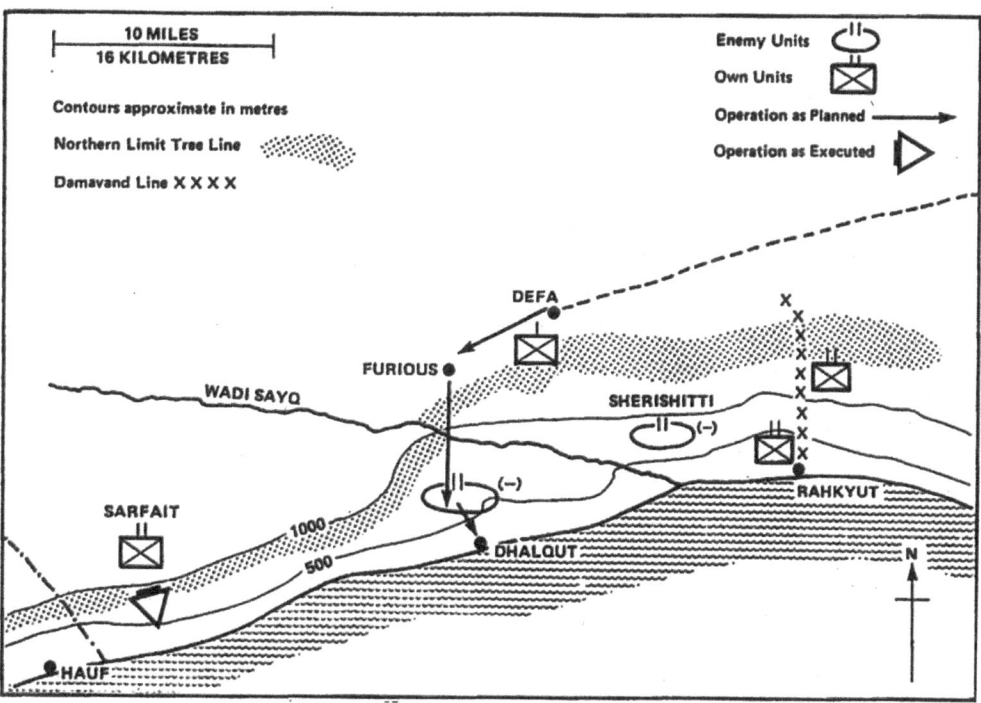

Figure 3: Map of Dhofar Operational Area – Final Operations.
Source: Perkins, K. "Oman 1975: The Year of Decision." *The RUSI Journal* 124, no. 1 (1979): 41. Reproduced courtesy of the RUSI journal.

Britain's influence on the development, operational execution and ultimately the Omani victory in the Dhofar COIN campaign is not in doubt. It was, however, not the same level of influence and control exerted over these aspects existing in 1975 as it did in 1964 when Colonel Lewis first deployed the SAF overground by Land Rover to Dhofar. For the many reasons outlined in this section, Britain should rightly be lauded as a, if not the, key external player in the Dhofar campaign. Oman itself aside, no other country exerted anywhere near the level of influence – both positive and negative – on the Dhofar COIN campaign. This can be even more clearly considered when the conflict is viewed as a decade-long struggle and not just a post-1970 or even a post-1973 military operation. When looking, however, at the decade-long timeframe of the war, the UK was not the only key player. Post-1970 its role in terms of relative influence and control diminished with surprising rapidity.

Final victory could not be assured or achieved without the expansive input, military numbers and fighting capability of a pre-revolutionary Iran. This was the case even with the SAF and allied forces technically under the command of a seconded serving British army general as the CSAF. In all it could be said that, "between 1968 and 1973, British assistance did not win the war in Dhofar, but it certainly prevented it from being lost", and that final victory was achieved by a British-engineered regional alliance and its control of war strategy.[59] These factors can ultimately be viewed as the UK's most significant achievements with regards to the Dhofar campaign, and was the UK's key strategic level 'management' or 'consultancy'-like role coming to the fore. The campaign was a highly UK-centric and influenced operation from its inception, but it was never completely, or even majority British in nature, unlike most, if not all of the previous classical-era UK COIN campaigns. Although the Dhofar campaign started off as an almost exclusively British-managed, run and funded venture, it was significantly less so towards the end of the campaign from 1973 to 1975; and Britain could not secure the final victory solely through its own efforts or influence.

Chapter 15

Conclusion

Although in many aspects very similar to previous classical-era UK COIN campaigns, many nuances or clear differences are apparent in the case of the Dhofar case. These, allied to its many singular circumstances which, like in the case of the Malayan campaign are unlikely ever to be repeated again, mean the Dhofar War should ultimately be considered unique in the history of British COIN.[1] In terms of success, although in many respects wasteful and more costly than envisioned at the outset, the war was eventually won, unlike many other cases of contemporary COIN campaign defeat for developed, ostensibly militarily powerful nations. It was a military success which had large scale strategic ramifications both on a regional and a worldwide basis. As to whether the Dhofar COIN campaign can be considered 'British', this is best seen through a shifting lens of influence, where the role for Britain changed from virtually complete control and influence to a somewhat weaker direct role, whilst retaining the most important levers of power and influence to control and affect the war's outcome. Throughout all aspects, the spectre of British Special Forces and primarily that of the SAS Regiment were writ large. Involved in a majority of the UK's classical-era COIN campaigns after its formation during the Second World War, Malaya was where the SAS found its role and justified its existence to the powers-that-be in the UK military and political establishments. Its role was key across multiple theatres in the prosecution of Britain's strategic aims over a decades-long timeframe. Its influence at the operational and tactical level was also no less significant. The Dhofar Conflict was no different in these respects.

Section 1 of this book establishes that there were certain key similarities which ran through most, if not all of Britain's classical-era campaigns. These ranged from background and strategic level circumstances to campaign-specific factors. On the surface Dhofar reflected closely previous UK COIN campaigns in these respects. At the same time, key fundamental differences are apparent, however, which means it cannot be considered a typical or archetypal British COIN campaign overall. Similarities with previous British COIN undertakings included those from a geostrategic background such as the common global Cold War/decolonisation background narrative. Also looming large was the issue of the UK withdrawal as a global power as well as specific actions like the drawdown East of Suez and from the Gulf region in the late 1960s and early 1970s. In terms of motivation and conduct of the Dhofar campaign, Britain's rationale for involvement was also similar to previous campaigns. Essentially this was based on general levels of expediency and calculations of self-interest, but was far from the Marxist-type view of colonial exploitation present in the wider war literature.[2] In terms of conduct of the war there were strong similarities also. The effectiveness of the operational conduct was generally competent and carried out in a manner which was arguably both humane, and true to the traditional 'minimum force' and restrained approach historically utilised by the British military in unconventional warfare campaigns.[3] The professionalism of the British officers involved meant the nature of the campaign was kept largely to disciplined UK-level expectations and past conduct which varied often with that of other COIN-conducting nations. This view is in contrast to the general narrative of several later revisionist writers on the subject who often emphasise the 'iron fist' elements of what is one of humankind's most base and violent pursuits.[4] Likewise, from an operational perspective, strong similarities are also apparent in terms of the type of terrain on which the COIN campaign was conducted (and resultant level of success), the classification of enemy being fought, and the typical mode of combat. Also similar are the eventual implementation (largely by the SAS) of elements of previously utilised 'hearts and minds' programmes and the utilisation for employment of indigenous forces to both provide intelligence as well as combatants. In addition, the relatively limited size, scope and general levels of cost of the Dhofar campaign was generally in keeping with most previous UK COIN operations. Minimum cost with maximum effect seems to be the British COIN maxim in general, and Dhofar was no different in this respect.

Although such similarities suggest the Dhofar campaign was much like its UK COIN predecessors, there were, however, fewer but fundamental differences which arguably negate such a classification. From a background perspective, key differences include the fact that unlike in all previous UK classical-era COIN operations the Dhofar campaign was not undertaken in sovereign UK or colonially-controlled territory. In addition, even though British military personnel were involved, the campaign was not carried out or executed either wholly or even primarily by sovereign UK, or British-controlled security forces.[5] Likewise in terms of campaign-specific factors, Dhofar can again be seen to be a standalone example. The higher quality of insurgent opposition faced in the province by COIN forces, for the most part the extreme low-tech nature of the conflict, and the fundamentally broader and larger-scope 'hearts and minds' campaign instigated to turn the campaign around from the low point of 1970/71 all differed. Also profoundly different in the case of Dhofar was the requirement to form an international coalition with British forces in the minority to enable the campaign to be turned from stalemate to winning ways. Conversely, the Dhofar campaign is also set apart by its outcome, being a clear COIN win in the end. Although with a record second-to-none in this respect, few, if any, of the UK's previous classical-era COIN campaigns replicated this level of operational success. Despite the clear similarities, these differences are so fundamental that the Dhofar COIN campaign can only be viewed as a standout or unique example in the history of classical-era UK COIN operations.

Section 2 of this book determines that, whilst many differences were apparent in the Dhofar campaign from a success perspective it was, however relatively typical of previous classical-era UK COIN actions. This was precisely because it was of mixed success. Notwithstanding the final result, far from being an all-embracing success, like its forebears, the campaign was significantly flawed and as such reflected the historical trend. Further, whilst it can undoubtedly be considered a success in overall relative terms, from an absolute success perspective this is less so. The Dhofar undertaking still exhibited many key absolute-level failures which detract from its traditional reputation as some sort of ideal or model-like campaign.[6] Although described as the best of any COIN campaign nation, in reality the British record was actually of very mixed success with highly successful campaigns waged in Malaya for example, but what can only be described as political (although not necessarily military per se) disasters such as Palestine or Aden also apparent.[7] As such, Dhofar was ultimately a relative or comparative success overall and led to a clear-cut win in 1975, whilst also exhibiting clear aspects of absolute failure.[8]

Dhofar was eventually a relative strategic and operational success. This can be seen when compared to both previous UK campaigns as well as to many of those of other COIN-undertaking nations of the classical era. It was also a success in terms of the relatively limited cost of the campaign for the UK. Likewise, it was also such for the continuing links achieved with COIN partners post-conflict, a military training and reputational boost for the country, and its overall reputation for military prowess. In addition, the campaign can be viewed as being a relative success for the Sultanate and the eventual coalition partners in several ways. The campaign did, however display many absolute-level operational failures which reappraises the traditional 'ideal' war narrative.[9] Poor pre-1970 military performance is apparent, allied to failures stemming from the SAF military structure and organisation, manning and equipment issues, and even from a theatre strategy and tactics perspective. In addition, even after the coup of July 1970 the traditional narrative that the campaign was quickly turned around to being successful or the revisionist-oriented view that it should be divided into unsuccessful pre-1970 and successful post-1970 phases can be considered flawed.[10] Although important in the long term, the 1970 coup was a 'false start' in terms of the hoped-for swift operation turnaround and success. It would not be until 1972 that the tide of the conflict had turned significantly. This resulted in a decade-plus long war and greater costs in terms of 'blood and treasure' than should have been the case if executed more efficiently or effectively. Like the overall historical classical British COIN record, the Dhofar campaign was similarly an amalgam of success and failure.

The Dhofar War was, however, from a relative perspective at least as successful as any UK COIN campaign of the classical era, or indeed compared to any other COIN-undertaking nation of the period.[11] This situation reinforces in a more nuanced manner the traditional view of the campaign whilst at the same time underlining the Dhofar War's unique status. Although significantly smaller in scale than the Malayan Emergency and many non-UK classical campaigns in both Africa and Asia, the fact remains that the strategic aims of the UK were achieved and a clear victory gained over a capable enemy. Further, it can be considered so in terms of a rare Cold War victory over communist insurgents in a relatively cost-efficient manner, and therefore can arguably be considered potentially the most successful UK COIN campaign of all time.[12] This not only makes it potentially 'best of class' in this respect but also the 'first of class' of a distinctly new type of COIN approach which additionally made it conceptually ground-breaking at the time and therefore, again, unique.[13]

Section 3 of this book establishes that fundamentally, the Dhofar campaign can be considered overwhelmingly 'British' in terms of inception and operational management. At the same time it also acts to clarify the narrative that somehow the Dhofar campaign was largely British in all key respects as with previous classical-era UK COIN campaigns. As such, Section 3 puts forward a more nuanced perspective that purports that the war was perhaps even more British-controlled (and won) than the general traditional literature views suggest. Importantly, the Dhofar campaign cannot, therefore, be considered a typical British 'classical-type' COIN campaign but can, however, concurrently be considered very much a UK COIN win.

Unlike in all previous classical-era British COIN operations the Dhofar campaign was not undertaken in UK-government-controlled territory but in that of a sovereign foreign nation. In addition, even though British military personnel were involved, the campaign was not carried out either wholly or even primarily by UK security forces but by the SAF and eventually by numerically similar or larger (than UK contribution) allied forces. Similarly, although the SAF was commanded by a serving officer of the UK armed forces, ultimately command lay with the Sultan of Oman and not the British Government. Further, the reality of Britain's influence or control of the Dhofar campaign is reflected in the 'sliding scale of influence' concept.[14] As such, this demonstrates that British influence was not an absolute phenomenon. It was actually a fluid, changing, or indeed dynamic situation with influence waning over the duration of the campaign to a situation of significantly less control/influence at its conclusion. Further, this book argues, however, that the Dhofar War was fundamentally still, a British-managed and led campaign. It was won precisely because of the input of hard-won COIN expertise of the UK.[15] The Dhofar undertaking was therefore very similar to previous classical-era UK COIN campaigns in numerous respects but its hybrid nature actually displayed too many differences overall to be described or considered as 'archetypal'. It was actually a new type of British anti-insurgency undertaking, or rather a metamorphosis to a more 'hands off' type of approach, whilst retaining the key levers of power and influence. This resembled more a proxy-type operation than ever before in the British COIN record. It has been said that, "This [Dhofar campaign] type of involvement with a foreign partner was unique at the time, even for Britain which was in the process of disengaging from the Middle East and relinquishing its strategic responsibilities across much of the globe."[16] Of this, the role of combined British forces, and especially that of the SAS was only a relatively small component. For the latter, it was also, however, an outsized one at the strategic, operational and tactical levels, i.e. at all the levels of warfare. This was similar to the unit's role in several prior UK COIN actions, be it in Malaya, or those in Brunei/Borneo or Aden.

The Dhofar War certainly does not provide a 'one size fits all' template for how to successfully undertake COIN. As has been established, and not unlike the Malayan campaign, it was undertaken under relatively unique and era-specific circumstances, was very limited in terms of comparative size, and was not even wholly consistent with the UK's worldwide experience of COIN since 1945.[17] Despite this it does, however, provide many pertinent lessons on how to best succeed at COIN. It clearly shows that 'choosing one's battles' carefully is key for success in COIN so as not to overextend resources. Following this, it requires unwavering long-term political commitment to enable the military component of COIN to prevail. With the exception of Northern Ireland, unlike other contemporary campaigns, the Dhofar case benefitted from a keen level of political judgement as to what was fundamentally 'winnable'.[18] The proof of such judgement and long-term commitment is in the proverbial 'pudding'. The Dhofar Campaign was not only a rare COIN win achieved months after the milestone Vietnam War loss, but was rare in COIN terms overall. Out of just 21 COIN wins achieved globally from 1945 out of over 70 campaigns undertaken, Britain can claim ownership of at least five and arguably six overall.[19] This is not to say Britain did everything right. Many mistakes were made along the way. It does, however, show an accumulation of learning and expertise by past generations of soldiers and politicians, all of which arguably reached its high point with the Dhofar win. It could be argued that the architects either side of the Atlantic of much less successful more recent COIN ventures in Afghanistan and Iraq for example, should perhaps have studied the Dhofar case in more detail.

In terms of ownership of the Dhofar COIN victory it is not clear-cut. Due to the nature of Britain's role it cannot be credited with solely fighting and winning the war. The positive aspects of the Omani leadership in the guise of Sultan Qaboos were certainly key. The fighting ability of the SAF was also a central factor, augmented by the combined military 'weight' of Jordan and especially Iran. All were key factors in achieving the insurgent defeat. Although it varied over the years and through different governments, Britain did provide the vital long-term political commitment to support the Sultanate in tangible terms. It also provided the deep military expertise, know-how, and – crucially – all-levels leadership, as well as key specific elements of support such as the deployment of the SAS, which finally 'broke' the insurgency. Much like the overall British role in the wider war, the SAS cannot be credited with the Dhofar victory, but without 'the Regiment's' input and the benefits brought by Operation STORM, the war would likely not have been won at all. In the words of Major General Tony Jeapes, in his 1980 book entitled *'SAS: Operation Oman'*:

> The Dhofar War was a classic of its type, in which every principle of counter-insurgency operations built up over the last fifty years in campaigns around the world by the British and other armies, often by trial and error, was employed. It was probably only the third campaign, after Greece in the 1940s and Malaya in the 1950s and early 1960s, to be won against a Communist armed insurrection. It came at an important time after the defeat in Vietnam of the most powerful nation in the world when many people in the free world became pessimistically resigned to the eventual victory of Communist revolution. Perhaps the most important lesson to come out of the Dhofar campaign is that the 'historic inevitability' of victory for Communist-inspired revolutions was exploded as the myth it is.[20]

Such observations reinforce the historical importance of the overall role of Britain and its armed forces – and especially the Special Air Service Regiment – in the Dhofar Conflict. They also serve to highlight the underrated success and collective historical implications of the Dhofar campaign victory. In the modern era it is clear that Insurgency as a concept and practice is not going away. It will likely be the dominant paradigm for years to come. As such, and despite its many limitations or caveats, the Dhofar example presents many both clear and important lessons for future such campaigns which are ignored by governments and their militaries at their peril.

Notes

Abstract
1. David Kilcullen, 'Counter-Insurgency Redux', *Survival*, 48 (2006) p.1
2. Thomas R. Mockaitis, *British Counterinsurgency in the Post-Imperial Era*, (Manchester: Manchester University Press, 1995) p.3

Chapter 1
1. Regional conflicts such as the 1967 Arab-Israeli war, the 1973 Yom Kippur War as well as those located outside the Middle East; i.e. the Vietnam War
2. Marc DeVore, 'The United Kingdom's Last Hot War of the Cold War: Oman 1963–75', *Cold War History*, Vol.11, Issue 3 (2011) p.1
3. "By September 1967 George Brown (UK Foreign Secretary) had clearly washed his hands of the South Arabian commitment, confiding 'it can't be helped – anyway, we want to be out of the whole of the Middle East as far and as fast as we possibly can'" Jonathan Walker, *Aden Insurgency, The Savage War in Yemen* 1962–67, (Barnsley: Pen & Sword, 2004)
4. Walter C. Ladwig III, 'Supporting allies in counterinsurgency: Britain and the Dhofar Rebellion', *Small Wars & Insurgencies*, Vol. 19, Issue 1 (2008) p.63
   Ranulph Fiennes, *Where Soldiers Fear to Tread*, (London: Hodder & Stoughton, 1975) p.9
   John Blashford-Snell, *A Taste for Adventure*, (London: Hutchinson & Co. (Publishers) Ltd., 1978) p.52
5. Marc DeVore, 'The United Kingdom's Last Hot War of the Cold War: Oman 1963–75', *Cold War History*, Vol.11, Issue 3 (2011) p.1
   Ian Beckett, *Modern Insurgencies and Counter-Insurgencies – Guerrillas and their Opponents since 1756*, (London: Routledge, 2001) p.230
   Geraint Hughes, 'A 'Model Campaign' Reappraised: The Counter-Insurgency War in Dhofar, Oman, 1965–1975', *Journal of Strategic Studies*, Vol.32 No.2 (2009) p.273
   David Charters, 'Counter-insurgency Intelligence: The Evolution of British Theory and Practice', *Journal of Conflict Studies*, Vol. 29 (2009) p.10
6. Fred Halliday, *Arabia without Sultans*, (Harmondsworth, Penguin, 1974) pp.350–51
   Karl Hack, 'Everyone lived in fear: Malaya and the British Way of counter-insurgency', *Small Wars & Insurgencies*, (2012) p.671
   Alan Hoskins, *A Contract Officer in the Oman*, (Tunbridge Wells: Costello, 1988) p.11
7. Marc DeVore, 'The United Kingdom's Last Hot War of the Cold War: Oman 1963–75', *Cold War History*, Vol.11, Issue 3 (2011) p.22
8. Sergey Plekhanov, *A Reformer on the Throne*, (Virginia: Trident Press, 2004) p.126
9. John Newsinger, *British Counterinsurgency*, (Basingstoke: Palgrave Macmillan) p.1
   Thomas R. Mockaitis, 'Low Intensity Conflict: The British Experience', *Conflict Quarterly*, (Winter 1993) pp.8–9
10. Douglas Porch, *Counterinsurgency: Exposing the Myths of the New Way of War*, (Cambridge: Cambridge University Press) p.266

Christopher Paul, Colin P. Clarke and Beth Grill, *Victory Has a Thousand Fathers: Sources of Success in Counterinsurgency*, (Santa Monica, CA: RAND Corporation, 2010) p.XX
11. Ken Perkins, 'Oman 1975: The Year of Decision', *The RUSI Journal*, Vol. 124, Issue 1 (1979) p.39
12. Marc DeVore, 'A more complex and conventional victory: revisiting the Dhofar counterinsurgency, 1963–1975', *Small Wars & Insurgencies*, Vol.23, Issue 1 (2012) p.144
13. Stewart Wilson, *Dhofar Voices: Frontier Force, Oman and its Life and Times 1970–1980*, (Kindle E-book, 2021) p.ii
14. John Akehurst, *We Won a War: The Campaign in Oman 1965–1975*, (Salisbury: M. Russell, 1982), pp.ix-x
    John Peterson, *Oman's Insurgencies : The Sultanate's Struggle for Supremacy*, (London: Saqi, 2007) p.486
15. Marc DeVore, 'The United Kingdom's Last Hot War of the Cold War: Oman, 1963–75', *Cold War History*, Vol.11, Issue 3 (2011) p.20
16. Christopher Paul, Colin P. Clarke, Beth Grill and Molly Dunigan, *Paths to Victory: Detailed Insurgency Case Studies*, (Santa Monica, CA: RAND Corporation, 2013) pp.285/6
17. Stephen Quick, 'Arabian Peninsula Histories: The Dhofar War in Oman 1965–1975: A Historical Perspective', *Nation Shield Journal*, Issue no. 559 (August 2018)
18. John Newsinger, *British Counterinsurgency*, (Basingstoke: Palgrave Macmillan, 2015) p.139
19. Sergey Plekhanov, *A Reformer on the Throne: Sultan Qaboos Bin Said Al Said*, (Trident Press Ltd, 2004)

Chapter 2
1. Ken Perkins, 'Oman 1975: The Year of Decision', *The RUSI Journal*, Vol. 124, Issue 1 (1979) p.38
2. Ibid.
3. Wilfred Thesiger, *Arabian Sands*, (London: Longmans, 1959)
4. Mick Dales, *SAS: A Storm Gathering*, (Kindle E-book, 2016) Chapter 8
5. Ian Gardiner, *In the Service of the Sultan*, (Barnsley: Pen and Sword, 2006) p.38
6. Marc DeVore, 'The United Kingdom's Last Hot War of the Cold War: Oman 1963–75', *Cold War History*, Vol. 11, Issue 3 (2011) pp.3–7
7. Marc Valeri, *Oman: Politics and Society in the Qaboos State*, (London: C. Hurst & Co., 2017) p.54
8. Donald Hawley, *Oman & Its Renaissance*, (London: Stacey International, 1995) p.59
9. Ibid., pp.59–60
10. John McKeown, 'The Dhofar War and Its Significance', (MA, Cambridge, 1981) p.10
11. Wendell Phillips, *Oman: A History*, (Beirut: Librarie du Lebanon, 1971) p.160
12. Ibid., pp.160–61
13. Ian Skeet, *Muscat & Oman: The End of an Era*, (London: Faber & Faber, 1974) p.196
    Marc Valeri, *Oman: Politics and Society in the Qaboos State*, (London: C. Hurst & Co., 2017) p.50
    David Neild, *A Soldier in Arabia*, (Surbiton: Medina Publishing Ltd., 2015) pp.40–41
14. Wendell Phillips, *Oman: A History*, (Beirut: Librarie du Lebanon, 1971) p.205
    David Smiley, *Arabian Assignment*, (London: Leo Cooper, 1975) p.87
15. Ibid., p.212
16. John Cloake, *Templer: Tiger of Malaya*, (London: Harrap, 1985)
17. J.E. Peterson, *Oman's Insurgencies: The Sultanate's Struggle for Supremacy*, (London: Saqi, 2007) p.102

18. Ibid., pp.102–104
19. Ibid.
20. Abdel Takriti, *Monsoon Revolution: Republicans, Sultans and Empires in Oman, 1965–1976*, (Oxford: Oxford University Press, 2016) p.8
21. Fred Halliday, *Arabia Without Sultans*, (Harmondsworth: Penguin, 1974) p.274
    Walter C. Ladwig III, 'Supporting allies in counterinsurgency: Britain and the Dhofar Rebellion', *Small Wars & Insurgencies*, Vol.19, Issue 1 (2008) p.65
22. Halliday states that, "In 1970 Oman had an infant mortality rate of 75%. It had [only] three small primary schools, one hospital, no press and a literacy rate of 5 per cent" Fred Halliday, *Arabia Without Sultans*, (Harmondsworth: Penguin, 1974) p.274
23. Calvin H. Allen and W. Lynn Rigsbee II, *Oman under Qaboos: From Coup to Constitution, 1970–1996*, (London: Frank Cass, 2002), p.24
24. Calvin H. Allen and W. Lynn Rigsbee II, *Oman Under Qaboos: From Coup to Constitution, 1970–1996*, (London: Frank Cass, 2002) p.24
    Fred Halliday, *Arabia Without Sultans*, (Harmondsworth: Penguin, 1974) p.276
25. Abdel Takriti, *Monsoon Revolution: Republicans, Sultans and Empires in Oman, 1965–1976*, (Oxford: Oxford University Press, 2016) p.36
26. S. Monick, 'Victory in Hades: The Forgotten Wars of the Oman 1957–1959 and 1970–1976. Part 2: The Dhofar Campaign 1970–1976', *Scientia Militaria, South African Journal of Military Studies*, Vol.12, No.4 (1982) p.1
    Corran Purdon, *List the Bugle: Reminiscences of an Irish Soldier*, (Antrim: Greystone Books, 1993) p.244
27. Jim White, 'Oman 1965–1976: From Certain Defeat to Decisive Victory', *Small Wars Journal*, (2008) p.3
28. Ibid., p.4
29. David Commins, *The Gulf States: A Modern History*, (London: I.B. Tauris, 2012) p.195
    Robert Alston and Stuart Laing, *Unshook Till the End of Time: A History of Relations Between Britain & Oman 1650–1970*, (London: Gilgamesh Publishing, 2012) p.251
30. Ibid.
31. Ranulph Fiennes, *Where Soldiers Fear to Tread*, (New English Library, 1976), pp.34–35
32. J.E. Peterson, *Oman's Insurgencies: The Sultanate's Struggle for Supremacy*, (London: Saqi, 2007) p.233
33. Ibid., p.476
34. Fred Halliday, *Arabia Without Sultans*, (Harmondsworth: Penguin, 1974) p.318
35. Ian Beckett, *Modern Insurgencies and Counter-Insurgencies – Guerrillas and their Opponents since 1756*, (London: Routledge, 2001) p.218
36. Abdel Takriti, *Monsoon Revolution: Republicans, Sultans and Empires in Oman, 1965–1976*, (Oxford: Oxford University Press, 2016) p.55
37. Marc Valeri, *Oman: Politics and Society in the Qaboos State*, (London: C. Hurst & Co., 2017) p.60
38. MEC – GRAHAM COLLECTION – Tony Lewis, 'The Story of the Sultan of Oman's Armed Forces 1964–67', *The Journal of the Sultan's Armed Forces Association*, Issue 37 (February 1988) Article p.35
39. Ibid., Jim White, 'Oman 1965–1976: From Certain Defeat to Decisive Victory', *Small Wars Journal*, (2008) p.7
    Peterson, p.284
40. Peterson, p.477
41. Ibid.

42. Tony Lewis, 'The Story of the Sultan of Oman's Armed Forces 1964–67', *The Journal of the Sultan's Armed Forces Association*, (1988) p.36
43. Ibid., p.33
44. White, p.7
    Peterson, p.284
45. S. Monick, 'Victory in Hades: The Forgotten Wars of the Oman 1957–1959 and 1970–1976. Part 2: The Dhofar Campaign 1970–1976', *Scientia Militaria, South African Journal of Military Studies*, Vol.12, No.4 (1982) p.5
46. Marc Valeri, *Oman: Politics and Society in the Qaboos State*, (London: C. Hurst & Co., 2017) p.57
    Robert Thompson, *Peace is not at Hand*, (London: Chatto & Windus, 1974) p.6
47. Christopher Paul, Colin P. Clarke, Beth Grill and Molly Dunigan, *Paths to Victory: Detailed Insurgency Case Studies*, (Santa Monica, CA: RAND Corporation, 2013) p.275
48. Walter C. Ladwig III, 'Supporting allies in counterinsurgency: Britain and the Dhofar Rebellion', *Small Wars & Insurgencies*, Vol.19, Issue 1 (2008) p.70
49. Ian Beckett (Ed.), *The Roots of Counter-Insurgency: Armies and Guerrilla Warfare 1900–1945*, (London: Blandford) p.6
50. Ian Beckett, *Modern Insurgencies and Counter-Insurgencies – Guerrillas and their Opponents since 1756*, (London: Routledge, 2001) p.vii
51. David Galula, *Counter-Insurgency Warfare: Theory and Practice*, (New York: Frederick A. Praeger, 1964) p.3
52. Ian Beckett, *Modern Insurgencies and Counter-Insurgencies – Guerrillas and their Opponents since 1756*, (London: Routledge, 2001) p.vii
53. Robert Thompson, *Defeating Communist Insurgency*, (London: Chatto & Windus, 1974)
    David Galula, *Counter-Insurgency Warfare: Theory and Practice*, (New York: Frederick A. Praeger, 1964)
    Julian Paget, *Counter-Insurgency Campaigning*, (London: Faber & Faber, 1967)
    Frank Kitson, *Low Intensity Operations: Subversion, Insurgency and Peacekeeping*, (London: Faber & Faber, 1971), Frank Kitson, *Bunch of Five*, (London: Faber & Faber, 1977)
54. Thomas R. Mockaitis, 'Low-Intensity Conflict: The British Experience', *Conflict Quarterly*, (Winter 1993)
    Thomas R. Mockaitis, 'The Iraq War: Learning from the Past, Adapting to the Present and Planning for the Future', *Strategic Studies Institute, US Army War College* (2007)
    Thomas R. Mockaitis, 'Minimum Force, British Counter-Insurgency and the Mau Mau Rebellion: A Reply', *Small Wars & Insurgencies*, Volume 3, Issue 2 (1992)
    Thomas R. Mockaitis, 'The Phoenix of Counterinsurgency', *Journal of Conflict Studies*, (Summer 2007)
    John A. Nagl, *Learning to Eat Soup with a Knife: Counterinsurgency Lessons from Malaya and Vietnam*, (Chicago: Chicago University Press, 2005)
    David Kilkullen, 'Counterinsurgency Redux', *Survival*, Vol. 48, Issue 4 (Winter 2006/7)
    David Kilkullen, 'Three Pillars of Counterinsurgency', Speech: US Government Counterinsurgency Conference, Washington D.C., (28 September 2006)
55. John Newsinger, *British Counterinsurgency*, (Basingstoke: Palgrave Macmillan, 2015)
    David French, 'Nasty not Nice: British Counterinsurgency Doctrine and Practice, 1945–1967', *Small Wars & Insurgencies*, Vol. 23, Issue 4–5 (2012)
    Douglas Porch, *Counterinsurgency: Exposing the Myths of the New Way of War*, (Cambridge: Cambridge University Press, 2013)
    Paul Dixon, "Hearts and Minds'? British Counter-Insurgency from Malaya to Iraq', *Journal of Strategic Studies*, Vol. 32, Issue 3 (2009)

56. Marc DeVore, 'The United Kingdom's Last Hot War of the Cold War: Oman 1963–75', *Cold War History*, Vol. 11, Issue 3 (2011) p.8
57. David Martin Jones and M.L.R. Smith, 'Myth and the Small War Tradition: Reassessing the discourse of British Counter-Insurgency', *Small Wars & Insurgencies*, Vol. 24, Issue 3 (2013), p.437
Karl Hack, 'Everyone Lived in Fear: Malaya and the British Way of Counter-Insurgency', *Small Wars & Insurgencies*, Vol. 23, Issue 4–5, (2012) p.673
58. Thomas R. Mockaitis, 'The Iraq War: Learning from the Past, Adapting to the Present and Planning for the Future', *Army War College Strategic Studies Institute* (2007) p.12
59. Francis Owtram, *Oman and the West: State Formation in Oman since 1920*, (London: University of London, 1999) pp.68–69
60. Wendell Phillips, *Oman: A History*, (Beirut: Librarie du Lebanon, 1971) pp.218–219
61. With reference to the wording of the 1800 treaty between the British government and the Sultan of Muscat and Oman. Donald Hawley, *Oman & Its Renaissance*, (London: Stacey International, 1995) p.61
62. Fred Halliday, *Arabia Without Sultans*, (Harmondsworth: Penguin, 1974) p.279
63. Marc DeVore, 'A more complex and conventional victory: revisiting the Dhofar counterinsurgency, 1963–1975', *Small Wars & Insurgencies*, Vol. 23, Issue 1 (2012) p.144
64. Geraint Hughes, 'A 'Model Campaign' Reappraised: The Counter-Insurgency War in Dhofar, Oman, 1965–1975', *Journal of Strategic Studies*, Vol. 32, Issue 2 (2009) p.281
65. Marc DeVore, 'A more complex and conventional victory: revisiting the Dhofar counterinsurgency, 1963–1975', *Small Wars & Insurgencies*, Vol. 23, Issue 1 (2012) p.144
66. David Charters, 'Counter-insurgency Intelligence: The Evolution of British Theory and Practice', *Journal of Conflict Studies*, Vol. 29 (2009) p.10
67. Ian Beckett, *Modern Insurgencies, Counter-Insurgencies, Guerillas and their Opponents since 1756*, (London: Routledge, 2001) p.230
68. "I felt that the British had no reason to feel proud of their attempts at running the Sultan's Armed Forces (SAF)... there were far too many 'easy riders' and potential and practicing alcoholics among the 'white faces'." Alan Hoskins, *A Contract Officer*, (Tunbridge Wells: DJ Costello, 1988) p.11
69. Geraint Hughes, 'A 'Model Campaign' Reappraised: The Counter-Insurgency War in Dhofar, Oman, 1965–1975', *Journal of Strategic Studies*, Vol. 32, Issue 2 (2009) p.281
70. Marc DeVore, 'The United Kingdom's Last Hot War of the Cold War: Oman 1963–75', *Cold War History*, Vol. 11, Issue 3 (2011) p.10
71. Sultanate of Oman NRAA – Records of Oman 1966–1971 (Cambridge Archive Editions, 2003) Vol. 4. Annual Review 1969 correspondence, D.G. Crawford to British Consulate-General dated 30 Dec 1969
72. James Worrall, *Statebuilding and Counterinsurgency in Oman: Political, Military and Diplomatic Relations at the End of Empire*, (London: I.B. Tauris, 2014) p.13
73. Stephen Quick, *The Dhofar War: British Covert Campaigning in Arabia 1965–1975*, (Exeter: Exeter University Press, 2024)
74. Geraint Hughes, 'A 'Model Campaign' Reappraised: The Counter-Insurgency War in Dhofar, Oman, 1965–1975', *Journal of Strategic Studies*, Vol.32, Issue 2 (2009) p.300
75. David Charters, 'Counter-insurgency Intelligence: The Evolution of British Theory and Practice', *Journal of Conflict Studies*, Vol. 29 (2009) p.10
David Benest, 'Ponder Anew: Brigadier Graham and the Dhofar War 1970–1972', (Oct 2015) https://thestrategybridge.org/the-bridge/2016/1/1/ponder-anew-brigadier-john-graham-the-dhofar-war-19701972 Accessed online 19 Apr 2023, p.9

Brigadier John Akehurst recalled how he had to remind two visiting senior British officials that it was not a 'British victory' as such. John Akehurst, *We Won a War: The Campaign in Oman 1965–75*, (Guildford: M. Russell, 1982) p.185

Tony Jeapes, *SAS Operation Oman*, (London: HarperCollins, 1980) p.12

Marc DeVore, 'The United Kingdom's Last Hot War of the Cold War: Oman 1963–75', *Cold War History*, Vol. 11, Issue 3 (2011) p.22

Geraint Hughes, 'A 'Model Campaign' Reappraised: The Counter-Insurgency War in Dhofar, Oman, 1965–1975', *Journal of Strategic Studies*, Vol. 32, Issue 2 (2009) p.300

Walter C. Ladwig III, 'Supporting allies in counterinsurgency: Britain and the Dhofar Rebellion', *Small Wars & Insurgencies*, Vol.19, Issue 1 (2008) p.38

76. Francis Owtram, *Oman and the West: State Formation in Oman since 1920*, (London: University of London, 1999) pp.68–69

    Fred Halliday, *Arabia Without Sultans*, (Harmondsworth: Penguin, 1974) p.344

77. Douglas Porch, *Counterinsurgency: Exposing the Myths of the New Way of War*, (Cambridge: Cambridge University Press, 2013) p.265

    John Newsinger, *British Counterinsurgency*, (Basingstoke: Palgrave Macmillan, 2015) p.139

78. Robert Alston and Stuart Laing, *Unshook Till the End of Time: A History of Relations Between Britain & Oman 1650–1970*, (London: Gilgamesh Publishing, 2012) p.299

    Marc DeVore, 'The United Kingdom's Last Hot War of the Cold War: Oman 1963–75', *Cold War History*, Vol. 11, Issue 3 (2011) p.17

79. Geraint Hughes, 'A Proxy War in Arabia: The Dhofar Emergency and Cross-Border Raids into South Yemen', *Middle East Journal*, Vol. 69, Issue 1 (Winter 2015) p.94

80. Marc DeVore, 'The United Kingdom's Last Hot War of the Cold War: Oman 1963–75', *Cold War History*, Vol. 11, Issue 3 (2011) p.22

81. James Goode, 'Assisting our Brothers, Defending Ourselves: The Iranian Intervention in Oman, 1972–75', *Iranian Studies*, Vol. 47, Issue 3 (2014) p.441

82. Ken Perkins, 'Oman 1975: The Year of Decision', *The RUSI Journal*, Vol. 124, Issue 1 (1979) p.39

83. Sergey Plekhanov, *A Reformer on the Throne*, (Virginia: Trident Press, 2004) p.126

84. Stephen Quick, *The Dhofar War: British Covert Campaigning in Arabia 1965–1975*, (Exeter: Exeter University Press, 2024)

85. Robert Alston and Stuart Laing, *Unshook Till the End of Time: A History of Relations Between Britain & Oman 1650–1970*, (London: Gilgamesh Publishing, 2012) p.299

86. Referring to Major General Creasey and Brigadier Fletcher, Ray states that, "They had been a great pair to have guided us through a crucial part of the Dhofar War, the country (Oman) was lucky to have had them and so was the SAF". Bryan Ray, *Dangerous Frontiers; Campaigning in Somaliland and Oman*, (Barnsley: Pen & Sword, 2008) p.197

    David Benest, 'Ponder Anew: Brigadier Graham and the Dhofar War 1970–1972', (Oct 2015) https://thestrategybridge.org/the-bridge/2016/1/1/ponder-anew-brigadier-john-graham-the-dhofar-war-19701972 Accessed online 19 Apr 23

Part I

1. Including in the comprehensive British COIN-related books/sections of former Sandhurst academic Aaron Edwards' *Defending the Realm? The Politics of Britain's Small Wars Since 1945*, (Manchester: Manchester University Press, 2012) and further Douglas Porch, *Counterinsurgency: Exposing the Myths of the New Way of War*, (Cambridge: Cambridge University Press, 2013)

2. Karl Hack, 'Everyone lived in fear: Malaya and the British Way of counter-insurgency', *Small Wars & Insurgencies*, Vol. 23, Issue 4–5, (2012) p.671
3. Ian Beckett, *Modern Insurgencies and Counter-Insurgencies – Guerrillas and their Opponents since 1756*, (London: Routledge, 2001) p.vii
4. Ibid.
5. Ian Beckett and John Pimlott, *Armed Forces & Modern Counter-Insurgency*, (New York: St. Martin's Press, 1985) p.1
6. Ibid.
7. Ian Beckett, *Modern Insurgencies and Counter-Insurgencies – Guerrillas and their Opponents since 1756*, (London: Routledge, 2001) p.vii
8. Ibid., David Galula, *Counter-Insurgency Warfare: Theory and Practice*, (New York: Frederick A. Praeger, 1964) p.4
9. Ian Beckett, *Modern Insurgencies and Counter-Insurgencies – Guerrillas and their Opponents since 1756*, (London: Routledge, 2001) p.viii
10. Robert Alston and Stuart Laing, *Unshook Till the End of Time: A History of Relations Between Britain & Oman 1650–1970*, (London: Gilgamesh Publishing, 2012) p.261
11. David Kilcullen, 'Counterinsurgency Redux', *International Institute of Strategic Studies*, Vol. 48, Issue 4 (Winter 2006/7) p.1
12. Ibid.
13. Ibid, p.4
14. Michael Crawshaw, 'The Evolution of British COIN', *Ministry of Defence Joint Doctrine Publication*, (JDP 3–40), (2012) p.2
15. Robert Thompson, *Defeating Communist Insurgency*, (London: Chatto & Windus, 1974)
Julian Paget, *Counter-Insurgency Campaigning*, (London: Faber & Faber, 1967)
Frank Kitson, *Low Intensity Operations: Subversion, Insurgency and Peacekeeping*, (London: Faber & Faber, 1971), Frank Kitson, *Bunch of Five*, (London: Faber & Faber, 1977)
David Galula, *Counter-Insurgency Warfare: Theory & Practice*, (New York: Frederick A. Praeger, 1964)
16. John Pimlott, *British Military Operations, 1945–85*, (London: Bison, 1986) p.20/p.50
17. Ibid, pp.86–91
18. Ibid.
19. Although only the early stages of the Brunei/Borneo/Indonesian Confrontation could strictly be considered an insurgency with the attempted coup in Brunei in Dec 1962 by the Indonesian supported North Kalimantan National Army, followed by Indonesian-backed Kalimantan Indonesians/Sarawak Chinese raiders. Robert Jackson, *The Malayan Emergency & Indonesian Confrontation – The Commonwealth's Wars 1948–1966*, (Barnsley: Pen & Sword, 2008) p.124/5
This situation remained until the Indonesian military took over responsibility for the campaign in Feb. 1964. Thomas R. Mockaitis, 'British Counterinsurgency in the Post-Imperial Era', (Manchester: Manchester University Press, 1995) p.16
20. AGDA FCO 8/2470, 'Military Assistance from UK to Oman', Treadwell to MODUK, 15 Mar 1975
AGDA FCO 8/2241, 'Iranian Military Assistance to Oman', Hawley to FCO, 5 May 1974
21. Thomas R. Mockaitis, 'The Origins of British Counterinsurgency', *Small Wars & Insurgencies*, Vol. 1, Issue 3 (1990) p.205 and p.2
Rod Thornton, 'The British Army and the Origins of its Minimum Force Philosophy', *Small Wars & Insurgencies*, Vol. 15, Issue 1 (2004) pp.85–95

22. Thomas R. Mockaitis, 'Low-Intensity Conflict: The British Experience', *Conflict Quarterly*, (Winter 1993) p.12
23. Ibid., p.8
24. Ibid.
    Thomas R. Mockaitis, 'The Phoenix of Counterinsurgency', *The Journal of Conflict Studies*, (Summer 2007) p.13
25. FCO 8/41 – 'Persian Gulf: Political Affairs (Ext.): Bilateral Effects on Aden' – Letter Balfour Paul (British Residency Bahrain) to M.S. Wier (Arabian Department, FO)
26. John Newsinger, *British Counterinsurgency*, (Basingstoke: Palgrave Macmillan, 2015) p.2 and David Jones and M.L.R. Smith, 'Myth and the Small War Tradition: Reassessing the discourse of British Counter-Insurgency', *Small Wars & Insurgencies*, Vol. 24, Issue 3 (2013) p.436
27. David M. Anderson, 'British Abuse and Torture in Kenya's Counter-Insurgency, 1952–1960', *Small Wars & Insurgencies*, Vol. 23, Issue 4–5 (2012) p.702
    Which has been collectively estimated to be well in excess of the officially-recognised 11,000 people. Caroline Elkins, 'Alchemy of Evidence: Mau Mau, the British Empire and the High Court of Justice', *The Journal of Imperial and Commonwealth History*, Vol. 39, Issue 5 (2011) p.739
28. Karl Hack, *The Malayan Emergency: Revolution and Counterinsurgency at the End of Empire*, (Cambridge: Cambridge University Press, 2021), p.300
29. Ian Beckett and John Pimlott, *Armed Forces & Modern Counter-Insurgency*, (New York: St. Martin's Press, 1985) p.64
    Applied to the Vietnam War where a key US Army General is quoted as stating, "We were indiscriminate in our application of firepower." Quoting Chief of Staff of the Army, General Harold K. Johnson, John A. Nagl, *Learning to Eat Soup with a Knife: Counterinsurgency Lessons from Malaya and Vietnam*, (Chicago: Chicago University Press, 2005) p.175
30. Bruno C. Reis, 'The Myth of British Minimum Force in Counterinsurgency Campaigns during Decolonization (1945–1970)', *Journal of Strategic Studies*, Vol. 34, Issue 2 (Apr. 2011) p.250
31. Thomas R. Mockaitis, 'Low-Intensity Conflict: The British Experience', *Conflict Quarterly*, (Winter 1993) p.8
    Thomas R. Mockaitis, 'The Origin of British Counter-insurgency', *Small Wars & Insurgencies*, Vol. 1, Issue 3 (1990) p.214
32. J.E. Peterson, *Oman's Insurgencies: The Sultanate's Struggle for Supremacy*, (London: Saqi, 2007) p.401
33. Ibid.
34. Christopher Paul and others, 'Paths to Victory: Detailed Insurgency Case Studies', (Santa Monica, CA: RAND Corporation, 2013) p.275
    Marc Valeri, *Oman: Politics and Society in the Qaboos State*, (London: C. Hurst & Co., 2017), p.57
35. Karl Hack, 'Everyone lived in fear: Malaya and the British Way of counter-insurgency', *Small Wars & Insurgencies*, Vol. 23, Issue 4-5 (2012) p.671
36. Thomas R. Mockaitis, 'The Iraq War: Learning from the Past, Adapting to the Present and Planning for the Future', *Army War College Strategic Studies Institute* (2007) p.12
37. Johnny Cooper, *One of the Originals: The Story of a Founder Member of the SAS*, (London: Pan Books Ltd., 1991)
38. Ibid
    David Smiley, *Arabian Assignment*, (London: Leo Cooper, 1975)

39. Tony Jeapes, *SAS Operation Oman*, (London: HarperCollins, 1980)
    Peter de la Billiere, *Looking for Trouble: SAS to Gulf Command*, (London: Harper Collins, 1995)
40. Mark Urban, *Big Boys' Rules*, (London: Faber & Faber, 1993)

Chapter 3
1. Christopher Paul, Colin P. Clarke, Beth Grill and Molly Dunigan, *Paths to Victory – Detailed Insurgency Case studies*, (Santa Monica, CA: RAND Corporation, 2013) p.VI
2. TNA CAB21/1681 – Cabinet Malaya Committee: Operation Against Bandits etc. (General) – "…part of the Kremlin's world-wide campaign against the Western Powers", Memorandum by the Secretary of State for the Colonies, 14 Jul 1950
3. TNA AIR 20/10377 – Review of the Emergency in Malaya from June 1948 to August 1957, Dated 24 Oct 1957. Average strength of Malayan terrorists for 1951 was 7,292
4. Robert Jackson, *The Malayan Emergency & Indonesian Confrontation – The Commonwealth's Wars 1948–1966*, (Barnsley: Pen & Sword, 2008) p.121
5. MEC – GRAHAM COLLECTION – Box 7/1 – John Graham, 'Point summary on Development of SAF for lecture to Anglo-Omani Society June 1996'
    John Akehurst, *We Won a War: The Campaign in Oman 1965–75*, (Guildford: M. Russell, 1982) p.29
6. TNA CAB21/1681 – Cabinet Malaya Committee: Operation Against Bandits etc. (General) –Memorandum by the Secretary of State for the Colonies, 14 Jul 1950
7. Jonathan Walker, *Aden Insurgency, The Savage War in Yemen 1962–67*, (Barnsley: Pen & Sword, 2004) p.127
8. Clive Jones, *Britain and the Yemen Civil War, 1962–65: Ministers, Mercenaries and Mandarins: Foreign Policy and the Limits of Covert Action*, (Eastbourne: Sussex Academic Press, 2010) p.191
9. Ibid. p.222
    MEC – GRAHAM COLLECTION – Box 5/2 John Graham, 'Thirty Months: A Brief History of Oman's Armed Forces April 1970 – September 1972'
10. Marc DeVore, 'The United Kingdom's Last Hot War of the Cold War: Oman 1963–75', *Cold War History*, Vol. 11, Issue 3 (2011) pp.1–2
    Tony Geraghty, *Who Dares Wins: The Story of the SAS 1950–1982*, (London: Fontana/Collins, 1990), p.99
11. Robert Alston and Stuart Laing, *Unshook Till the End of Time: A History of Relations Between Britain & Oman 1650–1970*, (London: Gilgamesh Publishing, 2012) p.322
12. Abdel Takriti, *Monsoon Revolution: Republicans, Sultans and Empires in Oman, 1965–1976*, (Oxford: Oxford University Press, 2016) p.79
13. Ibid.
14. Although there is substantial crossover between the two camps – Nationalist/Decolonisation and Cold War elements – as with the examples of Malaya, Borneo and Aden
15. TNA CAB/129/96 – "I feel that I should let my colleagues know that the Governor of Kenya, with my full support, is about to take certain measures to remove or minimise dangerous threats to security that exist now in the colony, particularly in Nairobi", 'Security Measures in Kenya', Memorandum by the Secretary of State for the Colonies, 5 Mar 1959
16. Chris Summers, 'Can Cyprus Overcome Its Bloody History?', BBC News Article (online), dated 23 Nov 2009   Accessed online 18 Jun 2018

17. TNA CAB/129/96 – 'Security Measures in Kenya', Memorandum by the Secretary of State for the Colonies, 5 Mar 1959
18. TNA CAB 21/1681 – Cabinet Malaya Committee On Operation Against Bandits etc. (General), 'Comment on the Defence of Malaya', Chiefs of Staff Joint Planning Staff Report, 10 Oct 1950
19. Ibid.
20. MEC–Granada TV 'End of Empire'–Archive list of Interview Transcripts; The Rt.Hon. J. Amery (Roll 4) p.5
21. TNA FCO 8/1688, 'Attachment of SAS Division of United Kingdom to Armed Forces of Oman', A. Ackland to Mr. Parsons, 1 Feb 1971
22. Marc DeVore 'A more complex and conventional victory: revisiting the Dhofar counterinsurgency, 1963–1975', *Small Wars & Insurgencies*, Vol. 23, Issue 1 (2012) p.144
    Marc DeVore, 'The United Kingdom's Last Hot War of the Cold War: Oman 1963–75', *Cold War History*, Vol. 11, Issue 3 (2011) p.2
23. Corran Purdon, *List the Bugle: Reminiscences of an Irish Soldier*, (Antrim: Greystone Books, 1993) p.277
    John Graham, *Ponder Anew: Reflections on the Twentieth Century*, (Staplehurst: Spellmount Limited, 1999), p.355
24. Aaron Edwards 'Defending the Realm? The Politics of Britain's Small Wars Since 1945', (Manchester: Manchester University Press, 2012) p.215
25. Walter C. Ladwig III, 'Supporting allies in counterinsurgency: Britain and the Dhofar Rebellion', *Small Wars & Insurgencies*, Vol.19, Issue 1 (2008) p.76
    TNA FCO 8/1688, 'Attachment of SAS Division of United Kingdom to Armed Forces of Oman', A. Ackland to Mr. Parsons, 1 Feb 1971
26. TNA FCO 8/2006 'Annual Review of Oman 1972', A.D Parsons to Mr. Le Quesne, 12 Feb 1973
27. Francis Owtram, *Oman and the West: State Formation in Oman since 1920*, (London: University of London, 1999) pp.68–69
28. MEC – GRAHAM COLLECTION – Box 6/3 – Sir Donald Hawley, 'Recollections of Muscat', *The Journal of the Sultan's Armed Forces Association*, Issue 42, March 1993
29. J.E. Peterson, *Oman's Insurgencies: The Sultanate's Struggle for Supremacy*, (London: Saqi, 2007) pp.102–3
30. Smiley, p.78
31. Colin Richardson, *Masirah – Tales from a Desert Island*, (Durham: Carnegie Publishing, 2001) p.219
    James Worrall, *Statebuilding and Counterinsurgency in Oman: Political, Military and Diplomatic Relations at the End of Empire*, (London: I.B. Tauris, 2014) p.200
32. Sultanate of Oman NRAA – Records of Oman 1966–1971 (Cambridge Archive Editions, 2003) Vol. 5: Annex 'A' to COS 96/68 /RAF Salalah: Introduction, p.6 and p.201
33. Donald Hawley, *Oman & Its Renaissance*, (London: Stacey International, 1995) p.59

Chapter 4

1. Marc DeVore 'A more complex and conventional victory: revisiting the Dhofar counterinsurgency, 1963–1975', *Small Wars & Insurgencies*, Vol.23, Issue 1 (2012) p.144
2. Douglas Porch, *Counterinsurgency: Exposing the Myths of the New Way of War*, (Cambridge: Cambridge University Press, 2013) p.265
   Marc DeVore, 'The United Kingdom's Last Hot War of the Cold War: Oman 1963–75', *Cold War History*, Vol. 11, Issue 3 (2011) p.2

3. TNA FCO 8/1669 – Annual Review of Oman, "Omanis were sullen under his (Sultan Said's) repressive regime… his ([Qaboos's] father's policies had brought the Sultanate to the brink of despair", Sultanate of Oman: Annual Review for 1970, HM Consul-General Muscat to HM Political Resident Persian Gulf, 4 Jan 1970
John Newsinger, *British Counterinsurgency*, (Basingstoke: Palgrave Macmillan, 2015) p.139
4. TNA AIR 10377, Some 700,000,000 million pounds up to 31 Aug 1957, of which over 500,000,000 came from the British government with the final cost over 600,000,000 more than normal operating costs – 'Review of the Emergency in Malaya from June 1948 to August 1957'
5. J.E. Peterson, *Oman's Insurgencies: The Sultanate's Struggle for Supremacy*, (London: Saqi, 2007) p.111
6. Corran Purdon, *List the Bugle: Reminiscences of an Irish Soldier*, (Antrim: Greystone Books, 1993) p.294
7. Walter C Ladwig III, 'Supporting allies in counterinsurgency: Britain and the Dhofar Rebellion', *Small Wars & Insurgencies*, Vol. 19, Issue 1 (2008) p.67
8. Marc DeVore, 'A more complex and conventional victory: revisiting the Dhofar counterinsurgency, 1963–1975', *Small Wars & Insurgencies*, Vol.23, Issue 1 (2012) p.150
9. Walter C. Ladwig III, 'Supporting allies in counterinsurgency: Britain and the Dhofar Rebellion', *Small Wars & Insurgencies*, Vol.19, Issue 1 (2008) p.72
10. David Benest, 'Ponder Anew: Brigadier Graham and the Dhofar War 1970–1972', (Oct 2015) https://thestrategybridge.org/the-bridge/2016/1/1/ponder-anew-brigadier-john-graham-the-dhofar-war-19701972 Accessed online 19 Apr 2023
11. Geraint Hughes, 'A 'Model Campaign' Reappraised: The Counter-Insurgency War in Dhofar, Oman, 1965–1975', *Journal of Strategic Studies*, Vol.32, Issue 2 (2009) p.283
12. Alluded to by writers including Halliday and Owtram and latterly John Newsinger
13. Walter C. Ladwig III, 'Supporting allies in counterinsurgency: Britain and the Dhofar Rebellion', *Small Wars & Insurgencies*, Vol.19, Issue 1 (2008) p.65
14. "To him [the Sultan] the Dhofaris were no better than animals", Ranulph Fiennes, *Where Soldiers Fear to Tread*, (London: The Travel Book Club, 1976) p.64
15. TNA FCO 8/1473, British Assistance to Sultan's Armed Forces of Oman – e.g. An enquiry as to whether British officers were being loaned to Muscat and Oman, "…a country in which slavery remains legal", Letter Mr. Toby Jessel MP to Sir James Dunnett dated 17th June 1970
16. Marc DeVore, 'The United Kingdom's Last Hot War of the Cold War: Oman 1963–75', *Cold War History*, Vol. 11, Issue 3 (2011) p.10
17. Quoting another revisionist scholar (who was sympathetic to the insurgent cause), Fred Halliday – John Newsinger, *British Counterinsurgency*, (Basingstoke: Palgrave Macmillan, 2015) p.149
18. Ranulph Fiennes, *Where Soldiers Fear to Tread*, (London: The Travel Book Club, 1976) p.59
19. David Arkless, *The Secret War – Dhofar 1971/72*, (London: William Kimber, 1988) pp.81/82
20. TNA DEFE 11/854 – 'Oman' – Letter Major General Perkins to Oman Minister of Interior/Dep. Min. of Defence, dated 18 March 1975
21. BBC 'Empire Warriors: The British Empire at War 1945–1967', BBC Documentary, 2004, Disc 1
22. Ibid., Disc 2

23. Ibid., Disc 2
24. Douglas Porch, *Counterinsurgency: Exposing the Myths of the New Way of War*, (Cambridge: Cambridge University Press, 2013) p.127 and p.265
John Newsinger, *British Counterinsurgency*, (Basingstoke: Palgrave Macmillan, 2015) p.1
25. Ian Beckett and John Pimlott, *Armed Forces & Modern Counter-Insurgency*, (New York: St. Martin's Press, 1985) p.64
26. Thomas R. Mockaitis, 'The Minimum Force Debate: Contemporary Sensibilities Meet Imperial Practice', *Small Wars and Insurgencies*, Vol.23, Issues 4–5 (Oct-Dec 2012) pp.762–780
27. Thomas R. Mockaitis, 'The Origins of British Counter-Insurgency', *Small Wars & Insurgencies*, Vol.1, Issue 3 (1990) p.214
28. J.E. Peterson, 'The Experience of British Counter-Insurgency Campaigns and Implications for Iraq', Arabian Peninsula Background Note, No. APBN-009. Published on www.JEPeterson.net (July 2009) p.10
29. Robert O. Tilman, 'The Non-Lessons of the Malayan Emergency', *Asian Survey*, Vol.6, No.8 (1966) p.408
30. Ian Gardiner, *In the Service of the Sultan*, (Barnsley: Pen & Sword, 2006) p.25
31. Ian Beckett, *Modern Insurgencies and Counter-Insurgencies – Guerrillas and their Opponents since 1756*, (London: Routledge, 2001) p.vii
32. PFLOAG's northern affiliate, NDFLOAG smuggled in arms and attacked the northern military bases at Izki and Nizwa and members (inc. Iraqis, Omanis and Bahrainis) of the Arab Action Party (AAP) landed on the Musandam Peninsula late 1970.
Marc DeVore, 'The United Kingdom's Last Hot War of the Cold War: Oman 1963–75', *Cold War History*, Vol. 11, Issue 3 (2011) p.7
Athol Yates and Geraint Hughes, 'Operation Intradon in the Musandam, 1970–1971: What This Counterinsurgency Operation Says About British Military Operations in the Arabian Gulf', *Small Wars & Insurgencies*, Vol. 33, Issue 7 (2022)
33. Ian Beckett and John Pimlott, *Armed Forces & Modern Counter-Insurgency*, (New York: St. Martin's Press, 1985)
34. Robert O. Tilman, 'The Non-Lessons of the Malayan Emergency', *Asian Survey*, Vol.6, No.8 (1966) p.412
35. Ibid. pp.90–95
36. J.E. Peterson, 'The Experience of British Counter-Insurgency Campaigns and Implications for Iraq', Arabian Peninsula Background Note, No. APBN-009. Published on www.JEPeterson.net (July 2009) p.10
37. Marc Valeri, *Oman: Politics and Society in the Qaboos State*, (London: C. Hurst & Co., 2017) p.2
38. TNA CAB 186/11 – 'The Subversive Threat from the People's Democratic Republic of Yemen (PDRY)' – Report by Joint Intelligence Committee, JIC(A)(72)7, dated 25 Feb 1972
39. Ian Beckett, 'The Future of Insurgency', *Small Wars & Insurgencies*, Vol.16, Issue 1 (2005) pp.23–24
40. Geraint Hughes, 'A Model Campaign Reappraised. The Counter-Insurgency War in Dhofar, Oman, 1965–1975', *Journal of Strategic Studies*, Vol. 32, Issue 2 (2009) p.278
41. Robert O. Tilman, 'The Non-Lessons of the Malayan Emergency', *Asian Survey*, Vol.6, No.8 (1966) p.413
42. "The most striking and apparent dissimilarities between Malaya and Vietnam stem from the political geography of the two countries. Malaya, a narrow peninsula of less

than 200 miles in width at its widest point, shares a common land border with only one country." Ibid.
43. Ian Beckett, *Modern Insurgencies and Counter-Insurgencies – Guerrillas and their Opponents since 1756*, (London: Routledge, 2001) p.218 and Marc DeVore, 'The United Kingdom's Last Hot War of the Cold War: Oman 1963–75', *Cold War History*, Vol. 11, Issue 3 (2011) p.20
44. Walter C. Ladwig III, 'Supporting allies in counterinsurgency: Britain and the Dhofar Rebellion', *Small Wars & Insurgencies*, Vol.19, Issue 1 (2008) p.72
    Ian Beckett, *Modern Insurgencies and Counter-Insurgencies – Guerrillas and their Opponents since 1756*, (London: Routledge, 2001) p.218
45. TNA AIR 20/10377 – 'Review of the Emergency in Malaya from June 1948 to August 1957', dated 24 Oct 1957. Average strength of Malayan terrorists for 1951 was 7,292 – p.4
46. Julian Paget, *Counter-Insurgency Campaigning*, (London: Faber & Faber, 1967) p.66
47. Ibid., pp.90–96
48. Ibid., p.123
49. Douglas Porch, *Counterinsurgency: Exposing the Myths of the New Way of War*, (Cambridge: Cambridge University Press, 2013) p.197
    Ian Beckett and John Pimlott, *Armed Forces & Modern Counter-Insurgency*, (New York: St. Martin's Press, 1985) p.82
50. Julian Paget, *Counter-Insurgency Campaigning*, (London: Faber & Faber, 1967) p.104
51. Ibid.
    TNA AIR20/10377 – (Chiefs of Staff Committee) Review of the Emergency in Malaya from June 1948 to August 1957
52. Jonathan Walker, *Aden Insurgency, The Savage War in Yemen 1962–67*, (Barnsley: Pen & Sword, 2004) p.285
53. Julian Paget, *Counter-Insurgency Campaigning*, (London: Faber & Faber, 1967) p.140
    Robert Jackson, *The Malayan Emergency & Indonesian Confrontation – The Commonwealth's Wars 1948–1966*, (Barnsley: Pen & Sword, 2008) p.139
54. John Newsinger, *British Counterinsurgency*, (Basingstoke: Palgrave Macmillan, 2015) p.193 – 103 British military personnel killed in 1972
55. Ibid.
56. Marc DeVore, 'The United Kingdom's Last Hot War of the Cold War: Oman 1963–75', *Cold War History*, Vol. 11, Issue 3 (2011) p.20
57. Ibid.
    Akehurst, pp.ix-x. and Dedication
    Peterson, p.486
58. J.E. Peterson, *Oman's Insurgencies: The Sultanate's Struggle for Supremacy*, (London: Saqi, 2007) pp.330–331 and p.384
59. Ian Beckett and John Pimlott, *Armed Forces & Modern Counter-Insurgency*, (New York: St. Martin's Press, 1985) p.54
    USNA – https://www.archives.gov/research/military/vietnam-war/casualty-statistics accessed 20 Aug 2018
60. Ibid., p.401
61. TNA – WO 305/4293 – 'Borneo Operations Feb – Jul 1965', *SAS Reports*, Volume 2 (Feb-Jul 1965) SAS Patrol Report dated 29 May, 1965
62. Tony Geraghty, *Who Dares Wins: The Story of the Special Air Service Regiment 1950–1982*, (London: Fontana/Collins, 1990) p.100

63. Julian Paget, *Counter-Insurgency Campaigning*, (London: Faber & Faber, 1967) p.102
    Frank Kitson, *Bunch of Five*, (London: Faber & Faber, 1977), p.34
64. Geraghty, pp.100–02
    Frank Kitson, *Low Intensity Operations: Subversion, Insurgency and Peacekeeping*, (London: Faber & Faber, 1991) p.95
65. Mark Urban, *Big Boys' Rules*, (London: Faber & Faber, 1993) pp.35–36 and p.109
66. Ibid, p.254
67. Marc DeVore, 'The United Kingdom's Last Hot War of the Cold War: Oman 1963–75', *Cold War History*, Vol. 11, Issue 3 (2011) p.9
68. Robert Jackson, *The Malayan Emergency & Indonesian Confrontation – The Commonwealth's Wars 1948–1966*, (Barnsley: Pen & Sword, 2008) p.38
69. Peter de la Billiere, *Looking for Trouble: SAS to Gulf Command*, (London: Harper Collins, 1995) pp.230–232
70. John Akehurst, *We Won a War: The Campaign in Oman 1965–75*, (Guildford: M. Russell, 1982) p.43
71. Fiennes, pp.34–35.
72. Ladwig III, p.73
73. Ibid.
74. John Akehurst, *We Won a War: The Campaign in Oman 1965–75*, (Guildford: M. Russell, 1982) p.42
    Marc DeVore, 'The United Kingdom's Last Hot War of the Cold War: Oman 1963–75', *Cold War History*, Vol. 11, Issue 3 (2011) p.20
75. MEC – GRAHAM COLLECTION – John Graham, 'Thirty Months: A Brief History of Oman's Armed Forces April 1970 – September 1972'
    Geraint Hughes, 'A Proxy War in Arabia: The Dhofar War Emergency and Cross-border Raids into South Yemen', *Middle East Journal*, Vol. 69, No.1 (Winter 2015) pp.92–96
76. Marc DeVore, The United Kingdom's Last Hot War of the Cold War: Oman 1963–75', *Cold War History*, Vol. 11, Issue 3 (2011) p.9
77. John Pimlott, *British Military Operations, 1945–85*, (London: Bison, 1986) p.50
    Corran Purdon, *List the Bugle: Reminiscences of an Irish Soldier*, (Antrim: Greystone Books, 1993) pp.188–191
78. Corran Purdon, *List the Bugle: Reminiscences of an Irish Soldier*, (Antrim: Greystone Books, 1993) pp.99–118
79. Ken Perkins, *A Fortunate Soldier*, (London: Brassy's, 1988) p.59
80. 'Korea Veterans Remember Fallen Comrades', BBC News World Service Online (20 Apr 2001) Accessed 6 Apr 2024
81. Obituary 'Brigadier Mike Harvey', *The Times*, 7 Aug 2007
82. Peter de la Billiere, *Looking for Trouble: SAS to Gulf Command*, (London: Harper Collins, 1995) pp.204–8
    TNA – WO 305/4293 – 'Borneo Operations Feb – Jul 1965', *SAS Reports*, Volume 2 (Feb-Jul 1965)
83. Quoting CO 22 SAS Tony Jeapes – Ian Beckett, *Modern Insurgencies and Counter-Insurgencies – Guerrillas and their Opponents Since 1756*, (London: Routledge, 2001) p.217
84. As highlighted by the various press cuttings collected by Graham during his secondment as CSAF and available to view in the MEC, Graham Collection, Boxes 7 and 8. An example being 'Oman – What does British Presence Mean', *The Daily Telegraph Magazine* (April 1971) pp.17–20
    Fred Halliday, *Arabia without Sultans*, (Harmondsworth: Penguin, 1974)

85. TNA – DEFE 25/186 – Muscat and Oman – General Secretary of State for Defence (Secret) Memorandum 'SAS Assistance to the Sultanate of Oman' (4 Sep 1970) p.4
86. J.E. Peterson, 'The Experience of British Counter-Insurgency Campaigns and Implications for Iraq', Arabian Peninsula Background Note, No. APBN-009. Published on www.JEPeterson.net (July 2009) p.9
87. Michael Crawshaw, 'The Evolution of British COIN', *Ministry of Defence Joint Doctrine Publication* (JDP 3–40), (2012) p.20
88. MEC – GURNEY COLLECTION – FILE 1/2 – Sir Henry Gurney, 'A Palestine Postscript, 15 March-13 May 1948'
TNA – WO 106/6020 – 'Report on Cyprus Emergency', Director of Operations Report on the Cyprus Emergency, 31 Jul 1959
89. Clive Jones, *Britain and the Yemen Civil War, 1962–65: Ministers, Mercenaries and Mandarins: Foreign Policy and the Limits of Covert Action*, (Eastbourne: Sussex Academic Press, 2010) p.191
Julian Paget, *Last Post: Aden 1964–67*, (London: Faber & Faber, 1969) pp.223–4
90. Colin Mitchell, *Having Been a Soldier*, (London: Hamish Hamilton, 1969), p.242
91. Ibid., p.151 and p.242
92. Ibid., p.207
93. Palestine 1948, and Aden/Southern Federation 1967 versus Malaya, Kenya and Cyprus
94. "[SAS founder, Colonel David] Stirling told [ADC to the Governor of Aden Flight Lieutenant Tony])
Boyle that with the authority of two government ministers [Amery and Sandys] and the knowledge of the Prime Minister [Macmillan], a group of former SAS soldiers was about to be infiltrated into the Yemen [to covertly assist Royalist forces]", Duff Hart-Davies, *The War That Never Was*, (London: Random House, 2011) p.15
95. TNA DEFE 11/533, 'Aden', 'Report on the Mutinies within the South Arabian Forces on 20 June 1967 (and the action taken to control them by British and South Arabian Forces)', HQ Middle East Command (22 Oct 67) p.15
96. MEC – GRAHAM COLLECTION – Box 5/2 – John Graham, 'Thirty Months: A Brief History of Oman's Armed Forces April 1970 – September 1972'
97. John Graham, *Ponder Anew: Reflections on the 20th Century*, (Spellmount, 1999) p.328
98. Ibid., p.344
99. Ian Beckett and John Pimlott, *Armed Forces & Modern Counter-Insurgency*, (New York: St. Martin's Press, 1985) p.100
100. Ibid.

Chapter 5

1. Fred Halliday, *Arabia Without Sultans*, (Harmondsworth: Penguin, 1974) pp.270/71
2. Julian Paget, *Counter-Insurgency Campaigning*, (London: Faber & Faber, 1967) p.78
3. "…Oman has been a de facto British colony…Britain imposed its will when it wanted to. The pretence of Omani 'independence'… is meant to hide what is in fact a pellucid arrangement."). Fred Halliday, *Arabia Without Sultans*, (Harmondsworth: Penguin, 1974) p.271
4. E.g. support for Royalist forces in North Yemen against UAR/Egyptian-installed regime in 1960s
5. TNA – FCO 8/1437 – British Assistance to the Sultan's Armed Forces of Oman - Inc. Charles Kendall & Partners Ltd. as Oman's official Chandlery and Airwork Services Ltd. for contract officer recruitment

6. MEC-GURNEY COLLECTION–FILE 1/2 - "…the undertaking by Britain… represents the only attempt by any nation to help the Jews. It ended in ingratitude, bitterness and tragedy only because the Zionists wanted more than had been given and turned against Britain". Sir Henry Gurney, 'A Palestine Postscript, 15 March-13 May 1948'
7. A situation not countered until post 1970 by SAS psyops efforts - "Until the last months of the war there was nothing in Dhofar to counter the powerful transmitters of Radio Aden and a constant flow of totally false propaganda was fed daily to the civilian inhabitants of the province." John Akehurst, *We Won a War: The Campaign in Oman 1965–75*, (Guildford: M. Russell, 1982) p.30
8. Often utilising pictures/diagrams as well as text to aid messaging due to widespread illiteracy levels
9. Toby Mattheisen, 'Anti-Colonialism, the Cold War and the Long Sixties in the Gulf States' in *The Routledge Handbook of the Global Sixties: Between Protest and Nation-Building*, (London/New York: Routledge, 2017) p.100, The Gulf Committee, 'Dhofar: Britain's Colonial War in the Gulf', (London: The Gulf Committee, 1972) p.5
10. Walter C. Ladwig III, 'Supporting allies in counterinsurgency: Britain and the Dhofar Rebellion', *Small Wars & Insurgencies*, Vol.19, Issue 1 (2008) p.65
11. "Meanwhile, hidden behind ever carefully layered veils of agents and intermediaries, the same powers which have distinctly ruled the region for hundreds of years are making sure their grip gets ever tighter". Christopher Davidson, *Shadow Wars: The Secret Struggle for the Middle East*, (London: Oneworld Publications, 2016) p.xiii
12. Fred Halliday, *Arabia Without Sultans*, (Harmondsworth: Penguin, 1974) p.265
MEC – GRAHAM COLLECTION – Box 6/3 – "Consequently there was an annual embarrassment for Britain at the United Nations when 'The Question of Oman' was dealt with (by the Marxist/Nationalist-driven UN lobby)". Sir Donald Hawley, 'Recollections of Muscat', *The Journal of the Sultan's Armed Forces Association*, Issue 42 (March 1993)

Chapter 6

1. TNA – KV5/41 – Irgun Zvai Leumi – National Military Organization in the Land of Israel –Herut Group. Loose Minute from MI1 to MI5, dated 15 Jan 1953. Units e.g. Stern Group and Irgun Zvai Leumi
Julian Paget, *Counter-Insurgency Campaigning*, (London: Faber & Faber, 1967) p.153
2. Simon Anglim, 'The Omani Djebel War 1957–59', *The Strategy Bridge* (1 Dec 2014) https://thestrategybridge.org/the-bridge/2014/12/1/the-oman-djebel-war-195759 Accessed online 19 Apr 2023
Smiley, pp.78–80
3. TNA – CAB21/1681 – Cabinet Malaya Committee on Operation against Bandits etc. (General). Meeting Minutes 25 Sep 1950
Colin Mitchell, *Having Been A Soldier*, (London: Hamish Hamilton, 1969) p.150
4. "Only about 12% of them (the Mau Mau 'Land Freedom Army' insurgent forces) were armed with precision weapons, and their deadliest tool was the razor-sharp machete, called a 'panga'. They had received virtually no military training but possessed a hunter's instincts and skill". Julian Paget, *Counter-Insurgency Campaigning*, (London: Faber & Faber, 1967) p.90
5. Frank Kitson, *Low Intensity Operations: Subversion, Insurgency and Peacekeeping*, (London: Faber & Faber, 1971) p.95

6. TNA – WO 305/4293 – Borneo Operations Feb-Jul 1965. Repeated arduous patrols deep into jungle areas yielded typical report comments such as, "There were no signs of military tracks in the area", (11 day SAS patrol 2 -13 Jun 1965, signed Major de la Billiere, OC A Sqn SAS, dated 15 Jun 1965) and (13 day SAS patrol 13 -16 Jun 1965, signed Major de la Billiere, OC A Sqn SAS, dated 19 Jun 1965) "…there were no signs of regular military uses of the areas"
7. Fiennes, p.35
8. Valeri, p.57
   Liddell Hart Archive, KCL – THWAITES COLLECTION – 'Operation Lance', *Guards Magazine; Journal of the Household Division* (Summer 1970) p.65
9. John Akehurst, *We Won a War: The Campaign in Oman 1965–75*, (Guildford: M. Russell, 1982) p.25
10. Walter C. Ladwig III, 'Supporting allies in counterinsurgency: Britain and the Dhofar Rebellion', *Small Wars & Insurgencies*, Vol.19, Issue 1 (2008) p.67
11. Ibid.
12. John Akehurst, *We Won a War: The Campaign in Oman 1965–75*, (Guildford: M. Russell, 1982) pp.24/25
13. TNA AIR20/10377 – Review of the Emergency in Malaya from June 1948 to August 1957 p.2
    Whose "atrocities were unbelievably brutal", such as the Lari massacre on 20 Mar 1953 where 1000 Kikuyu massacred 84 people – 2/3 of them women and children – and mutilated 31 others. Julian Paget, *Counter-Insurgency Campaigning*, (London: Faber & Faber, 1967) p.93
    MEC – JOHN GRAHAM COLLECTION, 5/6 – The Memoirs of Major General John Graham, Part 4, 1945–1947 Palestine, pp.13–16. The "shocking and atrocious act" of the King David Hotel bombing (91 killed) undertaken by IZL or the Stern Gang murder and booby-trapping of the bodies of Sergeants Pearce and Robinson developed in the troops "…a deep contempt for Jews of all sects, ages and backgrounds" which was "…so uncharacteristic of the British soldier in his normal dealings with civilians"
14. TNA AIR20/10377– (Chiefs of Staff Committee) Review of the Emergency in Malaya from June 1948 to August 1957, "The Emergency has been (purely) an infantry war fought by the rifle companies" p.27
15. c.18 hours to get off jebel by donkey and then to Bahrain for serious cases and no proper medical facilities in-country; just small ward at Bait Al Falaj HQ
16. Jonathan Walker, *Aden Insurgency, The Savage War in Yemen 1962–67*, (Barnsley: Pen & Sword, 2004) p.196
17. Ibid., p.97
18. Ian Beckett and John Pimlott, *Armed Forces & Modern Counter-Insurgency*, (New York: St. Martin's Press, 1985) pp.144/5
19. Walter C. Ladwig III, 'Supporting allies in counterinsurgency: Britain and the Dhofar Rebellion', *Small Wars & Insurgencies*, Vol.19, Issue 1 (2008) p.67
    John Blashford-Snell, *Something Lost Behind the Ranges*, (London: Harper Collins, 1995) p.162
20. J.E. Peterson, *Oman's Insurgencies: The Sultanate's Struggle for Supremacy*, (London: Saqi, 2007) p.369
21. Including state-of the-art combat medical services and the UK-manned Field Surgical Unit
22. J.E. Peterson, 'The Experience of British Counter-Insurgency Campaigns and Implications for Iraq', Arabian Peninsula Background Note, No.APBN-009. Published on www.JEPeterson.net (Jul 2009) p.10

23. "The crying need for helicopters was for casualty evacuation… Every officer had tales to tell of these long marches with stretchers being manhandled down perpendicular slopes while a man's lifeblood dripped slowly away", Peter Thwaites, *Muscat Command*, (Barnsley: Pen & Sword, 1995) p.40
24. Ian Beckett, *Modern Insurgencies and Counter-Insurgencies – Guerrillas and their Opponents Since 1756*, (London: Routledge, 2001) p.217
25. John Newsinger, *British Counterinsurgency*, (Basingstoke: Palgrave Macmillan, 2015) p.51
26. Ibid., p.76
27. Such as basic healthcare and education services. Marc DeVore, 'A more complex and conventional victory: revisiting the Dhofar counterinsurgency, 1963–1975', *Small Wars & Insurgencies*, Vol.23, Issue 1 (2012) p.152
28. Marc DeVore, 'A more complex and conventional victory: revisiting the Dhofar counterinsurgency, 1963–1975', *Small Wars & Insurgencies*, Vol.23, Issue 1 (2012) p.155
29. J.E. Peterson, *Oman's Insurgencies: The Sultanate's Struggle for Supremacy*, (London: Saqi, 2007) p.229
30. Ian Beckett, *Modern Insurgencies and Counter-Insurgencies – Guerrillas and their Opponents Since 1756*, (London: Routledge, 2001) p.218
31. TNA – DEFE 25/186 – Muscat and Oman – General. "..there will be a number of tasks for which the SAS are particularly suitable", 'An Appreciation of the Musandam Situation', HQ Land Forces Gulf, (1 Nov 70) p.6
    Marc DeVore, 'The United Kingdom's Last Hot War of the Cold War: Oman 1963–75', *Cold War History*, Vol. 11, Issue 3 (2011) p.22
32. As described by Peterson, J.E. Peterson, 'The Experience of British Counter-Insurgency Campaigns and Implications for Iraq', Arabian Peninsula Background Note, No. APBN-009. Published on www.JEPeterson.net (July 2009) p.8
33. John Graham, *Ponder Anew: Reflections on the Twentieth Century*, (Staplehurst: Spellmount Limited, 1999) p.321
34. Ibid., p.323
35. Marc DeVore, 'A More Complex and Conventional Victory: Revisiting the Dhofar Counterinsurgency, 1963–1975', *Small Wars & Insurgencies*, Vol. 23, Issue 1 (2012) p.155
36. Walter C. Ladwig III, 'Supporting allies in counterinsurgency: Britain and the Dhofar Rebellion', *Small Wars & Insurgencies*, Vol.19, Issue 1 (2008) p.74
    And seconded RAVC veterinary surgeons working alongside SAS soldiers. Sultanate of Oman NRAA – Records of Oman 1966–1971 (Cambridge Archive Editions, 2003) Vol. 6: Letter, British Consulate General, Muscat to Mr. G. Arthur (Bahrain), dated 15 Feb 1971 p.2
37. Walter C. Ladwig III, 'Supporting allies in counterinsurgency: Britain and the Dhofar Rebellion', *Small Wars & Insurgencies*, Vol.19, Issue 1 (2008) pp.72–74
38. John Newsinger, *British Counterinsurgency*, (Basingstoke: Palgrave Macmillan, 2015) p.78
39. United Arab Emirates (UAE) National Archives – FCO 8/1856 – Military Assistance to Oman from UK – Memorandum prepared by D.F. Hawley, British Ambassador, Muscat, dated 26 Feb 1972
40. Robert Alston and Stuart Laing, *Unshook Till the End of Time: A History of Relations Between Britain & Oman 1650–1970*, (London: Gilgamesh Publishing, 2012) p.252
41. Marc DeVore, 'A more complex and conventional victory: revisiting the Dhofar counterinsurgency, 1963–1975', *Small Wars & Insurgencies*, Vol.23, Issue 1 (2012) p.161
42. Peterson, pp.392–93
    M. Robb, The Anglo-Omani Society/Sultan's Armed Forces Association Lecture: 'Civil Aid in Dhofar; the Key to Peace', London, 15 Jun 2023

43. Ibid.
44. John Newsinger, *British Counterinsurgency*, (Basingstoke: Palgrave Macmillan, 2015) p.153
    Marc DeVore, 'A more complex and conventional victory: revisiting the Dhofar counterinsurgency, 1963–1975', *Small Wars & Insurgencies*, Vol.23, Issue 1 (2012) p.162
    M. Robb, The Anglo-Omani Society/Sultan's Armed Forces Association Lecture: 'Civil Aid in Dhofar; the Key to Peace', London, 15 Jun 2023
45. MEC – GRAHAM COLLECTION – Box 6/3 – Sir Donald Hawley, 'Recollections of Muscat', *The Journal of the Sultan's Armed Forces Association*, Issue 42 (March 1993)
46. MEC – GRAHAM COLLECTION – Briefing Document, Colonel M. Harvey, 'Dhofar Background', 27 June 1971
47. Robert Jackson, *The Malayan Emergency & Indonesian Confrontation – The Commonwealth's Wars 1948–1966*, (Barnsley: Pen & Sword, 2008) p.54
48. Marc DeVore, 'The United Kingdom's Last Hot War of the Cold War: Oman 1963–75', *Cold War History*, Vol. 11, Issue 3 (2011) p.10
49. J.E. Peterson, *Oman's Insurgencies: The Sultanate's Struggle for Supremacy*, (London: Saqi, 2007) p.329
50. TNA – CAB 186/11, JIC, 'Outlook for Oman (Delicate Source)', 1 Mar 72, Part 2, Main report
51. Walter C. Ladwig III, 'Supporting allies in counterinsurgency: Britain and the Dhofar Rebellion', *Small Wars & Insurgencies*, Vol.19, Issue 1 (2008) p.76
52. TNA – 11/854 – Oman, Chiefs of Staff Committee Defence Planning Staff, 'The Progress of Operations in Oman', 26 Feb 1975
53. United Arab Emirates NA – FCO 8/2022 – Annex to Oman Intelligence Report No. 56 (16–29 Dec 1973), dated 10 Jan 1974
    United Arab Emirates NA – FCO 8/2021 – Extracts from Correspondence: Muscat and Oman: Cooperation between armed forces of Oman and United Arab Emirates. Defence Attaché Muscat's TLM 621 (Deployment of ADDF Units in Oman) of 1 August to MOD
54. Ibid.
55. Marc DeVore, 'A more complex and conventional victory: revisiting the Dhofar counterinsurgency, 1963–1975', *Small Wars & Insurgencies*, Vol.23, Issue 1 (2012) p.163
56. Marc DeVore, 'The United Kingdom's Last Hot War of the Cold War: Oman 1963–75', *Cold War History*, Vol. 11, Issue 3 (2011) p.17
57. MEC – GURNEY COLLECTION – FILE 1/2 – Sir Henry Gurney, 'A Palestine Postscript, 15 March–13 May 1948'
58. Clive Jones, *Britain and the Yemen Civil War, 1962–65: Ministers, Mercenaries and Mandarins: Foreign Policy and the Limits of Covert Action*, (Eastbourne: Sussex Academic Press, 2010) p.191
59. Julian Paget, *Counter-Insurgency Campaigning*, (London: Faber & Faber, 1967) pp.141–148
60. Robert Jackson, *The Malayan Emergency & Indonesian Confrontation – The Commonwealth's Wars 1948–1966*, (Barnsley: Pen & Sword, 2008) p.140
    Marc DeVore, 'A more complex and conventional victory: revisiting the Dhofar counterinsurgency, 1963–1975', *Small Wars & Insurgencies*, Vol.23, Issue 1 (2012) p.144
61. Akehurst recalled how he had to remind two visiting senior British officials that it was not a 'British victory' as such, but an Omani/Allied undertaking. John Akehurst, *We Won a War: The Campaign in Oman 1965–75*, (Guildford: M. Russell, 1982) p.185
62. David Kilcullen, 'Counterinsurgency Redux', *International Institute of Strategic Studies*, Vol. 48, Issue 4 (Winter 2006/7) p.111

63. Marc DeVore, 'The United Kingdom's Last Hot War of the Cold War: Oman 1963–75', *Cold War History*, Vol. 11, Issue 3 (2011) p.2
64. Douglas Porch, *Counterinsurgency: Exposing the Myths of the New Way of War*, (Cambridge: Cambridge University Press, 2013) p.249
65. Walter C. Ladwig III, 'Supporting allies in counterinsurgency: Britain and the Dhofar Rebellion', *Small Wars & Insurgencies*, Vol.19, Issue 1 (2008) p.63 and p.77
66. Out of 30 worldwide (historical) COIN campaigns studied by this Rand study, only eight were considered wins for the COIN forces, the rest as losses. Christopher, P., Clarke, C., & Grill, B., *Victory Has A Thousand Fathers: Sources of Success in Counterinsurgency*, (Santa Monica, CA: RAND Corporation, 2010) p.87

Part III
1. Thomas R. Mockaitis, 'Low-Intensity Conflict: The British Experience', *Conflict Quarterly*, (1993) p.8
Ian Beckett and John Pimlott, *Counter-Insurgency; Lessons from History*, (Barnsley: Pen & Sword, 2011) p.16
John A. Nagl, *Learning to Eat Soup with a Knife: Counterinsurgency Lessons from Malaya and Vietnam*, (Chicago: Chicago University Press, 2005) p.43 and p.59
2. Ian Beckett and John Pimlott, *Counter-Insurgency; Lessons from History*, (Barnsley: Pen & Sword, 2011) p.13
3. Ibid.
David Benest, 'Ponder Anew: Brigadier Graham and the Dhofar War 1970–1972', (Oct 2015) https://thestrategybridge.org/the-bridge/2016/1/1/ponder-anew-brigadier-john-graham-the-dhofar-war-19701972   Accessed online 19 Apr 2023
John Newsinger, *British Counterinsurgency*, (Basingstoke: Palgrave Macmillan, 2015) p.1
Douglas Porch, *Counterinsurgency: Exposing the Myths of the New Way of War*, (Cambridge: Cambridge University Press, 2013) p.266
Thomas R. Mockaitis, 'The Phoenix of Counterinsurgency', *The Journal of Conflict Studies*, (Summer 2007) p.13
4. Douglas Porch, *Counterinsurgency: Exposing the Myths of the New Way of War*, (Cambridge: Cambridge University Press, 2013) p.249
5. Marc DeVore, 'A more complex and conventional victory: revisiting the Dhofar counterinsurgency, 1963–1975', *Small Wars & Insurgencies*, Vol.23, Issue 1 (2012) p.144
6. Tony Jeapes, *SAS Operation Oman*, (London: HarperCollins, 1980) p.14
7. Christopher Paul, Colin P. Clarke, Beth Grill and Molly Dunigan, *Paths to Victory – Detailed Insurgency Case studies*, (Santa Monica, CA: RAND Corporation, 2013) p.51, p.XV
8. Ian Beckett, *Modern Insurgencies and Counter-Insurgencies – Guerrillas and their Opponents since 1756*, (London: Routledge, 2001) p.viii
9. Christopher Paul, Colin P. Clarke, Beth Grill and Molly Dunigan, *Paths to Victory – Detailed Insurgency Case studies*, (Santa Monica, CA: RAND Corporation, 2013) p.51, pp.11–423
10. Ibid.
11. Marc DeVore, 'A more complex and conventional victory: revisiting the Dhofar counterinsurgency, 1963–1975', *Small Wars & Insurgencies*, Vol.23, Issue 1 (2012) p.144
Tony Jeapes, *SAS Operation Oman*, (London: HarperCollins, 1980) p.14
Marc DeVore, 'A more complex and conventional victory: revisiting the Dhofar counterinsurgency, 1963–1975', *Small Wars & Insurgencies*, Vol.23, Issue 1 (2012) p.144

John Akehurst, *We Won a War: The Campaign in Oman 1965–75*, (Guildford: M. Russell, 1982) p.183

Ian Beckett and John Pimlott, *Counter-Insurgency; Lessons from History*, (Barnsley: Pen & Sword, 2011) p.43

David Benest, 'Ponder Anew: Brigadier Graham and the Dhofar War 1970–1972', (Oct 2015) https://thestrategybridge.org/the-bridge/2016/1/1/ponder-anew-brigadier-john-graham-the-dhofar-war-19701972 Accessed online 19 Apr 2023 p.9

David Charters, 'Counter-insurgency Intelligence: The Evolution of British Theory and Practice', *Journal of Conflict Studies*, Vol. 29 (2009) p.10

Ian Beckett, *Modern Insurgencies and Counter-Insurgencies – Guerrillas and their Opponents Since 1756*, (London: Routledge, 2001) p.230

12. John Newsinger, *British Counterinsurgency*, (Basingstoke: Palgrave Macmillan) p.1

    Thomas R. Mockaitis, 'The Phoenix of Counterinsurgency', *The Journal of Conflict Studies*, (Summer 2007) p.13

13. Thomas R. Mockaitis, Low-Intensity Conflict: The British Experience, Conflict Quarterly, (1993) p.9 and David Benest, 'Ponder Anew: Brigadier Graham and the Dhofar War 1970–1972', (Oct 2015) https://thestrategybridge.org/the-bridge/2016/1/1/ponder-anew-brigadier-john-graham-the-dhofar-war-19701972 Accessed online 19 Apr 2023 p.9

14. 21 out of 71 COIN campaigns included in the study. Christopher, P., Clarke, C., Grill, B., & Dunigan, M., *Paths to Victory – Detailed Insurgency Case studies*, (Santa Monica: Rand Corporation, 2013) p.11–423

15. Thomas R. Mockaitis, 'The Origin of British Counter-insurgency', *Small Wars & Insurgencies*, Vol. 1, Issue 3 (1990) p.214

    Thomas R. Mockaitis, 'Low-Intensity Conflict: The British Experience', *Conflict Quarterly*, (Winter 1993) p.8

    Ian Beckett and John Pimlott, *Counter-Insurgency; Lessons from History*, (Barnsley: Pen & Sword, 2011) pp.136–189

16. John A. Nagl, *Learning to Eat Soup with a Knife: Counterinsurgency Lessons from Malaya and Vietnam*, (Chicago: Chicago University Press, 2005) Foreword

17. Robert O. Tilman, 'The Non-Lessons of the Malayan Emergency', *Asian Survey*, Vol.6, No.8 (1966) p.413

18. John Newsinger, *British Counterinsurgency*, (Basingstoke: Palgrave Macmillan, 2015) p.1

19. Douglas Porch, *Counterinsurgency: Exposing the Myths of the New Way of War*, (Cambridge: Cambridge University Press, 2013) p.266

20. Christopher Paul, Colin P. Clarke, Beth Grill and Molly Dunigan, *Paths to Victory – Detailed Insurgency Case studies*, (Santa Monica, CA: RAND Corporation, 2013) pp.64–94

21. Nori Katagiri, 'Winning Hearts and Minds to Lose Control: Exploring Various Consequences of Popular Support in COIN Missions', *Small Wars & Insurgencies*, Vol.22, Issue 1 (Mar 2011) p.171

22. Ibid., p.176

23. Douglas Porch, *Counterinsurgency: Exposing the Myths of the New Way of War*, (Cambridge: Cambridge University Press, 2013) p.249

24. MEC – GURNEY COLLECTION – FILE 1/2 – Sir Henry Gurney, 'A Palestine Postscript, 15 March-13 May 1948'

25. Thomas R. Mockaitis, 'Low Intensity Conflict: the British Experience', *Conflict Quarterly* (1993) pp.8–9

26. Nori Katagiri, 'Winning Hearts and Minds to Lose Control: Exploring Various Consequences of Popular Support in COIN Missions', *Small Wars & Insurgencies*, Vol.22, Issue 1 (Mar 2011) p.176
    Douglas Porch, *Counterinsurgency: Exposing the Myths of the New Way of War*, (Cambridge: Cambridge University Press, 2013) p.266
27. David Charters, 'Counter-insurgency Intelligence: The Evolution of British Theory and Practice', *Journal of Conflict Studies*, Vol. 29 (2009) p.10
28. Marc DeVore, 'A more complex and conventional victory: revisiting the Dhofar counterinsurgency, 1963–1975', *Small Wars & Insurgencies*, Vol.23, Issue 1 (2012) p.144
29. "During the post-war period only the Zionist insurgency in Palestine was a complete defeat" and "Only the evacuation of Aden in 1967 represents a clear defeat for Britain in the post-colonial era", Thomas R. Mockaitis, 'Low Intensity Conflict: the British Experience', *Conflict Quarterly* (1993) pp.8–9
30. Thomas R. Mockaitis, 'Low Intensity Conflict: the British Experience', *Conflict Quarterly* (1993) pp.8–9
31. Ibid., p.9
    Ian Beckett, *Modern Insurgencies and Counter-Insurgencies – Guerrillas and their Opponents since 1756*, (London: Routledge, 2001) p.217
    Aaron Edwards, *Defending the Realm? The Politics of Britain's Small Wars Since 1945*, (Manchester: Manchester University Press, 2012) p.6
    Douglas Porch, *Counterinsurgency: Exposing the Myths of the New Way of War*, (Cambridge: Cambridge University Press, 2013) p.249
    John Newsinger, *British Counterinsurgency*, (Basingstoke: Palgrave Macmillan, 2015) p.1
    Caroline Elkins, 'Alchemy of Evidence: Mau Mau, the British Empire and the High Court of Justice', *The Journal of Imperial and Commonwealth History*, Vol. 39, Issue 5 (2011) p.732
    David M. Anderson, 'British Abuse and Torture in Kenya's Counter-Insurgency, 1952–1960', *Small Wars & Insurgencies*, Vol. 23, Issues 4–5 (2012) p.700
32. John Newsinger, *British Counterinsurgency*, (Basingstoke: Palgrave Macmillan, 2015) p.2

Chapter 7
1. The five as listed in the study out of 71 cases covered and 21 considered COIN 'wins', but the sixth considered as Brunei/early stages of Borneo campaign.
   Christopher Paul, Colin P. Clarke, Beth Grill and Molly Dunigan, *Paths to Victory – Detailed Insurgency Case studies*, (Santa Monica, CA: RAND Corporation, 2013) p.XV
2. Marc Valeri, *Oman: Politics and Society in the Qaboos State*, (London: C. Hurst & Co., 2017) p.34
3. Walter C. Ladwig III, 'Supporting allies in counterinsurgency: Britain and the Dhofar Rebellion', *Small Wars & Insurgencies*, Vol.19, Issue 1 (2008) p.65
4. Corran Purdon, *List the Bugle: Reminiscences of an Irish Soldier*, (Antrim: Greystone Books, 1993) pp.188–189
5. Attacking MECOM company vehicles in 1963 but vehicles from RAF Salalah only from Aug 1964
6. MEC – GRAHAM COLLECTION – Tony Lewis, 'The Story of the Sultan of Oman's Armed Forces 1964–67', *The Journal of the Sultan's Armed Forces Association*, Issue 37 (February 1988) Article p.35
7. Ibid., p.4
8. Walter C. Ladwig III, 'Supporting allies in counterinsurgency: Britain and the Dhofar Rebellion', *Small Wars & Insurgencies*, Vol.19, Issue 1 (2008) p.68

9. MEC – GRAHAM COLLECTION – Tony Lewis, 'The Story of the Sultan of Oman's Armed Forces 1964–67', *The Journal of the Sultan's Armed Forces Association*, Issue 37 (February 1988) Article p.35
10. Ibid., p.3
11. Ibid.
12. MEC – GRAHAM COLLECTION – Tony Lewis, 'The Story of the Sultan of Oman's Armed Forces 1964–67', *The Journal of the Sultan's Armed Forces Association*, Issue 37 (February 1988) p.33
13. Ibid.
14. Ibid. p.8 and J.E. Peterson, *Oman's Insurgencies: The Sultanate's Struggle for Supremacy*, (London: Saqi, 2007) p.198
15. "…tribes of strange non-Arab peoples, often living in caves, almost naked, speaking languages of their own", Jan Morris, *Sultan In Oman*, (London: Arrow Books Ltd, 1990) p.27
16. Ibid., p.200
17. MEC – GRAHAM COLLECTION – Tony Lewis, 'The Story of the Sultan of Oman's Armed Forces 1964–67', *The Journal of the Sultan's Armed Forces Association*, Issue 37 (February 1988) Article p.39
18. James Worrall, *Statebuilding and Counterinsurgency in Oman: Political, Military and Diplomatic Relations at the End of Empire*, (London: I.B. Tauris & Co. Ltd., 2014) p.54
19. J.E. Peterson, *Oman's Insurgencies: The Sultanate's Struggle for Supremacy*, (London: Saqi, 2007) p.206
20. MEC – GRAHAM COLLECTION – Tony Lewis, 'The Story of the Sultan of Oman's Armed Forces 1964–67', *The Journal of the Sultan's Armed Forces Association*, Issue 37 (February 1988) Article p.39
21. Walter C. Ladwig III, 'Supporting allies in counterinsurgency: Britain and the Dhofar Rebellion', *Small Wars & Insurgencies*, Vol.19, Issue 1 (2008) p.70
    John Graham, *Ponder Anew: Reflections on the Twentieth Century*, (Staplehurst: Spellmount Limited, 1999) p.323
22. Geraint Hughes, 'A 'Model Campaign' Reappraised: The Counter-Insurgency War in Dhofar, Oman, 1965–1975', *Journal of Strategic Studies*, Vol.32, Issue 2 (2009) p.280
    Marc DeVore, 'The United Kingdom's Last Hot War of the Cold War: Oman 1963–75', *Cold War History*, Vol. 11, Issue 3 (2011) p.10
23. Tony Jeapes, *SAS Operation Oman*, (London: HarperCollins, 1980) p.11, and Marc DeVore, 'A more complex and conventional victory: revisiting the Dhofar counterinsurgency, 1963–1975', *Small Wars & Insurgencies*, Vol.23, Issue 1 (2012) p.144
24. Marc DeVore, 'The United Kingdom's Last Hot War of the Cold War: Oman 1963–75', *Cold War History*, Vol. 11, Issue 3 (2011) p.8
25. TNA – DEFE 46/609 – Defence Planning of UK Armed Forces in Muscat and Oman – "…the SAF might (only) be able to hold Salalah itself… and to keep open albeit with some difficulty the land routes between Salalah and the rest of the Sultanate to the north and east", Annex to secret memo 'SAS Assistance to the Sultanate of Oman', Alec-Douglas Home, 4 Sep 1970
26. "The British Foreign Office continues to suppress the documents pertaining to the coup", Abdel Takriti, 'The 1970 Coup in Oman Reconsidered', *Journal of Arabian Studies*, Vol. 3, Issue 2 (2013) p.156
    Marc DeVore, 'A more complex and conventional victory: revisiting the Dhofar counterinsurgency, 1963–1975', *Small Wars & Insurgencies*, Vol.23, Issue 1 (2012) p.151

Abdel Takriti, 'The 1970 Coup in Oman Reconsidered', *Journal of Arabian Studies*, Vol. 3, Issue 2 (2013) p.169 and pp.171–172 '23-11-2009', in BBC Sounds (Radio 4), ed. by Mike Thomson (UK: BBC, 2009)

27. John Graham, *Ponder Anew: Reflections on the Twentieth Century*, (Staplehurst: Spellmount Ltd, 1999) pp.378–379, John Beasant and Christopher Ling, *Sultan In Arabia: A Private Life*, (Edinburgh: Mainstream, 2004) p.102
28. Marc DeVore, 'A more complex and conventional victory: revisiting the Dhofar counterinsurgency, 1963–1975', *Small Wars & Insurgencies*, Vol.23, Issue 1 (2012) p.151
John Akehurst, *We Won a War: The Campaign in Oman 1965–75*, (Guildford: M. Russell, 1982) p.15
29. Ian Beckett, *Modern Insurgencies and Counter-Insurgencies – Guerrillas and their Opponents Since 1756*, (London: Routledge, 2001) p.218
Jim White, 'Oman 1965–1976: From Certain Defeat to Decisive Victory', *Small Wars Journal* (2008) p.12
J.E. Peterson, 'Guerrilla Warfare and Ideological Confrontation in the Arabian Peninsula: The Rebellion in Dhurfar', *World Affairs*, Vol. 139, No.4 (1977) p.282
30. John Beasant and Christopher Ling, *Sultan In Arabia: A Private Life*, (Edinburgh: Mainstream, 2004) p.173
31. J.E. Peterson, *Oman's Insurgencies: The Sultanate's Struggle for Supremacy*, (London: Saqi, 2007) p.279 and p.384
32. Small engagements and casualties encountered by SAF all the way up until 1980. Ibid., pp.486–487
33. Col Harvey had to request Firqa leaders be interviewed by the Sultan and be lectured about indiscipline. Tony Jeapes, *SAS Operation Oman*, (London: HarperCollins, 1980) p.140
Mick Dales, *SAS: A Storm Gathering*, (Kindle E-book, 2016) Chapter 10
34. John Akehurst, *We Won a War: The Campaign in Oman 1965–75*, (Guildford: M. Russell, 1982) p.43
35. Geraint Hughes, 'A 'Model Campaign' Reappraised: The Counter-Insurgency War in Dhofar, Oman, 1965–1975', *Journal of Strategic Studies*, Vol.32, Issue 2 (2009) p.283
Marc DeVore, 'A more complex and conventional victory: revisiting the Dhofar counterinsurgency, 1963–1975', *Small Wars & Insurgencies*, Vol.23, Issue 1 (2012) p.154
36. John Graham, *Ponder Anew: Reflections on the Twentieth Century*, (Staplehurst: Spellmount Limited, 1999) p.360
Marc DeVore, 'A more complex and conventional victory: revisiting the Dhofar counterinsurgency, 1963–1975', *Small Wars & Insurgencies*, Vol.23, Issue 1 (2012) pp.155–6
37. Marc DeVore, 'The United Kingdom's Last Hot War of the Cold War: Oman 1963–75', *Cold War History*, Vol. 11, Issue 3 (2011) p.12
38. John Graham, *Ponder Anew: Reflections on the Twentieth Century*, (Staplehurst: Spellmount Limited, 1999) p.347
J.E. Peterson, 'Guerrilla Warfare and Ideological Confrontation in the Arabian Peninsula: The Rebellion in Dhurfar', *World Affairs*, Vol. 139, No.4, (1977) p.279
39. Ian Beckett, *Modern Insurgencies and Counter-Insurgencies – Guerrillas and their Opponents Since 1756*, (London: Routledge, 2001) p.218
Jim White, 'Oman 1965–1976: From Certain Defeat to Decisive Victory', *Small Wars Journal* (2008) pp.12/13
J.E. Peterson, 'Guerrilla Warfare and Ideological Confrontation in the Arabian Peninsula: The Rebellion in Dhurfar', *World Affairs*, Vol. 139, No.4 (1977) p.282

Marc DeVore, 'The United Kingdom's Last Hot War of the Cold War: Oman 1963–75', *Cold War History*, Vol. 11, Issue 3 (2011) p.11
40. Marc DeVore, 'A more complex and conventional victory: revisiting the Dhofar counterinsurgency, 1963–1975', *Small Wars & Insurgencies*, Vol.23, Issue 1 (2012) p.150
41. MEC – GRAHAM COLLECTION – Tony Lewis, 'The Story of the Sultan of Oman's Armed Forces 1964–67', *The Journal of the Sultan's Armed Forces Association*, Issue 37 (February 1988) Article p.32
42. Ibid.
43. Approximately 100–120 men
44. Jim White, 'Oman 1965–1976: From Certain Defeat to Decisive Victory', *Small Wars Journal* (2008) p.7
45. MEC – GRAHAM COLLECTION – Tony Lewis, 'The Story of the Sultan of Oman's Armed Forces 1964–67', *The Journal of the Sultan's Armed Forces Association*, Issue 37 (February 1988) Article p.32
46. Walter C. Ladwig III, 'Supporting Allies in Counter-Insurgency: Britain and the Dhofar Rebellion', *Small Wars & Insurgencies*, Vol.19, Issue 1 (2008) p.68
47. Ibid., p.67
48. Jim White, 'Oman 1965–1976: From Certain Defeat to Decisive Victory', *Small Wars Journal* (2008) p.7
Walter C. Ladwig III, 'Supporting Allies in Counter-Insurgency: Britain and the Dhofar Rebellion', *Small Wars & Insurgencies*, Vol.19, Issue 1 (2008) p.67
49. John Graham, *Ponder Anew: Reflections on the Twentieth Century*, (Staplehurst: Spellmount Limited, 1999) p.320
50. Walter C. Ladwig III, 'Supporting Allies in Counter-Insurgency: Britain and the Dhofar Rebellion', *Small Wars & Insurgencies*, Vol.19, Issue 1 (2008) p.67
Peterson, p.486
51. Marc DeVore, 'A more complex and conventional victory: revisiting the Dhofar counterinsurgency, 1963–1975', *Small Wars & Insurgencies*, Vol.23, Issue 1 (2012) p.153
52. Marc DeVore, 'A more complex and conventional victory: revisiting the Dhofar counterinsurgency, 1963–1975', *Small Wars & Insurgencies*, Vol.23, Issue 1 (2012) p.150
53. Ibid., p.163
54. Referred to as 'Jebelitis', Tony Jeapes, *SAS Operation Oman*, (London: HarperCollins, 1980) p.29
55. MEC – GRAHAM COLLECTION – Tony Lewis, 'The Story of the Sultan of Oman's Armed Forces 1964–67', *The Journal of the Sultan's Armed Forces Association*, Issue 37 (February 1988) Article p.37
56. Graham, p.350
57. Walter C. Ladwig III, 'Supporting Allies in Counter-Insurgency: Britain and the Dhofar Rebellion', *Small Wars & Insurgencies*, Vol.19, Issue 1 (2008) p.70
58. MEC – GRAHAM COLLECTION – Tony Lewis, 'The Story of the Sultan of Oman's Armed Forces 1964–67', *The Journal of the Sultan's Armed Forces Association*, Issue 37 (February 1988) Article p.40
59. J.E. Peterson, 'The Experience of British COIN Campaigns and Implications for Iraq', Arabian Peninsula Background Note, No. APBN-009. Published on www.JEPeterson.net (July 2009) p.8
60. MEC – GRAHAM COLLECTION – Tony Lewis, 'The Story of the Sultan of Oman's Armed Forces 1964–67', *The Journal of the Sultan's Armed Forces Association*, Issue 37 (February 1988) Article p.39

Walter C. Ladwig III, 'Supporting Allies in Counter-Insurgency: Britain and the Dhofar Rebellion', *Small Wars & Insurgencies*, Vol.19, Issue 1 (2008) p.70
61. Ranulph Fiennes, *Where Soldiers Fear to Tread*, (London: The Travel Book Club, 1976) p.59
Robert Alston and Stuart Laing, *Unshook Till the End of Time: A History of Relations Between Britain & Oman 1650–1970*, (London: Gilgamesh Publishing, 2012) p.284
62. MEC – GRAHAM COLLECTION – Tony Lewis, 'The Story of the Sultan of Oman's Armed Forces 1964–67', *The Journal of the Sultan's Armed Forces Association*, Issue 37 (February 1988) Article p.40
63. Robert Alston and Stuart Laing, *Unshook Till the End of Time: A History of Relations Between Britain & Oman 1650–1970*, (London: Gilgamesh Publishing, 2012) p.284
64. MEC – GRAHAM COLLECTION – Tony Lewis, 'The Story of the Sultan of Oman's Armed Forces 1964–67', *The Journal of the Sultan's Armed Forces Association*, Issue 37 (February 1988) Article p.40
65. J.E. Peterson, 'The Experience of British COIN Campaigns and Implications for Iraq', Arabian Peninsula Background Note, No. APBN-009. Published on www.JEPeterson.net (July 2009) p.6
66. Geraghty, pp.100–102
67. MEC – GRAHAM COLLECTION – Tony Lewis, 'The Story of the Sultan of Oman's Armed Forces 1964–67', *The Journal of the Sultan's Armed Forces Association*, Issue 37 (February 1988) Article p.35
68. Corran Purdon, *List the Bugle: Reminiscences of an Irish Soldier*, (Antrim: Greystone Books, 1993) p.237
69. MEC – GRAHAM COLLECTION – Tony Lewis, 'The Story of the Sultan of Oman's Armed Forces 1964–67', *The Journal of the Sultan's Armed Forces Association*, Issue 37 (February 1988) Article p.38
70. Ibid., p.36
71. Ranulph Fiennes, *Where Soldiers Fear to Tread*, (London: The Travel Book Club, 1976) p.13
72. Corran Purdon, *List the Bugle: Reminiscences of an Irish Soldier*, (Antrim: Greystone Books, 1993) p.294
73. Robert Alston and Stuart Laing, *Unshook Till the End of Time: A History of Relations Between Britain & Oman 1650–1970*, (London: Gilgamesh Publishing, 2012) p.288
74. Corran Purdon, *List the Bugle: Reminiscences of an Irish Soldier*, (Antrim: Greystone Books, 1993) p.294

Chapter 8
1. Tony Jeapes, *SAS Operation Oman*, (London: HarperCollins, 1980) p.14
2. After the establishment of PDRY following the British withdrawal from Aden in 1967
3. Ian Beckett, *Modern Insurgencies and Counter-Insurgencies – Guerrillas and their Opponents Since 1756*, (London: Routledge, 2001) p.217
Ian Cobain, 'Britain's Secret Wars' in *The Guardian Newspaper*, 8 Sep 2016, p.8
Ranulph Fiennes, *Where Soldiers Fear to Tread*, (London: The Travel Book Club, 1976) p.9
4. James Goode, 'Assisting Our Brothers, Defending Ourselves: The Iranian Intervention in Oman 1972–75', *Iranian Studies*, Vol.47, Issue 3 (2014) p.443
5. Ibid., p.448

6. Christopher Paul, Colin P. Clarke, Beth Grill and Molly Dunigan, *Paths to Victory – Detailed Insurgency Case studies*, (Santa Monica, CA: RAND Corporation, 2013) p.51, p.64 and p.274
7. Jordan formed from Transjordan and the only part left of Hashemite dynasty enveloping Syria, Iraq and Jordan – and the Shah's grandfather has taken power only after a relatively recent military coup
8. James Goode, 'Assisting Our Brothers, Defending Ourselves: The Iranian Intervention in Oman 1972–75', *Iranian Studies*, Vol.47, Issue 3 (2014) p.450
9. TNA FCO 8/2020 – 'Military Assistance from UK to Oman'– Annex A to DP 20/73(C), and Clive Jones, *Britain and the Yemen Civil War, 1962–65: Ministers, Mercenaries and Mandarins: Foreign Policy and the Limits of Covert Action*, (Eastbourne: Sussex Academic Press, 2010) p.191
10. Regional stability was already under intense pressure – e.g. the 1967 and 1973 Arab-Israeli wars and political and military 'fallout'
11. Called Operation DHIB in UK military parlance. Geraint Hughes, 'A Proxy War in Arabia: The Dhofar War Emergency and Cross-border Raids into South Yemen', *Middle East Journal*, Vol. 69, No.1 (Winter 2015) p.92
12. Geraint Hughes, 'A Model Campaign Reappraised. The Counter-Insurgency War in Dhofar, Oman, 1965–1975', Journal of Strategic Studies, Vol. 32, Issue 2 (2009) p.301
13. Clive Jones, *Britain and the Yemen Civil War, 1962–65: Ministers, Mercenaries and Mandarins: Foreign Policy and the Limits of Covert Action*, (Eastbourne: Sussex Academic Press, 2010) p.191
14. Douglas Porch, *Counterinsurgency: Exposing the Myths of the New Way of War*, (Cambridge: Cambridge University Press, 2013) p.266

Chapter 9

1. TNA 25/186 – Muscat & Oman General – Memorandum by Secretary of State for Defence, dated 4 Sep 1970
2. TNA FCO 8/1688 – 'Attachment of SAS Division of United Kingdom to Armed Forces of Oman', A. Ackland to Mr. Parsons, 1 Feb 1971 and TNA FCO 8/2020 'Military Assistance from UK to Oman'– Annex B to DP 20/73(C), TNA FCO 8/2006 – 'Annual Review of Oman 1972', A.D. Parsons to Mr. Le Quesne, 12 Feb 1973
3. E.g. the maximum number of US troops in Vietnam (Jan 1969) being 542,000 John A. Nagl, *Learning to Eat Soup with a Knife: Counterinsurgency Lessons from Malaya and Vietnam*, (Chicago: Chicago University Press, 2005) p.173
4. Walter C. Ladwig III, 'Supporting allies in counterinsurgency: Britain and the Dhofar Rebellion', *Small Wars & Insurgencies*, Vol.19, Issue 1 (2008) p.75-6
5. J.E. Peterson, *Oman's Insurgencies: The Sultanate's Struggle for Supremacy*, (London: Saqi, 2007) p.330
6. Julian Paget, *Counter-Insurgency Campaigning*, (London: Faber & Faber, 1967) p.74 and p.104
7. John Newsinger, *British Counterinsurgency*, (Basingstoke: Palgrave Macmillan, 2015) p.193
8. Ian Beckett and John Pimlott, *Armed Forces & Modern Counter-Insurgency*, (New York: St. Martin's Press, 1985) p.54
   USNA – https://www.archives.gov/research/military/vietnam-war/casualty-statistics Accessed 14 Aug 2024
   Ian Beckett and John Pimlott, *Armed Forces & Modern Counter-Insurgency*, (New York: St. Martin's Press, 1985) p.54

9. Peterson, p.482
10. Graham, p.343
11. Ian Beckett, *Modern Insurgencies and Counter-Insurgencies – Guerrillas and their Opponents since 1756*, (London: Routledge, 2001) p.221
12. Geraint Hughes, 'A 'Model Campaign' Reappraised: The Counter-Insurgency War in Dhofar, Oman, 1965–1975', *Journal of Strategic Studies*, Vol.32, Issue 2 (2009) p.299
13. J.E. Peterson, *Oman's Insurgencies: The Sultanate's Struggle for Supremacy*, (London: Saqi, 2007) p.328
14. Ibid., p.292
    TNA – FCO 8/1688 – Attachment of SAS Division of United Kingdom to Armed Forces of Oman – Letter A. Ackland to Mr. Parsons, dated 1 Feb 1971
15. John Graham, *Ponder Anew: Reflections on the Twentieth Century*, (Staplehurst: Spellmount Limited, 1999) p.360
16. Ladwig III, p.65
17. J.E. Peterson, *Oman's Insurgencies: The Sultanate's Struggle for Supremacy*, (London: Saqi, 2007) p.330
18. Ibid., p.486
19. Ibid., p.330
    John Graham, *Ponder Anew: Reflections on the Twentieth Century*, (Staplehurst: Spellmount Limited, 1999) p.373
20. TNA – FCO8/2020 – Military Assistance from UK to Oman – Annex B to DP 20/73(C), 'UK Interests', dated 5 Oct 1973
21. Marc Valeri, *Oman: Politics and Society in the Qaboos State*, (London: C. Hurst & Co., 2017) pp. 37/38
    Abdel Takriti, 'The 1970 Coup in Oman Reconsidered', *Journal of Arabian Studies*, Vol. 3, Issue 2 (2013) p.172
22. Ibid., p.156
23. James Worrall, *Statebuilding and Counterinsurgency in Oman: Political, Military and Diplomatic Relations at the End of Empire*, (London: I.B. Tauris, 2014) p.209
    Calvin Allen and Lynn Rigsbee, *Oman Under Qaboos: From Coup to Constitution, 1970–1996*, (London: Frank Cass, 2002) p.75
    Potentially Mirage aircraft and Crotale missiles. Nikolas Gardner, 'The Limits of the Sandhurst Connection: The Evolution of Oman's Foreign and Defense Policy, 1970–1977', *The Journal of the Middle East and Africa*, Vol. 6, Issue 1 (2015) p.56
    Marc DeVore, 'The United Kingdom's Last Hot War of the Cold War: Oman 1963–75', *Cold War History*, Vol. 11, Issue 3 (2011) p.20
24. James Worrall, *Statebuilding and Counterinsurgency in Oman: Political, Military and Diplomatic Relations at the End of Empire*, (London: I.B. Tauris, 2014) p.173
25. Nikolas Gardner, 'The Limits of the Sandhurst Connection: The Evolution of Oman's Foreign and Defense Policy, 1970–1977', *The Journal of the Middle East and Africa*, Vol. 6, Issue 1 (2015) p.45
26. MEC – GRAHAM COLLECTION – Box 2/1 – John Graham, Dhofar Casualties table (as at 16 Oct 1971)
27. Ibid.
28. Ibid., p.384
    http://uca.edu/politicalscience/dadm-project/middle-eastnorth-africapersian-gulfregion/oman-1912-present/ Accessed 26 Mar 2023
    Peterson, p.222

29. Ranulph Fiennes, *Where Soldiers Fear to Tread*, (London: The Travel Book Club, 1976) p.127
30. TNA – CAB 186/11 – Cabinet JIC Report – 'The Subversive Threat from the People's Democratic Republic of the Yemen (PDRY) (Delicate Source)', dated 25 Feb 1972
31. Walter C. Ladwig III, 'Supporting allies in counterinsurgency: Britain and the Dhofar Rebellion', *Small Wars & Insurgencies*, Vol.19, Issue 1 (2008) p.76
32. Ibid.
    Calvin Allen and Lynn Rigsbee, *Oman Under Qaboos: From Coup to Constitution, 1970–1996*, (London: Frank Cass, 2002) p.75
33. J.E. Peterson, *Oman's Insurgencies: The Sultanate's Struggle for Supremacy*, (London: Saqi, 2007) p.420
34. Robert Alston and Stuart Laing, *Unshook Till the End of Time: A History of Relations Between Britain & Oman 1650–1970*, (London: Gilgamesh Publishing, 2012) p.19
35. James Worrall, *Statebuilding and Counterinsurgency in Oman : Political, Military and Diplomatic Relations at the End of Empire*, (London: I.B. Taurus, 2014) p.91
    Allen and Rigsbee, p.104
36. Robert Alston and Stuart Laing, *Unshook Till the End of Time: A History of Relations Between Britain & Oman 1650–1970*, (London: Gilgamesh Publishing, 2012) p.296
    Marc DeVore, 'The United Kingdom's Last Hot War of the Cold War: Oman 1963–75', *Cold War History*, Vol. 11, Issue 3 (2011) p.20
37. John Graham, *Ponder Anew: Reflections on the Twentieth Century*, (Staplehurst: Spellmount Limited, 1999) p.372
38. Ibid., Calvin Allen and Lynn Rigsbee, *Oman Under Qaboos: From Coup to Constitution, 1970–1996*, (London: Frank Cass, 2002) p.74
    Robert Jackson, *Hawker Hunter (Modern Combat Aircraft 15)*, (London: Ian Allen Ltd., 1982) pp.65–8
39. J.E. Peterson, *Oman's Insurgencies: The Sultanate's Struggle for Supremacy*, (London: Saqi, 2007) p.486
40. Ibid., p.331
41. James Worrall, *Statebuilding and Counterinsurgency in Oman: Political, Military and Diplomatic Relations at the End of Empire*, (London: I.B. Tauris & Co. Ltd., 2014) p.287
    Geraint Hughes, 'A 'Model Campaign' Reappraised: The Counter-Insurgency War in Dhofar, Oman, 1965–1975', *Journal of Strategic Studies*, Vol.32, Issue 2 (2009) p.300
42. Ibid., p.331
43. Geraint Hughes, 'A 'Model Campaign' Reappraised: The Counter-Insurgency War in Dhofar, Oman, 1965–1975', *Journal of Strategic Studies*, Vol.32, Issue 2 (2009) p.300
44. Geraint Hughes, 'Amateurs Who Play in Division One? – Anglo-Iranian Military Relations During the Dhofar War in Oman', *British Journal for Military History*, Vol.4, Issue 1 (2017) p.103
45. J.E. Peterson, *Oman's Insurgencies: The Sultanate's Struggle for Supremacy*, (London: Saqi, 2007) pp.366/486

Chapter 10
1. Obituary, Sir Donald Hawley, in *The Telegraph Newspaper*, 11 Feb 2008
2. Robert Alston and Stuart Laing, *Unshook Till the End of Time: A History of Relations Between Britain & Oman 1650–1970*, (London: Gilgamesh Publishing, 2012) pp.305/6
3. Keith McCloskey, *Airwork; A History*, (Stroud: The History Press, 2012) p.98
4. Ibid.

5. TNA – FCO 8/2687 – Oman – Annual Review 1975, Review summary page
6. Calvin Allen and Lynn Rigsbee, *Oman Under Qaboos: From Coup to Constitution, 1970–1996*, (London: Frank Cass, 2002) pp.75-77
7. Sultanate of Oman NRAA – Records of Oman 1966–1971 (Cambridge Archive Editions, 2003) Vol. 5: Letter, British Consulate General to Mr. M. Wier (Bahrain) dated 3 Aug 1970
   TNA FCO 8/1669 Annual Review of Oman, Letter: Consul General Muscat (D. Crawford) to PRPG, dated 4 Jan 1971
   TNA – FCO 8/2687 – Oman – Annual Review 1975, British Ambassador, Muscat (C. Treadwell) to Prime Minister (J. Callahan) 1 Jan 1976
   Calvin Allen and Lynn Rigsbee, *Oman Under Qaboos: From Coup to Constitution, 1970–1996*, (London: Frank Cass, 2002) p.75-77
8. TNA – FCO 8/2687 – Oman – Annual Review 1975, British Ambassador, Muscat (C. Treadwell) to Prime Minister (J. Callahan) 1 Jan 1976
9. Marc Valeri, *Oman: Politics and Society in the Qaboos State*, (London: C. Hurst & Co., 2017) p.158
   Michael Barber, 'Brigadier Tim Landon – Soldier of Fortune Who Helped Ease Oman into the Modern World', Obituary in *The Guardian Newspaper*, 26 Aug 2007
10. Vron Ware, *Return of a Native: Learning from the Land*, (London: Repeater Books, 2022) pp. 54–6
    John Beasant, *Oman: The True-Life Drama and Intrigue of an Arab State*, (RandomHouse, 2011) pp. 192–6
11. Ibid.
12. Marc Valeri, *Oman: Politics and Society in the Qaboos State*, (London: C. Hurst & Co., 2017) p.159 and Michael Barber, 'Brigadier Tim Landon – Soldier of Fortune Who Helped Ease Oman into the Modern World', Obituary in *The Guardian Newspaper*, 26 Aug 2007
13. Marc Valeri, *Oman: Politics and Society in the Qaboos State*, (London: C. Hurst & Co., 2017) p.159
14. Calvin Allen and Lynn Rigsbee, *Oman Under Qaboos: From Coup to Constitution, 1970–1996*, (London: Frank Cass, 2002) pp.74–5
15. Succeeded by Air Vice Marshall Talib bin Meran bin Zaman Al-Raeesi
16. J.E. Peterson, *Oman's Insurgencies: The Sultanate's Struggle for Supremacy*, (London: Saqi, 2007) p.330
    DeVore, p.20
17. Ian Gardiner, *In the Service of the Sultan*, (Barnsley: Pen & Sword, 2006) p.56
18. Robert Alston and Stuart Laing, *Unshook Till the End of Time: A History of Relations Between Britain & Oman 1650–1970*, (London: Gilgamesh Publishing, 2012) p.300
19. And later to become Commander in Chief UK land forces (1980–81)
20. 2 x squadron deployment was very rare and did not even occur in Iraq during the early days of Task Force Black/Knight where the standard deployment was maximum a single SAS squadron. Mark Urban, *Task Force Black*, (London: Little, Brown) p.13
21. Marc DeVore, 'The United Kingdom's Last Hot War of the Cold War: Oman 1963–75', *Cold War History*, Vol. 11, Issue 3 (2011) p.20
    J.E. Peterson, *Oman's Insurgencies: The Sultanate's Struggle for Supremacy*, (London: Saqi, 2007) p.329
22. James Goode, 'Assisting Our Brothers, Defending Ourselves: The Iranian Intervention in Oman 1972–75', *Iranian Studies*, Vol.47, Issue 3 (2014) p.451

23. Geraint Hughes, 'Amateurs Who Play in Division One? – Anglo-Iranian Military Relations During the Dhofar War in Oman', *British Journal for Military History*, Vol.4, Issue 1 (2017) p.105
24. J.E. Peterson, *Oman's Insurgencies: The Sultanate's Struggle for Supremacy*, (London: Saqi, 2007) p.331
Geraint Hughes, 'Amateurs Who Play in Division One? – Anglo-Iranian Military Relations During the Dhofar War in Oman', *British Journal for Military History*, Vol.4, Issue 1 (2017) p.105
25. James Goode, 'Assisting Our Brothers, Defending Ourselves: The Iranian Intervention in Oman 1972–75', *Iranian Studies*, Vol.47, Issue 3 (2014) p.458
26. Tony Jeapes, *SAS Operation Oman*, (London: HarperCollins, 1980) p.11
27. Jeapes, p.14
28. John Pimlott (Ed), *British Military Operations*, 1945–85, (London: Bison Books, 1986) pp.16–17
29. Ibid.
30. Christopher Paul, Colin P. Clarke, Beth Grill and Molly Dunigan, *Paths to Victory – Detailed Insurgency Case studies*, (Santa Monica, CA: RAND Corporation, 2013) p.51, p.64 and p.274 and Tony Jeapes, *SAS Operation Oman*, (London: HarperCollins, 1980) p.14
31. Ian Beckett and John Pimlott, *Armed Forces & Modern Counter-Insurgency*, (New York: St. Martin's Press, 1985) p.67
32. Ibid.
Christopher Paul, Colin P. Clarke, Beth Grill and Molly Dunigan, *Paths to Victory – Detailed Insurgency Case studies*, (Santa Monica, CA: RAND Corporation, 2013) p.226
33. Ibid., p.177
34. Walter C. Ladwig III, 'Supporting allies in counterinsurgency: Britain and the Dhofar Rebellion', *Small Wars & Insurgencies*, Vol.19, Issue 1 (2008) p.76
Calvin Allen and Lynn Rigsbee, *Oman Under Qaboos: From Coup to Constitution, 1970–1996*, (London: Frank Cass, 2002) p.181
35. Fred Halliday, *Arabia Without Sultans*, (Harmondsworth: Penguin, 1974) p.174
Abdel Takriti, *Monsoon Revolution: Republicans, Sultans and Empires in Oman, 1965–1976*, (Oxford: Oxford University Press, 2016) p.223
36. James Goodge, 'Assisting Our Brothers, Defending Ourselves: The Iranian Intervention in Oman 1972–75', *Iranian Studies*, Vol.47, Issue 3 (2014) p.446
TNA DEFE 24/1856 – Middle East/Africa: Muscat and Oman – Letter, Acting Chief of Defence Staff to Minister for Defence, dated 16 Jul 1970, and DMO Briefing Notes for Chiefs of Staff Meeting Wednesday 15 July 1970, dated 14 Jul 1970
MEC – GRAHAM COLLECTION – Point Summary in Development of SAF for Lecture to Anglo-Omani society, (June 1996) p.2
From 'Muscat and Oman' (to 'The Sultanate of Oman')
John Graham, *Ponder Anew: Reflections on the Twentieth Century*, (Staplehurst: Spellmount Limited, 1999) pp.340–341
Sultanate of Oman NRAA – *Records of Oman 1966–1971*, (Cambridge Archive Editions, 2003) Vol. 6: Letter, Bank of England to A. Ackland (copy of letter from Bank to Sultan Qaboos), dated 19 Mar 1971
37. Walter C. Ladwig III, 'Supporting allies in counterinsurgency: Britain and the Dhofar Rebellion', *Small Wars & Insurgencies*, Vol.19, Issue 1 (2008) p.72
Geraint Hughes, 'A 'Model Campaign' reappraised: The Counter-Insurgency War in Dhofar, Oman, 1965–1975', Journal of Strategic Studies, Vol.32, Issue 2 (2009) p.288

38. Tony Jeapes, *SAS Operation Oman*, (London: HarperCollins, 1980) p.134–142
39. Corran Purdon, *List the Bugle: Reminiscences of an Irish Soldier*, (Antrim: Greystone Books, 1993) p.294
40. Calvin Allen and Lynn Rigsbee, *Oman Under Qaboos: From Coup to Constitution, 1970–1996*, (London: Frank Cass, 2002) p.78
41. James Worrall, *Statebuilding and Counterinsurgency in Oman: Political, Military and Diplomatic Relations at the End of Empire*, (London: I.B. Tauris & Co. Ltd., 2014) p.106
42. Abdel Takriti, *Monsoon Revolution: Republicans, Sultans and Empires in Oman, 1965–1976*, (Oxford: Oxford University Press, 2016) p.224
43. J.E. Peterson, *Oman's Insurgencies: The Sultanate's Struggle for Supremacy*, (London: Saqi, 2007) p.428
44. Geraint Hughes, 'A 'Model Campaign' Reappraised: The Counter-Insurgency War in Dhofar, Oman, 1965–1975', Journal of Strategic Studies, Vol.32, Issue 2 (2009) p.292
45. Ian Beckett, *Modern Insurgencies and Counter-Insurgencies – Guerrillas and their Opponents Since 1756*, (London: Routledge, 2001) p.230
46. Walter C. Ladwig III, 'Supporting allies in counterinsurgency: Britain and the Dhofar Rebellion', *Small Wars & Insurgencies*, Vol.19, Issue 1 (2008) p.76
47. Marc Valeri, *Oman: Politics and Society in the Qaboos State*, (London: C. Hurst & Co., 2017) p.68
48. Marc DeVore, 'A more complex and conventional victory: revisiting the Dhofar counterinsurgency, 1963–1975', *Small Wars & Insurgencies*, Vol.23, Issue 1 (2012) p.161
49. Ibid.
50. Walter C. Ladwig III, 'Supporting allies in counterinsurgency: Britain and the Dhofar Rebellion', *Small Wars & Insurgencies*, Vol.19, Issue 1 (2008) p.65
51. Jim White, 'Oman 1965–1976: From Certain Defeat to Decisive Victory', *Small Wars Journal* (2008) p.3
52. John Akehurst, *We Won a War: The Campaign in Oman 1965–75*, (Guildford: M.Russell, 1982) p.12
53. Marc Valeri, *Oman: Politics and Society in the Qaboos State*, (London: C. Hurst & Co., 2017) p.225
54. Thomas R. Mockaitis, 'Low Intensity Conflict: the British Experience', *Conflict Quarterly* (Winter 1993) pp.8–9
55. Tony Jeapes, *SAS Operation Oman*, (London: HarperCollins, 1980) p.14
56. Ian Beckett, *Modern Insurgencies and Counter-Insurgencies – Guerrillas and their Opponents since 1756*, (London: Routledge, 2001) p.230 and p.14
57. Christopher Paul, Colin P. Clarke, Beth Grill and Molly Dunigan, *Paths to Victory – Detailed Insurgency Case studies*, (Santa Monica, CA: RAND Corporation, 2013) p.XV
58. TNA – FCO 8/2687 – Oman – Annual Review 1975, British Ambassador, Muscat (C. Treadwell) to Prime Minister (J. Callahan) 1 Jan 1976, p.13
59. Christopher Paul, Colin P. Clarke, Beth Grill and Molly Dunigan, *Paths to Victory – Detailed Insurgency Case studies*, (Santa Monica, CA: RAND Corporation, 2013) p.51 and p.286
60. Walter C. Ladwig III, 'Supporting allies in counterinsurgency: Britain and the Dhofar Rebellion', *Small Wars & Insurgencies*, Vol.19, Issue 1 (2008) p.77
    Marc DeVore, 'A more complex and conventional victory: revisiting the Dhofar counterinsurgency, 1963–1975', *Small Wars & Insurgencies*, Vol.23, Issue 1 (2012) p.144
    David Benest, 'Ponder Anew: Brigadier Graham and the Dhofar War 1970–1972' (Oct 2015) https://thestrategybridge.org/the-bridge/2016/1/1/ponder-anew-brigadier-john-graham-the-dhofar-war-19701972 Accessed online 19 Apr 2023

61. Ian Gardiner, *In the Service of the Sultan*, (Barnsley: Pen and Sword, 2006) p.17
    Robert Alston and Stuart Laing, *Unshook Till the End of Time: A History of Relations Between Britain & Oman 1650–1970*, (London: Gilgamesh Publishing, 2012) p.283
62. Thomas R. Mockaitis, 'Low-Intensity Conflict: The British Experience', *Conflict Quarterly*, (1993) p.8
63. David Charters, 'Counter-insurgency Intelligence: The Evolution of British Theory and Practice', *Journal of Conflict Studies*, Vol. 29 (2009) p.10
    Tony Jeapes, *SAS Operation Oman*, (London: HarperCollins, 1980) p.14
    Julian Paget, *Counter-Insurgency Campaigning*, (London: Faber & Faber, 1967) p.74
64. Ibid.
65. Thomas R. Mockaitis, 'Low Intensity Conflict: the British Experience', *Conflict Quarterly* (1993) pp.8–9

Part IV

1. Proponents of the Marxist or revisionist authors such as Owtram and Halliday
2. Marc DeVore, 'The United Kingdom's Last Hot War of the Cold War: Oman 1963–75', *Cold War History*, Vol. 11, Issue 3 (2011) p.22
3. MEC – GRAHAM COLLECTION – Tony Lewis, 'The Story of the Sultan of Oman's Armed Forces 1964–67', *The Journal of the Sultan's Armed Forces Association*, Issue 37, February 1988, Article p.35
4. Marc DeVore, 'The United Kingdom's Last Hot War of the Cold War: Oman 1963–75', *Cold War History*, Vol. 11, Issue 3 (2011) p.22
5. TNA AIR20/10377 – (Chiefs of Staff Committee) Review of the Emergency in Malaya from June 1948 to August 1957
6. Fred Halliday, *Arabia Without Sultans*, (Harmondsworth: Penguin, 1974) p.348
7. Geraint Hughes, 'Demythologising Dhofar: British Policy, Military Strategy and Counterinsurgency in Oman, 1963–1976', *Journal of Military History*, Vol. 79, Issue 2 (2015) p.455
8. Walter C. Ladwig III, 'Supporting allies in counterinsurgency: Britain and the Dhofar Rebellion', *Small Wars & Insurgencies*, Vol.19, Issue 1 (2008) p.72
9. Marc DeVore, 'The United Kingdom's Last Hot War of the Cold War: Oman 1963–75', *Cold War History*, Vol. 11, Issue 3 (2011) p.20
10. Walter C. Ladwig III, 'Supporting allies in counterinsurgency: Britain and the Dhofar Rebellion', *Small Wars & Insurgencies*, Vol.19, Issue 1 (2008) p.76
    J.E. Peterson, *Oman's Insurgencies: The Sultanate's Struggle for Supremacy*, (London: Saqi, 2007) p.329
11. James Goodge, 'Assisting Our Brothers, Defending Ourselves: The Iranian Intervention in Oman 1972–75', *Iranian Studies*, Vol.47, Issue 3 (2014) p.451
12. John Graham, *Ponder Anew: Reflections on the Twentieth Century*, (Staplehurst: Spellmount Limited, 1999) p.372
13. Ibid.
14. Geraint Hughes, 'Amateurs Who Play in Division One? – Anglo-Iranian Military Relations During the Dhofar War in Oman', *British Journal for Military History*, Vol.4, Issue 1 (2017) p.102
15. Peter Thwaites, *Muscat Command*, (Barnsley: Pen & Sword, 1995) p.40
16. Geraint Hughes, 'Amateurs Who Play in Division One? – Anglo-Iranian Military Relations During the Dhofar War in Oman', *British Journal for Military History*, Vol.4, Issue 1 (2017) p.103

J.E. Peterson, *Oman's Insurgencies: The Sultanate's Struggle for Supremacy*, (London: Saqi, 2007) p.331

John Akehurst, *We Won a War: The Campaign in Oman 1965–75*, (Guildford: M. Russell, 1982) p.83. An example being the death of Major Braddell-Smith due largely to poor Iranian tactics. Ibid., pp.83–84

17. Ian Gardiner, *In the Service of the Sultan*, (Barnsley: Pen & Sword, 2006) p.154
18. Ken Perkins, 'Oman 1975: The Year of Decision', *The RUSI Journal*, Vol.124, Issue 1 (1979) p.39
19. John Newsinger, *British Counterinsurgency*, (Basingstoke: Palgrave Macmillan, 2015) p.152
20. Marc DeVore, 'The United Kingdom's Last Hot War of the Cold War: Oman 1963–75', *Cold War History*, Vol. 11, Issue 3 (2011) p.22
21. David Charters, 'Counter-insurgency Intelligence: The Evolution of British Theory and Practice', *Journal of Conflict Studies*, Vol. 29 (2009) p.10

    David Benest, 'Ponder Anew: Brigadier Graham and the Dhofar War 1970–1972' (Oct 2015) https://thestrategybridge.org/the-bridge/2016/1/1/ponder-anew-brigadier-john-graham-the-dhofar-war-19701972 Accessed online 19 Apr 2023 p.9

    Tony Jeapes, *SAS Operation Oman*, (London: HarperCollins, 1980) p.12
22. Francis Owtram, *Oman and the West: State Formation in Oman since 1920*, (London: University of London, 1999) p.155
23. Geraint Hughes, 'A Proxy War in Arabia: The Dhofar War Emergency and Crossborder Raids into South Yemen', *Middle East Journal*, Vol. 69, No.1 (Winter 2015) p.94
24. Corran Purdon, *List the Bugle: Reminiscences of an Irish Soldier*, (Antrim: Greystone Books, 1993) pp.293–294
25. Ibid., p.244

    David Arkless, *The Secret War*, (London: William Kinber & Co. Ltd., 1988) p.81
26. MEC – GRAHAM COLLECTION – Tony Lewis, 'The Story of the Sultan of Oman's Armed Forces 1964–67', *The Journal of the Sultan's Armed Forces Association*, Issue 37 (February 1988) Article p.40
27. Ibid.
28. Liddell Hart Archive, KCL – THWAITES COLLECTION – Letter, Sultan Said to Lieutenant Colonel Peter Thwaites, dated 8 Jan 1970

    Liddell Hart Archive, KCL – THWAITES COLLECTION – Letter, Sultan Said to Lieutenant Colonel Peter Thwaites, dated 8 Jan 1970
29. Liddell Hart Archive, KCL – THWAITES COLLECTION – Letter, Sultan Said to Lieutenant Colonel Peter Thwaites, dated 8 Jan 1970
30. Corran Purdon, *List the Bugle: Reminiscences of an Irish Soldier*, (Antrim: Greystone Books, 1993) p.293. "The old Sultan used to tell me to look at what happened to those other monarchs and heads of state who promoted their officers: the colonels then get rid of their rulers!"
31. MEC – GRAHAM COLLECTION – Tony Lewis, 'The Story of the Sultan of Oman's Armed Forces 1964–67', *The Journal of the Sultan's Armed Forces Association*, Issue 37 (February 1988) Article p.35
32. Corran Purdon, *List the Bugle: Reminiscences of an Irish Soldier*, (Antrim: Greystone Books, 1993) p.237
33. Ibid., p.244
34. Sultanate of Oman NRAA – *Records of Oman 1966–1971* (Cambridge Archive Editions, 2003) Vol. 4: Annual Review 1969 correspondence, D.G. Crawford to British Consulate-General dated 30 Dec 1969

35. David Benest, 'Ponder Anew: Brigadier Graham and the Dhofar War 1970–1972' (Oct 2015) https://thestrategybridge.org/the-bridge/2016/1/1/ponder-anew-brigadier-john-graham-the-dhofar-war-19701972 Accessed online 19 Apr 2023 p.2
36. Marc DeVore, 'The United Kingdom's Last Hot War of the Cold War: Oman 1963–75', *Cold War History*, Vol. 11, Issue 3 (2011) p.10
37. Nikolas Gardner, 'The Limits of the Sandhurst Connection: The Evolution of Oman's Foreign and Defense Policy, 1970–1977', *The Journal of the Middle East and Africa*, Vol. 6, Issue 1 (2015) p.47
38. Ibid., p.50
39. Calvin Allen and Lynn Rigsbee, *Oman Under Qaboos: From Coup to Constitution, 1970–1996*, (London: Frank Cass, 2002) p.36
40. Nikolas Gardner, 'The Limits of the Sandhurst Connection: The Evolution of Oman's Foreign and Defense Policy, 1970–1977', *The Journal of the Middle East and Africa*, Vol. 6, Issue 1 (2015) p.50
41. Ibid., p.51
42. Geraint Hughes, 'A 'Model Campaign' Reappraised: The Counter-Insurgency War in Dhofar, Oman, 1965–1975', *Journal of Strategic Studies*, Vol. 32, Issue 2 (2009) p.289
43. United Arab Emirates NA – FCO 8/2020 – Summary of main points discussed in the meeting between DMO and CSAF on 12 July 1973
44. Nikolas Gardner, 'The Limits of the Sandhurst Connection: The Evolution of Oman's Foreign and Defense Policy, 1970–1977', *The Journal of the Middle East and Africa*, Vol. 6, Issue 1 (2015) p.55
45. John Beasant and Christopher Ling, *Sultan in Arabia: A Private Life*, (Edinburgh: Mainstream Publishing, 2004) p.129
46. Calvin Allen and Lynn Rigsbee, *Oman Under Qaboos: From Coup to Constitution, 1970–1996*, (London: Frank Cass, 2002) p.75
47. Ibid.
48. John Beasant and Christopher Ling, *Sultan in Arabia: A Private Life*, (Edinburgh: Mainstream Publishing, 2004) p.128
49. John Graham, *Ponder Anew: Reflections on the Twentieth Century*, (Staplehurst: Spellmount Limited, 1999) p.371
50. Nikolas Gardner, 'The Limits of the Sandhurst Connection: The Evolution of Oman's Foreign and Defense Policy, 1970–1977', *The Journal of the Middle East and Africa*, Vol. 6, Issue 1 (2015) p.58
51. Sergey Plekhanov, *A Reformer on the Throne*, (Virginia: Trident Press, 2004) p.126
52. Marc Valeri, *Oman: Politics and Society in the Qaboos State*, (London: C. Hurst & Co., 2017) p.54
    Sergey Plekhanov, *A Reformer on the Throne*, (Virginia: Trident Press, 2004) p.88
53. Ibid., p.121
54. John Beasant and Christopher Ling, *Sultan in Arabia: A Private Life*, (Edinburgh: Mainstream Publishing, 2004) p.174
55. Ibid., p.142
56. Pauline Searle, *Dawn Over Oman*, (London: George Allen & Unwin, 1979) p.3
57. Writers such as Owtram and Halliday
    The influence of other powers such as Iran, Jordan and even the USA

Chapter 11
1. MEC – GRAHAM COLLECTION – Tony Lewis, 'The Story of the Sultan of Oman's Armed Forces 1964–67', *The Journal of the Sultan's Armed Forces Association*, Issue 37 (February 1988) Article p.35

Marc DeVore, 'The United Kingdom's Last Hot War of the Cold War: Oman 1963–75', *Cold War History*, Vol. 11, Issue 3 (2011) p.22
2. TNA AIR20/10377– (COS Committee) – Review of the Emergency in Malaya from Jun 1948 to Aug 1957, p.6
3. Stephen Quick, *The Dhofar War: British Covert Campaigning in Arabia 1965–1975*, (Exeter: University of Exeter Press, 2024) p.8
4. (CSAF) Colonel Tony Lewis
5. Marc DeVore, 'The United Kingdom's Last Hot War of the Cold War: Oman 1963–75', *Cold War History*, Vol. 11, Issue 3 (2011) p.10
6. MEC – GRAHAM COLLECTION – Tony Lewis, 'The Story of the Sultan of Oman's Armed Forces 1964–67', *The Journal of the Sultan's Armed Forces Association*, Issue 37 (February 1988) Article p.40
David French, 'Nasty not Nice: British Counterinsurgency Doctrine and Practice, 1945–1967', *Small Wars & Insurgencies*, Vol. 23, Issues 4–5 (2012) p.744
7. Hack, p.414
8. Nikolas Gardner, 'The Limits of the Sandhurst Connection: The Evolution of Oman's Foreign and Defense Policy, 1970–1977', *The Journal of the Middle East and Africa*, Vol. 6, Issue 1 (2015) pp.48–50
9. J.E. Peterson, *Oman's Insurgencies: The Sultanate's Struggle for Supremacy*, (London: Saqi, 2007) p.417
10. Marc DeVore, 'The United Kingdom's Last Hot War of the Cold War: Oman 1963–75', *Cold War History*, Vol. 11, Issue 3 (2011) p.20
11. TNA – FCO 8/1688 – Letter A. Ackland to Mr. Parsons, dated 1 Feb 1971
12. Such as the increasing problems and British military commitment in Ulster
13. Nikolas Gardner, 'The Limits of the Sandhurst Connection: The Evolution of Oman's Foreign and Defense Policy, 1970–1977', *The Journal of the Middle East and Africa*, Vol. 6, Issue 1 (2015) pp.48–50
14. Marc DeVore, 'The United Kingdom's Last Hot War of the Cold War: Oman 1963–75', *Cold War History*, Vol. 11, Issue 3 (2011) p.20
15. James Goode, 'Assisting our Brothers, Defending Ourselves: The Iranian Intervention in Oman, 1972–75', *Iranian Studies*, Vol. 47, Issue 3 (2014) p.451
16. Geraint Hughes, 'Amateurs Who Play in Division One? – Anglo-Iranian Military Relations During the Dhofar War in Oman', *British Journal for Military History*, Vol.4, Issue 1 (2017) p.103, J.E. Peterson, *Oman's Insurgencies: The Sultanate's Struggle for Supremacy*, (London: Saqi, 2007) p.331
17. Marc DeVore, 'A more complex and conventional victory: revisiting the Dhofar counterinsurgency, 1963–1975', *Small Wars & Insurgencies*, Vol.23, Issue 1 (2012) p.144
18. Nikolas Gardner, 'The Limits of the Sandhurst Connection: The Evolution of Oman's Foreign and Defense Policy, 1970–1977', *The Journal of the Middle East and Africa*, Vol. 6, Issue 1 (2015) p.47 and p.56
19. Robert Alston and Stuart Laing, *Unshook Till the End of Time: A History of Relations Between Britain & Oman 1650–1970*, (London: Gilgamesh Publishing, 2012) p.249
20. Nikolas Gardner, 'The Limits of the Sandhurst Connection: The Evolution of Oman's Foreign and Defense Policy, 1970–1977', *The Journal of the Middle East and Africa*, Vol. 6, Issue 1 (2015) p.45
21. James Worrall, *Statebuilding and Counterinsurgency in Oman: Political, Military and Diplomatic Relations at the End of Empire*, (London: I.B. Tauris & Co. Ltd., 2014) pp.202–3

22. J.E. Peterson, *Oman's Insurgencies: The Sultanate's Struggle for Supremacy*, (London: Saqi, 2007) p.420
23. John Beasant and Christopher Ling, *Sultan in Arabia: A Private Life*, (Edinburgh: Mainstream Publishing, 2004) p.130
24. Calvin Allen and Lynn Rigsbee, *Oman Under Qaboos: From Coup to Constitution, 1970–1996*, (London: Frank Cass, 2002) p.104

Chapter 12
1. Robert Alston and Stuart Laing, *Unshook Till the End of Time: A History of Relations Between Britain & Oman 1650–1970*, (London: Gilgamesh Publishing, 2012) p.135
2. Ian Skeet, *Muscat & Oman: The End of an Era*, (London: Faber & Faber, 1974) p.38
3. Donald Hawley, *Oman & Its Renaissance*, (London: Stacey International, 1995) p.59
4. John McKeown, *Britain and Oman: The Dhofar War and its Significance*, (University of Cambridge MA Dissertation, 1981) p.6
   Donald Hawley, *Oman & Its Renaissance*, (London: Stacey International, 1995) pp.59–60
5. Sultan Salim was forced into exile in Bandar Abbas by a coalition of conservative Ibadi forces led by Azzan bin Qais and Said bin Khalfan al-Khalili; the former was elected Imam within weeks of the victory. Robert Alston and Stuart Laing, *Unshook Till the End of Time: A History of Relations Between Britain & Oman 1650–1970*, (London: Gilgamesh Publishing, 2012) p.150
6. Wendell Phillips, *Oman: A History*, (Beirut: Librarie du Lebanon, 1971) p.160
7. A direct descendant of the original 1798 Oman-Britain treaty. Ian Skeet, *Muscat & Oman: The End of an Era*, (London: Faber & Faber, 1974) p.196
8. Marc Valeri, *Oman: Politics and Society in the Qaboos State*, (London: C. Hurst & Co., 2017) p.50
9. Latterly the United Arab Emirates (from 1971)
10. Wendell Phillips, *Oman: A History*, (Beirut: Librarie du Lebanon, 1971) p.205
    Smiley, p.67
11. J.E. Peterson, *Oman's Insurgencies: The Sultanate's Struggle for Supremacy*, (London: Saqi, 2007) p.103
12. Ibid.
13. Initially agreed as 23 officers: 1 x colonel, 2 x lieutenant-colonels, 6 x majors and 14 x captains. Ibid., p.104
    Effectively the post of 'Minister of Defence'. J.E. Peterson, *Oman's Insurgencies: The Sultanate's Struggle for Supremacy*, (London: Saqi, 2007) p.104
14. Clive Jones, *The Clandestine Lives of Colonel David Smiley: Code Name 'Grin'*, (Edinburgh: Edinburgh University Press, 2019) p.70 and p.153
15. Sergey Plekhanov, *A Reformer on the Throne*, (Virginia: Trident Press, 2004) p.70
16. John Beasant and Christopher Ling, *Sultan in Arabia: A Private Life*, (Edinburgh: Mainstream Publishing, 2004) p.137
    Ray Peterson, 'A Legacy Enshrined in his Actions', *The Oman Daily Observer*, 15 Jan 2020
17. James Goodge, 'Assisting Our Brothers, Defending Ourselves: The Iranian Intervention in Oman 1972–75', Iranian Studies, Vol.47, Issue 3 (2014) p.446
18. Ray Peterson, 'A Legacy Enshrined in his Actions', *The Oman Daily Observer*, 15 Jan 2020
19. Sergey Plekhanov, *A Reformer on the Throne*, (Virginia: Trident Press, 2004) p.85

Calvin Allen and Lynn Rigsbee, *Oman Under Qaboos: From Coup to Constitution, 1970–1996*, (London: Frank Cass, 2002) p.28

Sergey Plekhanov, *A Reformer on the Throne*, (Virginia: Trident Press, 2004) p.88

John Beasant and Christopher Ling, *Sultan in Arabia: A Private Life*, (Edinburgh: Mainstream Publishing, 2004) p.89

20. Marc DeVore, 'A more complex and conventional victory: revisiting the Dhofar counterinsurgency, 1963–1975', *Small Wars & Insurgencies*, Vol.23, Issue 1 (2012) p.151
21. TNA – FCO 8/41 – Persian Gulf: Political Affairs (Ext.): Bilateral: Effects on Aden – Confidential briefing document 'Lessons from South Arabia?', Sir Richard Beaumont, dated 20 Nov 1967
22. Ibid. and Clive Jones, *Britain and the Yemen Civil War, 1962–65: Ministers, Mercenaries and Mandarins: Foreign Policy and the Limits of Covert Action*, (Eastbourne: Sussex Academic Press, 2010) p.191
23. TNA – FCO 8/41 – Persian Gulf: Political Affairs (Ext.): Bilateral: Effects on Aden – Letter, S. Crawford (PRPG) to Sir Richard Beaumont, dated 26 October 1967
24. Although used as a base of operations as early as 1965. J.E. Peterson, *Oman's Insurgencies: The Sultanate's Struggle for Supremacy*, (London: Saqi, 2007) p.197
25. John Graham, *Ponder Anew: Reflections on the Twentieth Century*, (Staplehurst: Spellmount Limited, 1999) p.355
26. Geraint Hughes, 'A 'Model Campaign' Reappraised: The Counter-Insurgency War in Dhofar, Oman, 1965–1975', Journal of Strategic Studies, Vol.32, Issue 2 (2009) p.283
27. MEC – GRAHAM COLLECTION – Tony Lewis, 'The Story of the Sultan of Oman's Armed Forces 1964–67', *The Journal of the Sultan's Armed Forces Association*, Issue 37 (February 1988) Article p.40

Corran Purdon, *List the Bugle: Reminiscences of an Irish Soldier*, (Antrim: Greystone Books, 1993) p.294

28. J.E. Peterson, *Oman's Insurgencies: The Sultanate's Struggle for Supremacy*, (London: Saqi, 2007) p.206

John Graham, *Ponder Anew: Reflections on the Twentieth Century*, (Staplehurst: Spellmount Limited, 1999) p.355

29. TNA FCO 8/2006 – 'Annual Review of Oman 1972', A.D. Parsons to Mr. Le Quesne, 12 Feb 1973

Marc DeVore, 'The United Kingdom's Last Hot War of the Cold War: Oman 1963–75', *Cold War History*, Vol. 11, Issue 3 (2011) p.2

30. John Graham, *Ponder Anew: Reflections on the Twentieth Century*, (Staplehurst: Spellmount Limited, 1999) p.355
31. Marc DeVore, 'A more complex and conventional victory: revisiting the Dhofar counterinsurgency, 1963–1975', *Small Wars & Insurgencies*, Vol.23, Issue 1 (2012) pp.153–55

James Worrall, *Statebuilding and Counterinsurgency in Oman: Political, Military and Diplomatic Relations at the End of Empire*, (London: I.B. Tauris & Co. Ltd., 2014) p.162

32. Ibid., p.156
33. Ibid., p.145
34. Nikolas Gardner, 'The Limits of the Sandhurst Connection: The Evolution of Oman's Foreign and Defense Policy, 1970–1977', *The Journal of the Middle East and Africa*, Vol. 6, Issue 1 (2015) p.47
35. Ibid., p.45 and p.55
36. J.E. Peterson, *Oman's Insurgencies: The Sultanate's Struggle for Supremacy*, (London: Saqi, 2007) p.420

Marc DeVore, 'A more complex and conventional victory: revisiting the Dhofar counterinsurgency, 1963–1975', Small Wars & Insurgencies, Vol.23, Issue 1 (2012) p.161
37. J.E. Peterson, 'Guerrilla Warfare and Ideological Confrontation in the Arabian Peninsula: The Rebellion in Dhurfar', *World Affairs*, Vol. 139, No.4, (1977) p.286
38. Nikolas Gardner, 'Defense Sales and British Security Assistance to Oman, 1975–81', *MCU Journal*, Vol.10, No.1 (Spring 2019) p.54
39. Marc DeVore, 'A more complex and conventional victory: revisiting the Dhofar counterinsurgency, 1963–1975', *Small Wars & Insurgencies*, Vol.23, Issue 1 (2012) p.161
40. Ibid., p.162
41. J.E. Peterson, *Oman's Insurgencies: The Sultanate's Struggle for Supremacy*, (London: Saqi, 2007) p.148
42. Ibid.
43. Ibid., p.104 and p.148
44. Walter C. Ladwig III, 'Supporting allies in counterinsurgency: Britain and the Dhofar Rebellion', *Small Wars & Insurgencies*, Vol.19, Issue 1 (2008) p.76. Including LSP salaries, although 'extra costs' only were charged for the SAS and the Field Medical Team situated in Salalah
45. Ibid.
46. TNA – CAB 186/11 – Joint Intelligence Committee (A) (JIC(A)): reports 1–16 – JIC 'The Outlook for Oman', dated 1 Mar 1972
47. Ibid.
48. Ranulph Fiennes, *Where Soldiers Fear to Tread*, (London: The Travel Book Club, 1976) p.57
49. Robert Alston and Stuart Laing, *Unshook Till the End of Time: A History of Relations Between Britain & Oman 1650–1970*, (London: Gilgamesh Publishing, 2012) p.135
50. Keith McCloskey, *Airwork: A History*, (Stroud: The History Press, 2012) pp.97–100
51. Sultanate of Oman NRAA – *Records of Oman 1966–1971*, (Cambridge Archive Editions, 2003) Vol. 4: Correspondence PRPG to British Consulate General, Muscat – Sultanate Balance Sheet – 3rd Quarter 1969
Alan Hoskins, *A Contract Officer*, (Tunbridge Wells: Costelloe, 1988) p.15
52. Nikolas Gardner, 'The Harold Wilson Government, Airwork Services Limited, and the Saudi Arabian Air Defence Scheme, 1965–73', *Journal of Contemporary History*, Vol. 42, No.2 (2007) pp.345–349
53. Ibid., p.350 – The Saudi Arabian Air Defence Scheme/'Magic Carpet Programme' of the 1960s and 1970s was worth tens of millions of pounds
54. Iran was the largest exporter (Trend Indicator Values (TIVs)) to Oman in 1972 with double the UK value in that year. SIPRI Arms Transfers Database: http://armstrade.sipri.org/armstrade/html/export_values.php Accessed online 21 Jan 2024
55. Marc DeVore, 'A more complex and conventional victory: revisiting the Dhofar counterinsurgency, 1963–1975', *Small Wars & Insurgencies*, Vol.23, Issue 1 (2012) p.144
56. Ian Cobain, 'Britain's Secret Wars', Thur 8 Sep 2016: *The Guardian* Online Accessed 1 Nov 2022 https://www.theguardian.com/uk-news/2016/sep/08/britains-secret-wars-oman
57. Lewis, p.32
58. Robert Alston and Stuart Laing, *Unshook Till the End of Time: A History of Relations Between Britain & Oman 1650–1970*, (London: Gilgamesh Publishing, 2012) p.251
59. Followed by Major D. Ogram from 1962–1967. Ibid., p.252
60. Ibid., p.249

61. TNA FCO 8/1669 – Annual Review of Oman – Letter Department of Defence, Muscat to Colonel Adler (Arabian Dept., FCO) dated 25 Apr 1970
62. TNA FCO 8/1437 – British Assistance to the Sultan of Oman's Armed Forces – Letter Charles Kendall and Partner's Ltd. (John Kendall) to Colonel Adler, FCO Arabian Department dated 21 Sep 1970, Letter Mr. T. Nissen (Director of Sales (Supply) MOD to J.M. Kendall esq. dated 15 Sep 1970 and letter Mr. T. Nissen (Deputy Director of Army Sales, MOD to Lieutenant Colonel Adler, FCO Arabian Department (cc. J. Kendall Esq) discussing request via Charles Kendall & Partners for supply from MOD of £290,000 worth of artillery ammunition over a 3-year period, dated 2 Jun 1970
63. Robert Alston and Stuart Laing, *Unshook Till the End of Time: A History of Relations Between Britain & Oman 1650–1970*, (London: Gilgamesh Publishing, 2012) p.256
64. Peterson, p.469
65. J.E. Peterson, *Oman's Insurgencies: The Sultanate's Struggle for Supremacy*, (London: Saqi, 2007) p.250
66. Geraint Hughes, 'Demythologising Dhofar: British Policy, Military Strategy and Counterinsurgency in Oman, 1963–1976', *Journal of Military History*, Vol. 79, Issue 2 (2015) p.439
67. Geraint Hughes, 'A 'Model Campaign' Reappraised: The Counter-Insurgency War in Dhofar, Oman, 1965–1975', *Journal of Strategic Studies*, Vol.32 Issue 2 (2009) p.279 Walter C. Ladwig III, 'Supporting allies in counterinsurgency: Britain and the Dhofar Rebellion', *Small Wars & Insurgencies*, Vol.19, No.1 (2008) p.73
68. John Graham, *Ponder Anew: Reflections on the Twentieth Century*, (Staplehurst: Spellmount Limited, 1999) p.343
69. Geraint Hughes, 'A Proxy War in Arabia: The Dhofar War Emergency and Crossborder Raids into South Yemen', *Middle East Journal*, Vol. 69, No.1 (Winter 2015) p.94
70. John McKeown, 'Britain and Oman: The Dhofar War and its Significance', University of Cambridge MA Dissertation (1981) p.105
71. Jim White, 'Oman 1965–1976: From Certain Defeat to Decisive Victory', *Small Wars Journal* (2008) p.8
72. '23-11-2009', in BBC Sounds (Radio 4), ed. by Mike Thomson (UK: BBC, 2009) Matthew Campbell, 'The Soldier Who Overthrew the Sultan of Oman in a Very British Coup', *The Sunday Times* (22 Nov 2020)
73. TNA – FCO 46/609 – Defence Planning of UK Armed Forces in Muscat and Oman – Annex to D/DS 6/7/155/13, dated 17 Aug 1970
74. Peterson, p.479
75. Graham, p.337
76. Peterson, p.479
77. Robert Alston and Stuart Laing, *Unshook Till the End of Time: A History of Relations Between Britain & Oman 1650–1970*, (London: Gilgamesh Publishing, 2012) p.249
78. Ibid.
79. Walter C. Ladwig III, 'Supporting allies in counterinsurgency: Britain and the Dhofar Rebellion', *Small Wars & Insurgencies*, Vol.19, Issue 1 (2008) p.76
80. James Worrall, *Statebuilding and Counterinsurgency in Oman: Political, Military and Diplomatic Relations at the End of Empire*, (London: I.B. Tauris, 2014) p.156
81. Graham, p.372
82. Ibid.
83. James Worrall, *Statebuilding and Counterinsurgency in Oman: Political, Military and Diplomatic Relations at the End of Empire*, (London: I.B. Tauris, 2014) p.58

84. Clive Jones, *Britain and the Yemen Civil War, 1962–65: Ministers, Mercenaries and Mandarins: Foreign Policy and the Limits of Covert Action*, (Eastbourne: Sussex Academic Press, 2010) p.191
85. James Worrall, *Statebuilding and Counterinsurgency in Oman: Political, Military and Diplomatic Relations at the End of Empire*, (London: I.B. Tauris, 2014) p.225 and p.212
86. United Arab Emirates (UAE) National Archive – FCO 8/2022 – 'Extracts from Intelligence Reports' Oman Intelligence Report no.50 (23 Sep – 6 Oct 1973)
87. John Graham, *Ponder Anew: Reflections on the Twentieth Century*, (Staplehurst: Spellmount Limited, 1999) p.372
    DeVore, p.20
88. Nikolas Gardner, 'The Limits of the Sandhurst Connection: The Evolution of Oman's Foreign and Defense Policy, 1970–1977', *The Journal of the Middle East and Africa*, Vol. 6, Issue 1 (2015) p.48
89. Ibid., p.50
90. United Arab Emirates (UAE) National Archives – FCO 8/1856 – Military Assistance to Oman from UK – Memorandum prepared by D.F. Hawley, British Ambassador, Muscat, dated 26 Feb 1972

Chapter 13

1. Marc DeVore, 'A more complex and conventional victory: revisiting the Dhofar counterinsurgency, 1963–1975', *Small Wars & Insurgencies*, Vol.23, Issue 1 (2012) p.144
2. Ibid., p.145
3. J.E. Peterson, *Oman's Insurgencies: The Sultanate's Struggle for Supremacy*, (London: Saqi, 2007) pp.228–229
4. Ibid.
5. Marc DeVore, 'A more complex and conventional victory: revisiting the Dhofar counterinsurgency, 1963–1975', *Small Wars & Insurgencies*, Vol.23, Issue 1 (2012) p.152
6. J.E. Peterson, *Oman's Insurgencies: The Sultanate's Struggle for Supremacy*, (London: Saqi, 2007) p.230
   Calvin Allen and Lynn Rigsbee, *Oman Under Qaboos: From Coup to Constitution, 1970–1996*, (London: Frank Cass, 2002) p.67
7. Walter C. Ladwig III, 'Supporting allies in counterinsurgency: Britain and the Dhofar Rebellion', *Small Wars & Insurgencies*, Vol.19, Issue 1 (2008) p.76
8. Peterson, pp.392–3
9. Marc DeVore, 'A more complex and conventional victory: revisiting the Dhofar counterinsurgency, 1963–1975', *Small Wars & Insurgencies*, Vol.23, Issue 1 (2012) p.152
   Peter de la Billiere, *Looking for Trouble: SAS to Gulf Command*, (London: Harper Collins, 1995) pp.131–150
10. Ranulph Fiennes, *Where Soldiers Fear to Tread*, (London: The Travel Book Club, 1976) p.29
    Marc DeVore, 'A more complex and conventional victory: revisiting the Dhofar counterinsurgency, 1963–1975', *Small Wars & Insurgencies*, Vol.23, Issue 1 (2012) p.153
11. TNA – DEFE 25/186– Muscat and Oman General. Update sit.rep. Brigadier Bond to VCDS, 'Psyops in Oman and Dhofar', dated 19 Mar 1971
12. Ibid.
13. Ibid.
    United Arab Emirates (UAE) National Archives – FCO 8/1856 – Military Assistance to Oman from UK – Memorandum prepared by D.F. Hawley, British Ambassador, Muscat, dated 26 Feb 1972, p.22

14. Fiennes, p.127
15. Marc DeVore, 'A more complex and conventional victory: revisiting the Dhofar counterinsurgency, 1963–1975', *Small Wars & Insurgencies*, Vol.23, Issue 1 (2012) p.166
    Peterson, p.279 and p.384
16. Ian Beckett and John Pimlott, *Counter-Insurgency: Lessons from History*, (Barnsley: Pen & Sword Military, 2011) p.64
17. Graham, p.362
18. Ian Beckett and John Pimlott, *Counter Insurgency: Lessons from History*, (Pen and Sword, 2011) p.64
19. David Charters, 'Counter-insurgency Intelligence: The Evolution of British Theory and Practice', *Journal of Conflict Studies*, Vol. 29 (2009) p.2
20. MEC – GRAHAM COLLECTION – Tony Lewis, 'The Story of the Sultan of Oman's Armed Forces 1964–67', *The Journal of the Sultan's Armed Forces Association*, Issue 37 (February 1988) Article p.35
21. Corran Purdon, *List the Bugle: Reminiscences of an Irish Soldier*, (Antrim: Greystone Books, 1993) p.237
22. Ibid.
23. Marc DeVore, 'The United Kingdom's Last Hot War of the Cold War: Oman 1963–75', *Cold War History*, Vol. 11, Issue 3 (2011) p.7
24. TNA – FCO 8/1688 – Attachment of SAS Division of United Kingdom to Armed Forces of Oman – Letter A. Ackland to Mr. Parsons, dated 1 Feb 1971
    John Graham, *Ponder Anew: Reflections on the Twentieth Century*, (Staplehurst: Spellmount Limited, 1999) p.346
25. David Charters, 'Counter-insurgency Intelligence: The Evolution of British Theory and Practice', *Journal of Conflict Studies*, Vol. 29 (2009) p.9
26. Ibid., p.3 and p.9
    Geraint Hughes, 'Demythologising Dhofar: British Policy, Military Strategy and Counterinsurgency in Oman, 1963–1976', *Journal of Military History*, Vol. 79, Issue 2 (2015) p.445
27. Ibid., p.444
28. Ibid.
    Obituary 'Malcolm Dennison', *The Scottish Herald*, 5 Sep 1996
29. David Charters, 'Counter-insurgency Intelligence: The Evolution of British Theory and Practice', *Journal of Conflict Studies*, Vol. 29 (2009) p.17
30. Ibid., p.17–19
31. Ibid.

Chapter 14

1. John Graham, *Ponder Anew: Reflections on the Twentieth Century*, (Staplehurst: Spellmount Limited, 1999) p.314
2. Corran Purdon, *List the Bugle: Reminiscences of an Irish Soldier*, (Antrim: Greystone Books, 1993) p.243
3. DeVore, p.163
4. TNA – DEFE 11/854– Oman, Chiefs of Staff Committee Defence Planning Staff, 'The Progress of Operations in Oman', dated 26 Feb 1975
   DeVore, p.21
5. Ibid., p.17
6. Ladwig III, p.72

7. John Graham, *Ponder Anew: Reflections on the Twentieth Century*, (Staplehurst: Spellmount Limited, 1999) p.343
8. Ibid.
9. Ibid. and Walter C. Ladwig III, 'Supporting allies in counterinsurgency: Britain and the Dhofar Rebellion', *Small Wars & Insurgencies*, Vol.19, Issue 1 (2008) p.73
10. Calvin Allen and Lynn Rigsbee, *Oman Under Qaboos: From Coup to Constitution, 1970–1996*, (London: Frank Cass, 2002) p.76
11. Geraint Hughes, 'A 'Model Campaign' Reappraised: The Counter-Insurgency War in Dhofar, Oman, 1965–1975', *Journal of Strategic Studies*, Vol.32, Issue 2 (2009) p.283
12. Ibid.
13. Tony Jeapes, *SAS Operation Oman*, (London: HarperCollins, 1980) p.231
14. Ibid.
15. Graham, p.315
    Purdon, p.195
16. Graham, pp.355–6
17. TNA – FCO 46/835 – 'Armed Forces of United Kingdom in Muscat and Oman' – Memo, 'Assessment of the Situation by Major-General Tim Creasey Commander Sultan's Armed Forces', 16 Oct 1972
18. John Graham, *Ponder Anew: Reflections on the Twentieth Century*, (Staplehurst: Spellmount Limited, 1999) p.315
19. Purdon, p. 235
20. TNA – FCO 8/2960, '"Soldier" Magazine Story on Royal Engineer Squadron in Oman + other Publication of the Dhofar War', (Secret) Memo, Douglas-Home to Secretary of State for Defence FCS/70/56, 'Special Air Service (SAS Assistance to the Sultanate of Oman)', (undated)
    TNA FCO 8/1688, 'Attachment of SAS Division of UK to Armed Forces of Oman', A. Ackland to Parsons, 1 Feb 1971
21. TNA – FCO 46/609 – Defence Planning of UK Armed Forces in Muscat and Oman – Memo from Foreign Secretary (Alec Douglas-Home) to Defence Secretary dated 4 Sep 1970, p.4
    TNA – FCO 46/609 – Defence Planning of UK Armed Forces in Muscat and Oman – Annex to D/DS 6/7/155/13, dated 17 Aug 1970
22. J.E. Peterson, *Oman's Insurgencies: The Sultanate's Struggle for Supremacy*, (London: Saqi, 2007) p.267
23. TNA – FCO 46/609 – Defence Planning of UK Armed Forces in Muscat and Oman – Memo from Foreign Secretary (Alec Douglas-Home) to Defence Secretary dated 4 Sep 1970
    TNA – FCO 46/609 – Defence Planning of UK Armed Forces in Muscat and Oman – Annex to D/DS 6/7/155/13, dated 17 Aug 1970
24. TNA – FCO 8/1688 – 'Attachment of SAS Division of United Kingdom to Armed Forces of Oman', Letter A. Ackland to Parsons, 1 Feb 1971
25. Ibid.
26. Ibid.
27. Marc DeVore 'A more complex and conventional victory: revisiting the Dhofar counterinsurgency, 1963–1975', *Small Wars & Insurgencies*, Vol.23, Issue 1 (2012) p.151
28. Fiennes, p.51 and p.93
29. Ibid., p.93
30. John Graham, *Ponder Anew: Reflections on the Twentieth Century*, (Staplehurst: Spellmount Limited, 1999) p.347 (Previously 2 i/c of the Muscat Regiment in 1974)

J.E. Peterson, *Oman's Insurgencies: The Sultanate's Struggle for Supremacy*, (London: Saqi, 2007) pp.392–3
31. Jeapes, p.204
    DeVore, p.162
    M. Robb, The Anglo-Omani Society/Sultan's Armed Forces Association Lecture: 'Civil Aid in Dhofar; the Key to Peace', London, 15 Jun 2023
32. de la Billiere, p.270
33. Graham, pp. 360–1
    DeVore, p.155
34. Walter C. Ladwig III, 'Supporting allies in counterinsurgency: Britain and the Dhofar Rebellion', *Small Wars & Insurgencies*, Vol.19, Issue 1 (2008) p.72
35. Geraghty, pp.176–77
    Arkless, p.92
36. John Graham, *Ponder Anew: Reflections on the Twentieth Century*, (Staplehurst: Spellmount Limited, 1999) p.351
37. John Akehurst, *We Won a War: The Campaign in Oman 1965–75*, (Guildford: M. Russell, 1982) p.43
38. Graham, p.347
39. Ibid, p.367
40. John Blashford-Snell, *A Taste for Adventure*, (London: Hutchinson & Co. (Publishers) Ltd., 1978) p.55
41. Marc DeVore, 'A more complex and conventional victory: revisiting the Dhofar counterinsurgency, 1963–1975', *Small Wars & Insurgencies*, Vol.23, Issue 1 (2012) p.144
    John Graham, *Ponder Anew: Reflections on the Twentieth Century*, (Staplehurst: Spellmount Limited, 1999) p.374
42. Peterson, p.298
43. Ibid.
    de la Billiere, p.276
    Beckett and Pimlott, p.39
44. de la Billiere, p.277
45. The aircraft of several pilots were hit by enemy fire during risky low level strafing runs
    J.E. Peterson, *Oman's Insurgencies: The Sultanate's Struggle for Supremacy*, (London: Saqi, 2007) p.300
46. MEC – GRAHAM COLLECTION – Box 2/5 John Graham, Personal Diary Entry, dated 19 July 1972, and Marc DeVore, 'A more complex and conventional victory: revisiting the Dhofar counterinsurgency, 1963–1975', *Small Wars & Insurgencies*, Vol.23, Issue 1 (2012) p.157
47. J.E. Peterson, *Oman's Insurgencies: The Sultanate's Struggle for Supremacy*, (London: Saqi, 2007) p.296
48. Ibid., John Graham, *Ponder Anew: Reflections on the Twentieth Century*, (Staplehurst: Spellmount Limited, 1999) p.375, Peter de la Billiere, *Looking for Trouble: SAS to Gulf Command*, (London: Harper Collins, 1995) p.277, John Newsinger, *British Counterinsurgency*, (Basingstoke: Palgrave Macmillan, 2015) p.151
49. MEC – GRAHAM COLLECTION – Box 7/1 – John Graham, 'Point summary on Development of SAF for lecture to Anglo-Omani Society June 1996'
    MEC – GRAHAM COLLECTION – Box 3/7 – Letter, Lieutenant Colonel de la Billiere to Brigadier Graham, dated 9 August 1972
50. Ibid., p.302

51. MEC – GRAHAM COLLECTION – Box 3/7 – Letter, Lieutenant Colonel de la Billiere to Brigadier Graham, dated 9th August 1972
52. Marc DeVore, 'The United Kingdom's Last Hot War of the Cold War: Oman 1963–75', *Cold War History*, Vol. 11, Issue 3 (2011) p.20
53. Ken Perkins, 'Oman 1975: The Year of Decision', *The RUSI Journal*, Vol. 124, Issue 1 (1979) p.38
54. Ibid., p.39
55. James Goodge, 'Assisting Our Brothers, Defending Ourselves: The Iranian Intervention in Oman 1972–75', *Iranian Studies*, Vol.47, Issue 3 (2014) p.446
56. Nikolas Gardner, 'The Limits of the Sandhurst Connection: The Evolution of Oman's Foreign and Defense Policy, 1970–1977', *The Journal of the Middle East and Africa*, Vol. 6, Issue 1 (2015) p.50
57. MEC – GRAHAM COLLECTION – Donald Hawley, 'Recollections of Muscat', *The Journal of the Sultan's Armed Forces Association*, Issue 42 (March 1993) Article p.16
58. Nikolas Gardner, 'The Limits of the Sandhurst Connection: The Evolution of Oman's Foreign and Defense Policy, 1970–1977', *The Journal of the Middle East and Africa*, Vol. 6, Issue 1 (2015) p.50
Robert Alston and Stuart Laing, *Unshook Till the End of Time: A History of Relations Between Britain & Oman 1650–1970*, (London: Gilgamesh Publishing, 2012) p.249
59. Marc DeVore, 'The United Kingdom's Last Hot War of the Cold War: Oman 1963–75', *Cold War History*, Vol. 11, Issue 3 (2011) p.22

Chapter 15

1. Thomas R. Mockaitis, 'The Iraq War: Learning from the Past, Adapting to the Present and Planning for the Future', *Army War College Strategic Studies Institute* (2007) p.12
2. Francis Owtram, *Oman and the West: State Formation in Oman since 1920*, (London: University of London, 1999) pp.68–69
3. Thomas R. Mockaitis, 'The Minimum Force Debate: Contemporary Sensibilities Meet Imperial Practice', *Small Wars and Insurgencies*, Vol.23, Issues 4–5 (Oct–Dec 2012) pp.762–780
4. Fred Halliday, *Arabia Without Sultans*, (Harmondsworth: Penguin, 1974) p.279
John Newsinger, *British Counterinsurgency*, (Basingstoke: Palgrave Macmillan, 2015) p.2 and David Jones and M.L.R. Smith, 'Myth and the Small War Tradition: Reassessing the discourse of British Counter-Insurgency', *Small Wars & Insurgencies*, Vol. 24, Issue 3 (2013) p.436, Douglas Porch, *Counterinsurgency: Exposing the Myths of the New Way of War*, (Cambridge: Cambridge University Press, 2013) p.266
5. In all other cases highlighted in the study, British Crown, or Crown-controlled forces were operating in British-controlled (by mandate, colonial administration or sovereign territory) areas/lands
6. Marc DeVore, 'A more complex and conventional victory: revisiting the Dhofar counterinsurgency, 1963–1975', *Small Wars & Insurgencies*, Vol.23, Issue 1 (2012) p.144
Tony Jeapes, *SAS Operation Oman*, (London: HarperCollins, 1980) p.14
Ian Beckett and John Pimlott, *Counter-Insurgency; Lessons from History*, (Barnsley: Pen & Sword, 2011) p.43
Ian Beckett, *Modern Insurgencies and Counter-Insurgencies – Guerrillas and their Opponents Since 1756*, (London: Routledge, 2001) p.230
7. Thomas R. Mockaitis, 'The Phoenix of Counterinsurgency', *The Journal of Conflict Studies* (Summer 2007) p.13

8. David Charters, 'Counter-insurgency Intelligence: The Evolution of British Theory and Practice', *Journal of Conflict Studies*, Vol. 29 (2009) p.10
9. Marc DeVore, 'A more complex and conventional victory: revisiting the Dhofar counterinsurgency, 1963–1975', *Small Wars & Insurgencies*, Vol.23, Issue 1 (2012) p.144 Tony Jeapes, *SAS Operation Oman*, (London: HarperCollins, 1980) p.14
10. David Benest, 'Ponder Anew: Brigadier Graham and the Dhofar War 1970–1972' (Oct 2015) https://thestrategybridge.org/the-bridge/2016/1/1/ponder-anew-brigadier-john-graham-the-dhofar-war-19701972 Accessed online 19 Apr 2023 p.9
11. Ibid.
12. Tony Jeapes, *SAS Operation Oman*, (London: HarperCollins, 1980) p.11, p.14
13. Christopher Paul, Colin P. Clarke, Beth Grill and Molly Dunigan, *Paths to Victory – Detailed Insurgency Case studies*, (Santa Monica, CA: RAND Corporation, 2013) p.286
14. Stephen Quick, *The Dhofar War: British Covert Campaigning in Arabia 1965–1975*, (Exeter: Exeter University Press, 2024) pp.7–8
15. Sultanate of Oman NRAA – *Records of Oman 1966–1971* (Cambridge Archive Editions, 2003) Vol. 6: Diplomatic Report from HM Ambassador to Muscat to Secretary of State for Foreign Affairs, dated 5 Aug 1971, p.6
16. Christopher Paul, Colin P. Clarke, Beth Grill and Molly Dunigan, *Paths to Victory: Detailed Insurgency Case*, (Washington DC: Rand, 2013) pp.285/6
17. Robert O. Tilman, 'The Non-Lessons of the Malayan Emergency', *Asian Survey*, Vol.6, Issue 8 (1966) p.413
18. Peterson, p. 401
19. The sixth could be considered as Brunei/early stages of Borneo campaign. Christopher Paul, Colin P. Clarke, Beth Grill and Molly Dunigan, *Paths to Victory – Detailed Insurgency Case studies*, (Santa Monica, CA: RAND Corporation, 2013) p.XV
20. Jeapes, p.14

Bibliography

Primary Sources
The National Archives (TNA), Kew, London
Sultanate of Oman, National Records & Archives Authority, Muscat, Oman
United Arab Emirates National Archives (NA), Abu Dhabi, UAE
Liddell Hart Centre for Military Archives (LHCMA), King's College London
Middle East Centre (MEC), St Anthony's College, Oxford
UAE Arabian Gulf Digital Archive (AGDA)
USA National Archives Catalog Collection

Official Publications
Crawshaw, M. (2012) 'The Evolution of British COIN' *UK Ministry of Defence Joint Doctrine Publication (JDP 3-40)*
Anon. (2007) US Army & Marine Corps Counterinsurgency Field Manual. US Army Field Manual No.3-24/Marine Corps Warfighting Publication No.3-33.5 (Chicago: University of Chicago Press)

Memoirs/Autobiographies
Akehurst, J. (1982) *We Won a War: The Campaign in Oman 1965–75* (Guildford: M. Russell)
Arkless, D. (1988) *The Secret War – Dhofar 1971/72* (London: William Kimber)
Cooper, J. (1991) *One of the Originals: The Story of a Founder Member of the SAS* (London: Pan Books Ltd.)
Dales, M. (2016) *SAS: A Storm Gathering* (Kindle E-book)
De La Billiere, P. (1995) *Looking for Trouble: SAS to Gulf Command* (London: Harper Collins)
Blashford-Snell, J. (1978) *A Taste for Adventure* (London: Hutchinson & Co. (Publishers) Ltd.)
Blashford-Snell, J. (1995) *Something Lost Behind the Ranges* (London: Harper Collins)
Fiennes, R. (1976) *Where Soldiers Fear to Tread* (London: The Travel Book Club)
Gardiner, I. (2006) *In the Service of the Sultan* (Barnsley: Pen and Sword)
Graham, G. (1999) *Ponder Anew: Reflections on the Twentieth Century* (Staplehurst: Spellmount Limited)
Hoskins, A. (1988) *A Contract Officer in the Oman* (Tunbridge Wells: DJ Costello)
Jeapes, T. (1980) *SAS Operation Oman* (London: HarperCollins)
Large, L. (2000) *Soldier Against the Odds: From the Korean War to SAS* (Edinburgh: Mainstream Publishing)
Mitchell, C. (1969) *Having Been A Soldier* (London: Hamish Hamilton)
Neild, D. (2015) *A Soldier in Arabia* (Surbiton: Medina)
Purdon, C. (1993) *List the Bugle: Reminiscences of an Irish Soldier* (Antrim: Greystone Books)
Ray, B. (2012) *Dangerous Frontiers: Campaigning in Somaliland & Oman* (Barnsley: Pen & Sword)
Smiley, D., (1975) *Arabian Assignment*, (London: Leo Cooper)

Thesiger, W (1991) *Arabian Sands* (London: Penguin)
Thomas, B. (1938) *Arabia Felix: Across the Empty Quarter of Arabia* (Oxford: Alden Press)
Thwaites, P. (1995) *Muscat Command* (London: Leo Cooper)
Wilson, S. (2021) *Dhofar Voices: Frontier Force, Oman and its Life and Times 1970–1980* (Kindle E-book)
White, R. (2011) *Storm Front* (New York: Bantam Press)

Secondary Sources
Books
Allen, C., Rigsbee, L. (2000) *Oman under Qaboos: From Coup to Constitution, 1970–1996* (London: Frank Cass)
Alston, R. and Laing, S. (2012) *Unshook Till the End of Time: A History of Relations Between Britain & Oman 1650–1970* (London: Gilgamesh Publishing)
Beasant, J. and Ling, C. (2004) *Sultan In Arabia: A Private Life* (Mainstream: Edinburgh)
Beckett, I. (2001) *Modern Insurgencies and Counter-insurgencies – Guerrillas and their opponents since 1756* (London: Routledge)
Beckett, I. (Ed.) (1988) *The Roots of Counter-Insurgency: Armies and Guerrilla Warfare 1900–1945* (London: Blandford)
Beckett, I., Pimlott, J. (1985) *Armed Forces & Modern Counter-Insurgency.* (New York: St. Martin's)
Christopher, P., Clarke, C., and Grill, B., (2010) *Victory has a Thousand Fathers: Sources of success in Counterinsurgency* (Santa Monica: RAND Corporation)
Christopher P, Clarke, C., Grill, B. and Dunigan, M. (2013) *Paths to Victory: Detailed Insurgency Case Studies* (Washington DC: Rand Corporation)
Cloake, J. (1985) *Templer: Tiger of Malaya* (London: Harrap)
Commins, D. (2012) *The Gulf States: A Modern History* (London: I.B. Tauris)
Edwards, A. (2012) *Defending the Realm? The Politics of Britain's Small Wars Since 1945* (Manchester: Manchester University Press)
Galula, D. (1964) *Counter-Insurgency Warfare; Theory and Practice* (New York: Frederick A. Praeger)
Geraghty, T. (1990) *Who Dares Wins: The Story of the Special Air Service Regiment 1950–1982* (London: Fontana/Collins)
Hack, K. (2021) *The Malayan Emergency: Revolution and Counterinsurgency at the End of Empire* (Cambridge: Cambridge University Press)
Halliday, F. (1974) *Arabia without Sultans* (Middlesex: Penguin)
Hart-Davies, D. (2011) *The War That Never Was* (London: Random House)
Hawley, D. (1995) *Oman & Its Renaissance* (London: Stacey International)
Jackson, R. (1982) *Hawker Hunter (Modern Combat Aircraft 15)* (London: Ian Allen Ltd)
Jackson, R. (2008) *The Malayan Emergency & Indonesian Confrontation – The Commonwealth's Wars 1948 – 1966* (Barnsley: Pen and Sword)
Jones, C. (2010) *Britain and the Yemen Civil War, 1962–65: Ministers, Mercenaries and Mandarins: Foreign Policy and the Limits of Covert Action* (Eastbourne: Sussex Academic Press)
Jones, C. (2019) *The Clandestine Lives of Colonel Davis Smiley; Codename Grin* (Edinburgh: Edinburgh University Press)
Kitson. F. (1977) *Bunch of Five*, (London: Faber & Faber)
Kitson, F. (1971) *Low intensity Operations: Subversion, Insurgency, Peace-Keeping* (London: Faber)

Mattheisen, T. (2017) *Anti-Colonialism, the Cold War and the Long Sixties in the Gulf States* in The Routledge Handbook of the Global Sixties: Between Protest and Nation-Building (London/New York: Routledge)

McCloskey, M. (2012) *Airwork; A History* (Stroud: The History Press)

Mockaitis, M. (1995) *'British Counterinsurgency in the Post-Imperial Era'* Manchester: Manchester University Press)

Nagl, J.A. (2005) Learning to Eat Soup with a Knife: Counterinsurgency Lesson from Malaya and Vietnam, (Chicago: Chicago University Press)

Newsinger, J. *(2015) British Counterinsurgency* (Basingstoke: Palgrave Macmillan)

Owtram, F. (1999) *Oman and the West: State Formation in Oman since 1920* (London: University of London)

Paget, J. (1967) *Counter-Insurgency Campaigning* (London: Faber & Faber)

Peterson, J. (2013) *Oman's Insurgencies: The Sultanate's Struggle for Supremacy* (London: Saqi)

Pimlott, J. (1986) *British Military Operations, 1945–85*, (London, Bison)

Plekhanov, S. (2004) *A Reformer on the Throne*, (Virginia: Trident Press)

Porch D. (2013) *Counterinsurgency: Exposing the Myths of the New Way of War* (Cambridge: Cambridge University Press)

Phillips, W. (1971) *Oman; A History* (Beirut: Librarie Du Lebanon)

Richardson, C. (2001) *Masirah – Tales from a Desert Island* (Durham: Carnegie Publishing)

Quick, S. (2024) *The Dhofar War: British Covert Campaigning in Arabia 1965–1975* (Exeter: Exeter University Press)

Searle, P. (1979) *Dawn Over Oman* (London, George Allen & Unwin)

Skeet, I (1974) *Muscat and Oman: The End of An Era.* (London: Faber and Faber)

Takriti, A. (2013). *Monsoon Revolution: Republicans, Sultans, and Empires in Oman, 1965–1976* (Oxford: Oxford University Press)

Thompson, R. (1974) *Defeating Communist Insurgency*, (London: Chatto & Windus)

Thompson, R. (1974) *Peace is not at Hand* (London: Chatto & Windus)

Urban, M. (1993) *Big Boys Rules* (London: Faber & Faber)

Urban, M. (2010) *Task Force Black* (London: Little, Brown)

Valeri, M. (2017) *Oman: Politics and Society in the Qaboos State* (London: C. Hurst & Co.)

Walker, J. (2004) *Aden Insurgency – The Savage War in Yemen 1962–67.* (Barnsley: Pen & Sword)

Ware, Y. *Return of a Native: Learning from the Land* (London: Repeater Books, 2022).

Worrall, J. (2014) *State-building and Counter-Insurgency in Oman: Political, Military and Diplomatic Relations at the End of Empire.* (London: I.B. Tauris & Co. Ltd.)

Articles

Anderson, D. British Abuse and Torture in Kenya's Counter-Insurgency, 1952–1960' *Small Wars & Insurgencies*, 23:4–5 700–719 (2012)

Beckett, I. 'The Future of Insurgency' *Small Wars & Insurgencies*, 16:1, 22–36 (2005)

Beckett, I. 'British Counterinsurgency: A Historiographical Reflection' *Small Wars & Insurgencies*, 23:4–5 (2012)

Beckett, I. 'Forward to the Past: Insurgency in Our Midst', *Harvard International Review*, Vol. 23, NO.2 (Summer 2001)

Charters, D. 'Counter-Insurgency Intelligence: The Evolution of British Theory and Practice' *Journal of Conflict Studies*, Vol. 29 (2009)

DeVore, M. 'A More Complex and Conventional Victory: Revisiting the Dhofar Counterinsurgency *1963–1975' Small Wars and Insurgencies*, Vol.23, Issue 1 (2012) 144–173

DeVore, M. 'The United Kingdom's Last Hot War of the Cold War: Oman 1963–75' *Cold War History* iFirst article 1–31, (2011)

Dixon, P. 'Hearts and Minds? British Counter-Insurgency from Malaya to Iraq' *Journal of Strategic Studies*, Vol. 32, Issue 3 (2009)

Elkins, C. 'Alchemy of Evidence: Mau, the British Empire and the High Court of Justice, *The Journal of Imperial and Commonwealth History*, 39:5, 731–748 (2011)

French, D. 'Nasty not Nice: British Counterinsurgency Doctrine and Practice, 1945–1967, *Small Wars & Insurgencies*, 23:4–5 (2012)

Gardner, N. 'The Harold Wilson Government, Airwork Services Ltd, and the Saudi Arabian Air Defence Scheme, 1965–73' *Journal of Contemporary History*, Vol. 42(2) 343–361 (2007)

Gardner, N. 'The limits of the Sandhurst Connection: The Evolution of Oman's Foreign and Defense Policy, *1970–1977' The Journal of the Middle East and Africa 6:1, 45–58 (2015)*

Gardner, N. 'Defense Sales and British Security Assistance to Oman, 1975–81' *MCU Journal* Vol.10, no.1, p.54 (2019)

Goodge, J. 'Assisting out Brothers, Defending Ourselves: The Iranian Intervention in Oman 1972–1975' *Iran Studies*, Vol 47, Issue 3 (2014)

Gustafsson, K. and Hagström, L. 'What is the Point? Teaching Graduate Students how to Construct Political Science Research Puzzles' *European Political Science* (2017)

Hack, K. 'Everyone lived in fear: Malaya and the British Way of counter-insurgency', *Small Wars & Insurgencies* (2012)

Hawley, D. 'Some Surprising Aspects of Omani History', Asian Affairs, 13:1, (1982)

Hughes, G. 'A Model Campaign Reappraised. The Counter-Insurgency War in Dhofar Oman, 1965–1975' *Journal of Strategic Studies*, Vol 32, Issue 2 (2009)

Hughes, G. 'A Proxy War in Arabia: The Dhofar Emergency and Cross-Border Raids into South Yemen', *Middle East Journal* Vol 69, No. 1, WINTER 2015

Hughes, G. 'Demythologising Dhofar: British Policy, Military Strategy and Counterinsurgency in Oman, 1963–1976' *Journal of Military History*, 79(2), (2015)

Hughes, G. 'Amateurs Who Play in Division One? – Anglo-Iranian Military Relations During the Dhofar War in Oman' *British Journal for Military History*, Vol.4, Issue 1, (2017)

Johnson, T. 'Writing for International Security: A Contributor's Guide' *International Security*, Vol.16, No.2 pp. 171–180 (1991)

Jones, C. 'Military intelligence in the war on Dhofar; an appraisal' *Small Wars and Insurgencies*, 25(3). pp. 628–646 (2014)

Jones, D. and Smith, M.L.R. 'Myth and the Small War Tradition: Reassessing the discourse of British Counter-Insurgency' *Small Wars & Insurgencies*, 24:3 (2013)

Katagiri, N. 'Winning Hearts and Minds to Lose Control: Exploring Various Consequences of Popular Support in Counterinsurgency Missions' *Small Wars & Insurgencies*, Vol.22, No.1 (Mar 2011)

Kilkullen, D. 'Counterinsurgency Redux', *Survival*, 48(4) (Winter 2006/7)

Ladwig, W. 'Supporting Allies in Counter-Insurgency: Britain and the Dhofar Rebellion' *Small Wars & Insurgencies*, Vol 19, Issue 1 (2008)

Mockaitis, T. Low Intensity Conflict: the British Experience, *Conflict Quarterly* (Winter 1993)

Mockaitis, T. 'The Phoenix of Counterinsurgency', *The Journal of Conflict Studies*, (Summer 2007)

Mockaitis, T. The Iraq War: Learning from the Past, Adapting to the Present and Planning for the Future, *Strategic Studies Institute, US Army War College* (2007)

Mockaitis, T. Minimum Force, British Counter-Insurgency and the Mau Mau Rebellion: A Reply, *Small Wars & Insurgencies*, 3:2 (1992)

Mockaitis, T. The Phoenix of Counterinsurgency, *Journal of Conflict Studies*, (Summer 2007)
Monick, S. 'Victory in Hades: The Forgotten Wars of the Oman 1957–1959 and 1970–1976. Part 2: The Dhofar Campaign 1970–1976' *Scientia Militaria, South African Journal of Military Studies*, Vol.12, Nr.4 (1982)
Nuri, M. 'Regional Military Involvement: A Cases Study of Iran Under the Shah' *Pakistan Horizon*, Vol 37, Issue 4 (1984)
Perkins, K 'Oman 1975: The Year of Decision' *The RUSI Journal*, Vol 124, Issue 1 (1979)
Peterson, J. 'Britain and the 'Oman War': An Arabian Entanglement' *Asian Affairs*, Vol. 7, No. 3 (1976)
Peterson, J. 'Guerrilla Warfare and Ideological Confrontation in the Arabian Peninsula: The Rebellion in Dhurfar' *World Affairs*, Vol. 139, No.4 (1977)
Quick, S. 'Arabian Peninsula Histories: The Dhofar War in Oman 1965–1975: A Historical Perspective. *Nation Shield Journal* (Issue no. 559, August 2018)
Reis, B. 'The Myth of British Minimum Force in Counterinsurgency Campaigns during Decolonization (1945–1970)' *Journal of Strategic Studies*, Vol. 34, No. 2 (Apr 2011)
Smiley, D. 'Muscat and Oman' Royal United Services *Institution Journal*, 105:617, 29–47 (1960)
Tillman, R. 'The Non-Lessons of the Malayan Emergency' *Asian Survey*, Vol. 6 No. 8 (Aug 1966)
Thornton, R. 'The British Army and the Origins of its Minimum Force Philosophy', *Small Wars and Insurgencies*, 15:1, 2004
White, J. 'Oman 1965–1975: From Certain Defeat to Decisive Victory' *Small Wars Journal* (2008)
Yates, A. and Hughes, G. 'Operation Intradon in the Musandam, 1970–1971: What This Counterinsurgency Operation Says About British Military Operations in the Arabian Gulf', *Small Wars & Insurgencies*, (2022).

Speeches/Lectures
Kilkullen, D 'Three Pillars of Counterinsurgency', Speech: US Government Counterinsurgency Conference, Washington D.C., 28 September 2006
Robb, M., The Anglo-Omani Society/Sultan's Armed Forces Association Lecture: 'Civil Aid in Dhofar: The Key to Peace', London, 15 Jun 2023

Newsletters/Independent Publications
The Gulf Committee Dhofar – Britain's Colonial War in the Gulf. (London: The Gulf Committee, 1972)
The Sultan's Armed Forces Association Newsletter (various)
The Journal of the Sultan's Armed Forces Association (various)

Newspaper Articles/Websites
Anglim, S. 'The Omani Djebel War 1957–59' *The Strategy Bridge*, 1 Dec 2014 https://thestrategybridge.org/the-bridge/2014/12/1/the-oman-djebel-war-195759 Accessed online 19 Apr 2023
Barber, M. 'Brigadier Tim Landon – Soldier of Fortune Who Helped Ease Oman into the Modern World' Obituary in *The Guardian Newspaper*, 26 Aug 2007. https://www.theguardian.com/news/2007/aug/28/guardianobituaries.military Accessed online 2 Jun 2024
Benest, D. 'Ponder Anew: Brigadier Graham and the Dhofar War 1970–1972' *The Strategy Bridge* (Oct 2015) https://thestrategybridge.org/the-bridge/2016/1/1/ponder-anew-brigadier-john-graham-the-dhofar-war-19701972 Accessed online 19 Apr 2023

Cobain, I. 'Britain's Secret Wars' in *The Guardian Newspaper*, 8 Sep 2016. https://www.theguardian.com/uk-news/2016/sep/08/britains-secret-wars-oman Accessed online 21 Jan 2023

'Korea Veterans Remember Fallen Comrades' *BBC News World Service Online*, 20 Apr 2001. http://news.bbc.co.uk/2/hi/uk_news/1288010.stm Accessed 6 Apr 2024

Obituary 'General Sir John Akehurst' *The Times*, 27 Feb 2007, Accessed online 10 Oct 2023

Obituary 'Brigadier Mike Harvey' *The Times*, 7 Aug 2007, Accessed online 9 Sep 2023

Obituary 'Brig. J. S. Fletcher, CBE' December 1976 (*anyflip.com*), Accessed online 29 Oct 2023

Obituary 'Malcolm Dennison' *The Scottish Herald*, 5 Sep 1996 https://www.heraldscotland.com/news/12033607.malcolm-dennison Accessed online 2 Mar 2024

Obituary 'Sir Donald Hawley' *The Telegraph Newspaper*, 11 Feb 2008, Accessed online 12 Feb 2022

Peterson, J. 'The Experience of British Counter-Insurgency Campaigns and Implications for Iraq'. *Arabian Peninsula Background Note, No. APBN-009. Published on* www.JEPeterson.net, *July 2009*. Accessed online 4 Feb 2022

Peterson, R. 'A Legacy Enshrined in his Actions', *The Oman Daily Observer*, 15 Jan 2020 https://www.omanobserver.om/article/18109/Local/a-legacy-enshrined-in-his-actions accessed online 26 Apr 2024

SIPRI Arms Transfers Database: http://armstrade.sipri.org/armstrade/html/export_values.php accessed online: 21 Jan 2024

Summers, C. 'Can Cyprus Overcome Its Bloody History' *BBC News Article* (online) dated 23 Nov 2009 http://news.bbc.co.uk/2/hi/europe/8321765.stm Accessed online 11 May 2024

http://uca.edu/politicalscience/dadm-project/middle-eastnorth-africapersian-gulf-region/oman-1912-present/ accessed 26 Mar 2023

– USNA – https://www.archives.gov/research/military/vietnam-war/casualty-statistics Accessed 14 Aug 2024

Other Media

BBC 'Empire Warriors: The British Empire at War 1945–1967' Documentary, 2004, Discs 1 and 2

'23/11/2009' Podcast by Mike Thomson on the British role in the 1970 Oman Coup *BBC Sounds (Radio 4)*, (UK: BBC, 2009).